CLASSICAL PRESENCES

General Editors
Lorna Hardwick   James I. Porter

CLASSICAL PRESENCES

The texts, ideas, images, and material culture of ancient Greece and Rome have always been crucial to attempts to appropriate the past in order to authenticate the present. They underlie the mapping of change and the assertion and challenging of values and identities, old and new. Classical Presences brings the latest scholarship to bear on the contexts, theory, and practice of such use, and abuse, of the classical past.

Dynamic Reading

Studies in the Reception of Epicureanism

EDITED BY
BROOKE HOLMES AND W. H. SHEARIN

OXFORD
UNIVERSITY PRESS

OXFORD
UNIVERSITY PRESS

Oxford University Press, Inc., publishes works that further
Oxford University's objective of excellence
in research, scholarship, and education.

Oxford New York
Auckland Cape Town Dar es Salaam Hong Kong Karachi
Kuala Lumpur Madrid Melbourne Mexico City Nairobi
New Delhi Shanghai Taipei Toronto

With offices in
Argentina Austria Brazil Chile Czech Republic France Greece
Guatemala Hungary Italy Japan Poland Portugal Singapore
South Korea Switzerland Thailand Turkey Ukraine Vietnam

Copyright (c) 2012 by Oxford University Press, Inc.

Published by Oxford University Press, Inc.
198 Madison Avenue, New York, New York 10016
www.oup.com

Library of Congress Cataloging-in-Publication Data
Dynamic reading : studies in the reception of Epicureanism /
edited by Brooke Holmes and W.H. Shearin.
p. cm. — (Classical presences)
Includes bibliographical references and index.
ISBN 978-0-19-979495-9 (hardcover : alk. paper)
1. Epicureans (Greek philosophy) I. Holmes, Brooke II. Shearin, W. H.
B512.D96 2012
187—dc23 2011031838

ISBN: 9780199794959

Printing number: 1 3 5 7 9 8 6 4 2

Contents

Acknowledgments

We wish to thank Éditions Kimé for permission to print a modified translation of Alain Gigandet's essay "Présences d'Épicure," first published in Frédéric Gros and Carlos Lévy (eds.), *Foucault et la philosophie antique* (Paris, 2003), and Vita & Pensiero for permission to print a revised version of Glenn Most's "The Sublime, Today?," first published in an Italian translation by Margherita Redaelli as "Il sublime oggi?" in Elisabetta Matelli (ed.), *Il Sublime: fortuna di un testo e di un'idea* (Milan, 2007).

We would also like to acknowledge the generous support of The Barr Ferree Fund, Department of Art and Archaeology, Princeton University and the Max Orovitz Research Award in the Humanities, University of Miami.

We are very grateful to the anonymous readers for the Press for their helpful comments. Special thanks are due to Jim Porter and Stefan Vranka, who unerringly guided the project from its beginning some years ago to its end. Deirdre Brady and Sarah Pirovitz both went beyond the call of duty in helping us secure permissions for the images and otherwise shepherding the manuscript to completion. Finally, we have been fortunate to have a wonderful production team. We would like to thank Natalie Johnson, our production editor at OUP, Kiran Kumar, our production manager, and especially our excellent copy editor, Katherine Ulrich.

Contributors

Anthony Curtis Adler is an Associate Professor of Comparative Literature at Yonsei University's Underwood International College, where he has been teaching since 2006. His translation of Fichte's *Closed Commercial State*, together with an interpretive essay, will be published by SUNY Press in Spring 2012, and he has also authored journal articles on a wide variety of topics in literary theory, German literature, and philosophy. He is presently working on a study of Friedrich Hölderlin's theory of the political.

Richard Fletcher is an Assistant Professor in the Department of Classics at The Ohio State University. His book, *Apuleius' Platonism: the Impersonation of Philosophy*, is forthcoming from Cambridge University Press.

Alain Gigandet studied philosophy at the École Normale Supérieure de la rue d'Ulm and took his Ph.D. in the History of Ancient Philosophy at the Sorbonne (Paris I). Currently, he teaches Ancient Philosophy at the University of Paris-East, Créteil (formerly Paris XII). His research focuses upon ancient Epicureanism, as well as its modern and contemporary reinterpretations. Published work includes *Fama deum. Lucrèce et les raisons du mythe* (Vrin, 1998), *Lucrèce, Atomes, mouvement* (PUF, 2001), and (with P.-M. Morel) *Lire Épicure et les épicuriens* (PUF, 2007) as well as numerous papers upon various aspects of ancient Epicurean philosophy and modern readings of Epicureanism (Montaigne, Diderot, Leopardi, Hegel, Strauss, Foucault).

Brooke Holmes is an Assistant Professor of Classics at Princeton University, where she currently holds the Elias Boudinot Preceptorship. She is the author of *The Symptom and the Subject: The Emergence of the Physical Body in Ancient Greece* (Princeton, 2010) and the co-editor, with W. V. Harris, of *Aelius Aristides between Greece, Rome, and the Gods* (Brill, 2008), as well as articles on Homer, Euripides, the history of medicine and the body, and Lucretius. Her book *Gender: Antiquity and Its Legacy* is forthcoming from I. B. Tauris and OUP in 2012.

Natania Meeker is an Associate Professor of French and Comparative Literature at the University of Southern California. She is the author of *Voluptuous Philosophy: Literary Materialism in the French Enlightenment* (Fordham, 2006) and a series of articles on femininity in the French Enlightenment. She is currently working on two book projects: a monograph on female libertinism, and a co-authored volume on plant horror from antiquity to the present day.

Glenn W. Most has taught at the Universities of Yale, Princeton, Michigan, Siena, Innsbruck, and Heidelberg. Since 2001 he has been Professor of Greek Philology at the Scuola Normale Superiore di Pisa, since 1996 he has been a visiting Professor on the Committee on Social Thought at the University of Chicago; recently he has also become an external scientific member of the Max Planck Institute for the History of Science in Berlin. He has published numerous books and articles on ancient and modern literature and philosophy, the history and methodology of classical studies, comparative literature, cultural studies, the history of religion, literary theory, and the history of art. Most recently he has co-edited a one-volume companion to the classical tradition, and is currently preparing a co-edited four-volume Loeb edition of the Presocratics, co-revising an English translation of the Greek tragedies, and co-editing and -translating the ancient and medieval commentaries to Hesiod's *Theogony*.

Gerard Passannante is Assistant Professor of English and Comparative Literature at the University of Maryland and the author of *The Lucretian Renaissance: Philology and the Afterlife of Tradition* (Chicago, 2011). He was the recipient of a Rome Prize in 2006-2007 and has held fellowships at the National Humanities Center and the Folger Shakespeare Library. He is currently at work on a project about the history of disaster and the humanist imagination.

Adam Rzepka recently received his Ph.D. in English from the University of Chicago, and teaches courses in Rhetoric and Comparative Literature at University of California, Berkeley. His dissertation and current book project investigate the category of "experience" in early modern culture and theater. His other research interests include early modern science, travel and utopian literature, and critical theory.

W. H. Shearin is Assistant Professor of Classics at the University of Miami. He has received various fellowships and awards, including a Fulbright and a postdoctoral award from the Andrew W. Mellon Fellowship of Scholars at Stanford University. Currently, he is completing two projects, one on performative language in the Epicurean poet Lucretius, the other on stupidity in Roman-period philosophical texts.

James A. Steintrager is Professor of English, Comparative Literature, and French at the University of California, Irvine. He is the author of *Cruel Delight: Enlightenment Culture and the Inhuman* (2004) and has published on a range of topics, from the theoretical and popular reception of the Marquis de Sade in the 1960s to Hong Kong horror cinema. His current book project is entitled *The First Sexual Revolution: Libertines, License, and the Autonomy of Pleasure* (forthcoming from Columbia University Press).

Benjamin Aldes Wurgaft is currently the Andrew W. Mellon Interdisciplinary Postdoctoral Fellow at the New School for Social Research. He received his doctorate in European Intellectual History from the University of California, Berkeley and his undergraduate degree from Swarthmore College. His writings on public intellectuals, critical theory, and food culture have appeared in *History and Theory*, *Gastronomica*, and other journals.

Note on Editions

The edition and translation used throughout is the second edition of W. H. D. Rouse's *Lucretius, De Rerum Natura* (Cambridge, Mass., 1992), revised by M. F. Smith.

To make the volume as accessible as possible, we have provided full information on all of the classical texts used in preparing it.

DYNAMIC READING

Introduction: Swerves, Events, and Unexpected Effects

W. H. Shearin and Brooke Holmes*

ὕστατος αὖ φυσικῶν καὶ κύντατος, ἐκ Σάμου ἐλθὼν
γραμμοδιδασκαλίδης, ἀναγωγότατος ζωόντων.

Last of the *physikoi* and most shameless, he came from Samos,
a teacher of letters, the most undisciplined of living creatures.[1]

So Timon of Phlius describes Epicurus.[2] However exaggerated these lines, they contain, like many fragments of ancient biography, elements of central importance for understanding not so much Epicurus himself but, rather, his historical and intellectual impact and the reception of his philosophy. The papers in this collection offer a series of engagements with Epicurus in this latter guise, that is, as the founder of a philosophy that has been transmitted, appropriated, and reanimated multiple times over the past two millennia.

Timon's remarks imply that Epicureanism's journey through history has been a bruising one. And, in fact, from its inception, it has been a philosophy that, while at times eagerly received, has also been subject to

* We are grateful to Constanze Güthenke and Glenn Most, as well as to the anonymous referees, for their very helpful feedback on the introduction.

[1] The term φυσικός (*physikos*) does not have an easy English equivalent. Perhaps the best rendering is "natural philosopher," one who studies φύσις (*physis*, "nature") as part of a tradition going back to the Preplatonic philosophers.

[2] This couplet is attributed to Timon at Diogenes Laërtius 10.3. All citations of Diogenes follow the edition of Marcovich (1999). In referring to Epicurus as a "teacher of letters," Timon is playing on his alleged conversion from schoolmaster to philosopher.

vicious attack. In the hands of both admirers and critics, moreover, Epicurus's ideas have appeared uncommonly vulnerable to misrepresentation, willful or otherwise. The present volume does not try to reverse the damage by reconstructing the ancient doctrines or offering philosophical justification for them. Rather, the essays included here take up Epicureanism as a catalytic object that must be read *together with* its effects. We approach Epicureanism not as a closed philosophical system but as a dynamic "text" that is capable of producing patterns of response—patterns that are nevertheless diversified by the temperaments (individual, cultural, historical) of those who encounter it—and that comes to incorporate those responses into itself.

To this end, the papers gathered here range over more than two millennia to plot reactions to Epicurus's legacy, from Cornelius Nepos and Diogenes Laërtius to Leo Strauss, Gilles Deleuze, and Michel Foucault. Some of the papers explore the ways in which Epicureanism disturbs and inhabits those who would critique it or reject it altogether. Others trace the various effects produced on Epicureanism's adherents, whose minds are as often unsettled by Epicurean texts as they are led toward *ataraxia*, the psychic calm at which Epicurean teaching aims. Extending these lines of inquiry, some contributors adopt concepts from Epicureanism, such as the swerve or the analogy between atoms and letters or the sublime, to reflect on the tradition of reading and response to which it gives rise and the very concepts of influence, impact, and imitation.

The volume thus takes up Epicureanism as a kind of text that has been thickened by a rich history of reading and rereading, a thickening that reshapes the "original" while also attesting its enduring creative powers. By referring to Epicureanism as a "text," we aim to capture its status as an interlocking, if not watertight, network of concepts that travels through history both as a relatively cohesive system (e.g., in the *De Rerum Natura*) and in fragments and paraphrases and sound bites to be cited, praised, appropriated, reinvented, critiqued, and mocked. The notion of a "text" captures, too, the idea that Epicureanism is under constant modification and expansion as the oldest stratum of texts by or about Epicurus generates new texts, both pro- and anti-Epicurus, that become part of the larger "text" of Epicureanism. With regard to these individual texts, we also understand the concept of "text" in more conventional terms as "the wording of anything written or printed; the structure formed by the words in their order, the very words, phrases, and sentences as written," on the one hand, and as a physical object encountered by a reader (e.g., "I am holding a text of Lucretius"), on the other.[3] For the two senses, "text" and text, it may be useful to compare the transmission of Platonism as opposed to the transmission of specific texts of Plato (recognizing that, in the case of Epicurus, one of the most important transmitting texts is authored by an uncommonly gifted disciple, namely, Lucretius).

What we might call "philosophical reception" need not, of course, be figured solely in textual terms. Rather, our deliberate decision to use "text" in this double sense when speaking of the Epicurean tradition reflects our sense that Epicureanism is also a valuable resource for thinking about reception more generally, that there is an "Epicurean" way of thinking about reception as well as a reception of Epicureanism. Among the powerful tools that Epicureanism has to offer the theorization of reception is the well-known analogy between letters and atoms, where the written word models the atomic compound. In referring to Epicureanism itself as a text, we have the atomist analogy in mind. This analogy facilitates the conceptualization of Epicureanism as something material and capable of impacting the minds of listeners and readers, as well as the conceptualization of a text as an interrelated and dynamic complex of ideas.

The aims of the volume are twofold. On the one hand, by offering a series of papers that explore the powerful impact of Epicurus's ideas on the Western tradition, we stake out ground for a renewed encounter with Epicureanism in the present. On the other hand, the volume suggests new directions for theorizing the interaction between ancients, moderns, and the many readers in between. In the introduction, we point out ways in which Epicureanism has already contributed to what "reception" means and offer suggestions as to how Epicureanism may continue to shape Reception Studies by turning scholarly concerns from an emphasis

---

[3] *Oxford English Dictionary*, 2nd ed. (1989), s.v. "text, n.," http://www.oed.com/ (online edition accessed 18 May 2011). We can imagine the physical position of the reader as the complement to that of the writer as Jane Bennett describes her in terms of what Deleuze and Guattari call an assemblage: "The sentences of this book also emerged from the confederate agency of many striving macro- and microactants: from 'my' memories, intentions, contentions, intestinal bacteria, eyeglasses, and blood sugar, as well as from the plastic computer keyboard, the bird song from the open window, or the air or particulates in the room, to name only a few of the participants. What is at work on the page is an animal-vegetable-mineral-sonority cluster with a particular degree and duration of power" ((2010) 23).

on epistemology (what we can *know* about a given work and its meaning) to an emphasis on affect and dynamic response (how a given idea, philosophical system, or text provokes us to think, imagine, and even feel in new ways).

Both aspects of the project, we hope, can contribute to a conversation about the reception of ancient philosophical ideas. While the field of Reception Studies has grown exponentially in the last decade or so, most of the attention has been directed toward the afterlife of literary and aesthetic works and to the ways in which the idea of classical antiquity has influenced the emergence of philology as a modern academic discipline. There has been less interest in the reception of philosophical systems, at least within Reception Studies, which has had little interaction with the history of philosophy.[4]

Historians of philosophy, conversely, have tended to engage with ancient philosophers and philosophies more at the level of doctrine and argument than at the level of their reception by later thinkers.[5] There are, however, important crosscurrents to this approach, some of which are becoming increasingly dominant. Historians of philosophy in the Hellenistic and Roman periods, in particular, have been highly sensitive to the transformation of positions and arguments within the philosophical schools under internal and external pressures.[6] Moreover, the inquiry into the reception of philosophical and scientific ideas *within* antiquity has been greatly enriched in recent years by the rapidly growing attention to doxography and the commentary tradition as objects of study in their own right.[7] Historians of philosophy, together with historians of science

---

[4] Philosophy is largely absent, for example, from the excellent survey of recent scholarship in Güthenke (2009). Modern scholarship on doxography is briefly mentioned at Porter (2008) 473.

[5] This approach to the history of philosophy is defended, for example, in Frede (1992).

[6] Historical—and historically informed—studies of ancient Epicureanism are numerous. Clay (1998), for example, in a series of specific case studies, considers much evidence, both material and textual, for the practices of the Epicurean school. See also Frischer (1982), where Frischer, a specialist in material culture, speculates (if not always convincingly) about the practices of philosophical recruitment within the ancient Epicurean school. Sedley (1973), in presenting a new edition of Epicurus's *On Nature* XXVIII, also offers much of interest on the historical development of Epicurus's own thought.

[7] For recent surveys of work on the doxographical tradition, see Mansfeld (1999a); (1999b); Mejer (2006); van der Eijk (2009). For case studies, see, e.g., Mansfeld and Runia

and medicine, have shifted away from an approach that mines later authors for fragments of earlier thinkers in order to bring to the foreground the context and structure of these citations, as well as the doctrinal and methodological commitments of the doxographer. By confronting head-on the mediated nature of so much of what we know about Greek philosophy, science, and medicine, these scholars have developed significant subfields within these disciplines, marked by their own concerns and debates.[8]

The present volume contributes to these larger projects in the history of ancient Greco-Roman philosophy while, at the same time, moving beyond the ancient world and the specific genre of doxography. By bringing together an inquiry into the impact of the Epicurean tradition on later authors with the theoretical concerns that have occupied those working primarily on aesthetic works from classical antiquity, we hope to open up space for greater interaction between the history of philosophy and science and the field that has come to be termed Reception Studies.

In what follows, we flesh out the overarching aims of the volume. We begin by outlining some contributions that Epicureanism can make to recent and current work in the field of Reception Studies before reviewing what this volume hopes to offer to the specific reception of Epicureanism. The introduction closes with a brief summary of the essays in the collection. These essays bear witness to the long afterlife of Timon's attack on Epicurus as the most "undisciplined" (*anagōgotatos*) of creatures, a word that, in Greek, describes both someone intemperate in his pleasures and someone unconstrained by *agōgē* ("training, discipline").[9] The word's double sense suggests that it is precisely *because* of Epicurus's lack of discipline that his legacy has proved so fascinating and so productive.

(1996–); Baltussen (2000); Wolfsdorf (2009). The essays in van der Eijk (1999) address doxography within the history of medicine. On the commentary tradition, see the essays in Gibson and Kraus (2002).

[8] See, for example, the competing positions of Zhmud (2001) and Mansfeld (2002).

[9] *Anagōgos* is a term Plutarch uses to describe a man who is "intemperate in his pleasures": Plutarch, *Moralia* 140B (*Precepts for Marriage*): ἀκρατὴς...περὶ τὰς ἡδονάς. This Plutarch passage is cited from Klaerr (1985).

RECEPTION STUDIES, EPICUREANISM,
AND EPICUREAN RECEPTION

> What has come to be called reception theory is by no means as
> uniform as it may seem. Its various ramifications are marked by a
> basic duality, incorporating both the reception of the literary text
> and its effects on its potential reader. . . . An aesthetics of reception
> explores reactions to the literary text by readers in different
> historical situations. . . . By delineating the historical conditionality
> of readers' reactions, an aesthetics of reception turns literature into
> a tool for reconstituting the past.
>
> While an aesthetics of reception deals with real readers, whose
> reactions testify to certain historically conditioned experiences of
> literature, my own theory of aesthetic response focuses on how a
> piece of literature impacts on its implied readers and elicits a
> response. A theory of aesthetic response has its roots in the text;
> an aesthetics of reception arises from a history of readers'
> judgments.[10]

Thus Wolfgang Iser, in a recent introduction to literary theory, characterizes reception theory, an approach to literature that, for all its still-
developing variety, remains chiefly identified with Iser himself and his
former Konstanz colleague, Hans Robert Jauß. Here Iser, while treating
"an aesthetics of reception" and his own "theory of aesthetic response"
as two parts of a single theory, nonetheless takes pains to draw a distinction between Jauß's more historical contribution (*Rezeptionsästhetik*)
and his own more textual one (*Wirkungsästhetik*). This distinction is
worth preserving, if for no other reason than that it fairly accurately characterizes the Anglo-American reception of the two scholars and their
work. Iser's textually driven "theory of aesthetic response" has long since
been received among, if not entirely subsumed into, other "reader-
response" theories; Jauß's historical work, on the other hand, has become
the basis, albeit in substantially modified form, of much that today is
termed simply "reception."[11]

---

[10] Iser (2006) 57.

[11] For the reception of Iser into the American academy, see, for example, Tompkins
(1980), which presents—among a set of essays penned largely by American-based critics—a

While any attempt to sever Iser's project too firmly from Jauß's does injustice to their shared development in Konstanz, Reception Studies as a field, particularly as conducted within the discipline of Classics, has developed largely in dialogue with Jauß rather than with Iser. Typical in this regard are the works of Charles Martindale, who has spearheaded much of the growing enthusiasm for Reception Studies in the United Kingdom and elsewhere. Two works in particular—*Redeeming the Text* and *Classics and the Uses of Reception* (an edited collection with Richard Thomas)—have established Martindale as a leading writer on theoretical problems of classical reception.[12] In both of these works, Martindale marries Jaußian reception to "other, more deconstructionist models of dissemination."[13] He thus adopts Jauß's historical approach, with its real, historical readers and its historically conditioned "horizon of expectations" (*Erwartungshorizont*), only to explode anything like a Jaußian notion of history. More specifically, Martindale criticizes the tenet, central to Jauß's notion of history (and inherited from the philosopher Hans-Georg Gadamer), that—despite any manifest plurality of interpretations—the text "remains the same work."[14] On the basis of this model, receptions differ entirely because of historical circumstance and not because of any difference that may be located within the text itself. Martindale, by contrast, prefers to understand reception on the model of musical performance, where each reception or performance—even if it bears a "family relationship" to other performances—is a distinct event.[15] In other words, for Martindale, different receptions (which effectively create different "texts" or "works") do not differ due to varying "horizons of expectations" but rather due to the fact that different receptions are distinct occurrences.

---

selection from Iser (1974). Iser eventually became an American-based critic, but most of his founding theoretical works were written in Germany. For Jauß, the canonical work is Jauß (1982), a collection and translation of several works largely from the 1970s.

[12] Martindale (1993) and Martindale and Thomas (2006). See further Martindale (2007).

[13] Martindale (1993) 10. Jauß is explicitly named and discussed in Martindale's work (e.g., Martindale (1993) 7–10 and Martindale (2006) 3). Iser, by contrast, appears only marginally in Martindale's writing. In Martindale (1993), for example, Iser appears only in one footnote (16n.22), where he is "dispos[ed] of" by Stanley Fish.

[14] Gadamer (1975) 336, cited at Martindale (1993) 17.

[15] The term "family relationship" is Martindale's, although it clearly echoes Wittgenstein's notion of "Familienähnlichkeiten." See Wittgenstein (1997) § 67.

What is so striking about the move to understand reception as performance is that it commits Martindale to a position that better resembles that of Iser than that of Jauß. Of course, Martindale (not unlike Stanley Fish[16]) would be displeased with some of the terms of Iser's textual theory. Iser continually divides up texts between their determinate portions, where there is no question as to the meaning of the text, and their indeterminate ones, where there are "blanks" to be filled in by the reader.[17] This division implicitly suggests precisely what Martindale aims to deny—that "texts" or "works" are, with regard to their interpretation, in some way fixed. Nonetheless, with a Derridean redefinition of history, a definition of history that locates reception in the event rather than in a given historical period with a given "horizon of expectations," Martindale changes the problematics of reception from a largely positivist attempt at the reconstruction of history to a problematics of reading. It is precisely this attention to reading that brings Martindale closer to Iser than to Jauß.[18]

This brief summary of Martindale's engagement with reception theory provides key terms for articulating both the specific contribution of the present volume and the contribution of Epicureanism more generally to Reception Studies. In the first instance, we suggest that the dichotomy presented by Iser and Jauß—aestheticizing *or* historical, textual *or* cultural—is, in many ways, false. Instead, we understand reading and interpretation as always already ideological and cultural. Even the most formal or aesthetically oriented readings of texts can be shown to be rife with historical and cultural meaning. To some extent, this position separates us not only from Jauß and Iser but also from Martindale, who, as Miriam Leonard has recently pointed out, privileges the formal or aesthetic dimension of Derrida's thought without taking his conceptualization of history sufficiently into account.[19]

Moreover, in place of a performance theory of reception, we prefer to speak of reception as an event. The term "event" better captures, we feel,

---

[16] See Fish (1989).

[17] For "blanks" in Iser's theory, see, e.g., Iser (1978) 182–203.

[18] Indeed, one might speculate that Martindale makes Jauß his primary forebear precisely because classical studies has such a long history as a positivist, historical discipline. That is, writing on (and revising) Jauß allows Martindale to attack positivist historiography in a way that writing on Iser would not.

[19] Leonard (2006).

the dynamics at play in reception, particularly the sense that interpretation is an affective transaction. This transaction may not be directed entirely by either the reader-performer or her text. Instead, we suggest, something complex happens in reception—namely, an event—and one of the most significant traces of this event is often its affective impact. Additionally—and here we turn to another significant focus of the present volume—"event," at least as it can be understood as an *eventum* ("accidental property"), is a term of Epicurean physics.

The recent history of literary and cultural theory has shown that Epicureanism—especially in the guise of Lucretius's poem *De Rerum Natura*—can be a productive resource for theorizing reading and interpretation. More specifically, Epicureanism has provided a number of recent philosophers and theorists with the figural vocabulary to characterize not only reading but also a number of the phenomena attending to reading, including, as we have just mentioned, the event itself.[20] In other words, Epicureanism's claim on Reception Studies is quite direct and organic: it is not merely yet another text whose history of readings we may trace but a "text" that in many instances helps define the terms of reading itself.

To catalogue all the ways in which modern critics and philosophers have deployed Epicurean or Lucretian themes (and tropes) in the characterization of reading (and interpreting) would be a vast undertaking. Yet a brief sampling of this work may give some sense of just how important Epicureanism has been for recent theoretical and philosophical work in this vein. In his book *La naissance de la physique dans le texte de Lucrèce*, the philosopher Michel Serres points to Lucretius's frequent comparison of letters to atoms (both, at times, *elementa* in Latin), as well as to his famous description of the *clinamen*, or atomic "swerve,"[21] in presenting discourse as defined by turbulence and movement.[22] The critic Jacques Lezra fastens upon the Lucretian notion of the *eventum*

---

[20] It is perhaps worth noting that Lucretius himself, if not Epicureanism more generally, makes a substantial contribution to our understanding of what *figura* (and "figural") may mean. See Auerbach (1984) 16–18.

[21] For passages within Lucretius that compare letters and atoms, see *De Rerum Natura* 1.197, 1.824, 1.912, 2.688, 2.1013. For the swerve, see *De Rerum Natura* 2.216–93 as well as the further discussion below.

[22] See Serres (1977) 168–71.

("accident" as in "accidental, rather than proper, attribute"),[23] turning it upon us, as readers and interpreters, in order to point out that there may be other ways of configuring the past than merely in terms of what is proper or accidental to period terms like "Renaissance."[24] In his last writings and interviews, the Marxist philosopher Louis Althusser speaks of an "aleatory materialism," which he traces back to Democritus, Epicurus, and Lucretius.[25] For Althusser, Epicureanism's anti-teleology, its denial of a first cause at the origin of the world, is a central element in displacing philosophical attempts to locate reason, sense, or necessity authoritatively. Finally, Jacques Derrida reads much of the ancient atomist tradition as a forerunner of modern psychoanalytic thought, focusing specifically on how "accidental" occurrences in Epicurus become "symptoms of the soul."[26] In each of these authors, Epicureanism, by teaching us to read through symptoms, swerves, anti-teleology, and *eventa*, functions not only as a philosophy whose reception we study but also as a theoretical resource informing and defining how we read.

Many of the pieces in the present volume likewise draw critical and theoretical tools from Epicureanism for pondering and figuring reception. W. H. Shearin, in studying the ancient Epicurean Titus Pomponius Atticus, looks at ways in which Epicurean anti-teleology may be not only a characterization of the natural world but also a descriptor of how we read and interpret texts. Adam Rzepka draws upon both Michel Serres and Jacques Lezra to consider the ways in which Epicureanism figures the terms of its own reception. Gerard Passannante explores the affective sympathy of one Renaissance reader with his text of Lucretius, studying tensions between this encounter and the stated aims of Epicurean doctrine. Brooke Holmes examines how Deleuze, in his reading of the *De Rerum Natura*, explores the function of the simulacrum as a mechanism for explaining not only how we view the physical world but also how philosophy and, more specifically, philosophical texts inform our ethical relationship to that world. Other essays in the volume may be seen

---

[23] See Lucretius *De Rerum Natura* 1.449–58.

[24] Lezra (1997) 4: "Disagreements over periodization quickly show themselves to be debates about what characteristics or attributes are definitionally proper (*coniuncta*) or accidental (*eventa*) to a thing or term. . . ."

[25] See, e.g., Althusser (1994) 35. Selections from Althusser (1994) are translated in Althusser (2006).

[26] Derrida (1984) 8.

to approach these—and related issues—on their own terms. With the remainder of this section, we aim to explore one particular way in which Epicureanism, ever a fertile resource for rethinking reading, can open up current discourse within the discipline of Reception Studies, namely, by bringing the physical recipient and her embodied experience back into the act of reading and receiving the text.

Recent writing about Reception Studies, especially within the discipline of Classics—with its largely historicist and positivist past—has tended to ponder reception in epistemological terms.[27] The theory of reception is concerned above all with what we, as readers, can *know*. In the first instance, this epistemological focus serves a primarily negative function: reception reveals to us the limits on our knowledge. In his afterword to *Classics and the Uses of Reception*, for example, Duncan Kennedy writes:

A position of *epistemological* [emphasis added] certainty is a comfortable one to inhabit, particularly if you are a scholar, but reception theory has the capacity to challenge that confidence if the predisposition to a retrospective view that the term "reception" encourages is set against the possibility that knowledge is *provisional* [emphasis original], in the strong sense: looking toward the future, toward a desired plenitude that is not yet there (and indeed may never be). . . .[28]

Kennedy's point that reception theory can undermine epistemological certainty is well taken.[29] The diversity of historical readings of the *De Rerum Natura*, coupled with, as Kennedy stresses, the text's potential for future readings, should make us question any reading that professes absolute, eternal certainty. But, without disagreeing with Kennedy,

---

[27] To be fair, there are certainly moments where Martindale and others point to non-epistemological concerns in reception; see, for example, Martindale (1993) 10; Batstone (2006) 19. Both Kennedy and Martindale tend, however, to revert to epistemology in their more general formulations about reception and its significance. For the idea of a "materialist" Reception Studies, see Porter (2008) 477.

[28] Kennedy (2006) 292.

[29] And it is echoed variously throughout the Martindale-Thomas volume. Martindale, for example, speaks in his introduction of the "situated, contingent . . . character of readings" ((2006) 3) and makes clear that, for him, reception "is a way of doing classics that is at odds with the positivism of much that is now labelled 'reception'" (12).

we must ask whether questions of epistemology are the only, or even the primary, ones at stake in the process named by reception.

A detour into the recent history of literary theory can help us reconsider the place of epistemology in Reception Studies, specifically by suggesting that affect has been an overlooked element in theorizing reception. Although the observation is not often made, reception (named by the more traditional term "influence") and Epicureanism collide productively within Harold Bloom's well-known theory of poetry, as presented in *The Anxiety of Influence*.[30] There Bloom articulates a number of what he calls "revisionary ratios," that is, figurations of poetic influence. He directly addresses himself to poet-readers—and indeed tends to concern himself with "strong poets" and "strong misreadings"—but there is no reason not to understand his theory as applying to all meaningful reading and reception. The chief of his models for influence is Lucretius's *clinamen*,[31] or atomic "swerve," the uncaused, minimal movement that, on one reading, is the basis for free will.[32] Bloom describes his use of the *clinamen* as follows:

Clinamen . . . is poetic misreading or misprision proper. . . . A poet swerves away from his precursor, by so reading his precursor's poem as to execute a *clinamen* in relation to it. This appears as a corrective movement in his own poem, which implies that the precursor poem went accurately up to a certain point, but then should have swerved, precisely in the direction that the new poem moves.[33]

---

[30] Bloom (2011) represents the most recent statement of Bloom's theory of poetic influence. This work, his "final reflection upon the influence process" (ix), shows just how much Epicureanism—and Lucretius in particular—lie at the heart of his thought. Here he devotes an entire section, nearly a quarter of the work, to "The Skeptical Sublime" (133–206), where he traces the "Lucretian tradition" (136) from Dryden, Milton, and Shelley through to Giacomo Leopardi, Merrill, and Yeats. In terms of defining his "revisionary ratios," this new book largely restates Bloom's previous views, but in terms of articulating a particularly "Lucretian sublime" (166)—a term that is also treated by Most in the current volume—it represents a powerful addition to Bloom's critical catalogue.

[31] See Wolfreys (2000) 23–26, who reads the "swerve" as a (if not the only) distinctively Bloomian trope of reading.

[32] Many modern philosophers have found the Epicurean doctrine of the swerve incoherent. See, for example, Purinton (1999). Classicists, even those heavily influenced by the Anglo-American philosophical tradition, tend to be more sympathetic to the notion: see inter alia Englert (1987) 64–66; Fowler (2002) 407–27 (and ad loc.). (This scholarly literature is largely ignored by those who appropriate the swerve for theorizing reading.)

[33] Bloom (1997) 14.

Here Bloom rereads the swerve, replacing the atoms in the traditional Lucretian account with poet-readers. This juxtaposition of human readers and atoms serves, we may suggest, to blur the boundaries between the two.[34] Bloom's use of the *clinamen* implicitly paints poets as atoms that move mechanically until liberated by a chance movement that occurs at "no fixed place and no fixed time" (*De Rerum Natura* 2.293). (Lucretius himself makes this figural move well before Bloom: readers of his poem will recall, among other moments, how, in his second book, atoms fight wars, while in his fifth, humans gather and dissipate mechanically like atoms.)[35] Juxtaposing humans and atoms raises many issues, but in the realm of reception one of the most obvious is that of agency and intention. Suggesting (if only indirectly) that poet-readers act like mindless matter seems to call into question their ability to act solely as autonomous, intentional agents, a point noted by Bloom himself: "the student of Poetic Influence . . . must understand that the *clinamen* always must be considered as though it were simultaneously *intentional and involuntary* . . ." (44–45, emphasis added).

Within the well-traveled terrain of literary theory, the topic of agency (or more familiarly, authorial intention) may seem an old one, but it may yet have something to teach us. Bloom, it should be noted, does not utterly discount intention; instead, he couples it together with the involuntary. If reception (or influence), as Bloom surmises, is a process that, for each individual reader, is at once intentional *and* involuntary, then— while it should hardly be taken for granted that these two components of the process (intention and the involuntary) act in conflict—reception cannot be understood as anything other than a complex transaction or event. On the one hand, then, it is no surprise that recent writers on reception such as Duncan Kennedy use this complexity to make an epistemological point, stressing our ignorance about the transaction.

---

[34] Some of the result of such blurring would undoubtedly be "psychoanalytic," at least in the weak sense that intentions would not be fully present. Scholars have perceived a certain loosely "psychoanalytic" element in Epicureanism, especially in Lucretius: see Jope (1983). While far from hostile toward psychoanalytic approaches, the present discussion aims to describe a type of reading, one that need not be psychoanalytic, where texts are engaged as opportunities for interlocking with an external, othered world that produces an experience of pleasurable or unpleasurable assimilation.

[35] Cabisius (1985) and Fowler (1989) both examine the representation of humans as atoms and *vice versa*. Shearin (2007) 106–56, building upon this work, examines, among other things, how human names become more atomic.

Whatever an interpreter's intentions—whether these include actively producing further poetry or simply coming to grips with words on the page—it is difficult to feel certain in the knowledge that, within such a complex event, those intentions are realized or that they can be isolated from the rest of the event of reception. Yet on the other hand, the complexity of reception need not be reduced entirely to an epistemological problem: instead, this very complexity can open up other avenues of thought.

We might, for example, think of Bloom's coupling of intention with the involuntary as a reminder of a somewhat intransigent material or bodily presence in reading, a presence that affects and is affected by reading in productive, if sometimes unpredictable, ways. In other words, Bloom's insistence that agency in influence (or reception) is not simply defined by authorial intention perhaps hints that this process is not governed by a rational, teleological structure but shaped by other factors whose logic is better understood in material terms. Reading and influence are obviously mental and intellectual, but there may well be a physics (or a physical component) of reading, too. From this perspective (which is at least in some ways Epicurean), the reader experiences not only a physical encounter with the text but also, through reading, a potentially transforming and transformative encounter with the material world. Epicurus himself often uses physics to get to ethics: eliminating divine intervention as a possible physical explanation of lightning, for example, leads to psychic calm. Can turning our attention toward a physics of reading—that is, asking material, physical questions of who or what acts on whom—provide avenues for understanding reception that extend beyond the epistemological?

Bloom's exchange with Paul de Man about the former's theory of poetic influence dramatizes some of these concerns. Their exchange is one, as we shall see, that has often been read as turning upon epistemology and the epistemological status of figural language, but there may be other, more material issues at work. In reviewing Bloom's work, de Man points out, in a move we may call Epicurean, that the matter of language, his analogue of Lucretius's swerving atom, may be the agent just as well as the poet:

If we admit that the term "influence" is itself a metaphor that dramatizes a linguistic structure into a diachronic narrative, then it follows that Bloom's categories of misreading not only operate between authors, but also between the various texts of a single author or, within a given text, between the different parts, down to each particular chapter, paragraph, sentence, and, finally, down to the interplay between literal and figurative meaning within a single word or grammatical sign. . . . The passage through rhetoric reveals that the traditional scheme, still much in evidence in *The Anxiety of Influence*, according to which language is a tool manipulated by extralinguistic impulses rooted in a subject, can be dislodged by the equally reasonable alternative that the affective appeal of text could just as well be the result of a linguistic structure. . . . The very scheme of things based on such terms as cause, effect, center, and meaning is put in question.[36]

Bloom reads this critique as an epistemological one:

. . . literature relies upon troping, a turning away not only from the literal but from prior tropes. . . . Any stance that anyone takes up towards a metaphorical work will itself be metaphorical. My . . . decades-long critical quarrel with Paul de Man, a radiant intelligence, finally centered upon just the contention stated in the previous sentence. He insisted that an *epistemological stance* in regard to a literary work was the only way out of the tropological labyrinth, while I replied that such a stance was no more or less a trope than any other.[37]

In other words, Bloom takes the force of de Man's critique to lie in the epistemological uncertainty created by the inability of the external reader to decide between the agency of the poet and the agency of his language.[38]

There are certainly grounds for reading de Man as Bloom does.[39] Essays such as "The Epistemology of Metaphor" show the emphasis on

---

[36] De Man (1983) 276.

[37] Bloom (1997) xix. Emphasis added.

[38] "Agency of his language" is a strange turn of phrase, particularly for those who are not well-acquainted with de Man's *œuvre*. Perhaps the best way of understanding the agency that de Man accords to language is on the analogy of the machine. Just as machines, which are in some sense nothing more than artificial products of human effort, nonetheless may "do" things, including things we do not wish, so language can act and even misfire. The scholar who has identified de Man most clearly as a thinker of the machine is Avital Ronell. See Ronell (2002) 97–98.

[39] But it should be noted that the position Bloom carves out for himself is what others would attribute to de Man. See Jameson (1991) 238: "Metaphor, in DeMan [*sic*], is therefore itself a metaphorical act. . . ." Jameson's reading of de Man is fascinating for trying

the epistemology of figural language in de Man's writing.[40] But there is also another presumption, a suggestion if not a developed argument, lurking in de Man's commentary: de Man is interested in explaining, whether by recourse to linguistic structures or to human agents, "the affective appeal of text."[41] This phrase is striking because it is absent from many recent, more purely epistemological treatments of reception. Whatever de Man here suggests we may know, he aims to explain the affective or emotional appeal of texts. While affective appeal is perhaps inseparable from knowledge in the case of reading and receiving, an emphasis on affect and emotions can call into question the persistent recourse to knowledge and epistemologically based formulations we have been tracking in some of the more theoretical writing on reception.

"Meaning," Charles Martindale writes, "is always realized at the point of reception."[42] Perhaps so, but texts and their readers do things other than realize meaning. In trying to locate Epicurean reception, it is worth remembering that Epicureanism has often been understood primarily as an ethical philosophy, one that aims at joy and pleasure, even if this latter term originally held a sense (*ataraxia*, "freedom from disturbance") unfamiliar to most modern pleasure-seekers. Indeed, pleasure possesses a striking, if potentially accidental, textual connection to the *clinamen*, the Lucretian swerve that Bloom chooses to figure poetic influence, the swerve that at once undermines and underwrites intentionality. There is a famous confusion, perhaps nothing more than the error of an inattentive scribe, in Lucretius's text in the very passage where he justifies the need for the swerve. At *De Rerum Natura* 2.257, Lucretius speaks, in most modern editions, of a "free will, turned away from fate," but in all of his reported manuscripts (most ninth- or tenth-century) this is a "free pleasure." That is, by what amounts in Latin to the change of a letter—from *voluptas* to *voluntas*—the intent of Lucretius's

---

to understand de Man's relationship to Epicureanism, primarily because it attributes to him an eighteenth-century epistemology and locates him, as a thinker, in close proximity to Rousseau. These two (related) observations are interesting because Rousseau, particularly the Rousseau of the *Second Discourse*, is arguably the most Lucretian writer since Lucretius himself. See, e.g., Lovejoy and Boas (1935) 240–42.

   [40] "The Epistemology of Metaphor" appears most conveniently at de Man (1996) 34–50, although it was originally published in 1978.

   [41] Terada (2001) presents a strong case for the centrality of emotions in de Man's work.

   [42] Martindale (1993) 3. This statement is echoed throughout Martindale and Thomas (2006). See, for example, Batstone (2006) 16.

swerve is moved from the characterization of affective appeal to the characterization of intention.[43] While there is no need to attribute this reading to Lucretius himself—the text certainly provides easier sense if corrected to *voluntas*—for an understanding of Epicureanism that values rather than rejects the history of reading and misreading Lucretius, it is worth holding onto the conjunction of will and affect that this textual "error" encapsulates.[44]

Natania Meeker, in a recent reading of this passage, has interpreted the textual conjunction of *voluptas* ("pleasure") and *voluntas* ("will") as creating a kind of choice in how we understand Lucretius's own intentions for the impact of the *De Rerum Natura* on the reader:

> Lucretius, for all his critique of theology as mass delusion, is less concerned with freedom as "enlightened" choice than he is with pleasure as giving rise to a moment in which one reader's experience of the world may be materially reconfigured. His intention is at least in part to give readers what they most want to receive—not an illusory freedom of pure choice—but the possibility of bodily reinvestment in the material autonomy of the *semina rerum* as the very substance of delight.[45]

By emphasizing the idea that our "experience of the world may be materially reconfigured" by encountering Lucretius's poem, Meeker gives a sense of the ways in which reinscribing the embodied reader into a theory of reception can fundamentally alter the parameters of what we mean by reception itself. For she suggests, through her reading of Lucretius's own understanding of "reception," that a reader's engagement with a text is not only affected by her cultural, historical, and physical situatedness but also has the potential to reconfigure our encounters with the world around us.

If Epicureanism holds unexpected resources for thinking about reception in general, what kinds of resources might it hold for an understanding of its own specific reception? Are there particular elements in the

---

[43] On this connection/vacillation between will and pleasure, see Derrida (1984) 7–8 and Meeker (2006) 30.

[44] For a consideration of classical texts that aims to keep them alive to the plurality represented by their transmission (e.g., the *voluntas-voluptas* conjunction here), see Gurd (2005).

[45] Meeker (2006) 31.

nature of Epicureanism that make it such a dynamic force in the history of thought? We turn now to a discussion of where the present volume stands in relationship to scholarship on the legacies of Epicurus and Lucretius in the West, before reviewing the contributions it makes to the study of Epicureanism's unsettled and unsettling *Nachleben*.

ENCOUNTERS WITH EPICUREANISM

The last few decades have seen a remarkable rise of interest in the afterlife of ancient materialism and Epicureanism, in particular. The reception of Lucretius's epic masterpiece, the *De Rerum Natura*, has received comparable attention.[46] It may be that we are coming to see more clearly the major role played by Epicureanism and Lucretius in the formation of modernity, thanks to the work of Catherine Wilson, Stephen Greenblatt, and others.[47] It may be, too, as the later twentieth-century theoretical interest in Epicureanism documented above suggests, that its conceptual resources hold particular potential in the twenty-first century.[48] Whatever the reason for its resurgence, evidence of a renewed sense of Epicureanism's significance in the West has been abundant in recent years.

Scholarship on the reception of both Epicureanism and Lucretius has focused primarily on specific periods and milieus (e.g., early imperial Rome; Renaissance Florence; eighteenth-century France).[49] Besides yielding all the advantages of thick histories, work in this vein

[46] The reception of Lucretius is, on our view, inseparable from the reception of Epicureanism. See also Gillespie and Hardie (2007a) 14, where they locate the reception of Lucretius within the reception of Epicureanism more generally, and Erler (1994) 477: "die Geschichte der Nachwirkung von Lukrez stellt sich zeitweise als eine Geschichte der Nachwirkung Epikurs dar."

[47] See esp. Wilson (2008) and (2009); Greenblatt (2011).

[48] See also Holmes in this volume on the reception of Lucretius and Epicureanism in the last hundred years.

[49] There is a large and rapidly growing bibliography here. Up through 1994, the most comprehensive bibliography on all aspects of the reception (or *Nachwirkung*) of both Epicurus and Lucretius may be found in Erler (1994), esp. 195–202, 482–90; see also the wide-ranging, if uneven, selection of papers in Scherer 1969. On Epicureanism in antiquity, see the papers in Erler (2000). On Lucretius's reception generally, see Poignault (1999); in Latin poetry, see Hardie (2009), which includes a chapter on Milton. On Epicureanism in the Renaissance, see Goldberg (2009); Brown (2010); Passannante (2011); in early modern

has amply demonstrated its capacity to provoke and revitalize conversations and debates in a range of climates by embedding Epicureanism in the intellectual, cultural, and political dynamics of a given period. Taken individually, however, such studies give little sense of Epicureanism as a transcultural, transhistorical phenomenon. For more comprehensive coverage, scholars have been well served by the recent *Cambridge Companions* on Epicurus and especially on Lucretius, volumes whose format joins synoptic scope with the specialized knowledge of the contributors.[50] Even at the level of the individual chapter, however, the aim of the *Companions* is largely to foster broad acquaintance rather than to provide in-depth analysis.[51]

The present volume combines elements from both these approaches— the detailed micro-history and the sweeping survey—while experimenting with a different strategy. In scope, it spans the full afterlife of Epicurus and Lucretius in the West, from Greco-Roman antiquity to the late decades of the twentieth century in Europe and America. But, while wide-ranging, it makes no claims to being exhaustive. On the contrary, the majority of the studies included here dwell on specific and at times unexpected points of impact within the reception of Epicureanism. These targeted interventions are grounded in the historical and cultural contexts of their subjects. They tend to favor close reading over survey without forfeiting a sense of the larger picture or an interest in the nature of Epicurean reception as a specific phenomenon. They thus adopt the methods of fine-grained historical and literary analysis characteristic of work on the reception of Epicureanism in given authors or periods. Yet it is precisely through such localized techniques, joined with an interest in the nature of reception itself, that these studies collectively explore the internal coherence, outside the boundaries of historical period or genre or cultural and intellectual context, of a tradition of thinking about and responding to Epicureanism.

Europe, see the papers in Osler (1991); Wilson (2008). On the recent reception of Lucretius, see Johnson (2000); Kennedy (2002).

[50] See Gillespie and Hardie (2007) for Lucretius; Warren (2009) for Epicureanism. For coverage of the whole tradition, see also Jones (1989). Gordon and Suits (2003) covers the tradition's historical range, loosely in the name of assessing its contemporary relevance.

[51] Moreover, the reception aspect is tilted heavily toward Lucretius. The material on reception in the Epicureanism volume is far less extensive.

Coherence here should not be understood along the lines of a closed or static system, as we emphasized above. We are interested, rather, in how Epicureanism functions as a *dynamic* entity, one that is transformed in the hands of new readers or critics or converts while at the same time producing reactions that, if not always predictable, nevertheless generate distinct series. From this perspective, as we have been arguing, reception unfolds through collisions between a body of ideas, most often transmitted through a text but also, say, through conversation and debate, and a reader (or listener). It is possible to understand such collisions in materialist terms, that is, as events triggered by the particular nature of the doctrines and the objects transmitting them but always realized more or less differently depending on who is reading, and when, and where, under which conditions, and for what purpose. The nomadic journey of Epicureanism through these many encounters changes, in turn, the "text" of Epicureanism itself as at least some of these encounters are folded into its future reception through the responses to which they give rise.

The idea of a collision or encounter between a material text and an embodied reader finds support in Epicureanism itself. It is not simply that Epicurus conceives of words as physical objects, born out of our simulacral contact with the world around us and productive of atomic changes in our interlocutors. His philosophy can be conceptualized as a form of medicine that acts on those exposed to it.[52] Describing his own attempt to shape the minds of his listeners through the *De Rerum Natura*, Lucretius famously speaks of his poem as a bitter but curative potion (Epicurean philosophy) delivered in a cup rimmed with honey (Lucretian verse and imagery).[53] Lucretius thus extends the medical analogy so prevalent in Hellenistic philosophy to describe reading (or, as would have been the case for many elite Romans, being read to) as physically engaging. Indeed, Lucretius crafts his poem in such a way so as to grab hold of his addressee, Memmius, with his verses, as Memmius is coming to see the world in a new way (1.948–50). He describes his poem as something that "labors" (*molitur*) to fall upon the ears of the

---

[52] On philosophy as a cure in Epicureanism, see esp. Nussbaum (1994) 110–11, 123–24; Tsouna (2009). Cf., e.g., Long (1996) 128–30.

[53] Lucretius *De Rerum Natura* 1.921–50=4.1–25 (with minor variations in ll. 4.11, 24, 25 and possibly 8, 17).

listener (2.1024–25). The poem, animated by this striving, not only engages Memmius but also, hopefully, transforms him, by delivering him to the state identified by Epicurus as the goal (*telos*) of a human life: *ataraxia*, freedom from disturbance in the soul (accompanied, ideally, by *aponia*, freedom from bodily pain).

It does not take long to notice, however, that neither Epicurus nor Lucretius tends to leave his readers at peace. That is not to say that Epicureanism's adherents have failed to find fulfillment through its teachings. It is only to recall the remarkably turbulent wake of Epicureanism through Western history. Rather than bringing prospective disciples to an enlightened state of calm, the Epicurean axiom that the gods are indifferent to us has often left them angry, despairing, and unsettled. Those who have encountered Lucretius's poem and its sublime vision of the cosmos are just as likely to be seized by restlessness, pleasure, and amazement (*horror ac divina voluptas*, in Lucretius's own words) as they are to achieve the tranquility promised by Epicureanism as an ethical philosophy.

The tumult of Epicureanism is due, too, of course, to an entrenched misunderstanding of what kind of pleasure Epicurus named as the goal of life. From antiquity to the present day, Epicureanism has been a byword for hedonism at its most sensual, as the quote from Timon at the beginning of this introduction indicates. It is true that even a brief acquaintance with the fragments of Epicurus undermines this characterization. It is neither drinking nor a gourmet meal nor sex with women and boys, he writes, that produces the pleasant life. These kinds of pleasures are fleeting; giving rise to the desire for more pleasure, they make satisfaction ever more costly.[54] Epicurus, then, was not a straightforward hedonist.[55] Nevertheless, he has more often than not been mistaken by both self-proclaimed adherents and sworn enemies for the archetypal defender of the pursuit of sensory pleasures, a verdict that has made those

---

[54] Epicurus *Letter to Menoeceus* 131. See also Plutarch *Moralia* 1088B-D (*Non Posse*); Cicero *De Finibus* II.3. Plutarch is cited here from Einarson and De Lacy (1967); Cicero is cited from Reynolds (1998).

[55] What kind of hedonist he was, of course, is still very much under discussion. The difficulty in large part stems from the uncertain status of sensory pleasures in Epicurean hedonism. For discussion of the problem, see Glidden (1980); Brunschwig (1986); Annas (1993) 337; Purinton (1993); Striker (1993); Cooper (1999); Porter (2003a); Woolf (2009).

pleasures among the most volatile elements within Epicureanism as it is transmitted both within and after antiquity.

The representation of Epicurus as a base hedonist is perhaps the most obvious case of "misreading" or "misreception" in the afterlife of Epicureanism. What should we do with such a misreading? Can we find a way to conceptualize a text or, here, a doctrinal system that would include its capacity to generate competing reactions, reactions that nevertheless cluster into patterns across diverse historical, intellectual, and cultural contexts? Can we formulate a model of reception that does not cut off some of these clusters as errors but, rather, finds a way of understanding them as realizing some potential, what the Greeks would call a *dynamis*, within the original textual object?

The present volume is an experiment in reading the reception of Epicureanism as the history of how different potentialities within the "text" of that philosophical system have been realized. In bringing together admirers alongside detractors, placing faithful and faithless readings next to each other, and attending closely to the dynamics of reaction and our own task of making sense of these dynamics, we have tried to open up a conversation about what it would mean to think of the reception of Epicureanism not in terms of successes or failures of interpretation, nor in terms of an unrelated string of individual performances, but as a history of encounters that say as much about the catalytic object as they do about those who meet with it. At the same time, we continue to insist that the affective and transformative potential of Epicureanism be read together with the specific circumstances under which it is realized, and especially in terms of the experiences of specific readers: both aspects are crucial to the model we are proposing. Such a conversation can, we hope, have something to say about the reception of ancient texts, including philosophical systems, more generally.

A complex model of materialist reception is implied, in fact, by Lucretius himself in his famous honeyed cup simile. For the transmission of the poem as it is described by the simile is not arrested at the lips. Lucretius imagines his work will have a physical impact, too, on the recesses of the mind, much as food acts on both the senses and the cavity of the body. The model of dynamic reception that we are suggesting also envisions different zones of impact and reactions that are both, as it were, conscious and unconscious, felt immediately and intensely on contact as pleasure or pain, as well as through changes that work themselves to the surface of our experience and transform our lives more slowly.

Such an affective model of reception would see the reactions at both levels, at the surface and in the depths, as determined at least in part by the specific physical and mental conditions of the reader, conditions created by individual temperament, historical setting, cultural context, intellectual background, and so on. Yet it is worth remembering that Lucretius, having observed the rich variability of constitutions among people, still concludes that these variations do not preclude anyone from being able to see the truths and achieve the states promised by Epicureanism: Epicureanism, in other words, is a kind of machine capable of producing a fairly uniform pattern of response in adherents.[56] In the same way, we can say that despite all the historical and cultural and temperamental and circumstantial differences that stratify the last two millennia of readers, those readers react to Epicureanism in similar ways across the centuries. Nevertheless, these differences ensure that reactions to Epicureanism will never be entirely uniform. They account, too, for the specific responses within certain intellectual communities or historical periods or philosophical traditions. Indeed, we should expect that at certain times and places—say, eighteenth-century France— the external influences on the temperament of the reader inform how she responds to particular aspects of Epicureanism, such as the status of sensory pleasure or the absence of providence, with particular force.

It is no great stretch to say that texts and ideas impact us. The challenge is to bring a more rigorous concept of impact into our thinking about reception, a concept that accounts, on the one hand, for the patterns created by a text through its influence both on readers who live under the historical, cultural, and intellectual conditions of the text's initial emergence and on those readers who live far removed from its point of origin; and, on the other hand, for the non-uniformity of reactions. It is to bring a concept of affect into our understanding of how we interact with texts and the power they exercise over us, without denying that texts affect us at many levels, both palpably and more subtly. The papers that follow explore in various ways how we can begin to imagine two millennia of

---

[56] Lucretius *De Rerum Natura* 3.314–22.

reactions to a body of ideas, sometimes quite tight, sometimes quite loose, as one part of the Epicureanism that we engage with today.

In "Haunting Nepos: *Atticus* and the Performance of Roman Epicurean Death," **W. H. Shearin** examines the death of a famous Epicurean, Titus Pomponius Atticus, during the later Roman Republic. This death, when read in the company of various Epicurean and Stoic deaths, exemplifies the central role that disease (particularly *sudden* disease) plays in the demise of famous Epicureans. By contrast with the deaths of Stoics, for whom death is largely about the exercise of the will (and for whom suicide—in Latin *mors voluntaria*, "voluntary death"—is the ideal), the death of Atticus—although in some sense a suicide—is accomplished through the frustration of any direct intention. Atticus starves himself in the face of a disease that is apparently no longer there, an act that drama-tizes the very "swerviness" of Epicurean nature.

In "Epicurus's Mistresses: Pleasure, Authority, and Gender in the Reception of the *Kuriai Doxai* in the Second Sophistic," **Richard Fletcher** faces head-on the "willful misrepresentation" of Epicureanism by some of its earliest critics, who were working in the lively intellectual milieu of the second-century-CE Greco-Roman world. Fletcher advocates a "con-textual" reading of Epicureanism, one that embeds it in the sexual and philosophical politics of self-fashioning in this period. By way of illustra-tion, he zeroes in on one of Alciphron's fictional *Letters of Courtesans*, purportedly written by the Epicurean courtesan Leontion. Fletcher shows how the common accusations against Epicurus at this time (and for centuries)—too little spirituality, too much sensuality—become creative and complex challenges to philosophical authority in Alciphron's playful text. Leontion complains not only about her sexual enslavement to Epicurus, but also, jealously, about her lover's devotion to the master's "windy doctrines." She thus draws an analogy between her subordination to her master's pleasures and her lover's blind attachment to the pleasure promised by his philosophical master.

Gerard Passannante's contribution, "Reading for Pleasure: Disaster and Digression in the First Renaissance Commentary on Lucretius," explores the reception of Epicurean pleasure in the early sixteenth century in the crucible of loss and melancholy. By carefully following the digres-sions that repeatedly take us away from the Lucretian text in the first commentary edition of the *De Rerum Natura*, published by Giambattista Pio in 1511, Passannante provides an exemplary demonstration of the interaction of philology and affective response, love of text and the bittersweet pleasures of Lucretius's lessons on disaster. As Passannante declares, these digressions must not be seen as minor asides, but rather as "a crucial entry into the mental world of the poem" as it was taking shape at the birth of humanism.

Exploring the limitations of current scholarly discourse on the presence of Lucretius in the literature of Elizabethan England, **Adam Rzepka**, in his paper "Discourse *Ex Nihilo*: Epicurus and Lucretius in Sixteenth-Century England," confronts the notion that the *De Rerum Natura* figures the poetics of its own subsequent transmission. Drawing upon Michel Serres and Jacques Lezra, who have both used Lucretian terms (swerve, *eventum* ["accident"]) to figure discourse, he urges the need for a more mobile, complex model of discursive interaction during the Elizabethan period, which heretofore has presented Lucretian influence as a sudden, *ex nihilo* (and therefore highly un-Lucretian) occurrence.

In "Engendering Modernity: Epicurean Women from Lucretius to Rousseau," **Natania Meeker** analyzes the role played by women in the figuration of Epicurean subjectivity in the writings of Rousseau as he seeks to envision a new political and social order for revolutionary France. For Rousseau, Meeker argues, women stand at the intersection of Epicureanism and a voluptuous modernity; they are subjects naturally in thrall to pleasures that refuse to yield to the discipline of reason. Women make visible the need for ideological controls that acknowledge the power of pleasure without allowing it to destabilize the social order. Rousseau thus deploys the figure of the Epicurean woman, Meeker points out, as the foil that allows the male subject to "imagine [himself] as free."

In "Oscillate and Reflect: La Mettrie, Materialist Physiology, and the Revival of the Epicurean Canonic," **James Steintrager** studies the radical wing of French Enlightenment philosophy, which tended toward implicit atheism and more open materialism, two positions often called (by proponents and scholars) "Epicurean." Intellectual historians have understood this Epicureanism to entail a materialist physics—chiefly, atomism—and an ethics that eschews above all fear of the gods. In its more libertine guise, this "Epicurean" ethics also advocates sensual pleasure as the sovereign good. Steintrager argues that while associating radical *philosophie* with Epicurean physics and ethics makes good sense, limiting ourselves to these branches of philosophy overlooks the crucial revival of the Epicurean "canonic" (its explanation of the empirical bases of knowledge) in the seventeenth and eighteenth centuries.

In "Sensual Idealism: The Spirit of Epicurus and the Politics of Finitude in Kant and Hölderlin," **Anthony Adler** studies Kant's idiosyncratic and surprisingly positive reception of Epicureanism. Adler argues that despite his rejection of Epicureanism as dogmatic doctrine, Kant nonetheless endorses, and remains engaged with, the spirit of Epicureanism throughout his critical philosophy. Particularly important to this discussion is Kant's reading of the Epicurean technical term, *prolēpsis*, which the German views as an anticipation of his own a priori concepts. As a coda to his study of Kant, Adler examines Hölderlin's largely unrecognized engagement with Kant's reformulation of Epicureanism in his *Death of Empedocles*.

In his contribution, "The Sublime, Today?", **Glenn Most** studies what he calls the "Lucretian sublime," a concept he contrasts with the more familiar ancient notion of the "Longinian sublime." As Most demonstrates, whereas the Longinian sublime depends upon a theistic perspective, the Lucretian sublime is rooted precisely in a rejection of that perspective. He then tests and works out this notion of the Lucretian sublime against a series of striking twentieth-century visual examples, especially drawn from the work of Mark Rothko. The positing and development of the Lucretian sublime allow us to understand the persistent presence of the sublime in modern art (as well as in critical discourse about that art) that itself rejects a theistic worldview.

Benjamin Aldes Wurgaft, with his paper "From Heresy to Nature: Leo Strauss's History of Modern Epicureanism," traces the varying roles of the "Epicurean" throughout Strauss's corpus. Wurgaft shows that, despite Strauss's leanings toward and frequent association with Platonism, Epicureanism nonetheless plays a substantial role in defining his conception of philosophy. In particular, Strauss's early reflection on Epicureanism as heretical religious critique suggests that Epicureanism bears a certain attraction (if only by implication) for Strauss, who denies philosophers the ability to submit to the "salutary law" of religion. At the heart of this attraction lies a particular cross-linguistic pun: *apikores* (Hbr. "heretic") phonetically (and perhaps etymologically) suggests Epicurean.

In his piece, "Epicurean Presences in Foucault's *The Hermeneutics of the Subject*," **Alain Gigandet** studies the ways in which Epicureanism, while providing some of the evidence for Foucault's 1981–82 course on the hermeneutics of the subject, nonetheless seems to posit a subject that operates in terms different than those articulated by Foucault's predominantly Stoic account. Specifically, Gigandet suggests that the Epicurean subject is defined above all by the image of the conquest of a place, especially in a defensive manner. To make his case, he examines some of the central metaphors in the *De Rerum Natura* and other Epicurean texts that define the nature of the subject. He considers, for example, the famous Epicurean dictum that because of our common mortality we inhabit a "city without walls," a metaphor that points to the ultimately precarious foundation of our happiness, as well as to famous Lucretian images of the wise man as "fortified" by his Epicurean doctrine. He thus defines an Epicurean "hermeneutics of the subject" that is perhaps necessarily marginalized in Foucault's writings, as it is not entirely reducible to Foucault's broader and largely Stoic portrait.

Brooke Holmes's paper, "Deleuze, Lucretius, and the Simulacrum of Naturalism" addresses the attraction exercised by what Gilles Deleuze spent his life critiquing as a particularly dangerous myth, the myth of Platonism. Given the seductive appeal of a philosophy of essences, Deleuze sees an urgent need to reiterate philosophical pluralism as a rival image of thought. One such reiteration is his early reading of the *De Rerum Natura*, at the heart of which lies the figure of the simulacrum. The Lucretian simulacrum gives rise to two ways of seeing, two ways of understanding "the infinite." On the one hand, the simulacrum, by concealing the "shocks" and "motions" through which it is produced, causes us to believe in the stable image and, hence, immortal forms. On the other, the simulacrum is the basis of an inferential seeing that allows us to go past the surface to glimpse the events and microbodies of the atomic world. Recognizing that this glimpse into atomic reality takes place through philosophy itself, since there is no naked disclosure of that world, Deleuze addresses the need for naturalism to "produce a phantom at the limit of a lengthened or unfolded experience."

1

Haunting Nepos: *Atticus* and the Performance of Roman Epicurean Death

W. H. Shearin

> Death is the sanction of all that the story-teller can report. He has
> borrowed his authority from death. In other words: his stories refer
> back to *the story of nature*.[1]

Ancient Rome was fascinated by the performance of death.[2] Apart from
any popular, modern-day image of conquering Romans or gladiatorial
contests, the classical literary record provides copious evidence of this
fascination. From the Punic Wars to the reign of Theodoric, from Naevius
and Ennius to Boethius, the literature of Rome is marked by countless
dramatic—and dramatically staged—murders and suicides. Perhaps
most famously within the traditional narrative of ancient philosophy,
Cato the Younger (Marcus Porcius Cato), a Stoic, kills himself with his

I thank Brooke Holmes, James Ker, and the members of the Andrew W. Mellon
Fellowship of Scholars in the Humanities at Stanford University (2008–2009) for commenting on earlier drafts of this essay. All errors are, of course, my own.

[1] Benjamin (1977) 450: "Der Tod ist die Sanktion von allem, was der Erzähler
berichten kann. Vom Tode hat er seine Autorität geliehen. Mit anderen Worten: *es ist
die Naturgeschichte*, auf welche seine Geschichten zurückverweisen." Emphasis added.
All translations (of both ancient and modern languages) are my own unless otherwise
noted.

[2] Death in ancient Rome has, accordingly, a large bibliography. To cite only a handful
of recent works, see Ker (2009), Edwards (2007), Edwards (2005), Connors (1994). Suicide
is a major concern of later sections in this paper; on that topic, see Grisé (1982), Hirzel
(1908), Griffin (1986a), Griffin (1986b). The most extensive treatment of Epicurean death
from a philosophical perspective is Warren (2004).

own sword rather than submit to the tyranny of Caesar.[3] Similarly, Tacitus, the great historian of Imperial Rome, recounts the prolonged, forced suicide of Lucius Annaeus Seneca, another Stoic and one-time tutor of the emperor Nero.[4] Given the prominence of such scenes, it is hardly surprising that Epicureanism in its Roman manifestation also focuses upon death. Of course, death—or, more properly, release from the fear of death—is a central concern of all Epicureanism,[5] but Roman Epicureanism, as voiced through texts like Philodemus's *De Morte* (*On Death*) and the third and sixth books of Lucretius's *De Rerum Natura* (*On the Nature of Things*), investigates this concern more intensely and with greater psychological depth than other moments in the history of Epicureanism.[6] The present essay, while it does not provide a full treatment of Roman Epicureanism, nonetheless examines a text for which that philosophy and its intense investigation of death is an essential backdrop.

To be more specific, this essay pursues a reading of Cornelius Nepos's *Atticus* that looks not at the ways in which Nepos directly presents Epicurean doctrines but rather at the ways his text is, we may say, "haunted" by those doctrines.[7] "Haunting" is an appropriate term for the type of textual performance traced here—both because it is connected

[3] This story will be discussed below. It is most thoroughly recounted at Plutarch *Cato Minor* 66–73, cited from Ziegler (1964). Other versions of it occur at Appian *Bellum Civile* 2.98–99, cited from Viereck (1905); Cassius Dio 43.11.4–5, cited from Boissevain (1895–1901); Florus 2.13, cited from Malcovati (1972); Livy *Periochae* 114, cited from Rossbach (1910); *Bellum Africanum* 88.3–4, cited from Klotz (1927). See Edwards (2007) and Martial 1.78 for a reading of this death as a (or even the) "Roman death" (*Romana mors*). Martial is cited from Shackleton Bailey (1990).

[4] Tacitus *Annales* 15.60–64, cited from Heubner (1983). See Ker (2009) for a treatment of Seneca's death both in the texts of Neronian Rome as well as in its later reception. Peter Paul Reubens immortalized this event in his painting *The Death of Seneca* (c. 1608), which depicts Seneca's final bath.

[5] For the oft-stated Epicurean tenet that "Death is nothing to us," see, e.g., Epicurus *Kuriai Doxai* 2 (ὁ θάνατος οὐδὲν πρὸς ἡμᾶς); Lucretius *De Rerum Natura* 3.830–31 (*nil igitur mors ad nos*). A convenient collection of Epicurean texts on death is Long and Sedley (1987) 1: 149–54; 2: 154–59.

[6] See Segal (1990), which, in comparing of Epicurus's and Lucretius's views of death, suggests that Lucretius "reveals, far more vividly than Epicurus does, how much additional and unnecessary agony we inflict on ourselves through our anxiety about death" (41). Philodemus's *De Morte* has recently been re-edited and translated in Henry (2009).

[7] One touchstone within recent critical discourse for the study of "haunting" is Jacques Derrida's *Specters of Marx* and the "hauntology" he develops there. While the use here made of "haunting" is my own, it is made with some debt to Derrida's work. See Derrida (1994).

with the thematics of death under study and because it captures the fact
that Nepos's biography is not, strictly speaking, an Epicurean work. Titus
Pomponius Atticus, the famous correspondent of Cicero depicted in
Atticus, was himself an Epicurean, but Nepos's representation of him
strikingly omits any explicit mention of this fact.[8] Moreover, Nepos's
writing, far from being a committed philosophical treatise, owes much
to tropes of the Roman biographical genre of which *Atticus* is, at least
within the surviving Latin record, one of the earliest examples.[9]
Epicureanism thus haunts *Atticus*, for without being a named force
behind the text, it nonetheless leaves undeniable textual traces.

The present essay reads the dramatic death scene that concludes
Atticus against an analysis of the role played by Epicurean doctrines in
the text. It first examines earlier portions of the biography as well as
other relevant cultural and philosophical material to set the terms negoti-
ated by the concluding death scene. Above all, the discussion suggests
ways in which Epicureanism undermines any simple notion of "natural,"
intentional action. *Atticus*'s presentation of biographical events, up to
and including the protagonist's death, is colored extensively by fortune
(*fortuna*)—a fortune whose movement is, if not synonymous with chance,
nonetheless difficult to assimilate fully, as the text once claims, to
the habits (*mores*) of Titus Pomponius Atticus. In other words, as the
following pages explore, the ghost of Epicureanism is perhaps felt most

---

[8] For references to Atticus's Epicureanism, see Cicero *ad Atticum* 4.6.1, cited from
Shackleton Bailey (1987); *De Legibus* 1.21, 1.54, 3.1, cited from Powell (2006); *De Finibus*
5.3, cited here and elsewhere from Reynolds (1998). See further Leslie (1950), with Bailey
(1951), and Castner (1988) 57–61, with her bibliography. Lindsay (1998) also comments on
the absence of explicit discussion of Epicureanism in *Atticus*, suggesting that this fact may
reveal an aversion to philosophy on the part of Nepos (See Lactantius *Diuinae Institutiones*
3.15.10, cited from Heck and Wlosok (2007)) or negative cultural associations of
Epicureanism.

[9] In attempting to define Nepos's authorial project, commentators often point to the
following passage, where he suggests a distinction between his own biographical genre and
history (*Pelopidas* 1.1): "Pelopidas the Theban is better known to historians than to the
public. I am unsure in what manner I should expound his virtues, for I fear that—if I should
begin to lay out events [*res*]—I would seem not to tell his biography [*vitam*] but to write
history [*historiam*]." The text of Nepos is cited here and throughout from Marshall (1977).
See Titchener (2003) 85–88. For more on Nepos's place in the ancient biographical tradition, see Geiger (1985), which is reviewed, with some strong criticisms, by Moles (1989),
and Tuplin (2000). The literary form of ancient biography more generally is treated in Leo
(1901) and Momigliano (1993).

strongly in *Atticus*'s inability to separate fortune (*fortuna*) from its ety-mological relative, chance (*fors/forte*).[10]

I. WRITING THE LIFE: NARRATIVE, EPICUREANISM, AND *FORTUNA*

Biography, including Roman biography, is perhaps the most teleologi-cally overdetermined genre of narrative.[11] As a "writing of the life," a writing that tries to represent and conform to the structure of life, it begins with birth, and it drives toward death. This fact explains, at least on a narrative level, the persistent presence of death in life. Even without a highly theorized model of life narratives (or life as narrative), it is impossible to ignore the role that the stopping point holds for the telling of a life. Solon the Athenian famously held that one cannot evaluate a life until it is over.[12] And while Nepos, in authoring his *Vitae*, may not have had so explicit a philosophy, a concluding death is still constantly anticipated throughout *Atticus*. Death—if not always Atticus's own—appears, quite literally, as early as the second chapter of the work, where Atticus's father "perish[es] early" (2.1: *mature decessit*), and it lingers in

---

[10] We might even say that *forte* is a "crypt-word" for *Atticus*, since—though it is never used explicitly—it seems to lie at the center of the work's concerns. "Crypt-word" is a term that owes something to Nicolas Abraham and Maria Torok and their study of Freud's Wolf Man (Abraham and Torok (1986)), where they develop their notion of "cryptonomy"; but *forte* in *Atticus* hardly has the phonic charge of the word-thing *tieret* that lies at the center of Abraham and Torok's analysis. The role and scope of chance in Epicureanism is a topic that has attracted a fair amount of scholarly discussion, particularly with regard to the *clina-men*, or "swerve"; however, the sense in which *forte* is used here—"undesigned, unintended, random"—needs little discussion. On the possibly limited scope of the *clinamen* itself in Epicureanism, see Long (2006) 157–77.

[11] The works of Peter Brooks, especially Brooks (1984) and (1994), constitute perhaps the most impressive modern attempt to describe the psychological functioning of narrative and teleological narrative drives. Although Brooks takes Freud (particularly the Freud of "Beyond the Pleasure Principle") as his primary theoretical touchstone in forming his model for narrative, it is possible that Hellenistic philosophy provides a similar, if still dis-tinctive, life narrative. For example, the natural pursuit of pleasure posited by Epicureanism (from the cradle onward) is reminiscent, in some ways, of psychoanalytic thinking.

[12] See Herodotus *Historiae* 1.32: "And if . . . he shall end his life well, this man is the one you seek: he is worthy of being called blessed..." (εἰ δὲ...τελευτήσει τὸν βίον εὖ, οὗτος ἐκεῖνος τὸν σὺ ζητέεις, <ὁ> ὄλβιος κεκλῆσθαι ἄξιός ἐστι) The Greek text of Herodotus follows Hude (1926).

the background throughout much of the biography. We learn that during the days of Cinna and Sulla, Atticus is not "apart from danger" (2.1: *expers . . . periculi*), and he appears to have gone into exile to escape possible death.[13] Moreover, Atticus later (10.1–2) fears finding his name on the list of those proscribed to death when Antony returns to Italy.

Yet if biographical narrative drives toward death, and if death lurks beneath much of Atticus's biography, Epicureanism, at least in *Atticus*, may serve to draw us away from death. Not only may Epicureanism, if successful in its oft-stated aims, assuage fear of impending death, but its anti-teleology, most commonly understood in connection with the world's aimlessness, its lack of designed order, may also be associated with a resistance to the drive of narrative and the order imposed upon life by narrative.[14] While it should not be assumed that the writing of a life, specifically the writing of Atticus's life, conforms to an Epicurean understanding of the un-designed nature of that life, ancient evidence suggests that anti-teleology was regularly read as operating within texts and language.

There are numerous instances, for example, where Lucretius's *De Rerum Natura*, a poem known to Nepos, suggests a connection between the composition of the world and the composition of his work, most famously through his comparison of letters and atoms.[15] Additional sources connect anti-teleology to the larger structure of written works. Cicero preserves the comment, openly anti-Epicurean but striking nonetheless,

---

[13] As Nepos puts it, he went into exile "after he perceived . . . that the means of living in accordance with dignity was not granted to him" *Atticus* 2.2: *posteaquam vidit . . . neque sibi dari facultatem pro dignitate vivendi . . .*). On Atticus's exile (esp. as a literary precursor to Ovid's exile), see Hallett (2003) 348–52.

[14] For Epicurean anti-teleology, see, e.g., Lucretius *De Rerum Natura* 2.1052–57, Long and Sedley (1987) 1: 57–65; 2: 54–64.

[15] For Nepos's knowledge of Lucretius, see Cornelius Nepos *Atticus* 12.4, which mentions the death of the poets Catullus and Lucretius. For the letter-atom passages, see Lucretius *De Rerum Natura* 1.197, 824, 912; 2.688, 1013. See, too, Gale (2004) 62, which explains the "abrupt" conclusion of Lucretius's *De Rerum Natura* by alluding to two Epicurean concerns—(1) freedom from the fear of death/religion (since death is final and unperceived) and (2) anti-teleology (since the world, and therefore the poem, lacks a "divine" creator): "I have already suggested that the framing of the poem as a whole . . . suggests that it represents the story of a life. In this sense, it makes sense for the poem to just stop: Lucretius has insisted that death is the end, and in the same way, nothing can follow the poem's last full stop. Again, if the poem represents the universe . . . the abruptness could be seen as appropriate: since the universe is infinite, but the poem cannot go on for ever, any stopping point is equally arbitrary . . . ."

that those who believe in anti-teleology at the atomic level should also believe that Ennius's *Annales*, the greatest poetic work of the day, could be constructed from a chance collocation of letters upon the earth.[16] Plutarch comments, again in a context hostile to Epicureanism, that the *Kuriai Doxai*, or *Master Sayings*, of Epicurus may have been the construction of chance (ἀπὸ τύχης καὶ αὐτομάτως).[17] None of this evidence establishes in any detailed way Nepos's own knowledge of, or engagement with, Epicureanism, but it does suggest that moderns who see tenets of Epicureanism at work in structuring texts like *Atticus* are not without ancient forebears.

It would thus not be anachronistic to see Epicureanism at work in the various narrative detours and evasions of *Atticus*, which resist the dramatic conclusion (the end or *telos*) that readers know, from the opening lines onward, surely awaits. The biography, it seems, constantly holds out the possibility that its inevitable end (*fortuna*) is subject to the whims of chance (*forte*). Although death is both the "natural" and expected conclusion to the biography, events appear as if by chance— civil war "intercedes" (7.1), further war is waged (9.1), fortune suddenly changes (10.1)—collectively creating a sense that, although the biography must end, its narrative is hardly governed by a logical, teleological progression.[18] Nicholas Horsfall, in particular, makes clear that the biography is, if at times roughly chronological, at other times hardly temporally structured at all, instead largely generalizing about Atticus's character.[19] Fortune (*fortuna*) and the question of chance (*fors/forte*) are thus formal preoccupations of *Atticus*, preoccupations that, as we shall soon see, also form central thematic concerns of the biography.

Before we further probe the ways in which chance appears both implicitly and explicitly within *Atticus*, though, it is worth reviewing one other

[16] Cicero *De Natura Deorum* 2.93. See Pease (1955–58) 781, which is also the edition of reference for this text.

[17] Plutarch *De Pythiae Oraculis* 11.399e, cited from Sieveking (1929). For the reception of the *Kuriai Doxai* in Plutarch's day, see Fletcher (this volume).

[18] Ancient biography as a whole, while its narratives do tend to begin with birth and conclude with death, may obey structural principles that are not purely chronological, a fact that renders *Atticus*'s turns somewhat less striking. Perhaps the greatest example of such wandering—one that abandons the structure of natural, biological life—comes from Plutarch's *Antony*, where Antony dies well before the conclusion of the narrative, which turns to follow Cleopatra. See Pelling (1988) 323.

[19] Horsfall (1989) 9–10.

significant set of Epicurean traces within the work, if only to suggest that the Epicurean associations of chance appear far from random. Indeed, if Nepos's own statement is correct (17.3), we should expect both that there are philosophical ghosts lurking in *Atticus* and that those ghosts will be submerged into the *life* of Atticus (rather than, say, explicitly expressed in a set of doctrines): "He [sc. Atticus] had so understood the teachings [*praecepta*] of the chief philosophers that he used them for leading his life [*ad uitam agendam*], not for show [*ad ostentationem*]." In this vein, perhaps the most obviously Epicurean feature of the biography is Atticus's "retreat from politics," his reluctance to commit himself to "the tides of civic life" (6.1: *civilibus fluctibus*).[20] This political retreat not only conjures up a famous image from Lucretius's *De Rerum Natura*—that of the wise man who gazes upon the troubles of another, watching from the shore "while winds disturb the waters on the great sea" (*De Rerum Natura* 2.1: *mari magno turbantibus aequora ventis*)— but it also calls to mind many of Epicurus's descriptions of the wise man. The wise man, for example, neither intends "to take part in government" (πολιτεύσεσθαι) nor "to rule as a monarch" (τυραννεύσειν).[21] Even the specific terms employed by Nepos to describe his politics may conjure up the Garden, for instance, "tranquility" (6.5: *tranquillitas*), "quiet" (7.3: *quies*).[22]

Whatever the validity of such arguments, if Nepos seems at times to encourage reading Atticus as an Epicurean, he balances that concern with a desire to resist misconceptions of Epicureanism—an indirect

[20] See Cornelius Nepos *Atticus* 7.3, 8.4; *De Rerum Natura* 1.31, 3.18; Griffin (1986a) 76 n. 6, who comments that the nautical imagery employed by Nepos is "in no way exclusive to the [Epicurean] sect" but "very reminiscent of . . . Cicero's version of the Epicurean doctrine of abstention" at *De Re Publica* 1.1, 1.4, 1.9, cited from Powell (2006).

[21] Diogenes Laërtius 10.119, cited from Marcovich (1999). For discussion of this tenet of Epicureanism, with a fuller list and discussion of ancient sources, see Fowler (1989) 122–26.

[22] See Bailey (1951) 164. It is even possible to suggest that Nepos's much-remarked (and much-maligned) prose style could be, if not Epicurean, at least satisfactory when viewed through an Epicurean lens. His style is, after all, clear, the chief attribute that Epicurus demanded in his *On Rhetoric* (as reported at Diogenes Laërtius 10.13). For a standard assessment of Nepos's style, see Horsfall (1989) 8: "The flat, awkward prose of a man with no taste, or time, or capacity for elegance . . . is in its way also telling: N. is uninventive, and his graceless language augments our sense of his essential honesty."

confirmation of Epicureanism's unstated presence.[23] Atticus's Epicurean retreat from politics is thus accompanied by details limiting his Epicureanism, or at least limiting any perception of stereotypical, so-called Epicurean excess. At the same time that Atticus avoids formal public office for the pleasures of his tranquil home, that home is certainly not—as stereotypes may suggest—a debauched pleasure garden. "There was never a dinner at his home," Nepos writes, "without some reading— so that his guests might be delighted no less in their minds than in their stomachs" (14.1). Atticus has "no gardens" and "no sumptuous villa" (14.3). Nepos's descriptions seem, then, to anticipate and resist contemporary images of Epicurean pleasure, images—for example—of Epicureans as (fat, well-fed) pigs.[24]

But if *Atticus* balances Epicurean and anti-Epicurean with regard to politics, the situation with regard to "fortune" (*fortuna*) is more complex. Although "fortune" (*fortuna*, sometimes *Fortuna*, a Roman deity), especially in the translated Greek form *tuchē* (τύχη), is a common player in ancient biography of all periods, the term takes on a special significance in Nepos's *Atticus*.[25] Unlike in Nepos's other surviving biographies, *fortuna* appears repeatedly, in many guises, throughout the life of the Roman Epicurean, with meanings ranging from "material wealth" to "fate."[26] Most strikingly, two interrelated passages suggest it is within the

---

[23] "Balancing" seems to be a key feature of the rhetorical articulation of *Atticus*, which—as commentators have noted—is dominated by the figure of antithesis. See Norden (1971) 206: " . . . Die Antithese, sowohl die der Gedanken wie die der Form, beherrscht die Darstellung . . . " (" . . . antithesis—both of thoughts and of form—governs the presentation . . . ").

[24] For descriptions of Epicureans as pigs, see, e.g., Cicero *In Pisonem* 37 (an attack), Horace *Epistulae* 1.4 (Epicurean self-mockery). Cicero is cited from Nisbet (1961); Horace from Klingner (1959). The fullest scholarly discussion is Warren (2002) 129–49.

[25] *Tuchē* (the Greek equivalent of *fortuna*) plays a particularly prominent role in Plutarch; see Swain (1989a), Swain (1989b). For attempts to trace (or deny) a more general trajectory in Nepos' use of *fortuna* (including works other than *Atticus*), see Havas (1985) and Jefferis (1943). As the rest of the present discussion makes clear, I have sympathies with Havas's suggestion (503–504) that *fortuna* is strongly tied to "nature" (*die Natur*).

[26] *Fortuna* occurs fifteen times within *Atticus* (2.3, 3.3, 9.5 *bis*, 10.1, 10.2, 10.5, 11.1, 11.6 *bis*, 14.2, 19.1, 19.2, 19.3, 21.1). For comparison, *fortuna* appears no more than four times in any of the other *Vitae*, although it should be noted that *Atticus* is nearly twice the length of any other surviving biography from Nepos.

power of men to shape their own "fortunes." The first occurs concentrated in an unattributed poetic line:[27]

He also recalled the good turns he received with an undying memory; and the favors, which he himself had granted, he remembered to the extent that the recipient was pleased. He thus brought it about that the saying appears true:

> "For each among men, his habits [*mores*] fashion [*fingunt*] his fate [*fortunam*]."

Nevertheless, he did not fashion his fate [*fortunam*] before he fashioned himself—he, who feared lest he be blamed justly in any matter. (Nepos *Atticus* 11.5–6)

Several chapters later, in a pointedly repetitive gesture, Nepos refers back to this earlier claim:

I published the account to this point while Atticus was alive.[28] Now, since fortune [*fortuna*] has desired [*voluit*] us to survive him, we shall continue with the remainder and, as much as we can, we shall teach [*docebimus*] readers with examples of things [*rerum exemplis*] that, just as we indicated above, quite often, for each, his habits [*mores*] match his fate [*fortuna*] (Nepos *Atticus* 19.1).

These two passages constitute Nepos's most forceful, general attempts to read the *life* of Atticus, and they therefore serve as important clues as to how to read his death.

The first passage—through the vehicle of citation—describes a particular kind of ancient self-fashioning (*fingunt*).[29] The very notion of

---

[27] This line (which in Latin runs *sui cuique mores fingunt fortunam hominibus*) appears as fr. xix of the uncertain lines at Ribbeck (1897–98) 125. Horsfall (1989) 82–83 suggests the line may stem from the Comic poet Philemon.

[28] As James Ker helpfully points out to me (*per litteras*), Nepos's assertion that he published the first eighteen chapters of the biography while Atticus was still alive is a "striking admission." It has several implications but perhaps the most significant for the present study are: it demonstrates, on the one hand, that the narrative detours and wandering structure of the biography in fact at one point lacked their "inevitable" conclusion and, on the other, that the work—which could only recount Atticus's heroic death after he died—is clearly shaped by an active attempt to conform to Atticus's life.

[29] The literature on ancient self-fashioning is large (and growing), but any discussion must begin with the work of Michel Foucault. See Foucault (1984) and (2005). (The work

self-fashioning implicitly invests much into the (fashioning) agency of a subject. Yet here we find not, at least not initially, the notion that an individual (*homo*) creates himself (or even fashions his life) but that he, through his habits, creates his fate, his end, his "fortune" (even his "death"). This, at any rate, is the interpretation we reach if we take *fortuna* (here rendered by "fate") as "what befalls or is destined to befall one, one's fate, destiny, fortunes."[30] But the passage also suggests that there is continuity between the fashioning of fate and the fashioning of the individual. That is, an individual dies as he lives, and he—or so Nepos comments of Atticus—is, in some sense, *free* to fashion (and in the process of fashioning) himself.[31] This conjunction of the freedom of self-fashioning and a congruous, fashioned, if also fixed, "fate" has an undeniable Stoic coloring. Indeed, elsewhere, in explaining the Stoic tenet "that only the wise man is free, and every foolish man is a slave," Cicero conjures up the same poetic line as Nepos:

What is freedom (*libertas*)? The ability to live as you wish (*ut velis*). Who, then, lives as he wishes except he who follows the correct path; he who delights in duty; he for whom the path of living has been considered and foreseen; he who obeys not even the laws out of fear but follows them and cultivates them because he judges this to be greatly beneficial; he who says nothing, does nothing, thinks, finally, nothing if not willingly and freely; he for whom all plans and all he does set out from and return to the same thing—nothing holds greater sway with him than his own will [*voluntas*] and judgment? To him even fortune herself [*fortuna ipsa*]—she who, it is said, possesses the greatest power—yields, if, as the wise [*sapiens*] poet has

---

of Pierre Hadot, e.g., Hadot (1987), has a similar focus on practice, on "philosophy as a way of life.") My own brief intervention into this topic has some resonances with Foucault's discussion ((2005) 477–80) of the *meletē thanatou* ("preparation for death"), which emphasizes the comments of Seneca and Marcus Aurelius that one should live each day as if it were the last, that, moreover, one should view oneself from the perspective of death. But my project is rather to show some of the dissonances between the (narrated) life and the (narrated) death of Atticus, to upset, so to speak, an easy equation between the way one lives and the way one dies.

[30] *Oxford Latin Dictionary*, s. v. *fortuna* 8. Horsfall (1989) 22 renders *fortuna* with "fortune."

[31] This sentence articulates my understanding of the remark that Atticus "did not fashion fortune before himself" (*neque . . . prius fortunam quam se ipse finxit*). Atticus is thus, in a certain (Stoic) sense, "free" to fashion his fortune and himself simultaneously, even as these terms retain some fixity.

said, she is fashioned for each by his own habits [*moribus*]. (Cicero *Paradoxa Stoicorum* 5.34)[32]

This passage introduces the key term "freedom" (*libertas*)—which, as we shall soon see, plays a substantial role in the present study of Atticus's death. Cicero's definition of this term works to link "freedom" (*libertas*) to "will" (*voluntas*), but it does so in (Stoic) "paradoxical" fashion: "freedom" (*libertas*) is doing what one wants (*voluntas*), yet what one wants is "correct" and in accord with "duty" (*officium*). Will is "free" yet in accord with expectation and law. What is striking here is that, since "freedom" is effectively equated to "will," while "will" is constrained "willingly" by "duty," the movement from "habits" to "fate" (or "fortune") becomes trivial and natural.

Yet is it possible that *fortuna* ("fate," "fortune") in *Atticus* is more than this Stoic gloss suggests? Are there other ways of configuring *fortuna* and *voluntas*? *Fortuna* can, of course, refer not only to fate but also to less intended or intentional consequences, that is, "the way in which events fall out, the workings of fortune, chance(s), hazard(s)."[33] Indeed, while it is hardly a refutation of the Stoic position, we may note that in the second passage it is *fortuna* ("fortune") that "wished" (*voluit*) Nepos to survive Atticus rather than an individual human agent. On the basis of such a description, some "will" (*voluntas*) may coincide with "fate" (*fortuna*), but it is hardly presented as the free volition of a unique human self-fashioner. Such turns of phrase may be dismissed as conventional—*fortuna* ("fortune"), not unlike *natura* ("nature"), is regularly personified in Latin; but it is precisely this linguistic convention that should give us pause: the question of where to locate agency within self-fashioning does not seem—at least when considered on the material level of the written letter—entirely settled. (Is *fortuna* here an agent? A mere stand-in for chance?) The second passage above gives us, moreover, an arena in which to further probe this issue: it sets up Atticus's death as an *exemplum* ("example"), an exemplary presentation of its own Stoicizing analysis.[34] Parsing the role of agency within Atticus's death

[32] Although the identity of the poet is unknown, the term "wise" (*sapiens*) often has Stoic connotations.

[33] *Oxford Latin Dictionary*, s.v. *fortuna* 5.

[34] It is worth noting that Nepos wrote another work entitled *Exempla*. See Marshall (1977) 102–108.

thus offers an opportunity to further analyze the operation of "fortune" (*fortuna*) within Nepos's text, and it therefore forms a central concern of the following section.[35]

II. THE ART OF DYING: NARRATIVES OF EPICUREANISM AND STOICISM

As suggested at the outset of this essay, Atticus's death is but one among many within the surviving Roman literary corpus. The exemplary Roman death, one could say, forms a genre unto itself. And any literary consideration of Atticus's final moments must attend to the tropes of the genre. The present section thus provides a brief, selective sketch of ancient philosophical deaths, specifically Stoic and Epicurean deaths, alongside its reading of Atticus's own. It traces the details of various Stoic and Epicurean deaths in an attempt to locate the place, if any, of willful self-fashioning (and therefore "fortune")—what we might call the art of dying—within those events. The analysis suggests, in contrast to Nepos's own explicit reading, not only that there are Epicurean ghosts lurking in the byways of his account but also that these ghosts manifest themselves most strongly in the sudden operation of disease.

To construct a framework for Epicurean death, let us begin at the beginning, with the first Epicurean death—that of Epicurus himself. There are in fact multiple accounts of Epicurus's demise, but one in particular—as we can see clearly below—was current during the later Roman Republic.[36] Two letters—one from Epicurus, one from Cicero—give the essential details:

Already dying, Epicurus writes this letter to Idomenes:

"Enjoying a blessed day, a day that is also the final one of my life, I write you the following: strangury and dysentery dog me, withholding nothing from their attack. But, against all these things, the joy in my soul at the memory of

---

[35] See Ker (2009) 262–66 on the role of agency within Seneca's death.

[36] I present Epicurus's death through this letter, as it seems to be the account Cicero had in mind in writing his own. For other versions of Epicurus's death, see Diogenes Laërtius 10.15 (a narrative account attributed to Hermarchus) and 10.16 (a poem by Diogenes himself). In both of those accounts, the founder of the Kepos dies (from illness) in a hot bath.

our past dialogues is drawn up for battle. And you, in a fashion worthy of your attendance at my side from boyhood and of philosophy, attend to Metrodorus's children." (Diogenes Laërtius 10.22)

Since I've been suffering from intestinal pain for nine days and since I failed to prove to those who want to enjoy my help that I am not well (because I didn't have a fever), I fled to my Tusculan villa, though for two days I had been so far from eating that I did not even taste water; and so, stricken with weakness and hunger, I desired your kindness more than I thought mine to be sought by you. I fear, moreover, all disease but especially that which the Stoics allow your master, Epicurus, with difficulty, since he says strangury and dysentery were burdensome for him; the first disease, they think, is from gluttony, the second from shameful intemperance. I had quite thoroughly dreaded dysentery; but it seemed to me that either a change of scenery or a relaxation of the mind or perhaps even the remission of a disease already growing old would be worth it. (Cicero *Letters to his Friends* 7.26.1, to Marcus Fabius Gallus)

Two features of these epistolary texts stand out: (1) the presence (and importance) of disease in Epicurus's text and (2) the corresponding Stoic interpretation of that disease offered by Cicero's letter.[37] On the one hand, dysentery and strangury dog Epicurus in his final moments, moments that, Epicurus's letter suggests, the philosopher heroically greeted with equanimity by virtue of recalling friendly dialogues. On the other hand, Cicero, addressing and no doubt gently needling his friend Marcus Fabius Gallus, an Epicurean, conjures up a decidedly less heroic Epicurus as a haunting precursor of his own guilty disease: he presents the Stoic sentiment that Epicurus's final moments were not a portrait of courage in the face of bodily revolt but the result of a life of gluttony and hedonistic living.[38] This Stoic interpretation, an unsympathetic overreading if not an outright misreading of the original symptoms, nonetheless throws into relief a debate we shall develop and pursue throughout this section: Stoic encounters with death emphasize the intentional control of the agent confronting death, while Epicurean accounts tend to portray, if not a helplessness, an indifferent acceptance of death.[39] Epicurus is thus,

---

[37] Cicero also translates this letter of Epicurus at *De Finibus* 2.30 [96].

[38] The Stoic interpretation of course also indicts Cicero of hedonistic living.

[39] Indeed, the portrait offered in Epicurus's letter, where Epicurus joyfully thinks of past friendly conversations, operates not by choosing some proper death but rather by ignoring death altogether (through memory).

in Stoic eyes, the agent who brings about his own suffering rather than a serene observer of his body naturally taking its course.

Deaths of Stoic heroes are therefore generally not disease-filled, bed-ridden affairs but manly suicides.[40] Cato the Younger, perhaps the most famous Roman Stoic suicide, takes his own life instead of submitting to Julius Caesar for pardon. His final moments are portrayed by Seneca as follows:

I do not see, I declare, what Jupiter has more beautiful on Earth, if he should desire to pay attention to it, than that he regard Cato, although his sides were broken many times, nonetheless standing upright amid public destruction. "Although everything has fallen to the sovereignty of one man," he says, "although the lands are guarded by legions, the seas by fleets, although a Caesarian soldier blockades the city gates, Cato has a way out: a single hand will create a broad avenue [*latam . . . viam*] for liberty [*libertati*]. This sword, though unharmed and unstained by civil war, at last will provide good, noble deeds: that liberty [*libertatem*] which it could not provide for its country, it will grant to Cato. Draw near, O soul, the long-anticipated deed; remove yourself from human affairs. . . ." (Seneca *De Providentia* 2.9–11)[41]

In its portrayal of perhaps *the* Roman death, this passage theatrically recreates Cato's dying words, emphasizing a single, familiar theme— *libertas* ("freedom"). *Libertas* here refers not merely to abstract liberty but to an ability to step outside the domain of Caesar's rule, an ability, that is, to *choose* (*voluntas*) not to be governed. The strong geographical imagery—blockades, guarded lands, a broad avenue—vividly depicts the paradoxical Stoic theme: an internal, intentional choice reconfigures a menacing external landscape. The interior will is mapped onto the geo-graphical exterior, symbolically conflating death with intentional choice (*voluntas*), a choice that belongs to the agent desiring to step outside Caesar's realm.

Such analysis makes it clearer why suicide (often called *mors volun-taria*, "voluntary death") occupies a central place in Stoic mythology,

---

[40] Among well-known Stoics, Cleanthes—who (like Atticus) perishes from self-starvation—seems to be an exception to this general tendency. For the life of Cleanthes, see Diogenes Laërtius 7.168–76 (death at 176). The masculine "gendering" of Stoicism is occasionally made quite explicit. See, for example, Seneca *De Constantia Sapientis* 1 on the "manly path" (*via virilis*) of the Stoics. Seneca is cited from Reynolds (1977).

[41] I translate the text of Reynolds (1977). See Plutarch *Cato Minor* 66 for a similar version of this narrative.

while disease—although hardly absent from Stoic accounts—responds more readily to Epicurean fascination.[42] If suicide (*mors voluntaria*), the swift stroke of one's own sword, seemingly provides concrete manifestation of the will (*voluntas*), disease is murkier terrain for such intentional, willed action. Another text of Seneca, which addresses his asthma and its relation to death, throws this point into stark relief:

But I—even in the throes of an asthma attack—never ceased to find comfort in cheerful and courageous thoughts. "What's this?" I said. "Does death try me so often, then? Let him! I had a try at him a long while ago myself." "When?" you ask. Before I was born. Death is not being. . . .

. . . I am being cast out, yes, but just as if I were going out. The wise man is never cast out for this reason: to be cast out is to be expelled from a place one departs unwillingly (*invitus*). The wise man does nothing unwillingly (*invitus*); he escapes necessity, he wants (*vult*) what it will compel. (Seneca *Epistulae* 54.3–4; 7)[43]

On the one hand, Seneca here consoles himself with Epicurean rather than Stoic platitudes. The so-called symmetry argument, the claim that death is just not-being and is therefore, at least with regard to one's own existence, the same as the state prior to birth is a well-known Epicurean contention.[44] On the other hand, Seneca still concludes his letter (and thus adjudicates his struggle with asthma) with claims about the will of the wise man, implying that he still models his combat with asthma not on peaceful acceptance but on willed, intentional action. His vacillation between Stoic and Epicurean claims shows how hard it is to marry

---

[42] While only a few instances of Epicurean disease are studied within the present essay, it is worth noting briefly the existence of further evidence on disease within surviving *Epicurea*. Plutarch (*Non Posse* 1103a, cited here and elsewhere from Pohlenz and Westman (1959)), for example, records that Epicurus cared for Metrodorus, Polyainos, and Aristoboulos during their final illnesses. The Epicurean Metrodorus, moreover, wrote a work *On the Illness of Epicurus* (according to Diogenes Laërtius 10.24), and we have reports of his own illness (Plutarch *Non Posse* 1097e; Celsus *De Medicina* 3.21, cited from Marx (1915)), which Körte (1890) took to derive from a work *De Morbo Suo* (*On His Own Illness*). This evidence (hardly a comprehensive selection) already gives a sense of how frequently Epicureans discuss disease. (For a treatment of this evidence within the context of Epicurean school history, see Clay (1998) 64–67.)

[43] I translate the text of Reynolds (1965).

[44] On Epicurean symmetry arguments, see Warren (2004) 57–108.

certain Stoic tenets to the unclear vagaries of illness. As he makes clear elsewhere, Seneca needs to reassure us—and himself—that one *can* show valor (and therefore perhaps will, *voluntas*) in bed:

There is—trust me on this point—place for courage even in bed. Not only do arms and battle-lines give proof of a spirit keen and unconquered by fear: in bed-clothes, too, the brave man is visible. You have something to do: wrestle well with your disease. (Seneca *Epistulae* 78.21)[45]

This reassurance, we might say, is necessary because disease is an uneasy fit for Stoic thinking: it is neither, as we shall see in the case of Atticus, entirely in nor entirely out of our control.

This backdrop of Stoic and Epicurean thinking at last prepares us to read Nepos's portrayal of the death of Atticus, a scene that—although it depicts the heroic death of a well-known Epicurean—nonetheless seems to borrow from both Stoic and Epicurean *exempla*:[46]

When he had filled seventy-seven years [*septem et septuaginta annos*] in this fashion and grown to extreme old age no less through his dignity than through his kindness and good fortune—indeed, he obtained his many inheritances through nothing other than his goodness—and when he had enjoyed such greatly favorable health that he had not needed medicine for thirty years [*annis triginta*], he acquired an illness, which initially both he himself and his doctors disregarded; for they thought that it was "tenesmos" [Gk. τεινεσμός: a gripping pain in the bowels[47]], for which swift, easy cures [*remedia celeria faciliaque*] were proposed. When he had passed three months [*tres menses*] in this condition without any pain (beyond what he felt from the cure itself), suddenly [*subito*] such a great, powerful sickness burst forth in his lower intestine that in the end [*extremo tempore*] pus-filled ulcers broke out across his loins. But before this happened to him, after he felt the onset of his fever and his pains increasing day by day [*in dies*], he ordered his son-in-law Agrippa to approach him and, with him, Lucius Cornelius Balbus

---

[45] On this letter (and more generally on disease and the question of how Seneca writes the body in pain), see Edwards (1998), which is influenced by Scarry (1985).

[46] Such apparent philosophical "eclecticism," if in itself uncomfortable, fits nicely with what we have seen thus far in *Atticus*: the biography combines Stoic analyses with (submerged) Epicurean details.

[47] See Pliny *Naturalis Historia* 28.211, cited from Mayhoff (1892–1909): "*Tenesmos*, that is, a constant, vain desire for moving the bowels . . . " (*Tenesmos, id est crebra et inanis voluntas desurgendi, . . .*)

and Sextus Peducaeus. When he saw these were present, he leaned on his bed and said, "How much care and diligence I have applied in watching over my health in this time [*hoc tempore*]—since I have you as witnesses—it is in no way necessary to recall at length. Since, with these endeavors, I have made certain, I hope, that I have left nothing undone that pertains to improving my health, it remains that I take counsel with myself. All this, I did not want you to ignore; for it is my decision to leave off nourishing my disease. And I say this because—whatever food I have eaten these last days [*his diebus*]—I have prolonged my life in such a fashion that I have increased my pains without hope of health. Wherefore I seek from you, first that you approve my plan, then that you not try in vain [*frustra*] to obstruct me through dissuasion."

He gave this speech with such constancy of voice [*constantia vocis*] and appearance that it seemed that he was departing not from life, but from one home for another. When Agrippa specifically, crying over him and kissing him, begged and beseeched that he not himself hasten [*acceleraret*] that death toward which nature was goading him, and—since even at this moment he could live beyond the crisis [*temporibus*]—that he preserve himself both for himself and his family, Atticus quelled Agrippa's requests with quiet stubbornness. Thus, when he had abstained from food for two days [*biduum*], straightaway [*subito*] his fever subsided and his disease began to be lighter. Nevertheless, he carried out his plan all the same. And so on the fifth day [*die quinto*] after he had entered into his plan, the last day of March [*pridie kal. Aprilis*] when Gnaeus Domitius and Gaius Sosius were consuls, he died. He was carried away on a modest bier, as he himself had ordered, without any funeral procession, accompanied by all good men, with a great crowd. He was buried next to the Appian Way at the fifth stone in the memorial of Quintus Caecilius, his maternal uncle. (Nepos *Atticus* 21–22)

This lengthy scene, aside from its obvious fascination with sickness, manifests an Epicurean character in its emphasis on the *sudden* action of disease. Disease appears or disappears for Atticus suddenly (*subito*), a characterization put into relief by the extensive temporal accounting within the passage ("seventy-seven years," "thirty years," "three months," "day by day," "last days," etc.).[48] Such suddenness is, moreover, hardly

---

[48] Alongside the temporal accounting, it is worth paying attention to the various references to speed within the passage ("swift remedies" [*remedia celeria*]; "hasten[ing]" of death [*acceleraret*]). *Subito* itself carries the double sense of "suddenly" (*Oxford Latin Dictionary*, s.v. *subito* 1) and "quickly" (*Oxford Latin Dictionary*, s.v. *subito* 2), thus manifesting notions of speed, unexpectedness, and short, abbreviated temporality.

foreign to other tales of Epicurean illness. One of Lucretius's character-izations of disease in his sixth book makes a similar point, explaining how the seeds, the atoms, of death can rapidly collide and suddenly (*repente*) manufacture illness.[49] Likewise, although it provides an initial attempt at diagnosis, Atticus's death scene avoids any ultimate solution to the problem of disease, lingering instead in the vivid description of symptoms. As one stretch of Lucretius's famous account of the great Athenian plague shows, his account often prefers vividly cataloguing symptoms to the deeper reading, the reading "through" or "behind" of diagnosis, lingering upon surfaces rather than explaining them away.[50] Of course, disease for Lucretius has a reason, a principle, a *ratio*, but

---

[49] Lucretius *De Rerum Natura* 6.1090–97:

> Now I shall lay clear what the principle (*ratio*) is for diseases,
> or whence it's possible that the power of disease, straight from (*repente*) having arisen,
> causes death-dealing slaughter, for humankind and packs of beasts.
> First, I've shown above what are the life-bringing seeds of many things
> for us, and—by contrast—it is necessary that there are many seeds
> that fly about for death and disease. These, when they have arisen
> by chance [*casu . . . forte*] and disturbed thoroughly the heavens, disease-filled air
> is made.

On the later fate of this "seed" explanation of disease, see Nutton (1983), who also treats the question of "cause," "responsibility," and "individual predisposition" in disease. (See especially 4–7, 9–11, where he discusses Lucretius.)

[50] One exemplary presentation of the symptoms of plague may be found at Lucretius *De Rerum Natura* 6.1145–62:

> First their heads were burning with heat
> and both eyes were red with fire welling up from below.
> Then their jaws were sweating, black with blood,
> and the path of the voice was closing, fenced in with sores,
> and the tongue, translator of the mind, was dripping with blood,
> weakened by disease, slow to move, rough to the touch.
> From there, when—by the throat—the chest had filled and
> when the disease-bearing power had flowed even into the sad hearts of the sick,
> then truly all hold on life was slipping.
> Breath was pushing a foul odor from the mouth,
> like the scent of rancid, exposed corpses.
> And the very powers of the whole mind, the
> whole body already was drooping at the very doorstep of death.
> For these insupportable ills, both distressing anxiety
> and complaints mingled with groans were constant companions.
> Thick retching through night and day,
> constantly compelling muscles and limbs to tighten,
> was destroying them with fatigue, already exhausted as they were.

this *ratio* is nothing other than the chance (*casu, forte*) collision of atoms.

Alongside these identifiably, if not exclusively, Epicurean features, there are aspects of Atticus's death that remind one more of Stoicism. "Constancy" (*constantia*), Atticus's even voice and appearance in the face of death, is at least as Stoic as it is Epicurean, and perhaps the most dramatic feature of Atticus's death scene, his decision—made with great resolve—to starve himself rather than to continue enduring treatment and disease seems not wholly unlike Cato the Younger's refusal to submit to Caesar for pardon.[51] The decision, as the text puts it, "to leave off nourishing his disease" (*alere morbum desinere*) may perhaps be taken as a revolt against the tyranny of disease, an attempt to step away from an undesired governance of his body. Whether this particular metaphor is present, though, the choice certainly reads much like the rational, intentional choice that characterizes the death of Stoic heroes. (In addition, the suggestion that Atticus departs life as if "departing from one home for another" echoes a Stoic motif that life is analogous to a banquet—and that suicide is thus analogous to choosing to leave a banquet.)[52]

Yet—even as Atticus makes the choice to perish—his disease swerves into remission, a fact no doubt designed, within Nepos's narrative, to test the constancy of his resolve but one that also reminds us of the ways in which disease remains hidden and unknown, a manifestation whose principle (*ratio*) is chance (*casu*). His death thus remains a picture of constancy but perhaps also a picture of senseless obstinacy, starvation in the face of a receding illness. I point to this fact because, in reading through these concluding paragraphs of *Atticus*, one is struck by the fact that Atticus's death, while perhaps more Epicurean than Stoic, dwells uncomfortably and incompletely within a traditional assessment of the doctrines of either philosophical school. Indeed, this final swerve of Atticus's illness calls into question Nepos's own reading of Atticus's death in so far as it does not allow the simple, easy conclusion that Atticus's choices and habits shape his final moments.

What I want to say of Atticus coincides rather uncannily with a no doubt unrelated statement of Maurice Blanchot. Blanchot, in *L'espace*

---

[51] Seneca's *De Constantia Sapientis* forms perhaps the easiest *locus* for the discussion of "constancy" in Stoicism.

[52] See Ker (2009) 173 (with n. 85) on Seneca *Epistulae* 61.

littéraire (*The Space of Literature*), connects suicide with artistic production, noting that this connection arises because "the artist is linked to
his work in the same strange way in which the man who takes death for
a goal is linked to death."[53] In developing this connection, Blanchot
writes:

> Voluntary death is the refusal to see the other death, the death one cannot
> grasp, which one never reaches. It is a kind of sovereign negligence, an
> alliance made with visible death in order to exclude the invisible one, a pact
> with the good, faithful death which I use constantly in the world, an effort
> to expand its sphere, to make it still viable and true beyond itself, where it
> is no longer anything but the other death. The expression "I kill myself"
> suggests this doubling that is not taken into account. For "I" is a self in the
> plenitude of its action and resolution, capable of acting sovereignly upon
> itself, always strong enough to reach itself with its blow. And yet the one
> who is thus struck is no longer I, but another, so that when I kill myself,
> perhaps it is "I" who does the killing, but it is not done to me. Nor is it my
> death—the one I have dealt—that I have now to die, but rather the death
> which I refused, which I neglected, and which is this very negligence—
> perpetual flight and inertia.[54]

Here he describes suicide as functioning, in a sense, like artistic production: the suicide, like the artist, engages in an intentional act but does
so falsely. An "I" acts in Blanchot's analysis, but it does not act upon itself.
It acts upon another that does not receive the death given but rather
the death refused, neglected. And it is in this negligence, this neglected
death, that "the work"—artistic creation—"wants to dwell."

Not all of what Blanchot says translates easily to Atticus's death.
Blanchot illuminates artistic production through the figure of suicide and
not the reverse. Yet some aspects of Blanchot's statement resonate: the
frustration of intentional action that characterizes his model, the "I" that
attempts but fails to act upon itself, resembles the figure of Atticus who
chooses to throw off the sovereignty of his disease, a disease that may
have meanwhile decided to abdicate its position of authority. What
Atticus chose to kill, "to leave off nourishing," was his diseased body,
though he may ultimately have killed something else. And what he leaves

---

[53] Blanchot (1982) 105.
[54] Blanchot (1982) 106–107, translation slightly modified.

behind—though traditional Epicurean doctrine would perhaps suggest it is nothing more than atoms—is a creative work of sorts, an *exemplum* mediated through the pen of Nepos, an *exemplum* neither fully Epicurean nor Stoic (but entirely Roman). In the words of the famous Epicurean saying, death may indeed be nothing to us in so far as we are individual agents confronting a sensory experience, yet it—as Atticus shows—also may leave behind creative works, *exempla*, that, variously represented, may in fact be something for an "us" that thinks and reads, even if it cannot feel, beyond individual sensory experience.

Moreover, Blanchot's analysis also gives us a figure for negotiating the primary concern of the present essay—Cornelius Nepos's relation to his subject, Titus Pomponius Atticus, and more specifically, his relation to Atticus's Epicureanism.[55] Nepos himself is not entirely unlike Blanchot's suicide in so far as his work, his depiction of Atticus's death, evades the analysis it explicitly provides. He repeatedly claims that, for Atticus, "his habits fashion his fate"; yet, in the end, it is difficult to see how this explanation holds. Atticus's final moments are colored by a complex set of details, including both his intention "to leave off nourishing his disease" (and ultimately to starve himself) and the rapid appearance and disappearance of his disease. Depending upon which details we choose to emphasize, depending, that is, on which story of nature we choose to tell, Atticus's death both permits and denies Stoic and Epicurean accounts.

Given the Epicurean traces found elsewhere in *Atticus*, we may be tempted to emphasize any Epicurean resonances, above all the presence of Atticus's disease and its unpredictable nature. But such an emphasis risks ignoring Atticus's final constancy and resolve. And it is perhaps here that Blanchot helps most: he speaks of dying "the death which I neglected"; and we may similarly think of Nepos penning an *exemplum* that is intended but that hardly provides the intended textual performance, hardly produces the intended effect on its audience. J. Hillis Miller has written that "an example, it may be, . . . legislates or constitutes, but what it does is to disrupt the cognitive clarity of the argument it was

---

[55] Implicitly, then, Blanchot's figure of suicide as a model for artistic production turns Atticus and Nepos into doubles.

meant to clarify."[56] Such a description may well apply to the *exemplum* of Atticus's death, which—despite its inconsistently Stoic and Epicurean performance—is perhaps most Epicurean (anti-teleological) in its ability to disrupt the clear, teleological structure that would grant Nepos's narrative (and Atticus's death) a singular meaning. Epicurean ghosts, as we have seen, can always be disruptive creatures but perhaps never more so than when they haunt the resolve of seemingly Stoic agents.

---

[56] Miller (1995) 163–64. On Roman exemplarity more generally, see Roller (2004). (Roller is at work on a larger monograph on exemplarity.)

2

Epicurus's *Mistresses*: Pleasure, Authority, and Gender in the Reception of the *Kuriai Doxai* in the Second Sophistic

Richard Fletcher

> Taurus autem noster, quotiens facta mentio Epicuri erat, in ore atque in lingua habebat verba haec Hieroclis Stoici, viri sancti et gravis: Ἡδονὴ τέλος, πόρνης δόγμα· οὐκ ἔστιν πρόνοια, οὐδὲ πόρνης δόγμα.
>
> —Aulus Gellius *Noctes Atticae* 9.5.8

> Our Taurus, whenever mention was made of Epicurus, used to have on his lips and tongue these words of Hierocles the Stoic, a holy and austere man: "Pleasure is the goal, a whore's doctrine; there is no providence, not even a whore's doctrine."

Hierocles' pithy remark (*verba*) cuts Epicurean philosophy down to size as having too much sensuality and too little spirituality. The Stoic dismisses the Epicurean doctrine (*dogma*) of pleasure as the final goal (*telos*) by claiming that it was adhered to by the lowest rank of female prostitute (*pornē*).[1] While the joke works only if we consider Epicurean atheism a qualitatively worse doctrine than Epicurean hedonism, even if the quip fails, the perennially pleasure-seeking figure of the female prostitute acts as a locus for articulating its twin-attack against both hedonism

---

[1] For a discussion of difficulties of defining ranks of prostitution in ancient Greece, see Cohen (2006).

and atheism.[2] Like so many anti-Epicureans before and after him, Hierocles, with his *verba*, trades on the infamous early history of the Garden and, more specifically, on the presence of female courtesans (*hetairai*) such as Leontion and Themista within the school as a comment on the doctrine of pleasure as the final end.[3] The critical content and formal wit of Hierocles' *verba* is not, however, the end of the story. As so often in Gellius, we are invited to eavesdrop on a satirical drama of scholarly one-upmanship.[4] We are told not only of Hierocles' original saying but also of how the Platonist Taurus repeated it when confronted with someone mentioning Epicurus. One way to interpret Gellius's retelling of this anecdote about "our" (*noster*) Taurus is to see a shared disdain for the contemporary Epicurean school through a shared commitment to Platonist authority. Yet there are two related reasons for questioning Gellius's anti-Epicureanism and his commitment to the authority of the Platonist Taurus both in this passage and in his work more generally.

In the first place, Gellius does not present consistently anti-Epicurean views elsewhere in the *Noctes Atticae*.[5] On two occasions, he in fact defends Epicurus against the word-picking of the Platonist Plutarch.[6] Even if these instances could be construed simply as one Platonist squabbling with another, they make clear that any consideration of Gellius's supposed anti-Epicureanism demands equal consideration of Plutarch. Scholarly understanding of the Epicurean quotation (i.e., pleasure is the "well-balanced condition of the body") that opens the lemma (9.5.1) in which Hierocles' *verba* appear necessarily depends upon a parallel passage in Plutarch's anti-Epicurean polemic *Against the Epicurean Idea of Happiness*. Put simply, we only know that these words derive from

---

[2] Fischel (1973) 47–48 notes how this functions at a linguistic level too in the pun in Greek (*pron-/porn-*) and offers evidence for the inseparability of these two Epicurean doctrines, for example, from Dio of Prusa (*Orationes* 12.36), who has the Epicureans making Pleasure a goddess at the same time as getting rid of the gods. Dio is cited from von Arnim (1893–96).

[3] See P. Gordon (2004) for the most extended account of the role of prostitutes (*hetairai*) in the Epicurean Garden in the later reception of the school.

[4] On the satiric side of Gellius, see Gunderson (2009) and Keulen (2009).

[5] *Contra* Fitzgibbon (2001) 102–105, who argues that discussion of this lemma and the fact that Taurus and Hierocles have the final word signals Gellius's approval and, thus, his anti-Epicureanism.

[6] Gellius *Noctes Atticae* 2.8.7 and 2.9.4, cited from Marshall (1968).

Epicurus's *On the Telos* because of Plutarch, a fact that confirms the need to read this passage alongside the latter's anti-Epicureanism.

Secondly, as Erik Gunderson notes, "even as Gellius' relationship to philosophy may be read by the hostile as dilettantish and muddle-headed, the portrait of Taurus clearly authorizes a failure to commit oneself exclusively to philosophy."[7] If Gellius the philologist is sending up the philosopher Taurus, he does so by pointing out the excesses of philo-sophical doctrinal wrangling and the philosopher's dubious authority: a Platonist quotes a Stoic to attack Epicureans. The relish with which the Platonist Taurus cites the words of the Stoic Hierocles to denounce his Epicurean rivals reveals not only an authoritative verbal form that was a leading characteristic of the Epicurean school (the pithy remark or *sententia*) but also an undeniable pleasure in the sententiousness of his saying, which is perhaps a fetish of all authoritarian philosophers and philosophies.[8] Gellius the philologist thus critiques not only the whole back and forth of philosophical doctrinal wrangling but also the dubious claims to philosophical authority through the citation of other men's *sententiae* that this entails. The very reliance on the authoritative words of a master of the school, whether Stoic, Platonic, or Epicurean, ensures the passivity of the pupil speaker. Looked at in this way, Gellius turns Hierocles' *verba* about pleasure and prostitution in Epicureanism back on Taurus and his act of citation, implying that in philosophical communities there is always a dynamic of mastery and submission at work. Gellius asks: whether you cite Hierocles or Epicurus, what does it mean for your own autonomy to have another man's *verba* always on your lips? Furthermore, the particular emphasis on the role of the body in citation (*in ore atque in lingua*) perhaps even suggests that Gellius questions the very (gendered) dynamic of that act: who, that is, is the (male) master and who is the (female) prostitute?

Gellius is not alone among writers in the cultural milieu of the Second Sophistic (second to third centuries CE) in making gendered claims

---

[7] Gunderson (2009) 171.

[8] On the pleasure of sententiousness in general, see Morales (2001). Obviously, the *sententia* was a wide-spread philosophical and rhetorical form beyond the limits of the Epicurean school: from the sayings of Diogenes the Cynic in Diogenes Laërtius to Porphyry's *Sententiae*. For *sententiae* in rhetorical theory, see the helpful summary in Kirchner (2001) 20–43. On the Epicurean *sententia* within a wider generic context see Fischel (1973) 50.

about the performative role of *sententiae* in both the masculinized mastery of philosophical discursive authority and in the pupil's effeminized passivity in its reception.[9] In this essay, I contextualize Gellius's anecdote within this nexus of ideas in the Second Sophistic reception of the famous collection of Epicurean *sententiae*, Epicurus's *Kuriai Doxai* ("Principal Doctrines"/"Masterful Opinions"). I show how pro- and anti-Epicurean writing of the period becomes part of contemporary debates surrounding the autonomy of the (male) subject (Michel Foucault's "care of the self") through a specifically gendered reception of the pleasures that adherence to (Epicurean) philosophical authority creates. After a brief discussion of the key themes in the composition and reception of the *Kuriai Doxai* in general, paying particular attention to how the very title of the *Kuriai Doxai* becomes a site of contestation for issues of mastery and authority, I turn to Foucault's influential work and the place of Epicureanism in his conception of the "care of the self" in the Second Sophistic. I suggest that the gendering of these issues of mastery through the figure of the *hetaira* in the Epicurean Garden supplements the feminist critique of Foucault's discussion of the male-centered subject of the "care of the self."

I go on to consider four Second Sophistic authors and their respective responses to the *Kuriai Doxai* in two groups, organized according to their generally assumed relationship to Epicureanism: first, the ostensibly anti-Epicurean figures of Aelian and Alciphron; and second, the ostensibly pro-Epicurean Diogenes of Oenoanda and Diogenes Laërtius. Focusing on their respective treatments of the *Kuriai Doxai*, I claim that, in spite of their traditionally accepted philosophical allegiances, there is considerable contact between all of these authors based on their shared cultural contexts in the Second Sophistic. More specifically, these authors approach the gendering of pleasure and authority within the central issues of cultural learning (*paideia*) and political autonomy in similar ways. Aelian attacks the Epicureans for their atheism and shows how they are metaphorically "feminized" by their reading of the authoritative

---

[9] For the gendered discursive authority of the citation, see Derrida (1988) and Butler (1997). Cixous (1981) 51 remarks that "the moment women open their mouths— women more often than men—they are immediately asked in whose name and from what theoretical standpoint they are speaking, who is their master and where they are coming from."

Kuriai Doxai as "wicked sayings"; Alciphron's fictional *Letter* of Leontion, the famed philosopher-*hetaira* of the original Epicurean Garden, both challenges Epicurus's authority by pitting her own autonomy as a mistress (*kuria*) against the *Kuriai Doxai* and affirms his authority by bewailing the loss of her lover Timarchus to Epicurus's "sheltering doctrines." Diogenes of Oenoanda makes the *Kuriai Doxai* the most prominent text on his inscription, reworking the sayings as the core of his "fictional" *Letter* from Epicurus to his mother as a means not only of counteracting the *hetaira*-figure of the original Garden but also of steering her away from exponents of mainstream *paideia* and into the enclosure of the Epicurean community. Finally, Diogenes Laërtius, who ends his whole work by quoting the *Kuriai Doxai*, does so while focalizing his addressee, the female "lover of Plato," in a way that in the process acknowledges her philosophical (and perhaps, political) authority.

In each of these encounters between female readers and Epicurus's *sententiae*, we experience variations on Gellius's drama of the mastery of philosophical discursive authority and the pupil's passivity in its reception, variations that consistently blur the boundaries between polemic and apology, satire and encomium, pro- and anti-Epicureanism in the Second Sophistic, while, at the same time, articulating a major shift in the gender politics of the subject in this period.

I. "THE OPINIONS THEY CALL MASTER": THE PERFORMATIVE AUTHORITY OF THE *KURIAI DOXAI*

> Performativity is a luxury of authority. To be able to have the right and the power to produce the performative, there must naturally exist a right and a condition.[10]

The *Kuriai Doxai* are a collection of *sententiae* (maxims or sayings) attributed to Epicurus.[11] Even though Epicurus's original text is lost,

---

[10] Derrida (2000) 468. The quotation of my subtitle originates in Aelian fr. 64a (Domingo-Forasté), on which see below.

[11] We also have the other collection of maxims called the *Sententiae Vaticanae* or *The Voice of Epicurus* in which there is some crossover with the *Kuriai Doxai*. All texts of Epicurus are cited from Usener (1887) unless otherwise noted. The *Kuriai Doxai* are generally cited from Marcovich (1999).

collections of the *Kuriai Doxai* were preserved in two forms in the Roman Empire during the height of the Second Sophistic (second and third centuries CE): at the end of Diogenes Laërtius's tenth (and final) book and in fragmentary form running along the base of the inscription of Diogenes of Oenoanda. While reconstructions of Epicurus's original text have been attempted by means of a comparison of the collections preserved in these two authors, such attempts have been ultimately unsuccessful on account of both textual differences (of individual *sententiae*) and differences in ordering (of the collection as a whole).[12] Scholars have explained away the textual and organizational differences between the surviving collections either by emphasizing the role of the memorization of the *Kuriai Doxai* for the dissemination of Epicureanism or by questioning the individuality of an original Epicurean collection, distinct from excerpts from other works.[13] As we shall see, while these processes of memorization and excerption fail to provide a complete understanding of the textual history of the *Kuriai Doxai*, they are nevertheless significant for the performance of authority that marks the *Doxai* in their reception as a distinctively Epicurean text.[14]

Despite the absence of a surviving collection of the *Kuriai Doxai* before the Second Sophistic period, the maxims were clearly known to earlier Epicurean communities and their critics. Our earliest testimonies, from Cicero and Philodemus, stem from the first-century BCE.[15] Cicero, addressing the Epicurean Torquatus in *De Finibus*, asks rhetorically: "Who of those in your club has not learned Epicurus's *Kuriai Doxai* by heart?" (*quis enim vestrum non edidicit Epicuri* κύριας δόξας),[16] while Philodemus, in his *On Anger*, refers to people criticizing the *Kuriai Doxai*.[17] Cicero's reference to Epicureans learning the *Kuriai Doxai* is at

---

[12] See Gordon (1996) 59–65; Smith (2006).

[13] For discussion of the *Kuriai Doxai* and its psychagogic effects in Lucretius and beyond see Reinhardt (2002) 303 n. 37, with bibliography.

[14] I thank David Sedley for making me rethink these questions of memorization and excerption in the textual history of the *Kuriai Doxai*.

[15] For a helpful summary, see Gordon 1996 60–63. Lucretius's reference to the "golden sayings" (*aurea dicta*, *De Rerum Natura* 3.12) may refer to the *Kuriai Doxai* or to all of Epicurus's writings.

[16] Cicero *De Finibus* 2.20. I use the Latin text of Reynolds (1998); translations are my own, although they are made in consultation with Woolf in Annas (2001).

[17] Philodemus *De Ira*, col. 43 (Indelli). In addition, we have two testimonies from unknown Epicurean authors: *Vol. Herc.* col. XV and *Vol. Herc.* col. XXVII.

the center of a debate concerning the relationship between the *Kuriai Doxai* and the so-called *tetrapharmakos* (the "four-part cure"):

ἄφοβον ὁ θεός,
ἀνύποπτον ὁ θάνατος
καὶ τἀγαθόν μὲν εὔκτητον,
τὸ δὲ δεινὸν εὐκαρτέρητον.

God—not fearful
Death—not riskful
Virtue—obtained cheerfully
Evil—endured steadfastly. (Philodemus *Herculaneum Papyrus* 1005, 4.9–14)[18]

This brief, rhyming mnemonic has been understood as distilling the first four of the *Kuriai Doxai* of our extant collection, Diogenes Laërtius (10.139–40)[19]:

1. Τὸ μακάριον καὶ ἄφθαρτον οὔτε αὐτὸ πράγματα ἔχει οὔτε ἄλλῳ παρέχει, ὥστε οὔτε ὀργαῖς οὔτε χάρισι συνέχεται·ἐν ἀσθενεῖ γὰρ πᾶν τὸ τοιοῦτον.

2. Ὁ θάνατος οὐδὲν πρὸς ἡμᾶς· τὸ γὰρ διαλυθὲν ἀναισθητεῖ· τὸ δ' ἀναισθητοῦν οὐδὲν πρὸς ἡμᾶς.

3. Ὅρος τοῦ μεγέθους τῶν ἡδονῶν ἡ παντὸς τοῦ ἀλγοῦντος ὑπεξαίρεσις. ὅπου δ' ἂν τὸ ἡδόμενον ἐνῇ, καθ' ὃν ἂν χρόνον ᾖ, οὐκ ἔστι τὸ ἀλγοῦν ἢ τὸ λυπούμενον ἢ τὸ συναμφότερον.

4. Οὐ χρονίζει τὸ ἀλγοῦν συνεχῶς ἐν τῇ σαρκί, ἀλλὰ τὸ μὲν ἄκρον τὸν ἐλάχιστον χρόνον πάρεστι, τὸ δὲ μόνον ὑπερτεῖνον τὸ ἡδόμενον κατὰ σάρκα οὐ πολλὰς ἡμέρας συμμένει. αἱ δὲ πολυχρόνιοι τῶν ἀρρωστιῶν πλεονάζον ἔχουσι τὸ ἡδόμενον ἐν τῇ σαρκὶ ἤπερ τὸ ἀλγοῦν.

---

[18] Free rhyming translation of Fischel (1973) 33.
[19] I use the text of Marcovich (1999). All translations are my own, although I have consulted Hicks (1925).

1. A blessed and indestructible being neither has trouble himself nor brings any trouble to others, so that he is neither restrained by anger nor by partiality, for all things of this kind imply weakness.

2. Death is nothing to us; for what has been dissolved into its elements has no sensation, and what has no sensation is nothing to us.

3. The limit of the magnitude of pleasures is the removal of all pain. When such pleasure is present, for as long as it is present, there is no pain either of body or of mind or of both together.

4. Continuous pain does not last long in the body; instead, pain, if extreme, is present a very short time, and even that degree of pain that slightly exceeds bodily pleasure does not last for many days at once. Diseases of long duration allow an excess of pleasure in the body over pain.

There is some dispute as to which of our surviving *Kuriai Doxai* correspond to the *tetrapharmakos*. While *Kuriai Doxai* 1 and 2 are explicitly referenced, 3 and 4 are less easily identified by the third and fourth lines of the mnemonic. Indeed the reference to "the good" (*t'agathon*) in the *tetrapharmakos* could refer to the discussion of the "natural good" (*kata phusin agathon; to tēs phuseōs agathon*) and its lack in *Kuriai Doxai* 6 and 7:

6. Ἕνεκα τοῦ θαρρεῖν ἐξ ἀνθρώπων <πάντα> ἦν κατὰ φύσιν [ἀρχῆς καὶ βασιλείας] ἀγαθά, ἐξ ὧν ἄν ποτε τοῦτο οἷός τ' ᾖ παρασκευάζεσθαι.

7. Ἔνδοξοι καὶ περίβλεπτοί τινες ἐβουλήθησαν γενέσθαι, τὴν ἐξ ἀνθρώπων ἀσφάλειαν οὕτω νομίζοντες περιποιήσεσθαι. ὥστ' εἰ μὲν ἀσφαλὴς ὁ τῶν τοιούτων βίος, ἀπέλαβον τὸ τῆς φύσεως ἀγαθόν· εἰ δὲ μὴ ἀσφαλής, οὐκ ἔχουσιν οὗ ἕνεκα ἐξ ἀρχῆς κατὰ τὸ τῆς φύσεως οἰκεῖον ὠρέχθησαν.

6. For the purpose of feeling secure from men all things are natural goods out of which this end can be procured.

7. Some people seek fame and status, thinking that they could in
this way protect themselves against other men. If their lives really
are secure, then they have attained a natural good; if, however, they
are insecure, they still lack what they originally sought by natural
instinct.

This latter possibility is hinted at by an anonymous papyrus from
Herculaneum, which refers to "the most important" (τὰ κυριώτατα) of
the *Kuriai Doxai* as appearing at the beginning of the work.[20] But the
tetrapharmakos also could offer evidence for an alternative ordering to
the original Epicurean collection (1, 2, 6, 7) and one that, as we shall see,
may have been followed by the inscription of Diogenes of Oenoanda.[21]

This debate surrounding how the *tetrapharmakos* relates to the *Kuriai
Doxai* also has implications for the question of whether the *Kuriai Doxai*
were themselves memorized by Epicurean communities.[22] While memorization of the *tetrapharmakos* is explicitly encouraged by its formal features (brevity, rhyme), and while it may be based on the opening *doxai*
(1–4 or 1, 2, 6, 7), we cannot therefore be sure that the original work
by Epicurus was either limited to a small number of *doxai* or meant to be
memorized. Hence, it would be rash to posit the process of memorization
as the primary force enabling the textual fluidity of our two Second
Sophistic collections.[23] More significant for the present discussion is that
the reception of the *Kuriai Doxai* (including the very title of the work)
evokes the voice of the original master (*kurios*). Thus, memorization,
to whatever extent it occurred, would explain not so much the textual
history of the *Kuriai Doxai* as their performative textual authority.
Epicureans, that is, were defined by having the master's doctrines "on
their lips and tongues."

---

[20] *PHerc.* 1251 (Schmid) col. xv (cited from Usener (1887) 68); cf. Clay (1998) 23.

[21] To support this ordering, Philodemus's *Against [the Sophists]* 4.6–14, cited from
Sbordone (1947), refers to *Kuriai Doxai* 6 with the statement that a "good is easy to
secure."

[22] On memorization, see Gordon (1996) 60–65; Erler and Schofield (1999) 670, with
n. 64; and Mansfeld (1999a) 5: "The *KD* is a sort of catechism."

[23] Gordon (1996) 65: "The *doxai* were meant to represent the authoritative utterances
of Epicurus, but they were open to change." The fact of two conflicting collections does
not necessarily mean that there was never one text of the *Kuriai Doxai*. Fluidity is more a
matter of the role of performative authority in the reception history of the text than of the
text itself.

In addition to memorization, another debate on the textual history of the *Kuriai Doxai* concerns excerption.[24] In spite of the evidence that Epicurus composed an individual work called *Kuriai Doxai*, its absence as a text until the Second Sophistic has allowed for speculation about the origin of the collection. One of the most compelling theories is that these were Epicurus's "Greatest Hits," which originated in other works, such as Epicurus's *On Nature* and, possibly, the *Letter to Menoeceus*. Nonetheless, despite similar wording, no single *sententia* is found whole-sale in another work of Epicurus.[25] Once again, as with memorization, excerption perhaps tells us more about the cultural forces at play in the reception of the *sententiae* than their textual history. Fusing Epicurus's sayings with his total literary output perhaps suggests that Epicureans (and their critics) conceptualized the *Kuriai Doxai* as emanating from the singular authority of the master Epicurus himself. In this light, it is not surprising that Lucretius's phrases *patria praecepta* and *aurea dicta* have been understood as alluding to either the *Kuriai Doxai* specifically or to Epicurus's doctrines in general.

While memorization and excerption cannot conclusively account for the textual differences between Diogenes Laërtius and Diogenes of Oenoanda, both processes privilege the ultimate authority of Epicurus. Memorization demands the immediate recollection of the master's voice, while excerption proves the consistency of the master's thought by seeing his "opinions" as part of his total thought. This tension between Epicurus's authority and textual instability plays out in two interrelated debates in the reception of Epicurean philosophy and philosophy in general in the Hellenistic and Roman periods. First, how do ideas of *auctoritas* operate within a specifically Roman cultural context? Second, how are conceptions of philosophical authority constituted after the "decentralization" of the Athenian philosophical schools following Rome's

---

[24] Clay (1998) 22 refers to the "prehistory" of both the *Kuriai Doxai* and the *Letter of Menoeceus* in *On Nature*, but also asserts that the *Letter* is the "source" of some of the *Kuriai Doxai*. Clay (2009) 21 mentions how the *Letter of Menoeceus* "expands on many of the precepts abbreviated in the forty *Kyriai Doxai* that Diogenes [Laërtius] reproduces." These statements can mean either that the *Kuriai Doxai* preempted the *Letter* ("expands") or the *Letter* preempted the *Kuriai Doxai* ("abbreviated"). At a minimum, they seem to leave open the question as to whether the *Kuriai Doxai* precede the letter. The idea that the *Kuriai Doxai* originated in *On Nature* is intriguingly alluded to in Alciphron's *Letter*.

[25] Compare *Kuriai Doxai* 5 and the *Letter to Menoeceus* (Diogenes Laërtius 10.132).

conquest of Greece?[26] These two debates meet, I contend, in the idea of performative authority.[27] Performative authority means an authority that does not merely come from the words themselves—that is, from their manifest semantic or philosophical content—but from their status as words to be recalled (i.e., memorized) and cited (i.e., excerpted) in a given context. As we saw with the Epicurean who confronts Taurus in Gellius's anecdote, the "performative" aspect of recalling the *Kuriai Doxai* offers the authority to present a united front or to trump textual differences within the *Kuriai Doxai*.

This form of authority is not only at work in the dissemination of Epicurean philosophy: it also offers a prominent target for opponents of the philosophy.[28] For example, the following scene in Cicero's *De Finibus* displays how the *Kuriai Doxai* can be attacked for their content as well as for the performative authority with which they are imbued. When the interlocutor Torquatus defends Epicurean ethics, the argument pivots on the issue of pleasure as the final aim (Cicero *De Finibus* 2.18–22). The text of Epicurus's *On the Telos* is vital here, but the authority of the *Kuriai Doxai* is also strikingly evoked to highlight one aspect of Epicurean pleasure in Cicero's critique:[29]

In alio vero libro, in quo breviter comprehensis gravissimis sententiis quasi oracula edidisse sapientiae dicitur, scribit his verbis, quae nota tibi profecto, Torquate, sunt (quis enim vestrum non edidicit Epicuri κύριας δόξας, id est quasi maxime ratas, quia gravissimae sint ad beate vivendum breviter enuntiatae sententiae?). Animadverte igitur rectene hanc sententiam interpreter. (Cicero *De Finibus* 2.20–21)

Indeed, in another book, in which since he digested his most important opinions pithily, Epicurus is said to have pronounced oracles, as it were, of wisdom, he writes with the following words, which are surely well-known to you, Torquatus (for who of your club has not learned by heart

---

[26] On the idea that *auctor* and *auctoritas* are specifically Roman cultural concepts, see Cassius Dio 55.3.5, cited from and the discussion initiated by the seminal Heinze (1925). More recently, see Lincoln (1994) 1–13 and Lowrie (2009) 279–308. On the related ideas of philosophical *auctoritas* and the decentralization of Athenian school philosophy, see Sedley (1997) and (2003).

[27] Lincoln (1994).

[28] I owe these insights on authority to the editors.

[29] For Cicero's account of Epicurean pleasures in general, see Stokes (1995).

Epicurus's *Kuriai Doxai*—that is, his, as it were, especially authoritative opinions—because these briefly pronounced maxims are most important for
living the happy life?) Pay attention, then, to whether I translate this saying
correctly.

Cicero then renders the tenth *Kuriai Doxai*, which states that if indulgent
people were actually finding the pleasure required to free them from
pain, we would have no complaint with them. Triarius bursts in, outraged
that Epicurus really said such a thing, to which Torquatus retorts that
he has misread his master's words. This exchange is followed by
Cicero's extended critique. The passage thus addresses the *Kuriai Doxai*
through Cicero's translation and commentary as well as through
Torquatus's Epicurean response in his attempt to hide behind his master's (recalled) authority. Further, the nature of the authority of the *Kuriai
Doxai* themselves is put into question, not merely by Triarius's disbelief
that Epicurus actually *said* this *sententia* ("saying") or by the critique of
Torquatus's defense of Epicurus, but also by the constant playing or
punning on the title of the *Kuriai Doxai* themselves. This play ranges
from literal translation (*gravissimae sententiae*; *enuntiatae sententiae*)
to metaphorical reconception (*oracula*), but it consistently emphasizes
the pithiness of the maxims (the repetition of *breviter*).[30] Within this
punning on the title of the *Kuriai Doxai*, there is a marked critique of
Epicurean memorization and excerption as the "performative authority"
of Epicurus's words, which are here glossed by the phrase *maxime ratas*
(the *sententiae* that are "especially authoritative"). With Cicero's punning
in mind, I now want to explore further play on the title of the *Kuriai
Doxai* in Seneca and Plutarch as a potent way in which the performative
authority of the *Kuriai Doxai* as memorization and excerption comes
together in the very title of the work.

[30] Clay (1998) 22, "*gravissimae* comes closest to the Greek description of these doctrines as κυριώτατα." Cicero refers to the oracular nature of the *Kuriai Doxai* elsewhere,
including *De Finibus* 2.102 and *De Natura Deorum* 1.66, cited from Pease (1955–58), which
is a "faint and deformed echo" (Clay (1998) 22) of *Kuriai Doxai* 29. See the discussion of
Foucault (2005) below for a "positive" account of the oracle.

II. "HE WHO PUNS . . .": TITULAR PLAY IN SENECA AND PLUTARCH

the maymeaminning of maimoomeining[31]

Cicero's critique notwithstanding, the practice of punning on the title of the *Kuriai Doxai* is one that actually bridges pro- and anti-Epicurean texts.[32] The Epicurean Lucretius refers to Epicurus's *patria praecepta* and *aurea dicta*. Whether these terms refer to the *Kuriai Doxai* specifically or to all of Epicurus's doctrines more generally, they still highlight authority through qualitative metaphors (of paternity and metallurgy).[33] Amongst anti-Epicureans, as we have seen, Cicero puns on the title of the *Kuriai Doxai* to satirize Torquatus's claims to their "singular" authority in the figure of Epicurus and the "oracular" nature of that authority. This practice of punning continues into the ostensibly anti-Epicurean writing of the first two centuries CE, beginning with the work of Seneca and Plutarch. There is a marked difference, however, between the later anti-Epicurean polemic of Plutarch and the more nuanced critique of Epicureanism in Seneca, a difference that paves the way for our reading of later works in the second and third centuries CE of the Second Sophistic.

Plutarch's extended critique of Epicurus, carried out across several works, raises several issues for the *Kuriai Doxai*.[34] In *On the Pythian Oracles* (399e), Plutarch follows Cicero's pun on the oracular nature of the *Kuriai Doxai* by challenging an Epicurean to either deny the chance composition of oracles (i.e., to admit to providence) or to accept that the same process took place for the *Kuriai Doxai*.[35] Yet, as with Cicero, the attack on oracular pronouncement is not as forceful as the emphasis on the title of the collections as "masterful," which is made more directly in Plutarch's *Against Colotes*:

---

[31] *Finnegans Wake* 267.3, cited from Joyce (1939). Joyce's pun on the title of Ogden and Richards's book *The Meaning of Meaning*, which McHugh (2006) 267 explicates as containing *Meinung* ("opinion") *minne* ("love") and stuttering ("I meann, minne") and the popular song "The Young May Moon." My title for this section mimes Derrida (1986).

[32] The most extended discussion of the title of the *Kuriai Doxai* is Clay (1998) 22–24.

[33] Lucretius *De Rerum Natura* 3.9–13, on which see Gordon (1996) 60, with n. 77.

[34] For Plutarch's polemics against Epicureanism in general, see Boulogne (2003).

[35] See Snyder (1980) 37.

τοῦτο μέντοι τὸ συνεκτικὸν ἁπάσης κοινωνίας καὶ νομοθεσίας ἔρεισμα καὶ βάθρον οὐ κύκλῳ περιιόντες οὐδὲ κρύφα καὶ δι᾽ αἰνιγμάτων, ἀλλὰ τὴν πρώτην τῶν κυριωτάτων δοξῶν προσβαλόντες εὐθὺς ἀνατρέπουσιν. (Plutarch *Against Colotes* 1125e–f)

Now it is this belief, the underpinning and base that holds all society and legislation together, that the Epicureans, not by encirclement or covertly in riddles, but by launching against it the first of their most masterful opinions, proceed directly to demolish.

Plutarch then accuses Epicureans of attacking others for doing the same thing that they do (i.e., undermining religious institutions) and comments directly on the limits of the idea of *doxa* beyond the authority of Epicurus and in the recollection of his disciples (τὸ μὲν γὰρ ἁμαρτάνειν περὶ δόξαν, εἰ καὶ μὴ σοφῶν, ὅμως ἀνθρώπινόν ἐστι, "erring in one's opinion, although it does not befall wise men, nevertheless is a human failing," Plutarch *Against Colotes* 1125–26. This discrepancy between the *doxa* of a sage (Epicurus) and his blind followers is pressed further by Plutarch, who emphasizes not only *what* Epicurus teaches but *how* he teaches it. This emphasis is apparent in Plutarch's most explicit reference to an Epicurean maxim in his brief essay *Is "Live Unknown" a Wise Precept?* While this essay refers to an independent saying that does not occur in our extant works of Epicurus, its content hints at a series extant sayings (*Kuriai Doxai* 6, 7, 14).[36] Throughout this brief but biting polemic, Plutarch plays on conflicting ideas of authority behind Epicurus's *sententia*. For example, he opens the essay by remarking on the contradiction between the content of the maxim and its means of expression, stating that Epicurus fails to follow his own advice ("Live unknown") precisely by making it known. Furthermore, Plutarch ventriloquizes Epicurus himself in proving the direct association between the maxim and the biographical tradition of *hetairai* in the Garden where to "live unknown" is to live in the shadowy world of prostitutes. As with the passage on the oracular nature of the *Kuriai Doxai*, the Epicurean is put in a position of either renouncing the *sententia* (as in itself disproving the doctrine) or its content (based on the shadowy dealings of the Garden).

---

[36] For an expansive analysis of this saying, see Roskam (2007).

Such ad hominem polemic is avoided by Seneca, who quotes various "sayings" of Epicurus while playing on the title of the collection to undercut their status as the unique *sententiae* of Epicurus.[37] His emphasis on the authority of Epicurus is shown by how in several of the *Epistulae Morales* in Books 1–3, Seneca introduces a saying of Epicurus with reference to the "voice of Epicurus" (*vox Epicuri*). In his eighth *Epistle*, Seneca refers to the "voice" of Epicurus, which he read, and quotes the saying about being the slave to philosophy.[38] He proceeds to answer the complaint by Lucilius that he is quoting from the enemy by stating that "but is there any reason why you should regard them as sayings of Epicurus and not common property?" (*quid est tamen quare tu istas Epicuri voces putes esse, non publicas*, Seneca *Epistulae Morales* 8.7). This recourse to the voice of Epicurus is used elsewhere when he quotes Epicurus's "voice" as saying "imagine Epicurus is always watching you."[39] These passages, while they may not be literally from the *Kuriai Doxai*, participate in the rhetorical personification of Epicurus's opinions through his voice. A standard analysis of Seneca's use of the *vox Epicuri* is that it distances authority from Seneca, instead projecting it onto the philosophical tradition.[40] Yet it may also, I contend, be read as a critique, like that of Cicero, of the way in which Epicurean philosophy operates through the authority of its master's voice. In this light, Seneca's desire to make the voice "public" is a direct challenge to the "private" role played by the *Kuriai Doxai* in highlighting the singular authority of Epicurus for the individual Epicurean. Perhaps the clearest expression of Seneca's attempt to make public the voice of Epicurean speech-acts is in the following passage of the thirty-third *Epistle*:

non sumus sub rege: sibi quisque se vindicat. apud istos quidquid Hermarchus dixit, quidquid Metrodorus, ad unum refertur; omnia quae quisquam in illo contubernio locutus est unius ductu et auspiciis dicta sunt. (Seneca *Epistulae Morales* 33.4)

---

[37] On the quotations of Epicurus in the *Epistulae Morales* in general, see Griffin (2007) 90–93 with further references.

[38] Elsewhere Seneca refers to these sayings as *dicta* (16.7) or "Epicurus, who says" (Epicurus, qui ait, 26.8) or just quotes Epicurus (20.9) without introduction.

[39] Seneca *Epistulae Morales* 23.9 and 25.5, cited from Reynolds (1965).

[40] Wilson (2001) 176.

We are not under the rule of a king: each defends himself for himself. Among them [the Epicureans], whatever Hermarchus said, whatever Metrodorus said, is referred to one man [i.e., Epicurus]; all that anyone in that camp said was spoken under the leadership and auspices of that one man.

Here the political analogy and the autonomy of the subject are reiterated as a denial of the Epicurean practice of always using the voice and authority of Epicurus.

It is worth keeping in mind this more nuanced and suggestive anti-Epicureanism of Seneca as we move into the anti-Epicurean writing of Aelian and Alciphron in the second and third centuries CE. Both authors offer a less sustained critique of Epicureanism than either Cicero or Plutarch, yet they continue to pun on the title of the *Kuriai Doxai* as a way of satirizing Epicurean submission to the master's authority. Before considering any further titular play, however, I want to introduce these authors by considering the range of sources for Epicureanism in this period, viewed particularly through the lens of the late work of Michel Foucault.

III. SUBJECTIVE OPINIONS: FOUCAULT AND EPICUREANISM IN THE LATER SECOND SOPHISTIC

> The *doxa* is current opinion, meaning repeated as *if nothing has happened*.[41]

As we have seen, punning on the title of the *Kuriai Doxai* raises issues of their performative authority within both pro- and anti-Epicurean texts of the Roman Republic and early Empire. Yet as we move later into the height of the Second Sophistic (second and third centuries CE), the basic division of texts into pro- and anti-Epicurean becomes more muddled due chiefly to two related factors. First, the problematic nature of our sources for Epicureanism in this period makes delineating a clear division between pro- and anti-Epicurean perspectives more difficult. Second, there are recurring themes within accounts of Epicureanism in this period, as emphasized by the late work of Michel Foucault on the

[41] Barthes (1977) 122.

so-called "crisis of the subject," themes that similarly complicate any neat division between pro- and anti-Epicureanism.

Unlike during the Republic and early Empire, the quality and quantity of responses to Epicureanism in the second and third centuries CE make it harder to tie down pro- and anti-approaches to Epicureanism. Within this period, we have neither the sustained polemic of Plutarch nor the expansive critique of Seneca. Instead, we have, on the one hand, more anecdotal, often satiric, caricatures of the Epicurean school, some seemingly positive (Lucian, Aulus Gellius), some negative (Athenaeus, Aelian), and some in between (Alciphron).[42] On the other hand, we also have two of the most extended descriptions of Epicureanism, both important documents for the school's later survival (the inscription of Diogenes of Oenoanda and the tenth book of Diogenes Laërtius).

In general, surveys of this period maintain a division between these two types of sources: one (Diogenes of Oenoanda, Diogenes Laërtius) is valued as philosophical source material for Epicureanism, while the other (Aelian, Lucian, et al.) offers literary representations of contemporary or historical Epicureans. Yet this division of sources does not immediately coincide with the division between pro- and anti-Epicurean camps.[43] For example, Pamela Gordon's contextualization of Diogenes of Oenoanda within the Epicureanism of the Second Sophistic focuses on his relation to Diogenes Laërtius because the latter's tenth book offers a "source" for Epicurean philosophy comparable to the former's inscription. Yet her contextualization passes over the satiric caricatures of Epicureanism found in Athenaeus and Aelian and even the less hostile account of Alciphron.[44] Conversely, a recent study of authors of anti-Epicurean caricature understandably leaves out Diogenes of Oenoanda, a card-carrying Epicurean, but it also overlooks Diogenes Laërtius, whose Epicureanism is not so assured and whose biography of Epicurus adds much to our knowledge of the satire of Epicureans in general.[45] This division in how scholars approach these sources for Epicureanism is largely underwritten by the flawed assumption that to discuss

---

[42] In many ways, this satiric approach has its roots in Plutarch's polemics, which satirize contemporary Epicureans while denouncing Epicureanism as a whole. On this link, see Fitzgibbon (2001).

[43] For the former, see Gordon (1996) and Erler (2009); for the latter, Fitzgibbon (2001).

[44] Gordon (1996).

[45] Fitzgibbon (2001) 12.

Epicureanism and cite Epicurus makes one a bona fide Epicurean, while to satirize Epicureanism is clear proof of anti-Epicureanism.[46] As we have already seen in the opening Gellius quotation (and in the case of Seneca), such an assumption can lead one astray. In these passages, the boundaries of pro- and anti-Epicurean positions are confused when we simply class punning and creative engagement with the *Kuriai Doxai* as satirical.

To cast new light on our sources for Epicureanism in this period, there needs to be more emphasis on the shared concerns brought to bear on all approaches to Epicureanism. Here Michel Foucault can help. In his later work—the third volume of *The History of Sexuality: The Care of the Self* and especially his lectures on *The Hermeneutics of the Subject*—Foucault explores the philosophical legacy of the Hellenistic schools in the Roman Empire in terms of how they develop and promote practices of working on the self, seeing the period of the Second Sophistic as one marking a "crisis of the subject" in which the self and its relations to others were transformed by political changes.[47] Within this crisis, Foucault sees an important role for the Epicurean school; but unlike in his treatment of the Stoics, he lays emphasis on the earlier works of Epicurus and Philodemus rather than on writings produced under the Roman Empire.[48] In articulating the general concept of the "care of the self," for example, Foucault quotes Epicurus's *Letter to Menoeceus* to show how "philosophy should be considered as a permanent exercise of the care of the self."[49] Similarly, in his extended discussion of Epicureanism in *The Hermeneutics of the Subject*, Foucault depicts the school's conception of *physiologia* ("the study of nature") as opposed to *paideia* ("education, culture") by citing *Vatican Sayings* (29 and 45), the *Letter to Herodotus*, and the *Letter to Pythocles*. His portrait of the collective care of the self within the Epicurean community is likewise reliant on Marcello Gigante's Italian edition of Philodemus's *On Parrhesia*.[50] These two aspects of the Epicurean school, its devotion to

---

[46] Conversely, the idea that to *not* satirize Epicurus somehow makes you an Epicurean is shown to be flawed for both Gellius and Lucian.

[47] Foucault (1986) 81–95.

[48] Foucault's reading of Epicureanism in *The Care of the Self* and *The Hermeneutics of the Subject*, unlike his accounts of Stoicism in the same works, has not entered into general discussions of the school in the period.

[49] Foucault (1986) 46, quoting the *Letter to Menoeceus* 122.

[50] See the comments at Foucault (2005) 387.

physiologia and the collective care of the self, are especially important for Foucault's conception of the "crisis of the subject." Not coincidentally, these two ideas are united in the practice of *parrhesia* ("frank-speaking"), so central to Foucault's work of this period. In addition, feminist scholarly response to Foucault's work has opened up another avenue for the reception of the *Kuriai Doxai*: the figure of the courtesan (*hetaira*) allows critique of Foucault's bias toward the male subject. Before examining the figure of the *hetaira*, however, let us consider the role of Epicureanism in *The Hermeneutics of the Subject*.[51]

During the second hour of a lecture delivered on February 10, 1982, Foucault offers a theoretical framework for his discussion of the subject in terms of the difference between veridiction and subjectivation. He asks: "How is the relationship between truth-telling (veridiction) and the practice of the subject established, fixed, and defined? Or, more generally, how are truth-telling and governing (governing oneself and others) linked and connected to each other?" In answering this question, Foucault looks to the Hellenistic schools of the Roman Empire, first to the Cynics through Demetrius, then to the Epicureans, and finally to the Stoics, specifically Seneca and Epictetus. The Epicureans are key to Foucault's analysis, but they have often been overlooked to emphasize the later Stoic section.[52]

As we have already mentioned, Epicurean *physiologia* is a crucial concept for Foucault. By contrast with *paideia*, which creates "a culture of boasters, developed merely by concoctors of words whose only aim is to be admired by the masses," *physiologia* develops, on Foucault's reading, autonomy and self-mastery in the subject.[53] It thus operates on an individual level. Yet when the Epicurean individual is faced with others in the Epicurean community who cultivate their own autonomy, then *parrhesia* ("frank speaking") enters the equation. This term signifies a technique that "allows the master to make proper use, from the true things he knows, of that which is useful and effective for his disciple's

---

[51] For a focused and nuanced reading of the limits of Foucault's account of Epicureanism in *The Hermeneutics of the Subject*, see Gigandet (this volume, ch. 10).

[52] For example, Inwood (2005) 322–52 offers a nuanced reading of Foucault, the *Alcibiades*, and Stoicism.

[53] Foucault (2005) 239.

work of transformation."[54] Through *parrhesia*, then, the quest for individual autonomy becomes the "collective" care of the self.

Foucault again discusses *parrhesia* later in *The Hermeneutics of the Subject*, where he returns to the Epicureans, studying them this time even more explicitly as a community.[55] He discusses the centrality of the guide (*kathegetes* or *kathegoumenos*) for the Epicurean community. The guide draws his authority from a succession leading back to the original guide, Epicurus himself. This authority allows him to use *parrhesia* in his own discourse, a "discourse of truth" deriving ultimately from Epicurus. The practice of *parrhesia* is not, however, limited to guides. It is also produced by students as a novel form of confession. The *parrhesia* of the master thus demands a reciprocal *parrhesia* on the part of the student. This dynamic makes the Epicurean community the ideal "community model" for the care of the self.

It is not surprising that Foucault develops his conception of *phusiologia* chiefly from Epicurus's own texts, especially his maxims.[56] But to extend Foucault's analysis of *parrhesia* to the Second Sophistic, we can observe first that the role of the *sententia* is especially privileged within the Epicurean community in terms of its "performative authority." Further, *parrhesia* practiced on the part of the student (that is, confessional self-criticism) offers us an instance where traditionally anti-Epicurean (critical) and pro-Epicurean (affirmative) positions may be mingled. As I show, this case obtains in the manipulation of the *Kuriai Doxai* in our most explicitly pro-Epicurean text: the *Letter to Mother* of Diogenes of Oenoanda. Before turning to our full set of Second Sophistic texts, however, I want to discuss briefly the feminist critique of Foucault's male subject and how it can aid our reading of the gendered responses to the *Kuriai Doxai*.

One important aspect of the reception of Epicureanism in general and the *Kuriai Doxai* specifically in the Second Sophistic offers an essential challenge to the Foucauldian account of the Epicurean subject. As we

---

[54] Foucault (2005) 242.

[55] The end of the lecture on 10 March 1982, Foucault (2005) 386–91.

[56] Strozier (2002) 156 takes Foucault's brief discussion of *doxa* in the *Care of the Self* (Foucault (1986) 134–35, 139) as what exists in consciousness and reads it in terms of the practice of memorizing the *Kuriai Doxai*, wherein "they, *doxai*, are 'opinions' that are to be taken into consciousness and held there for a specific purpose," i.e., "for use toward countering disturbing influences."

have already seen with Gellius's anecdote, one of the major attacks on Epicurean theories of pleasure subsumes them under the figure of the female prostitute. At the same time, a major theme in the critical reception of Foucault's analysis has been his blinkered focus on the male subject.[57] In response to this critique, recent work has considered how the (male-constructed) female subject of the *hetaira* can be read in terms of Foucauldian conceptions of subjectivity.[58] When considered in relation to Foucault's interest in the Epicurean community, the figure of the *hetaira* adds a further dimension.[59] Synonymous with dissolute pleasure and therefore often emblematic of the Epicurean final end, the courtesan operates as the agent of Epicurus's doctrines, especially for his critics.[60] Yet in the Second Sophistic there is a new twist. The *hetaira* becomes a representative of the aims of *paideia*, who thus directly challenges the anti-*paideia* stance of Epicureanism. Perhaps as a result of this ambiguity, there is also a move in this period to replace the *hetaira* with other models of the female philosopher, both within the Epicurean community and within other institutions, such as those of patronage. This nexus of related issues explored in Foucault's account of Epicureanism and his feminist reception is at play in different ways in the texts I shall now discuss.

IV. SEX-SLAVES AND MISTRESSES: THE *KURIAI DOXAI* IN AELIAN AND ALCIPHRON

The venomous critique of Epicureans in the fragments of Aelian's *Divine Manifestations* and *Divine Providence* and the humorous letter of Epicurus's mistress Leontion in Alciphron's *Letters of Courtesans* at first glance appear to be completely different species of anti-Epicureanism. One ostensibly critiques the atheistic tenets of Epicureanism via damning satiric portraits of contemporary Epicureans, while the other highlights the pleasure-seeking basis of Epicurus himself though the fictional letter

---

[57] See especially Richlin (1991) and (1998), Dean-Jones (1992), Greene (1996) and Foxhall (1998).

[58] Gilhuly (1997).

[59] Funke (2008) successfully applies this feminist reception of Foucault to the *hetairai* of Alciphron's *Letters of Courtesans*.

[60] McClure (2003) 103 on Alciphron *Letter* 4.7.

of a classical Athenian *hetaira*. Yet the fusion of atheism and hedonism is enacted, as in Gellius's anecdote, around the role of the *Kuriai Doxai*, the punning on their title, and their performative authority for their readers.

The dating of and relationship between Aelian and Alciphron is a disputed issue.[61] The fact that both wrote *Letters of Farmers* has been read as a linking feature, with the general acceptance that Aelian's *Letters* are based on Alciphron's. In spite of these comparisons, little has been made of their responses to philosophy generally, let alone Epicureanism specifically.[62] For the present study, there is an intriguing connection in their shared depiction of philosophy in terms of prostitution. In an anecdote contained in his *Various History*, Aelian juxtaposes philosophy with prostitution. Relating an encounter of Socrates with the *hetaira* Callisto, he describes how Socrates once stated that it is easier for her, as a prostitute, to steal his pupils because the path toward virtue is steep (Aelian *Various History* 13.32).[63] A similar association of philosophy and *hetairai* is found in Alciphron's seventh *Letter of Courtesans*, from Thais to the philosopher Euthydemus, in which Aelian's model is playfully reversed. This time the prostitute claims that she, like Aspasia, can teach young men wisdom more successfully than "Socrates the sophist" (Alciphron *Letter* 4.7.8). This point of contact between Aelian and Alciphron is expanded by their respective accounts of Epicureanism, where once again the *Kuriai Doxai* play a significant role.

As Patricia Fitzgibbon has shown, Aelian draws "caricatures of Epicureans who are polemically cast as effeminate because of their adherence to the doctrines of Epicurus."[64] This critique is traditional and in line with Seneca's jibe at Epicureans who believe that to become free one has to become a slave to the master's philosophy.[65] Aelian, in a fragment belonging to either *Divine Manifestations* or *Divine Providence*, treats Epicurus himself as a "slave to pleasure" (*hēdonēs hēttōn*) on account of

[61] For a summary, see Easterling and Knox (1989) 119–22.

[62] There are passing references to Alciphron in P. Gordon (2004) 233 and 237 but no mention of Aelian, while Fitzgibbon (2001) 121–35 offers an extended account of Aelian, but not Alciphron.

[63] Quoted in McClure (2003) 102. Aelian's account follows Xenophon.

[64] Fitzgibbon (2001) 122.

[65] *Epistulae Morales* 8.7. See Clay (1998) 24.

his lavish arrangements in his will on his death.[66] Within this line of attack—that is, the assertion that Epicureans are slaves to Epicurus who was a slave to pleasure—what is novel is the way in which the physical text of the *Kuriai Doxai* and the memorization of and adherence to these maxims are attacked as the *direct* cause of effeminacy. Elsewhere, Aelian describes an Epicurean with his copy of the *Kuriai Doxai* as follows:

εἶχε δὲ ἄρα τὸ βιβλίον τὰς Ἐπικούρου δόξας, ἃς ἐκεῖνοι κυρίας οὕτω καλοῦσιν, Ἐπικούρου κακὰ γνωρίσματα. (Aelian 64a (Domingo-Forasté))[67]

And he had the book, the maxims of Epicurus, which those men [the Epicureans] call "master," the wicked hallmarks of Epicurus. [68]

While the description of the *Kuriai Doxai* in the text that follows and the tale of the Epicurean that quotes from the *Kuriai Doxai* is exclusively associated with atheism, in *Divine Providence*, we are given an Epicurean who is attacked for following the "evil wisdom" of Epicurus and specifically Epicurean ideas on pleasure:

κακὴν σοφίαν μετιὼν καὶ τοὺς ἀθέους Ἐπικούρου λόγους καὶ γύννιδας ἐπασκῶν κἀκ τῆς ἡδονῆς, ἣν ἐκεῖνος ὕμνει ὁ χλούνης τε καὶ γύννις . . . (Aelian 10e (Domingo-Forasté))[69]

Following evil wisdom and the godless words of Epicurus and even cultivating womanish men for pleasure, which that castrated, womanish man used to harp upon [*humnei*, lit. "hymn"] . . . .[70]

---

[66] Aelian fr. 39 (Hercher)/ 42a (Domingo-Forasté), quoted and translated by Clay (1998) 92–94; discussed by Fitzgibbon (2001) 122–24. Note that all the fragments of Aelian I discuss are from the *Suda*. See Fitzgibbon (2001) 121–33 for further references.

[67] This fragment forms part of the entry at *Suda* ε2406.

[68] For discussion of this fragment, see Fitzgibbon (2001) 127–29, whose translation informs the present rendering.

[69] This fragment is part of the entry at *Suda* γ504. The full set of relevant fragments is collected as Aelian ff. 10a–l (Domingo-Forasté). In addition to 10e, 10b and 10c make explicit reference to the feminizing effects of Epicurus's words.

[70] Text, translation, and discussion in Fitzgibbon (2001) 124–27. The idea that the Epicurean is an effeminate, castrated male is also present in the saying of Arcesilaus preserved by Diogenes Laërtius 4.43. When asked why people convert to Epicureanism from other schools but not the other way around, he retorts: "Men become Galli [i.e., castrated priests of Isis], but Galli never become men." See also Plutarch *Against Colotes* 1127c, cited from Pohlenz and Westman (1959).

This passage, one of several similar descriptions in the tenth-century (CE) historical lexicon known as the *Suda*, alludes to an episode where a torch-bearer at the Eleusinian mysteries was rendered effeminate through "the godless words of Epicurus."[71] Aelian combines the attack of atheism with excessive pleasure, just as in Gellius's anecdote.[72] Furthermore, by claiming that reading Epicurus and "hymning" his hedonistic doctrine somehow enacts a process of effeminization, Aelian seems to parody the fact that Epicurus encouraged women to become Epicureans.[73] Indeed, this idea of "hymning" Epicurus's doctrines is a consistent theme in both anti- and pro-Epicurean literature. In Plutarch's essay *That Epicurus Actually Makes a Pleasant Life Impossible*, he quotes Epicurus's pupil Metrodorus as representative of all Epicureans, who "tell us bellowing that they have not only lived a life of pleasure, but also exult and sing hymns in the praise of their own living" (ἀλλ' ἡδέως τε βεβιωκέναι καὶ βρυάζειν καὶ καθυμνεῖν τὸν ἑαυτῶν βίον ἐκκραυγάζοντες λέγουσι, 1098b). While Plutarch no doubt intends to paint a negative portrait here (as his use of the harsh term "bellowing" demonstrates), the passage also makes clear that praising (or "hymning") the Epicurean lifestyle and its doctrines is positively Epicurean. Diogenes Laërtius preserves further evidence that Epicurus himself manipulated and invoked hymnic language. The biographer refers to a negative portrayal of Epicurus, where a term for flattery (*kolakeuein*) is used to describe the philosopher's redeployment of cult titles for Apollo, precisely the same titles that are often invoked in hymns:

Μιθρῆν τε αἰσχρῶς κολακεύειν τὸν Λυσιμάχου διοικητήν, ἐν ταῖς ἐπιστολαῖς Παιᾶνα καὶ Ἄνακτα καλοῦντα· ἀλλὰ καὶ Ἰδομενέα καὶ Ἡρόδοτον καὶ Τιμοκράτην τοὺς ἔκπυστα αὐτοῦ τὰ κρύφια ποιήσαντας ἐγκωμιάζειν καὶ κολακεύειν <δι'> αὐτὸ τοῦτο. ἔν τε ταῖς ἐπιστολαῖς πρὸς μὲν Λεόντιον· 'Παιὰν ἄναξ,' <φησί,> 'φίλον Λεοντάριον, οἵου κροτοθορύβου ἡμᾶς ἐνέπλησας ἀναγνόντας σου τὸ ἐπιστόλιον'. (Diogenes Laërtius 10.4–5)

---

[71] Compare Epictetus's description of Epicurus as a *kinaidologos* recorded by Diogenes Laërtius (10.6).

[72] In order to send up religious belief in providence, Lucian showers praise on the *Kuriai Doxai* in his *Alexander*.

[73] Fitzgibbon (2001) 133 does not go this far, stating that Aelian "says nothing" about female Epicureans, but it seems that the effeminized reader has its origins in the standard critique of the Garden.

Epicurus shamefully flatters Mithras, the minister of Lysimachus, in his letters, calling him Healer and Lord.[74] Furthermore, he praises Idomeneus, Herodotus, and Timocrates, who had published his esoteric doctrines, and flattered them for that very reason. And in his letters to Leontion, "O Lord Apollo," he says, "my dear little Leontion, with what tumultuous applause you filled us as we read your letter."

As we shall see shortly, this idea of "hymning" also links Aelian's attack on Epicurus and Epicureanism to Alciphron's letter from Leontion. Yet the way in which Alciphron adopts this theme renders questionable any interpretation of his letter as straightforwardly anti-Epicurean. Toward the end of the letter, Alciphron's Leontion bewails the fact that on account of her own "slavery" to Epicurus, her young lover, Timarchus, has been brainwashed into becoming an Epicurean himself:[75]

ἀλλὰ καὶ δι' ἐμὲ πάντα ἠνάγκασται ὁ νεανίσκος καταλιπών, τὸ Λύκειον καὶ τὴν ἑαυτοῦ νεότητα καὶ τοὺς συνεφήβους καὶ τὴν ἑταιρείαν, μετ' αὐτοῦ ζῆν καὶ κολακεύειν αὐτὸν καὶ καθυμνεῖν τὰς ὑπηνέμους αὐτοῦ δόξας. (Alciphron *Letters* 4.17.7)

Furthermore, because of me the young man has been forced to abandon everything—the Lyceum, and his own youth, his young comrades and the club—to live with that man [Epicurus] and flatter him and hymn (*kathumnein*) the praises of his windy/sheltering *Doctrines*.

The "hymning" of praises links this passage with that of Aelian, but while there the Epicurean becomes effeminate because he "hymns" the "wicked sayings" of Epicurus, for Alciphron's Leontion, the young lover has been ruined by the same praise in becoming an Epicurean.[76] Furthermore, as Aelian refers to the "wicked sayings," in Alciphron the *Kuriai Doxai* are characterized as *tas hupēnemous doxas*, where the use of the meaning of the adjective *hupēnemos* is ambiguous. Benner and Fobes translate the phrase *hupēnemous doxas as* "wind-bag doctrines," but that rendering misses a further connotation that is important for appreciating the humor

---

[74] It is worth noting that these cult titles of Apollo often appear in hymns.

[75] I use the text and translation of Benner and Fobes (1949), with some modifications.

[76] Could this be the same Timarchus as addressed by Metrodorus (F38 Körte), cited in Plutarch *Against Colotes* 1117b, as suggested by Benner and Forbes (1949) 311n?

of the passage. Since the adjective *hupēnemos* does not mean exactly the same as the related *hupēnemios,* "windy," but "sheltered from the wind," we can see that Lenotion is not merely criticizing the nature of Epicurean doctrine, but also her Timarchus for running off to the "shelter" of the Epicurean school (and away from her). Perhaps a compromise that would register both meanings is "shady," whereby the "shady" doctrines would then reference what Pamela Gordon describes as "the shady, women-filled disrepute of the Garden."[77]

Yet there is a twist to Alciphron that is missing from the outright polemic of Aelian and that can be found in the countering critique of Leontion as she complains about the doctrines of Epicurus. While Aelian's caricatures of the "feminizing" force of Epicurean doctrine may have its origins in the popular riff on the presence of *hetairai* in the Garden, this connection is made explicit in Leontion's letter through her basic complaint against Epicurus and his philosophy for suppressing her pleasure. Elsewhere in the collection of *Letters,* Alciphron explicitly associates the role of the *hetaira* with the Epicurean concept of pleasure as the *telos:*

κατάβαλλε τὴν μωρίαν ταύτην καὶ ἀηδίαν, ὁ ἐμὸς ἔρως Εὐθύδημε—οὐ πρέπει σκυθρωποῖς εἶναι τοιούτοις ὄμμασι—καὶ πρὸς τὴν ἐρωμένην ἧκε τὴν ἑαυτοῦ οἷος ἐπανελθὼν ἀπὸ τοῦ Λυκείου πολλάκις τὸν ἱδρῶτα ἀποψώμενος, ἵνα μικρὰ κραιπαλήσαντες ἐπιδειξώμεθα ἀλλήλοις τὸ καλὸν τέλος τῆς ἡδονῆς. (Alciphron *Letters* 4.7.8)

Abandon this foolish, odious pose, my lover Euthydemus—eyes such as yours ought not to be solemn—and come back to your sweetheart as you are when you have come back, for instance, from the Lyceum wiping off the sweat, that we may carouse a bit and give each other a demonstration of that noble end, pleasure.

Leontion is proving herself to be a better Epicurean than Epicurus in enabling Timarchus to reach the *telos* of pleasure. Yet the humor of the Leontion letter also relies on her account of the sexual pleasure of her lover as being diametrically opposed to the "opinion/fame" (*doxa*) of Epicurus:

---

[77] P. Gordon (2004) 228. For ὑπηνέμος as "shady" (σκεπηνός), see Hesychius *Lexicon* U537, cited from Schmidt (1867).

τί σὺ λέγεις, Λάμια; οὐκ ἀληθῆ ταῦτα; οὐ δίκαιά φημι; καὶ μὴ δή, δέομαί σου πρὸς τῆς Ἀφροδίτης, μή σοι ταῦτα ἐπελθέτω· ʾἀλλὰ φιλόσοφος, ἀλλὰ ἐπιφανής, ἀλλὰ πολλοῖς φίλοις κεχρημένοςʾ. λαβέτω καὶ ἀγὼ ἔχω, διδασκέτω δ᾽ ἄλλους. ἐμὲ γὰρ οὐδὲν θάλπει ἡ δόξα, ἀλλ᾽ ὃν θέλω δὸς Τίμαρχον, Δάματερ. (Alciphron *Letters* 4.17.6)

What do you say, Lamia? Is not all this true? Am I not right? And do not, I beg of you by Aphrodite, do not let this answer enter your mind: "But he is a philosopher, he is distinguished, he has many friends." I say, let him take what I have too, but let him save his lessons for other people. "Fame/opinion" does not keep me warm at all, no, Demeter, give me Timarchus, it's what I want.

In this passage, *doxa* literally means fame or the opinion of others, but it also alludes to the *Kuriai Doxai* and the fact that Timarchus's choice between the shelter of Epicurus's philosophy or Leontion's warmth hinges on the authority of the *Kuriai Doxai*. But at the very beginning of the letter, Leontion, speaking of her own relationship with Epicurus, attacks his authority through yet another pun on the title of the *Kuriai Doxai*:

Οὐδὲν δυσαρεστότερον, ὡς ἔοικεν, ἐστὶν ἄρτι πάλιν μειρακευομένου πρεσβύτου. οἷά με Ἐπίκουρος οὗτος διοικεῖ πάντα λοιδορῶν, πάντα ὑποπτεύων, ἐπιστολὰς ἀδιαλύτους μοι γράφων, ἐκδιώκων ἐκ τοῦ κήπου. μὰ τὴν Ἀφροδίτην, εἰ Ἄδωνις ἦν, ἤδη ἐγγὺς ὀγδοήκοντα γεγονὼς ἔτη, οὐκ ἂν αὐτοῦ ἠνεσχόμην φθειριῶντος καὶ φιλονοσοῦντος καὶ καταπεπιλημένου εὖ μάλα πόκοις ἀντὶ πίλων. μέχρι τίνος ὑπομενεῖ τις τὸν φιλόσοφον τοῦτον; ἐχέτω τὰς περὶ φύσεως αὐτοῦ κυρίας δόξας καὶ τοὺς διεστραμμένους κανόνας, ἐμὲ δὲ ἀφέτω τὴν φυσικῶς κυρίαν ἐμαυτῆς ἀστομάχητον καὶ ἀνύβριστον. (Alciphron *Letters* 4.17.1)

Nothing is harder to please, it seems, than an old man who starts to play at being a boy again. How that Epicurus tries to manage me, scolding me for everything, suspecting me of everything, writing me well-sealed letters, chasing me out of his school garden! I swear by Aphrodite that if he were an Adonis—he's already nearly eighty—I would not put up with him, a louse-ridden valetudinarian all wrapped up in fleeces in place of woolens. To what point will anyone endure this "philosopher?" Let him keep his *Principal Doctrines on Nature* and his cross-eyed *Canons*; and let him allow me to be mistress of myself, as nature intended, the object neither of his anger nor his insolence.

The list of works by Epicurus—*On Nature,* the *Kuriai Doxai* and the *Canon*—is manipulated twice by Leontion. First, she conflates the two works—*On Nature* (Περὶ Φύσεως) and the *Kuriai Doxai*—into one: τὰς περὶ φύσεως αὐτοῦ κυρίας δόξας ("the principal opinions of him concerning nature") and adds the medical epithet διεστραμμένος ("crosseyed") to the Canons (plural). Second, she reworks these titles into her own challenging response, as the *Kuriai Doxai on Nature* of Epicurus has become appropriated as: "mistress to myself according to nature" (τὴν φυσικῶς κυρίαν ἐμαυτῆς). As for the two negative portrayals of anger and insolence, this could either allude to the main thesis of the *Canon*—that "the sensations, the prolepses, and the passions are the criteria of truth" and their rejection, or perhaps, to the first of the *Kuriai Doxai* and the conception of the divine being exempt from "anger and partiality."[78] Unlike her lover Timarchus, Leontion resists the authority of Epicurean philosophy, becoming her own *kuria* ("mistress").[79] Yet, and here is the twist, she does so in accordance to Epicurean principles. In rejecting Epicurus, she faithfully follows his guidelines.

While Timarchus shuns the institutions of *paideia*—the Lyceum, the gym, and his aristocratic club—Leontion manages to resist the advances of Epicurus through his own doctrine to maintain a "care of the self." Nonetheless, as an Epicurean, Leontion also displays appropriate *parrhesia* toward her master Epicurus and his doctrines, exemplifying the role of *parrhesia* in the Epicurean community by teacher and students alike, as outlined by Foucault's analysis.[80]

Thus, while Aelian's attack sees the authority of the *Kuriai Doxai* as an unambiguously dangerous, "feminizing" force to the male subject, Alciphron's fictional letter dramatizes the ironies of a *hetaira*, so often the symbol of the "feminized" pleasure in parodies of Epicureanism, showing resistance to the master's teachings in the name of anti-Epicurean *paideia*, but also perhaps the ultimate adherence to them in the form of

[78] Diogenes Laërtius 10.31.

[79] On the idea of being a *kuria* of oneself, see the comments on Glykera in Omitowoju (2002) 216, who refers to the discussion of Konstan (1987) 122–37.

[80] There are possible hints at Philodemus's *On Parrhesia* in the opening of the work. For example, there is the proverb—used by Philodemus in *On Parrhesia* col. 24b, cited from Konstan et al. (1998)—that old men are a second time children, although Alciphron could have found this in Epicurus as well: "both old and young alike ought to seek wisdom, the former in order that, as age comes over him, he may be young in good things because of the grace of what has been" (*Letter to Menoeceus* = Diogenes Laërtius 10.122).

Epicurean *parrhesia*. Alciphron's Leontion, therefore, adds an Epicurean twist to Gilhuly's point that "the *hetaira* provides an opportunity to see how a consideration of gender complicates Foucault's notion of subjectivity in terms of self-mastery and erotic objectification."[81] Yet, rather than being a mere symbol of Epicurean pleasure, Alciphron's Leontion presents herself as a *hetaira*, who is *kuria* ("mistress" of herself), and it is specifically through this parodic punning on the *Kuriai Doxai*, that she offers her own version of Epicurean *parrhesia* to her "pupil" Timarchus.

V. MOTHERS AND PLATO-LOVERS: DIOGENES OF OENOANDA AND DIOGENES LAËRTIUS

Alciphron's Leontion, unlike the explicit anti-Epicureanism of Aelian, reads the *Kuriai Doxai* as a key means of critiquing Epicurean hedonism from within and also displaying the contemporary force of the *hetaira* image for conceptions of *paideia* and Epicurean *parrhesia*. Yet, as we have seen, the *Kuriai Doxai* are also empowered in Leontion's acknowledgement of them as a major tool in Epicurean proselytizing, since the Epicurean student Timarchus shelters under them, rather than under the typical institutions of Hellenic *paideia*. The *hetaira*'s complaint offers a unique anti-Epicurean text that, therefore, speaks to the successes of Epicurean enrollment and its tools within the Epicurean community of the Garden.

If Alciphron's Leontion offers a retrospective account of the community model of the "care of the self" in the Second Sophistic, it is the inscription of Diogenes of Oenoanda that gives us a contemporary account of an Epicurean community in practice. In this section, I want to expand on a claim made by Pamela Gordon in which she argues that the part of the inscription known as *Letter to Mother* is a fictional text set to challenge the caricature of the female Epicurean as prostitute in the discussion of Epicurean pleasure, as a work that is meant to convert (female) members of the philosophical community.[82] If Alciphron can insert a contemporary model of the *hetaira* into his fictional letter set

[81] Gilhuly (2007) 64.
[82] Gordon (1996) 88–89 and (2004) 237–38.

in the classical Epicurean Garden, Diogenes can also use a feature of contemporary *paideia* in the figure of the contemporary rhetorician or sophist as an antithesis to the (female) philosopher. Once again the role of the
Kuriai Doxai is key.

Gordon argues that the *Letter to Mother* is a fictional text imagined to
have been written by Epicurus to his mother.[83] As a fictional text, it has
the plasticity to work as, on the one hand, a medium for Epicurean ideas
and, on the other hand, a caricature of Epicurus's biography as well as
Epicurean texts.[84] In terms of Diogenes' treatment of Epicurean texts,
Gordon sees the prominence of the *Kuriai Doxai* on the inscription as
bleeding into the *Letter*: "the letter quotes or alludes to *Principal Doctrines*
1 and 2, and if more fragments turn up, we may find the whole *tetrapharmakos* in the letter."[85] In this way, the *Letter* sees Epicurus utilize the
main tenets of his philosophy to show his own mother how to achieve
freedom from pain (*ataraxia*). While I would argue Gordon is on the
right track here, I see two problems. First, in hoping for the remainder of
the *tetrapharmakos* to appear in future fragments, she is not only simpli-
fying the relationship between the *tetrapharmakos* and the *Kuriai Doxai*,
but also mapping the order of the *Kuriai Doxai* found in Diogenes
Laërtius onto the inscription. Second, while it is important to her general
argument, she does not extend this analysis of the *Kuriai Doxai* onto the
final fragment we have of the *Letter* (fr. 127). My argument is that if we
consider the role of the *Kuriai Doxai* in the inscription as a whole and
then return to Gordon's idea, we can put it on firmer footing.

Aside from the tenth book of Diogenes Laërtius, the inscription of
Diogenes of Oenoanda is the most important Epicurean text of the
Second Sophistic period.[86] It is comprised of works by Diogenes on
Physics and *Ethics*, old age, and a series of his own *Maxims* and *Letters*.
It also contains several works attributed to Epicurus, among which the
Kuriai Doxai have pride of place, running along the bottom of the inscrip-
tion, in large letters. The prominence of the *Kuriai Doxai* in the physical
layout of the inscription is further affirmed by the presence of Diogenes'

---

[83] Gordon (1996) 66–93.

[84] For example, it plays upon the tradition that Epicurus's mother was superstitious,
known to us through Diogenes Laërtius's biography (10.4).

[85] Gordon (1996) 90.

[86] For a helpful summary of the contents of the inscription and its significance for
Epicureanism under the Roman Empire, see Erler (2009) 54–59.

own *Maxims*—imitating the genre of his master—and the way in which several of the sections above it themselves seem to respond to the *Kuriai Doxai*—and not only the *Letter to Mother*, as argued by Gordon. For example, while the *Kuriai Doxai* literally underline the *Ethics* epitome, it has been argued that the *Kuriai Doxai* line up with pertinent points of the immediately above *Ethics* section.[87]

Now, to return to the role of the *Kuriai Doxai* in the *Letter to Mother*, if we follow the order of the *Kuriai Doxai* that Diogenes has at the base of the inscription with the *Letter for Mother*, we see that after *Kuriai Doxai* 1 and 2 we have what seems to be *Kuriai Doxai* 6:[88]

[ἕνεκα τοῦ θαρρεῖν ἐξ ἀνθρώπων, ἦν κατὰ φύσιν ἀρχῆς καὶ βασιλείας ἀγαθόν, ἐξ ὧν ἄν ποτε τοῦτο οἷός τ'] ᾗ παρασκευ[άζε]σθαι. (Diogenes of Oenoanda fr. 32)

For the purpose of gaining security from men (government and kingship) are a natural good, so long as this end can be procured from them.

This sentiment is then fleshed out in *Kuriai Doxai* 7, as recorded by Diogenes Laërtius, which, though missing, may have been in the lacuna in the fragments. The problematic end of achieving security from men through fame or reputation articulated in *Kuriai Doxai* 7 is a theme touched on elsewhere in the inscription, especially at the beginning of the *Ethics* (fr. 29–30). Also, as in the order of the *Kuriai Doxai* moving onto the issue of pleasure, in the *Ethics* there is a swift movement onto the issue of pleasures. This reading makes more sense of fr. 127 and adds weight to it belonging to the *Letter to Mother*.[89]

col. I   τῶν ῥητορικῶν ἀπο-

5   κάμψεις λόγων ὅπως

         ἀκούσῃς τι τῶν ἡμεῖν

         ἀρεσκόντων. υ ἔνθεν

---

[87] Clay (1990) 2532–36; Smith (1996) 471–72.

[88] I use the text and translation of Smith (1996) 201.

[89] For the debate on its place in the *Letter*, see Clay (1990) 2442, Gordon (1996) 89, and Smith (1996) 559–60.

σε καὶ κατελπίζομεν

τὴν ταχίστην τὰς φι-

10   λοσοφίας κρούσειν θύ-

col. II [ρας

You will veer away from the speeches of the rhetoricians in order to listen to some of our doctrines. And from then on it is our firm hope that you will come as quickly as you can to knock at the doors of philosophy . . . .[90]

In asking his mother to steer clear of the speeches of rhetoricians, "Epicurus" is reiterating the point that the "goods of philosophy" (i.e., Epicureanism) are sufficient. This all amounts to the *Letter*, at fr. 127, working in the basic Epicurean idea of "living unknown."[91] The whole metaphorical force of the fragment is set at bringing Epicurus's mother "in doors" to the Epicurean fold. Here is where we pick up with Gordon, this time in her later work on the role of *hetairai* in the Garden. Amid a discussion of the poles of Plutarch's polemic *Is "Live Unknown" a Wise Precept?* she refers to "the public glory of intellectual, political and military achievement on one side and the shady, women-filled disrepute of the Garden on the other."[92] For Diogenes, these poles are the same, but as an Epicurean their emphasis is reversed. This is where the Second Sophistic context of the *Letter* is important. Gordon notes:

Perhaps the strain is not so heavy if we imagine that the *Letter to Mother* was composed not in the late fourth century B.C.E., when a woman could study neither philosophy nor rhetoric without being called a *hetaira*, but during Diogenes's era, when another Diogenes dedicated to a woman his "Lives and Opinions of Famous Philosophers and According to Their Sects," and when women were often visible in the public life of the Greek cities of Asia Minor, especially as magistrates and important *patronissai*.[93]

---

[90] I use the text and translation in Clay (1990) 2542.

[91] See Roskam (2007) 37–39 on the *Kuriai Doxai* 6, 7, and 14 on the theme of "living unknown."

[92] P. Gordon (2004) 228.

[93] Gordon (1996) 89.

The option for Epicurus's mother is to either listen to the speeches of rhetoricians or to the tenets of (Epicurean) philosophy. What is interesting is that she has already been "listening" to the paraphrase of the first two *Kuriai Doxai* earlier in the *Letter* and that this latest piece of advice follows the theme of the *Ethics* and their own model, the *Kuriai Doxai*. As in Alciphron's Leontion, we see in the *Letter* a conflict between the pervasive forces of contemporary *paideia*, as exemplified in the speeches of rhetoricians, and the shelter of the Epicurean community. Furthermore, if the *Kuriai Doxai* running along the bottom of the inscription has the order 1, 2, 6, 7, the latter two *doxai* reiterated could fill in the gap before fr. 127 and the focus on the needs of security (*asphaleia*) beyond that of fame and political institutions. Here we see Foucault's focus on the community model of the "care of the self" at work. In addition, as Gordon's comment elucidates, Diogenes has returned to the original Garden to show the way for contemporary female philosophers to become Epicureans and not to be labeled *hetairai*.

Diogenes of Oenoanda, therefore, reworks the *Kuriai Doxai* into his *Letter to Mother* to offer the fantasy, for his contemporary Epicurean readership, to return to their original moment of practical use, as words of wisdom from Epicurus to his mother. This fantasy, in turn, operates as a powerful calling card for the presence of female philosophers within the contemporary Epicurean community. Diogenes' return to the Garden acts as a foil to the parody of Alciphron to show the presence of (potential) female philosophers in the contemporary sect.

Now, given that Gordon uses a reference to Diogenes Laërtius to support her claim about the resonance of the *Letter to Mother* for contemporary female Epicureans, I want now to turn to this other Diogenes and his addressee, the female "lover of Plato."[94] In terms of our discussion, Diogenes Laërtius includes both genres of anti-Epicurean polemic and pro-Epicurean apologetic within his *Life*. The former is focused on the biography of Epicurus and his rivals; the latter, on the faithful recounting of the master's works and words. Yet if we can uncover Epicurean doctrines in Alciphon's fictional account of Epicurus's biography and appreciate how Diogenes of Oenoanda fictionalizes the origins of the *Kuriai Doxai* in the *Letter to Mother*, then Diogenes Laërtius's text become all the more intriguing. In addition, the oft-noted link between the third

---

[94] For this debate, see Warren (2007).

book on Plato and the tenth on Epicurus via the figure of the female addressee as a "lover of Plato" in the former can now be seen within the context of the role of gendering reception in Aelian, Alciphron, and Diogenes of Oenoanda.

Just before quoting the three Epicurean *Letters*, Diogenes calls upon his addressee for the first and only time since the third book on Plato:

Ἃ δὲ αὐτῷ δοκεῖ ἐν αὐτοῖς ἐκθέσθαι πειράσομαι τρεῖς ἐπιστολὰς αὐτοῦ παραθέμενος, ἐν αἷς πᾶσαν τὴν ἑαυτοῦ φιλοσοφίαν ἐπιτέτμηται·θήσομεν δὲ καὶ τὰς Κυρίας αὐτοῦ δόξας καὶ εἴ τι ἔδοξεν ἐκλογῆς ἀξίως ἀνεφθέγχθαι, ὥστε σὲ πανταχόθεν καταμαθεῖν τὸν ἄνδρα καὶ κρίνειν εἰδέναι [κρίνειν]. (Diogenes Laërtius 10.28–29)

I will attempt to present the views expressed in these works by transmitting three of his letters, in which he has summarized his entire philosophy. I will also transmit his *Principal Doctrines* and some other sayings which are worth citing, so that you yourself may acquire thorough mastery of the man, and know how to judge him.

Why would Diogenes recall his addressee right at this point? The answer, I believe, is apparent at the very end of the work, before he quotes the *Kuriai Doxai*:

Καὶ φέρε οὖν δὴ νῦν τὸν κολοφῶνα, ὡς ἄν εἴποι τις, ἐπιθῶμεν καὶ τοῦ παντὸς συγγράμματος καὶ τοῦ βίου τοῦ φιλοσόφου, τὰς Κυρίας αὐτοῦ δόξας παραθέμενοι καὶ ταύταις τὸ πᾶν σύγγραμμα κατακλείσαντες, τέλει χρησάμενοι τῇ τῆς εὐδαιμονίας ἀρχῇ. (Diogenes Laërtius 10.138)

Come, then, let me set the colophon, so to say, both on my entire work and on the life of this philosopher by transmitting his *Principal Doctrines*, therewith bringing the whole work to a close and making the end of it the beginning of happiness.

These closing remarks allude to a specifically Epicurean image—the idea of the end of the work meaning the beginning of happiness alludes to Epicurus's conception of pleasure as articulated in the *Letter to Menoeceus* (129): καὶ διὰ τοῦτο τὴν ἡδονὴν ἀρχὴν καὶ τέλος λέγομεν εἶναι τοῦ μακαρίως ζῆν ("And for this reason we say that pleasure is the beginning and end of living blessedly.") Yet the reference to putting a seal, a *kolophon*, to his work, and the phrase "so to say" that follows it, is made in such a way to evoke a specifically Platonic technique of closure. While the term kolophon alone, which appears in Plato as the "summit" of an argument at the end of *Laws* Book 3 and concludes a specific line of argument in the *Theaetetus*, may not be uniquely Platonic, its collocation with the phrase "so to say" is revealing.[95] The specific phrase ὡς ἂν εἴποι τις is used elsewhere by Diogenes (4.64) to pun on the Stoic doctrine of "cosmic sympathy," which Carneades famously opposed. The phrase comes straight after the alluded to doctrine (*sumpathein*).[96] Beyond Diogenes, it is also used by Aelius Aristides in his *To Plato: In Defense of Rhetoric* when he states, "I shall now come to the very *kolophon*, as one might say, of Plato's argument."[97] Therefore, the collocation of the *kolophon* and the aside "so to say" (ὡς ἂν εἴποι τις) in Diogenes' text seems to enact an impersonation of Platonic phraseology within the presentation of Epicurean doctrine. Now, I would argue that this gesture is an oblique focalization of his Platonist addressee in which the author is employing her beloved Plato to introduce his Epicurean *telos*. But why would Diogenes do this? One answer could be that he is undercutting any Epicurean affiliation he may be said to have to remain separate from any philosophical school's authority. Another answer, and one that chimes with the other punning responses to the *Kuriai Doxai* in the Second Sophistic from both pro- and anti-Epicureans that I have discussed, is that Diogenes is setting two different types of authority against one another. In her comparison between Diogenes of Oenoanda's fictionalized mother of Epicurus and Diogenes Laërtius's female Platonic addressee, Gordon makes the point of powerful female patrons (*patronissai*) operating during the period. When scholars have attempted to identify the female Platonist addressee of Diogenes's work, various *patronissai* have been suggested, including the wife of Septimius Severus, Julia Domna.[98] Now, I still believe that it is impossible to support any one candidate for Diogenes' addressee, but if we read Diogenes' evocation of her at the moment of citing the *Kuriai Doxai* alongside the other uses of this text in

---

[95] Plato *Theaetetus* 153c. *Laws* 673d–674c. *Theaetetus* is cited from Duke et al. (1995); *Laws* from Burnet (1922).

[96] Cicero *De Divinatione*. 2.34, cited from Pease (1920–23).

[97] Aristides *To Plato: In Defence of Rhetoric* 304: εἶμι δ᾽ ἐπ᾽ αὐτὸν ἤδη τὸν κολοφῶνα τῶν Πλάτωνος, ὡς ἄν τις εἴποι, ῥημάτων. Aristides is cited from Dindorf (1829).

[98] Perhaps most convincingly, yet still tentatively and speculatively, by Hemelrijk (1999).

Aelian, Alciphron, and Diogenes of Oenoanda, a picture emerges of a correlation unique to the Second Sophistic between the performative authority of these *sententiae* and the role of Epicureanism in the changing roles of gender dynamics in the period.

CONCLUSIONS

The four responses to the *Kuriai Doxai* in the Second Sophistic I have discussed (Aelian, Alciphron, Diogenes of Oenoanda, and Diogenes Laërtius) all utilize the performative authority of Epicurus's sententious text to ground their discussions of the interaction between Epicurean hedonistic philosophy and contemporary debates of the "care of the self." Aelian's "feminized" reader of the *Kuriai Doxai*, although opposed to the less polemic projection of female readers of the *Kuriai Doxai* shared by the rest of these authors, nonetheless underlines the dynamic of mastery and submission that surrounded these powerful *sententiae* since Epicurus's day. In fact, Gellius's anecdote about Taurus and the *verba* of Hierocles with which I began this essay reiterates Aelian's extreme position in a more playful tone. Both of these authors articulate the power of the *Kuriai Doxai* as reflecting on the crisis of the (male) subject in the Roman Empire. The philosophical authority in general, for Gellius, and of Epicureanism, for Aelian, will only lead to a disempowered individual. In a related way, Alciphron and Diogenes of Oenoanda each articulate a contemporary concern surrounding the autonomy of the subject through the performative authority of the Epicurean text, specifically in debating the role of *paideia* in society and in relation to the Epicurean community. In different ways, both authors return to the original Epicurean Garden to fictionalize Epicurean women (the *hetaira* Leontion and the philosopher's mother) to dramatize opposing positions in debates surrounding the contemporary conception of *paideia*. Alciphron's Leontion valorizes *paideia* through the figure of the *hetaira* in the face of her master Epicurus's "masterful opinions," stating her claim to being her own "mistress" (*kuria*), but also playfully teaches Epicureans appropriate *parrhesia* at the same time. While Diogenes of Oenoanda imagines the original use of the *Kuriai Doxai* in Epicurus's advice to his mother and in doing so, warns against the "security" of the institutions of *paideia*, calling for her to come within the doors of the school. In this context, we can better

Dynamic Reading

make sense of Diogenes Laërtius's address to a Platonic female reader in his work. His Platonic focalization of her at the very moment the Epicurean *Kuriai Doxai* are quoted not only makes a statement about the problems of philosophical autonomy, in which his addressee's Platonism appears at the moment of quoting the pinnacle of Epicurean philosophy, but also of political autonomy. In this context, when writing under the patronage of a "Plato-loving" patroness, quoting the *Kuriai Doxai*, even cushioned with Platonic resonances, shows a balancing of the pressures of philosophical and political authority. For this argument to work, Diogenes Laërtius does not need to be a card-carrying Epicurean: his work is simply another example of how the performative authority of the *Kuriai Doxai* bridges pro-Epicurean apologetic and anti-Epicurean polemic to articulate key contemporary debates surrounding pleasure, gender, and authority in the Second Sophistic.[99]

[99] I want to thank both editors for their telling comments and constant encouragement throughout the process from presentation to publication.

3

Reading for Pleasure: Disaster and Digression in the First Renaissance Commentary on Lucretius

Gerard Passannante

The art of losing isn't hard to master.

—Elizabeth Bishop, "One Art"

In his *Remedies for Fortune Fair and Foul*, Petrarch recommends the "diligent reading of outstanding writers" as a physic to earthquakes, plagues, and other disasters that remind us (as if anyone needs reminding) that "life changes in the instant."[1] Like Petrarch's *Remedies*, this essay also concerns what it means to read for "pleasure" with disaster on the mind, and, in particular, what it means to encounter Lucretius's *De Rerum Natura*—a poem in so many ways about disaster management, at least in the philosophical sense. Over the six books of the poem, the Epicurean poet teaches us that by understanding the "nature of things"—namely, the atoms that make up the phenomenal world and its effects—we can achieve this state of "pleasure" or *ataraxia*, a mind serenely removed from the fear of death. As Virgil once famously put it in a line that is thought to weigh heavily with Lucretian influence: "Happy is the man who knows

I would like to thank Julia Haig Gaisser for her generous comments, Anthony Grafton, James I. Porter, Marc Schachter, and my friends and colleagues at the American Academy in Rome who heard an early version of this essay as a talk. I dedicate this piece to the memory of my friend James McMackin. Translations are my own unless otherwise noted.

[1] Petrarch (1991) 1: 3; the second quotation is from Didion (2005) 3.

the causes of things" (*Georgics* 2.490). But the question is: how exactly does one learn from a poet such as Lucretius who was either "happy" in this sense, or who, paradoxically, had a reputation for melancholy, madness, and suicide and was said to have written his poems in the intervals between his madness? In what follows, I want to explore how one particular reader—Giambattista Pio, the author of the poem's first annotated edition—made sense of Lucretius and his philosophy in the shadow of his own pointed experience of disaster and loss in early sixteenth-century Bologna.

While Pio's edition of the *De Rerum Natura* has long been the subject of scholarly attention, my own interest is in a somewhat forgotten corner of the commentary.[2] I am thinking here of the various personal "digressions" the commentator scatters throughout his learned notes—occasional thoughts on the earthquakes he experienced in 1505, the death of his father and teacher the same year, and the memory of his beloved mother who died, he tells us, of the kind of fever that Lucretius describes in book 6. Modern readers of the edition have for the most part found Pio's *excursus* histrionic or simply ignored them altogether. For the Italian scholar Ezio Raimondi, for example, the commentator's digressions amount to little more than a "minor chapter" in the work compared to his more erudite musings, and their author was a "consummate actor, a little bit of a ham."[3] Charlotte Goddard does not mention the digressions at all in her reading of Pio's edition, but insists that his "style of commentary does not stem from an interest in Lucretius or Epicureanism. It does not lend itself to reflecting the spirit of the *De Rerum Natura* or to exploring the meaning of the work."[4] In what follows here, I will take a different approach. By reconsidering the curious place of these digressions in Pio's commentary and also within a larger history of Epicurean reading, I want to begin to put some pressure on the notion of the poem's "spirit" and the ways a commentator might be imagined to have absorbed it. At the same time, I would like to explore how Pio's seemingly unimportant wanderings from the philological path may reflect a very real engagement with the poem—an engagement that emerges in the mixing of

---

[2] See, for example, Dionisotti (1968) 78–110; Raimondi (1974); Del Nero (1985); Del Nero (1986); Del Nero (1990); Goddard (1991); Gambino Longo (2004) 38–41.

[3] Raimondi (1974) 658–59.

[4] Goddard (1991) 216.

philosophy and philology that Pio advocates as a style of commentary and a habit of mind.

In the very broadest terms, this is a story about the reception of Epicureanism in the Renaissance, the often difficult relationship between sentiment and philosophy, and the history of humanist reading and textual practice. In trying to pin down the function of Pio's digressions (if one can speak of a function with regard to a practice that, as we shall see, is hardly consistent and that sometimes calls its own utility into question), I will show how they took shape both as a response to habits that Pio inherited from his teacher, the great Bolognese humanist Filippo Beroaldo, and as a self-conscious answer to the poem's narrative of didactic instruction. I have broken down the discussion into three parts, each of which considers the problem from a slightly different perspective, but which are closely connected. In the first section, we will look at the digression as a form of historical abstraction and the ambivalence it generates with regard to the poem's Epicurean lessons. The second part will examine the history of the digressive form itself and the nature of Pio's own "Lucretian" take on it. In the last section, we will consider the digressive plot of mourning in the commentator's engagement with the poet's philosophy. In the end, Pio's occasional thoughts begin to look like more than merely idiosyncratic or meaningless diversions from the real work of writing a learned commentary. Rather, they constitute, in their own decidedly literary way, a complex and unfolding dialogue about the proper relation a philologist should assume with regard to his text, the place of loss in Epicurean philosophy, and the ethical dimensions (and limits) of Lucretius's art.

EARTHQUAKES OF THE MIND

Hidden in a corner of the Palazzo Communale in Bologna is a fresco by the humanist-painter Francesco Francia, *The Madonna of the Earthquake*, a monument to the miraculous survival of a city—and to how easily some disasters are forgotten.[5] Often considered the earliest perspectival view of Bologna outside the hand of its patron saint, the fresco pictures a

---

[5] On Francia and and the culture of humanism in Bologna, see Faietti and Oberhuber (1988).

round-headed Madonna hovering blithely over the city and shielding it from the three tremors that shook the earth beginning on December 31, 1504. While most of the city's inhabitants survived the quakes, the same unfortunately could not be said for some of its buildings, though it was not the trembling that caused the damage—at least not directly.[6] In a short treatise on earthquakes and plagues published the same year, Francia's friend, Filippo Beroaldo, would explain how the great Bentivoglio tower that rose above the palazzo was unceremoniously dismantled in response to the fears of men who thought it safer to live without it:[7] a fitting conclusion to a longstanding anxiety that the pilgrim Dante had expressed more than two centuries earlier when he encountered the giant Antaeus frozen in ice at the bottom of hell and remembered another of Bologna's famous towers falling in perpetual suspension, "thus did Antaeus seem to my fixed gaze / as I watched him bend—that was indeed a time / I wished that I had gone another road" (*tal parve Antëo a me che stava a bada / di vederlo chinare, e fu tal ora / ch'i' avrei voluto ir per altra strada*).[8]

The Bolognese skyline, however, was not the only thing that would bear the mark of disaster. One comes across another mention of the earthquakes again six years later in the pages of Pio's commentary on the *De Rerum Natura*. Buried amid the deep learning and erudition of the notes is a long digression that recounts the catastrophes that befell Bologna in 1505, a digression that breaks up the usual philological commentary. Pio begins this digression rather curiously by telling the story of an apparition in the salty fields of Bologna: figures of two "giants" fighting that were witnessed by "all of Italy."[9] The commentator himself did not witness the spectacle personally, he says, because he was busy entertaining a "certain prince" who mocked such superstitions, hinting perhaps that he was also somewhat skeptical of the story.[10] "Still,"

---

[6] For a more detailed account of the aftermath of the earthquakes, see Muzzi (1845) 5: 465–66.

[7] Beroaldo (1505) sig. B 5ᵛ.

[8] Dante, *Inferno* 31.139–41. Trans. Robert and Jean Hollander in Hollander and Hollander (2000).

[9] Pio (1511) 123ᵛ. Raimondi fails to see the historical significance of this passage or its relation to the larger note, describing the fighting giants simply as "uno spettacolo per così dire sportive" ((1974) 658).

[10] Pio (1511) 123ᵛ.

he wrote, "misfortunes followed of every kind" (*sequuta tamen sunt omnis generis infortunia*),

> quae miserrimam patriam omni calamitatis genere confecerunt. Tremores videlicet terrae formidolosissimi, quibus ter ingenti omnium pavore noctu Bononia et Bononiensis ager intremuit: nec statim finis, verum spatio menstruo solum et si non perniciose, fluitavit tamen, peiorque motu fuit timor ipse motus. Aestate deincipiti patritii plebeique ingenio divitiisque conspicui decesserunt, et humanis valere dixerunt. Inter quos Beroaldus praeceptor meus vir, cui musae latinae haerebant genitorque Iacobus Andalus Pius fide, animi praestantia, robore, sinceritate, pulchritudine nemini secundus. Secuta est caeli miseranda lues, pestisque contagiosis malis reliquias absumens.[11]

which consumed our most miserable country with all manner of disaster. Clearly tremors of the earth are the most terrifying, and by these Bologna and its territory trembled three times during the night, to the great terror of all. Nor did it end all at once, but within the space of a month the ground, even if not dangerously, shook nevertheless, and worse than the motion was the fear of the motion itself. The following summer both patricians and plebeians notable for their talent and wealth bid farewell to their fellow man. Among them was Filippo Beroaldo my teacher, a man to whom the muses of Latin clung, and my father Jacob Pio, second to no one in faith, excellence of spirit, strength, sincerity, and beauty. Misery-bringing plague spread from the sky, eating away at survivors with the wicked contagion of disease.

After recounting these disasters, which he experienced on a personal level, the commentator shifts to an account of the political instabilities of Bologna, finally panning out to a lesson on the history of the city—a digression within a digression on the wars that unfolded in the year of the earthquake, the story of Theodosius's founding, and the tomb of the tyrant Censorinus, which was said to be located just outside the city's walls.[12] Both for the range of topics covered in such a compressed space and for its seeming irrelevance to the matter at hand the digression is

---

[11] Ibid.

[12] Ibid. On the unstable political history of Bologna in this period, see Muzzi (1845) 5: 467–71; Farolfi (1977).

stunning. But what is the purpose of this wandering note in the commentary, and, moreover, we might ask, of the act of digressing itself?

At first glance, the relationship between the text and the note seems almost arbitrary. Pio mentions an apparition of giants that refers back loosely to the poet's description of the accidental formation of images in the clouds. As Lucretius has it:

> nam saepe Gigantum
> ora volare videntur et umbram ducere late,
> interdum magni montes avolsaque saxa
> montibus anteire et solem succedere praeter,
> inde alios trahere atque inducere belua nimbus.
> (*De Rerum Natura* 4.136–40)

For often giants' countenances appear to fly over and draw their shadow afar, sometimes great mountains and rocks torn from the mountains to go before and to pass by the sun, after them some monster pulling and dragging other clouds.[13]

Pio's list of natural and historical events almost seems to mimic the periodic flow of images in the clouds, changing, transforming—a stream of thought. In the place in the poem to which the note is attached, Lucretius is explaining to us the spontaneous formation of figures that we may mistake for ghosts or apparitions—figures or, as he calls them, *simulacra*, which "never cease to dissolve and change their shapes and turn themselves into the outlines of figures of every kind" (*nec speciem mutare suam liquentia cessant / et cuisque modi formarum vertere in oras*, 4.141–42). With the randomness of the giants passing in the clouds and the sense of contingency they brought with them, was Pio suggesting that perhaps the apparitions outside Bologna, too, were merely random images or *simulacra*—specters with no reality beyond the stories we project upon them as we forget our own hand in the art?

This would seem like a reasonable explanation, and one close to the poem's own heart. As the digression continues to unfold, however, this question about the giants becomes slightly more difficult to answer because it unlocks another question about the relation between the

---

[13] Translations for Lucretius are from Rouse-Smith unless otherwise noted.

apparition and the disasters that followed. What may seem at first like an arbitrary link between giants and earthquakes reflects a logic that would have been familiar to Pio's contemporary readers and would have needed no explanation. When Pio writes "still misfortunes followed of every kind," for example, he is recalling the idea that ghostly apparitions like the battling giants in the field were commonly connected to future events of disaster and were even thought to foretell the imminent wrath of God, as Ottavia Niccoli has shown was the case in the many pamphlets printed in this period.[14] In writing the digression, Pio may even have been thinking of one work in particular, a narrative ballad that was published in Bologna the same year as his edition of Lucretius, and likely by the same printer, Girolamo Benedetii or his brother Giovanni Antonio.[15] Among the signs that are reported in the ballad are the sounds of ghostly battles not unlike the one Pio recounts, a vision of a serpent, and the figures of two angels.[16] By invoking this popular tradition in the context of Lucretius's poem, Pio was in his own way opening up a space of dialogue between the skepticism of that "certain prince" whose name he conspicuously leaves out and the prophetic logic that connects ghostly apparitions to a providential history of disaster.

In this sense, the very form of the digression becomes a mode of analysis that reflects the work of historical narrative-making and a deep analogy between understanding the causes of natural and human events. For if the commentator is holding the divinatory power of these apparitions or *simulacra* in suspension (in other words, introducing an Epicurean critique), he is also posing a question about the desire to find meaning in seemingly random events and to place them within a personal and historical framework.[17] Here in the cloud-like shift from an account of contemporary earthquakes and plague to the political contingencies that befell Bologna to a grade school lesson in the city's history, we may catch

---

[14] Niccoli (1990).

[15] *Memoria della novi segni* (1511). See Niccoli (1990) 28.

[16] As Niccoli has pointed out, all of the prodigies in the *Memoria* were linked to specific political instabilities in Italy, suggesting "an unconscious but clear connection between war, political disintegration, and prophecy" ((1990) 28).

[17] What Charles Edward Trinkaus once wrote of Pio's teacher Beroaldo might also be said here of him: "Beroaldo's city, Bologna, was one of the objects of French, Papal, and Venetian ambition, so that Beroaldo was particularly aware of the difficulties and calamities of the times and was, perhaps, compelled to assume a resigned attitude . . ." ((1940) 135).

a glimpse of a reader thinking seriously about the relation between natural and historical causes, the interdependence of events, and the nature of causality itself.[18] This is clearly not the pious consolation or moralizing that a reader might have expected or wanted from a Christian commentator responding to a poem so closely associated with atheism.[19] That Pio himself would actively refrain from the typical response of his more pious contemporaries might just be the point after all.[20] In this regard, the very matter-of-factness of the digression carries its own expressive force. But has Pio reached the peace of mind the poet describes and hopes to instill in his readers, found pleasure in contemplating the flux of history and matter? Is the digression itself a reflection of this peace of mind or, rather, an index to the very difficulty of achieving it?

By dragging the reader back to the microcosm of Bologna and its troubles from the cosmological scale of the poem, the commentator was no doubt wandering from the path. But he was also, I would suggest, bringing us back to the poem in another way. Cast in the shadow of catastrophes and strife, Pio's note subtly reminds us that the very poem we are reading was written in view of the Roman civil wars (and perhaps even during them).[21] As Lucretius writes at the start of the *De Rerum Natura*:

> nam neque nos agere hoc patriai tempore iniquo
> possumus aequo animo nec Memmi clara propago
> talibus in rebus communi desse saluti.
> omnis enim per se divom natura necessest
> immortali aevo summa cum pace fruatur
> semota ab nostris rebus seiunctaque longe. (*De Rerum*
> *Natura* 1.41–46)

---

[18] Del Nero (1985) 160.

[19] Compare Pio's response, for example, to that of his contemporaries who held processions to ward off God's wrath: see Muzzi (1845) 5: 465–66.

[20] Like his teacher, Pio was in his own way critiquing the *religiosiores* who instilled fear in the hearts of Bologna's citizens. See Beroaldo (1505) sig. C i. As Trinkaus (1940) 135, points out, Beroaldo himself attributed the unhappy state of man "to the power of fortune, which, blind to human defects and merits, arbitrarily raises men up, only to cast them down."

[21] Gregory Hutchinson has argued that the *De Rerum Natura* was written later than scholars have previously thought (ca. 48 BCE), thus making the poem refer more immediately to actual civil war: see G. O. Hutchinson (2001).

For in this time of our country's troubles neither can I do my part with untroubled mind, nor can the noble scion of the Memmii at such a season be wanting to the common weal. [I pray to you for peace,] for the very nature of divinity must necessarily enjoy immortal life in the deepest peace, far removed and separated from our affairs.

Here, in this early passage, Lucretius is laying the foundation of the idea of the poem as a kind of medicine. Reading the poem, we are meant, like the gods, to find pleasure in the clash of atoms and men viewed from a distance: "when great legions cover the outspread plains in their maneuvers, evoking war in mimicry . . . there is a place on the high mountains, from which they seem to stand still, and to be a brightness at rest on a plain" (*praeterea magnae legiones cum loca cursu / camporum complent belli simulacra cientes . . . et tamen est quidam locus altis montibus unde / stare videntur et in campis consistere fulgor*, 2.323–32).[22]

At the same time, in digressing on the event of earthquakes, Pio may have had in mind another moment in the *De Rerum Natura*—a moment in which Lucretius himself interrupts the studied façade of his own Epicurean sangfroid with an apprehensiveness that seems decidedly out of place. The passage in question concerns the experience of earthquakes (or, in this case, rather, the mere thought of them):

> . . . dictis dabit ipsa fidem res
> forsitan, et graviter terrarum motibus ortis
> omnia conquassari in parvo tempore cernes.
> quod procul a nobis flectat fortuna gubernans,
> et ratio potius quam res persuadeat ipsa
> succidere horrisono posse omnia victa fragore.
> (*De Rerum Natura* 5.104–109)

My words will perhaps win credit by plain facts, and within some short time you will see violent earthquakes arise and all things convulsed with shocks. But may pilot fortune steer this far from us, and may pure reason rather than experience persuade that the whole world can collapse borne down with a frightful-sounding crash.

---

[22] For a discussion of Lucretius and images of atoms and warfare, see Cabisius (1985); Fowler (1989); Gale (2000), 232–69.

Lucretius is here extending his argument about the power of reason to make sense of things without visible evidence. In a rare use of the first person, he is also acknowledging the difficulty of being an Epicurean in the face of disaster, of laying aside fear and submitting oneself to the whims of blind fortune.[23] As the poet seems to suggest, the bitter pill of philosophy is not always easily swallowed—even, it turns out, with the honey of poetry.[24]

At the end of the day, the Bolognese disasters that Pio describes naturally did not lead to the end of the world, but they no doubt shook up the commentator—and the memory of them lingers in the commentary in small tremors. Before his edition comes to a close, in fact, Pio will digress on the earthquakes explicitly for a second time, he says, "so that I might console myself and my fatherland Bologna which trembled three times, shaken almost to the root" (*tum ut me consoler et patriam Bononiam quae ter radicitus paene convulsa tremuit*).[25] If in the earlier digression that we looked at the commentator had claimed the disasters had done very little damage (the fear, he said, was worse than the trembling itself), here we are told the earthquakes shook Bologna almost to the root—a disaster magnified, it would seem, the more he thinks about it. The occasion now is Lucretius's own description and explanation of earthquakes—a powerful evocation of the winds that cause the earth to tremble beneath the ground and the fear that the shaking generates in the minds of men (*De Rerum Natura* 6.535–607). Nearly three full pages of commentary on earthquakes and their causes accompany the text, and Pio now seems to be taking the Epicurean lesson to heart: to understand the causes of things is to be released from the grip of fear. At the same time, however, the "pleasure" he achieves here is not exactly what one could call Epicurean. Pio concludes the passage on earthquakes on a strangely cheerful note, reminding his readers (and perhaps himself) that the trembling had indeed been very mild. He even

---

[23] By using the phrase *fortuna gubernans*, for example, Lucretius, one might argue, is dramatizing a reversion to traditional ways of thinking and speaking when fear comes into play, rehearsing in miniature the etiology of superstition he describes in the same book. By contrast, A. A. Long has suggested that we should simply allow Lucretius some "poetic license" ((1977) 73).

[24] As Porter (2003b) reminds us, in the cosmic world of the poem, "the spectacle of earthquakes evokes that of bodies rushing through the unresisting void" (213).

[25] Pio (1511) 200[r].

recounts again the wars that followed and the capture of Bologna, "but for good," he insists: "The genial comic actor having left the stage completely, with all having gained" (*comicum prorsus et iucundum cunctis adeptis exitum*).[26] If here, however, the commentator is able to transmute the experience of tragedy into comedy and "console" himself, the memory of loss and disaster is not too far in the background. Pio, of course, knew as well as Lucretius how quickly a scene could change.

POETICUS AFFLATUS

Pio himself leaves us a clue as to the meaning and function of his digressions in the first note on earthquakes when he bears witness to the death of his teacher, Filippo Beroaldo. The form of the digression itself was, in fact, a subtle homage to Beroaldo, a man famous for scattering his own "little flowers" throughout his lectures and learned commentaries.[27] As a celebrated teacher lecturing to sometimes three hundred students at a time, Beroaldo often told stories, no doubt to keep his students listening and awake or, as he put it, to refresh the weary spirit—a benefit that translated directly into the work of the commentary. "I have made an effort quite intentionally," he wrote in his notes on Suetonius, "that the work be marked here and there with various little flowers plucked out of untrampled verdant fields" (*dedi operam, et quidem ex industria, ut flosculis hic et inde complusculis ex virore pratorum nondum conculcato decerptis insignirentur*).[28] At the same time, however, the digressions also served a somewhat deeper function, as Maria Teresa Casella has explained, providing a space of "total adhesion" between the text and its reader.[29] A good commentator, Beroaldo insisted, was like a Platonic rhapsode—inspired by a *poeticus afflatus* that allowed him to participate in the subtle mysteries of the text as he carefully unfolded it and penetrated its hidden

---

[26] Ibid.

[27] On the history and form of Beroaldo's digressions in his commentaries, see especially Krautter (1971); Casella (1975); Gaisser (2008) 197–242.

[28] Beroaldo (1493) fol. A iv^v. Trans. Ciapponi (1995) 13–14 n. 3, slightly modified. For a brief discussion of this trope, see Raimondi (1950) 106.

[29] Casella (1975) 669. On the nature of Beroaldo's intimacy with his texts, see, in general, Gaisser (2008) 197–242.

recesses.[30] As Plato had described the rhapsode overtaken as if by the invisible hooks of a magnet, the Renaissance commenter, too, was part and parcel of this extended chain of sympathetic knowledge.[31]

This explains why so many of Beroaldo's own digressions were composed in the style of the author he was working on: a kind of *imitatio* that, as Konrad Krautter has suggested, almost represents its own literary genre.[32] Different authors required different styles and there were, of course, many ways to be possessed by a poetic *furor*. In the commentary on Apuleius, for example, the Bolognese humanist wrote gleefully in the author's eccentric style of his marriage to his wife, anticipated the birth of his child he hoped would be a son, talked politics and aesthetics, and described the details of a palazzo outside Bologna in a note accompanying the section on the house of Cupid and Psyche.[33] In demonstrating his ability to imitate Apuleius while bringing the author to bear on his own world, Beroaldo made the past speak to the present. As Petrarch once wrote letters to the ancients and absorbed their work so thoroughly that he sometimes forgot he was imitating them, Beroaldo found his own way of communing with the dead and losing himself to books.[34]

Beroaldo's charismatic influence significantly influenced Pio's development as a philologist, though the two certainly had their differences.[35] Pio was apparently something of a difficult student—as Raimondi has described him, "obstinate, closed, and proud"—and little by little we find the student straying from school.[36] In the pages of his edition of Fulgentius, for example, Pio would declare his methodological independence between the lines, reaching, as Valerio Del Nero has put it, "an irreparable break" with his teacher, a "point of no return."[37] Slightly later, just before

---

[30] Beroaldo (1487) fol. A 2^r. See Ciapponi (1995) 7–9.

[31] Beroaldo was clearly drinking from the Platonic wells of Marsilio Ficino and Angelo Poliziano when he described his interpreter as a kind of rhapsode. See Coppini (1998). On Ficino's active idea of the rhapsode, see M. J. B. Allen (1993).

[32] Krautter (1971) 40–52; Gaisser (2008) 224.

[33] For Beroaldo's discussion of art and the work of Francia in a digression, see Baxandall and Gombrich (1962) 113–15.

[34] Beroaldo knew Petrarch's poetry well and even translated some of it into Latin. See Krautter (1971) 190–92.

[35] On Pio's complex relation to Beroaldo, see Dionisotti (1968) 78–94; Raimondi (1974). On the taste for the archaic, see especially D'Amico (1984).

[36] Raimondi (1974) 644.

[37] Del Nero (1981) 251.

Beroaldo's death, Pio would go even further, renouncing the famous Beroaldan style so much admired and extravagantly lampooned by his contemporaries.

Redeamus ad annotamenta nostra bene favente virtutis genio, stylo non Asio, non florido, non tumenti, non obscuro, non desito, sicut antea consuevimus, utentes, sed potius dicendi genus Grammaticum aggrediamur supra crepidam (ut aiunt) non se tollens, ingeniis nostri temporis, perinde ac moribus, inservientes, quos non improbo, quippe cum illis obtemperare necesse sit. . . .[38]

Let's go back to a commentary without that Asiatic, puffed up, pompous, obscure and out-of-fashion style we were so used to. Let us pursue instead a grammatical manner of speaking, which does not (as they say) lift itself from its last, making ourselves serve the talents of our day, in accord with our customs, which I do not reproach, for we must conform to those. . . .

It was finally this style and not his teacher's that Pio would use when he wrote his commentary on the *De Rerum Natura*.

Pio and Beroaldo had other differences too. By the time Pio was writing his commentary, the text of the *De Rerum Natura* had already become a heated object of contention. First, Lucretius's poem posed a difficult question about the relation between philology and philosophy, or rather, the proper decorum that a commentator should observe in working with the two disciplines. Whereas Beroaldo, for example, had insisted on keeping problems of philology and philosophy separate in his commentaries, Pio would take the *De Rerum Natura* as the ideal opportunity to celebrate their marriage, pointing out the necessity for the commentator to understand philosophy in order to emend the text correctly.[39]

---

[38] Gruter (1602–34) 1: 388. Cited in Raimondi (1974) 644 and Dionisotti (1968) 93. Dionisotti describes this passage as a "sottomissione forzata . . . al gusto dei contemporanei."

[39] In the same place where he disagrees with Beroaldo on the state of the Lucretian text, Pio, in his *Annotamenta* (1505), draws upon the authority of Quintilian to make his point about the union of grammar and philosophy and quotes a passage directly from the *De Rerum Natura*. See Gruter (1602–34) 1: 397. On Beroaldo's response to Pio's method in his commentary on *Apuleius*, see Gaisser (2008) 232. As Dionisotti (1968) 91, points out, while Beroaldo said he did not want to seem more of a philosopher than a commentator, his own work is riddled with language borrowed from the Platonism of Ficino. See also Raimondi (1974) 648–49.

The second thing they disagreed about with regard to Lucretius was the text itself. In a passing remark in his *Annotationes Centum*, Beroaldo had complained bitterly that the poetry of Lucretius was left in ruins, "consigned to oblivion by the all-consuming darkness of error," and hardly showing "the many lights of genius," as Cicero once wrote.[40] Disagreeing with Beroaldo on this point, Pio himself saw the bad state of the text as both a challenge and an opportunity. When he responded in his *Annotamenta*, as if in dialogue with his teacher, he would also quote Cicero, but would emphasize not what was lost, but rather the parts of the poem that had swum to safety through seas of barbarous and illiterate opinion. Even the fragments of the poem that have reached us, Pio insisted, were anointed with "the many lights of genius."[41]

It was finally in spite of all these subtle and not-so-subtle differences that Pio would come to scatter digressions throughout his Lucretius commentary in a kind of formal gesture to Beroaldo—a gesture that would have been unmistakable to his learned contemporaries.[42] At the same time, the form of the digressions would provide Pio with another occasion to distinguish himself from his teacher and continue the dialogue. As we have begun to see, Pio's digressions are not exactly the happy flights of Beroaldo running through the pages of the *Golden Ass* at high speed, scattering flowers here and there.[43] Nor are they quite what Julia Haig Gaisser has described as the commentator's attempt to inhabit the skin of his author and affirm himself as an artistic counterpart—at least not on

---

[40] Gruter (1602–34) 1: 308: *Sed de Lucretii locis obscurioribus alibi plura, cum eius poemata adeo mendosa circumferantur, ut non lita multis luminibus ingenii videri possint, sicut Q. Ciceroni videbantur, sed oblita tenebris errorum praescatentibus* (But I will have more to say elsewhere about the obscure passages in Lucretius, since his poems circulate with so many flaws that seem impossible to erase even by the "many lights of genius," as they seemed to Quintus Cicero, but instead are consigned to oblivion by the all-consuming darkness of error). Cf. Cicero *Letters to His Brother Quintus* 2.10.3 (cited and trans. from Shackleton Bailey (2002)): *Lucreti poemata ut scribis ita sunt, multis luminibus ingeni, multae tamen artis* (Lucretius's poetry is as you say—sparkling with natural genius, but plenty of technical skill). I have altered the translation slightly. Cited in Raimondi (1974) 649.

[41] Gruter (1602–34) 1: 396–97. See Raimondi (1974) 649.

[42] On the longer history of this kind of commentary digression in Bologna, see Casella (1975).

[43] Raimondi (1974) 658: "Al pari del Beroaldo il Pio giudica che i 'digressus' e i 'diverticula' debbano ristorare il 'lector vegetus', e fa quindi ricorso agli episodi della propria esistenza, alla realtà bolognese che gli vive intorno, sebbene non possieda più il gusto comico ed estroverso del maestro . . . ."

first glance.[44] His digressions, in fact, seem closer to the kind of remarks Beroaldo had scattered in his 1505 treatise on earthquakes and plagues— for example, an acknowledgment of anxiety about the safety of his family and the report of a man who supposedly went mad with compulsive fear, which would later attract the attention of Robert Burton in the *Anatomy of Melancholy*.[45] When Pio himself wrote of the "sweetness" of diverting his attention at the end of his first note on the Bolognese earthquakes, the sweetness seems less the feeling the poet famously describes in the proem to book 2, watching ships toil at sea, than the bitter sweetness of nostalgia, a longing for things past.[46]

In what sense, then, could Pio be said to have absorbed the *afflatus* of his author as Beroaldo had dictated, if at all? What would it even mean to talk about the "spirit" of a poet who argued vehemently that the soul was mortal? Looking back to the world of Florentine humanism, which Beroaldo so much admired, Pio could have found at least one answer in the work of the Platonist Marsilio Ficino, who had taken up this very question in his *Platonic Theology*, using the Epicurean poet as an example of one of those illustrious men who had been seized by a divine frenzy.[47] Like the unlearned and unskilled poets who had been inspired by the muses, the poem of an Epicurean madman was another testimony to the fact that "[the poets] had not pronounced the words themselves but

[44] As Gaisser (2008) 224 says, " . . . Beroaldo both presents himself as a worthy emulator of Apuleius and creates his own small but self-conscious work of literary art."

[45] See Burton (2001) 338: "At Bologna in Italy, Anno 1504, there was such a fearful earthquake about eleven o'clock in the night (as Beroaldus, in his book *de terræ motu*, hath commended to posterity) that all the city trembled, the people thought the world was at an end, *actum de mortalibus*, such a fearful noise, it made such a detestable smell, the inhabitants were infinitely affrighted, and some ran mad. *Audi rem atrocem, at annalibus memorandam* (mine author adds), hear a strange story, and worthy to be chronicled: I had a servant at the same time called Fulco Argelanus, a bold and proper man, so grievously terrified with it, that he was first melancholy, after doted, at last mad, and made away himself."

[46] Pio (1511) 123[v]: *Si datur occasio: etiam si non datur in patriae nostrae memoriam nobis divertere dulce est* (If the occasion is given [*sc.* for digression], even if it is not given, it is sweet to divert ourselves in the memory of our country). Cf. Lucretius *De Rerum Natura* 2.1–2: *Suave, mari magno turbantibus aequora ventis, / e terra magnum alterius spectare laborem* (Pleasant it is, when over a great sea the winds trouble the waters, to gaze from shore upon another's great tribulation).

[47] For all his interest in the Platonic dialogues and in later traditions of Platonism in the commentary, it is curious to note that Pio himself mentions Ficino only once: see Pio (1511) 95[r]. On Pio's use of Platonism in the commentary, see Del Nero (1985) 164–65.

rather God had spoken loudly through them as through trumpets" (*quasi non ipsi pronuntiaverint, sed deus per eos ceu tubas clamaverit*).[48] This might be reason enough to think about the *afflatus* of Lucretius. The story, however, changes slightly later in the same text when Ficino warns us not to take Lucretius's philosophy to heart. There is, Ficino implies, a fine line between a Platonic *furor* and a Lucretian melancholy, one that should be carefully observed:

Ceterum meminisse oportet eam opinionem sive affectionem non satis habere fidei, quae sequitur aut ingenium melancholicum, aegrum et quo-dammodo vitae contrarium, aut indecentem et noxiam positionem siderum, quae etiam complexionem pervertit humanam ac defectum affert secum, non modo quantum spectat ad vitae fiduciam, sed etiam quantum ad humanarum rerum gubernationem. Unde impii homines plurimum vel ignavissimi sunt, qualis fuisse dicitur Epicurus, vel flagitiosi, qualis Aristippus, vel insani, qualis sectator eorum Lucretius. Qui dum insania propter atram bilem concitaretur, animam suam primo conatus est verbis perdere in libro De natura rerum tertio, deinde corpus suum gladio perdidit.

For the rest, we must remember not to put full trust in that opinion or affection which results either from a melancholic genius (*ingenium melan-cholicum*), one sick and contrary in a way to life, or from an inappropriate and harmful position of the stars that both perverts the human temperament and brings with it a weakness with regard not only to our confidence in life but also to the governance of human affairs. Hence impious men are for the most part either extremely idle as Epicurus was said to be, or profligate like Aristippus, or mad as was their follower Lucretius. When his madness was roused on account of his black bile, Lucretius first tried to slaughter his soul verbally in the third book of his *On the Nature of Things*; then slaughtered his body with a sword.[49]

Ficino here is playing fast and loose with a famous chapter of Lucretius's biography as it was reported dubiously by Saint Jerome.[50] As Jerome has it, Lucretius drank a love philter administered by his wife that caused him to go mad, wrote his poem in rare moments of lucidity between the bouts

[48] Trans. Allen and Hankins in Ficino (2001–2006) 4: 126–27.
[49] Trans. Allen and Hankins in Ficino (2001–2006) 4: 308–309, slightly modified.
[50] On the troubled reception history of the life of Lucretius, see Canfora (1993); Holford-Strevens (2002).

of madness (*per intervalla insaniae*), and afterward committed suicide.[51] Though the story seems straight forward, what *per intervalla insaniae* means exactly is hard to pin down, and Ficino takes advantage of the ambiguity.[52] By recycling the anecdote for his own polemical purposes, the Platonic philosopher seems to be implying that Lucretius's poem was not written "between moments of insanity" but, rather, was the product of his so-called madness or "melancholic genius."[53]

Pio himself, of course, knew the poet's biography from Jerome and Lactantius and, I would suspect, from Ficino's discussion here as well.[54] When he later bore witness to the earthquakes, plagues, and deaths he experienced personally in his digressions, he was in his own way attempting to capture the "spirit" of the poet—at least as Ficino had understood it before him and as Goethe would later understand it when he described Lucretius as a "gloomy, fierce spirit" (*finstern, ingrimmischen Geist*).[55] It was, indeed, almost a kind of serious joke, for if his teacher, Beroaldo, had famously said one must be possessed by the *afflatus* of an author like a Platonic rhapsode, to absorb the *afflatus* of Lucretius, that most un-Platonic of poets, was ironically to confront the poet's "melancholic genius" and, as it were, to confront one's own.

THE ART OF LOSING

Nowhere is the subtle trace of the commentator's own melancholy more evident or deeply felt than in his account in the notes of his mother's death, another of his personal digressions written in the shadow of disaster. This strange figure of personal loss emerges again like another

---

[51] Fotheringham (1923) 231: *Titus Lucretius poeta nascitur. Qui postea amatorio poculo in furorem versus, cum aliquot libros per intervalla insaniae conscripsisset, quos postea Cicero emendavit, propia se manu interfecit anno aetatis XLIIII* (Titus Lucretius, the poet, was born. Later he was driven mad by a love-philtre, after he had written several books in the intervals of insanity; Cicero subsequently corrected these books; Lucretius died by his own hand in the forty-fourth year of his life). Cited and translated in Hadzsits (1935) 5.

[52] See Canfora (1993) in general for the ambiguities of the story and its interpretations.

[53] As Hankins (2011) argues, melancholy for Ficino was a cause of religious atheism.

[54] Pio mentions the biographical tradition of Jerome and Lactantius explicitly in the preface to his edition. See Pio (1511) 2[r].

[55] Cited and translated in Clay (1983) 251.

apparition in the sixth book of the *De Rerum Natura* where the poet
describes the symptoms of a fever. Here are the verses in question and the
commentator's memorial to his mother:

> Numquis enim nostrum miratur, siquis in artus
> accepit calido febrim fervore coortam
> aut alium quemvis morbi per membra dolorem?
> opturgescit enim subito pes, arripit acer
> saepe dolor dentes, oculos invadit in ipsos,
> existit sacer ignis et urit corpore serpens
> quam cumque arripuit partem repitque per artus,
> nimirum quia sunt multarum semina rerum,
> et satis haec tellus morbi caelumque mali fert,
> unde queat vis immensi procrescere morbi. (*De Rerum
> Natura* 6.655–64)

For is there any of us who feels wonder, if someone has got into his limbs a
fever that gathers with burning heat, or any other pain from disease throughout his body? For the foot suddenly swells, a sharp aching often seizes the
teeth, or invades the eyes themselves, the accursed fire appears creeping over
the body and burning each part it takes hold on, and crawls over the limbs,
assuredly because there are seeds of many things, and this earth and sky produce enough noxious disease that from it may grow forth an immeasurable
quantity of disease.

[Pio's commentary] quali morbo sanctae Memoriae genetrix mea Helena
diem clausit: qua: pace caeterarum dixerim: nulla pientior: modestior: aut
religiosior fuit digna priscis matronarum caetibus inferi: qua viva vivere
dulce mihi fuit: qua extincta nullum non diem egimus atrum et lugubrem.[56]

With such a sickness my mother Helena of blessed memory died; and by
leave of the other women I would say that none was more pious, more modest,
or more religious, worthy of the other ancient matrons of the afterlife. With
her alive, living was sweet to me; with her dead we passed no day that was not
black and lugubrious.

Pio goes on to credit his mother with his early education and success as
a humanist, and from this one gets the sense that he thinks of her often

---

[56] Pio (1511) 202[r].

as he works. What may seem here, however, like a purely personal moment invites us once again to think about the commentator's relationship to the poem, or rather to the poem and its didactic lesson. In his note, Pio seems to be doing exactly the opposite of what the poet is asking us to do in the lines just before the fever *excursus*—namely, to cast our view "wide and deep, and survey all quarters far abroad," so that we "may remember how profound is the sum of things" (*hisce tibi in rebus latest alteque videndum / et longe cunctas in partis dispiciendum, / ut reminiscaris summam rerum esse profundam*, 6.647–49). In this part of the poem, the fever-ridden body is not used to invoke personal or even collective grief (as Pio implies in the move from *mihi* to *egimus*, that is, from a first-person-singular pronoun to a first-person-plural verb), but rather as an analogy to help the reader understand "that a supply of all things is brought up from the infinite" (*ex infinito satis omnia suppeditare*, 6.666). As the body suffers a fever, so, too, the earth and the universe are subject to violent upheavals, strong "enough to enable the earth on a sudden to quake and move, the swift whirlwind to scour over land and sea, Etna's fires to overflow, the heaven to burst in a blaze" (*unde repente queat tellus concussa moveri / perque mare ac terras rapidus percurrere turbo, / ignis abundare Aetnaeus, flammescere caelum*, 6.667–69). In making it personal, the commentator effectively interrupts the logic of the poem that would help us ideally widen our gaze, and we experience a different kind of tremor. Cast in the pall of his mother's death, the images of eruption and quaking lend a peculiar force to the memory of pain and mourning and to an excess of emotion that, as anyone knows, can feel like an earthquake.

In a note like this one, Pio is not simply digressing casually or arbitrarily, but rather posing a very real question about the place of loss and mourning in Epicurean philosophy—a question perhaps with which the poet might have struggled himself.[57] As Pio knew, Epicurean philosophy generally advocates a studied abstinence from excessive emotion and, as some Renaissance readers complained, from any emotion altogether. In his *Dialogus de Consolatione* (1463), for example, Bartolomeo Scala has his interlocutor Cosimo de' Medici describe the severe limitations of Epicureanism with regard to sorrow, loss, and the experience

---

[57] For Lucretius's treatment of death and dying, see especially Segal (1990).

of human suffering. Written on the mournful occasion of the death of Cosimo's son, the text critiques the Epicurean position as untenable—impossibly cold and inhuman:

Nam et Epicurei, qui etsi mihi penitus improbandi videntur, tamen audio a quibusdam non omnino contemni, dum voluptati faventes, dolorem dicunt non solum malum sed etiam summum, minus etiam quam Stoici tolerabilia videntur afferre. Qui enim ita dicit, idem dicat necesse est ab iustitia, ab fortitudine, ab omni fere honestate frequentissime, ne in dolorem incidant, esse recedendum. Quid autem est minus tolerandum in publicis et privatis actionibus ea voce, quae deserendam praecipiat honestatem quaeque ceteris omnibus et amicorum et parentum et patriae utilitatibus commodisque ne quid doleat anteponat? Utrum tandem, Epicure, ut dolorem fugias, incendes patriam sacrasque aedes et templa Dei profanabis? . . . quandoquidem sine omni penitus incommoditate tota non traduci vita potest. . . .

And even though the Epicureans seem to me to merit utter rejection I hear that some do not altogether despise them. As defenders of pleasure, they say that sorrow and pain not only are bad, but are actually the worst things, and seem to regard them as even less tolerable than the Stoics did. If you say this, you must necessarily say that we should regularly step back from justice, fortitude, and every sort of honor so as to avoid pain and sorrow. What could be less acceptable in public and private life than such a point of view, urging men to desert honor and all other things, and not serve the interests of friends and parents and country lest they themselves get hurt? Would you, Epicurus, in order to escape suffering, set fire to your country and profane the sacred chambers and temples of God? . . . we cannot go through life with no experience at all of suffering. . . .[58]

For Scala's Cosimo, the opinion of Epicurus on suffering was decidedly vacuous.[59] Are we to never suffer anything, "which is impossible by nature" (*quod natura fieri non potest*)?[60] Will we allow ourselves no form

<hr>

[58] Trans. Watkins in Scala (2008) 104–105.

[59] On the role of Lucretius and Epicureanism in Quattrocento Florence, see A. Brown (2010); on mourning and humanism in the Quattrocento, see especially King (1994).

[60] The full passage reads: *Ad idque videntur perducere, ut aut nihil unquam doleamus, quod natura fieri non potest, aut postea quam dolore inceperimus, intelligentes nos in summo esse malorum omnium, nullam admittere consolationem possimus* (They seem to bring us to the conclusion either that we never suffer anything—which is impossible by nature—or that after we begin to be in pain, we understand that we are subject to the worst of all evils, and we cannot allow of any consolation, trans. Watkins in Scala (2008) 106–107).

of consolation? "For," he continues, "what sort of solace can there be for one who has convinced himself that the worst has happened, that having lost pleasure, i.e., the highest good, he thinks he has fallen into the extreme of misery?" (*Quid enim afferri solacii ei poterit qui ita sibi persuaserit accidere sibi peius nihil posse quam acciderit et, voluptate amissa, id est summo bono, extrema se in miseria collocatum putarit?*).[61] Reading Pio's commentary in the light of this passage, we may begin to see why the commentator's mournful *excursus* seem so out of Epicurean character, and so out of place. How, after all, does one reconcile the death of one's parents with the poet's insistence that we "see how very small a part, how infinitesimal a fraction of the whole universe is one sky" (*et videas caelum summai totius unum / quam sit parvula pars et quam multesima constet*, 6.650–51), and by extension one's loss? Pio's answer in the digression—like Cosimo's in Scala's dialogue—seems to be "not easily."

It is with this sense of difficulty that I want to conclude now with one final passage, this time not a digression in the formal sense but a question of philology that engages some of the larger themes we have been exploring here. The passage I have in mind comes from book 6 of the poem, where Lucretius describes yet another natural disaster: the ravages of the Athenian plague. Scholars have understood this extended passage, borrowed and adapted from Thucydides, as a test of the Epicurean lesson the poet has introduced.[62] Is it possible, Lucretius seems to ask his readers, to find pleasure in the wake of a disaster that terrorizes the world indiscriminately, devours whole communities from the inside out, and fills temples with corpses? Is it possible for the reader or, as it were, even the poet himself to maintain calm in the face of vivid descriptions of sick and decomposing bodies and the world reduced to chaos? Take, for example, these lines:

> nam quicumque suos fugitabant visere ad aegros
> vitai nimium cupidos mortisque timentis
> poenibat paulo post turpi morte malaque,
> desertos, opis expertis, incuria mactans. (*De Rerum Natura* 6.1238–41)[63]

---

[61] Trans. Watkins in Scala (2008) 106–107.

[62] See, for example, Commager (1957); Segal (1990) 234.

[63] These are lines 1239–42 in Rouse-Smith, a difference generated by the transposition of line 1245 before 1237.

For if any shirked the visitation of their own sick (*aegros*), avenging
Neglectfulness not long after would punish them for their too great greed of
life and their fear of death, by a death foul and evil, deserted and without help.

In the words of Diskin Clay, the poet here "forces his readers into close
contact with the distant Athenians," introducing a powerful affective and
moralizing dimension to the impersonal account of the plague that he
imports from Thucydides.[64] As H. S. Commager Jr. has suggested, the
poet here reverses the idea that those who help the sick catch the plague,
making the contagion a punishment for those who exhibit fear.[65] It is
Lucretius here, rather than his source, who insists upon a kind of personal eyewitnessing, who asks us to take the plague home. "On occasion,"
the poet writes, "*you* could see the bodies of parents stretched out on
their dead children, and contrariwise children yielding up their life upon
the bodies of mother and father" (*exanimis pueris super exanimate parentum* / *corpora nonnumquam posses retroque videre* / *matribus et patribus
natos super edere vitam, De Rerum Natura* 6.1256–58).[66] In the wake of so
much personal misfortune, we might ask, could Pio have failed to think
of himself or his family when he got to this disastrous end of the poem?
Are we able to put Pio or, as it were, our own misfortunes out of mind?

Pio, as it turns out, did struggle with these lines in his edition, proposing the change of one letter in one word (*aegros*, "sick ones," to *agros*,
"fields") and thereby making the moral condemnation of the people who
deserted their sick into a rebuke of those who abandoned their fields.[67]
While the commentator here insists he is emending the word on the
authority of various unnamed *antiqua exemplaria*, he was, in fact, working against both commonly received readings of the text and, as some
have said, against common sense itself.[68] The note that follows offers us
no good explanation as to why Pio would go out of his way to make the
change as he did, though it is difficult not to be reminded of the bitterness

---

[64] Clay (1983) 262.

[65] Commager (1957) 108.

[66] I am borrowing Clay's translation and emphasis here. Clay ((1983) 262) describes
these lines as part of the "heightening of affect" in the plague section of book 6.

[67] Pio (1511) 214ᵛ: *Scribo ex antiquis exemplaribus: agros non aegros.*

[68] See, for example, Wakefield (1796–97) 3: 383. Charlotte Goddard has rightly put it,
"if Pius wanted to persist with '*agros*,' then he ought to have suggested why evacuation to the
countryside was such a punishable offense" ((1991) xx).

that preceded this moment—the death of his father and teacher in the year of the plague in Bologna, the passing of his mother from a fever. Throughout the commentary, Pio himself has instructed us how to think in this way. Indeed, one of the most important effects of the commentator's digressions (as few and as random as they may seem) is that they unlock a dynamic mode of exchange between the text and the reader and lead to what we might even call a habit of thought in the commentary. If we are tempted to psychologize the philologist's choices here, to use a modern term, it is only because Pio has already invited us to see him (and ourselves) in the making of the text and in a sentimental economy of the poet's Epicurean instruction.

This moment should also remind us of Pio's insistence that the philology and philosophy are inseparable. To correct the text entails understanding what it means; understanding what it means requires taking the poet's position as one's own (if perhaps only begrudgingly). In the second edition of Pio's commentary on *De Rerum Natura* published a few years later in 1514, the French humanist Nicolas Bérault would put an interesting point on the question of sympathy for the poet. As he put it:

Qua re factum ut qui antehac ab eius scriptis ceu morosis nimium &, ut eorum ipsorum verbo utar, putidulis non aliter que ab infami aliqua ac pestilente domo abhorruerant novam hanc in Lucretium interpretationem, Lucretiumque ipsum avide nunc legant & amplectantur . . . .[69]

Therefore it happened that those who had previously recoiled from [the poet's] works as being overly gloomy and, in their own words, infected, as though from a disreputable and plague-ridden house, now eagerly read and embrace this new commentary on Lucretius and Lucretius himself. . . .

In the light of Pio's emendation above, however, one might well ask: did the commentator himself ever really "embrace" Lucretius? There is perhaps no one answer to this question—or rather Pio does not allow us one in his aloofness. If his sometimes poignant reflections on disaster and expressions of loss appear to jar with the poem's Epicurean narrative (and in the last instance with the text itself), there are other ways in which they might be said to lay bare a sympathy for the poet. As James I. Porter has

---

[69] Pio (1514) dedication.

put it: "Lucretius's unique achievement may lie in the way he reminds us of the precariousness of [the Epicurean] balance and its hard-won character."[70] One might very well say the same thing of Pio in his digressions.

In the end, it was precisely in trying to "embrace" the spirit of the poet, to borrow Bérault's word again, that Pio himself ends up posing some difficult questions about the human value of the poem and about the ethical work of reading—questions that at once glance backward to his teacher's example and forward in a way to the ironic, digressive, and deeply Epicurean engagement of Michel de Montaigne's *Essais*.[71] As Montaigne himself once famously wrote: "Anyone I regard with attention easily imprints on me something of himself" (*Qui que je regarde avec attention, m'imprime facilement quelque chose du sien*).[72] In all their peculiarity and historical specificity, Pio's personalizing digressions raise a question about what Lucretius may have "imprinted" on Pio and open an affective window onto what it might mean to inhabit Lucretius's seemingly untenable position as one's own. In this sense, the digressions lend a powerful expression to the practice of a certain mode of humanistic *imitatio* or what I am calling sympathy at its limits. When we arrive at the final moments of the plague in book 6—to Lucretius's all-too-intimate account of a disaster that is, by its nature, barely imaginable—who can say if Pio has cultivated a reading of Lucretius that exposes an underlying tension in the poem or whether the relation he develops is ultimately one of resistance or failed identification? Perhaps it is merely in making room for this ambivalence that his digressions are most meaningful.

---

[70] Porter (2003b) 225. Porter has traced Lucretius's own hesitations in the face of Epicureanism back to a more fundamental fear of the void that pervades the poem and that appears to have troubled Epicurus himself.

[71] On Montaigne's Epicurean engagement, see especially MacPhail (2000); Passannante (2009).

[72] Montaigne (1978) 875. The translation follows Frame in Montaigne (1958) 667.

4

Discourse *Ex Nihilo*: Epicurus and Lucretius in Sixteenth-Century England

Adam Rzepka

Over sixty years have passed since L. C. Martin, listing a number of strik-ing textual convergences in a brief article for the *Review of English Studies*, suggested that "Lucretius, at first or second or tenth hand, may have been among the influences which affected Shakespeare during his mainly tragic period."[1] Martin's most persuasive examples come from *King Lear* and *Measure for Measure*; both plays had their first recorded perfor-mances in 1606, and a passing reference to Lucretius has become a criti-cal commonplace for both of them. Yet the chain of English hands through which Lucretius's sweeping Epicurean poem *De Rerum Natura* passed before 1606 remains, like the constellation of ideas and strategies that is supposed to have constituted his particular influence, significantly untraced. Before the 1650s, the map of Lucretius's dissemination in England is remarkably fragmentary, riddled with documentary gaps, ambiguities between public and private discourse, thorny problems of chronology, and fundamental questions about how we might distinguish Lucretian influences from Epicurean ones. The turbulent zone of critical and historiographical uncertainty surrounding the uses of atomism in sixteenth-century England has made it consistently difficult to see those uses as discursively related in any substantive sense. Howard Jones offers a typically sweeping gloss of the problem in *The Epicurean Tradition*,

---

[1] Martin (1945) 178.

where he argues that Epicurus "plays no other role than that of a rhetorical shuttlecock" in England before the seventeenth century and has no "positive impact" until the 1640s.[2] That assessment, formulated in 1989, advances the issue of Epicurean transmission in Elizabethan England no further than Martin's "at first or second or tenth hand" in 1945; indeed, it represents an implicit rejection even of Martin's modest claims, leaving us with little more than Thomas Mayo's strict, parenthetical periodization of the issue in the title of his foundational 1934 study: *Epicurus in England (1650–1725)*.[3] More recently, scholars have incrementally rolled this threshold back to the 1630s, but the contours of an atomist discursive formation in England before the middle decades of the seventeenth century remain, perhaps permanently, sub-visible.[4] Thus, concrete instances of influence like the ones Martin lists can seem to emerge *ex nihilo*, their discursive preconditions at work, like the Lucretian atomic motions that generate apparently solid objects, "far beneath our senses" (. . . *longe nostris ab sensibus infra*).[5]

The 1650s certainly saw a crucial expansion of the range of Epicurean and (especially) Lucretian ideas in England. This was when the first known English translation of *De Rerum Natura*, by Lucy Hutchinson, was undertaken, and also when atomism first became a pervasive public factor in the development of the English sciences; it is in 1653, for example, that Francis Bacon's first sustained treatment of a Lucretius-inflected atomism sees print in the *Cogitationes De Natura Rerum*.[6] Yet even in these relatively clear instances, the scholarly commonplace that Lucretius

---

[2] Jones (1989) 156.

[3] Mayo (1934). "There is," Mayo writes, an "almost complete absence during these two centuries (1476 to 1650) of [English] books concerned with Epicurus and his followers" (xi). He also argues that, "as a rule, Englishmen who wrote, before the middle of the seventeenth century, of 'Epicureanism,' meant some form of abandoned Sensuality" (xxii). These statements of the issue are, for my purposes here, exemplary: they are both quite accurate, but only if we take whole books as the smallest discursive unit that counts and a nominal, doctrinal "Epicurean*ism*" as the criterion for the visibility of influence.

[4] Kroll (1991) uses "a starting date of 1640" for its emergence (3). Barbour (1998) treats Epicurean thought in the early Stuart period, though this turns out to mean a working threshold of the 1630s. Even then, Barbour writes, English readers "lacked a systematic understanding of the relations between Democritus, Epicurus, and Lucretius so that their notions of the atomist, hedonist, or 'epicure' were tendentious and misinformed. . . " (23).

[5] Lucretius *De Rerum Natura* 2.312.

[6] On atomism and Bacon's *Cogitationes De Natura Rerum*, see Schuler (1992).

arrives in England in the mid-seventeenth century must contend with a set of curious lags, historical disparities through which that arrival keeps slipping backward in time. Hutchinson composes her translation in response to what has already been, she writes, "so much discourse" on Epicurean atomism, and the extent and chronology of this discourse remains largely unexplored.[7] Bacon's published assessment of atomism gestures backward as well: *Cogitationes De Natura Rerum* was written not in the 1650s but in 1604, before the increasing disillusionment with regard to ancient atomism that Bacon expresses in his 1620 *Novum Organum*.[8]

These chronological cross-currents already present serious challenges to the coherence of the mid-century threshold identified by Mayo and Jones, but this is only a prelude to greater complexity and ambiguity earlier in the same story. As we work back toward the start of the seventeenth century, further from the critical mass of Epicurean engagements in the 1650s, we begin to encounter an atomist discourse that is increasingly scattered in its enunciations and increasingly tangled in its networks of transmission. John Donne describes a fallen world "crumbled out again to his Atomies" in his "First Anniversary" in 1610. The Epicurean premise that "nothing can come of nothing" appears, as Martin reminds us, in *Lear* in 1605; and we find a personal existence composed of "many a thousand grains / That issue out of dust" in *Measure for Measure* in the same year.[9] Perhaps, then, we should shift our chronology and say, with Martin, that atomism "hardly affects Elizabethan literature before *1600*" rather than fifty years later.[10] But then what are we to make of Queen Mab's "team of little atomi" in *Romeo and Juliet* in 1595?[11] What of

---

[7] L. Hutchinson (1996).

[8] In the *Cogitationes*, Bacon writes that the theory of atoms "is either true or useful for demonstration, for it is not easy either to grasp in thought or to express in words the genuine subtlety of nature, such as it is found in things, without supposing an atom" (Jones (1989) 193). Despite the opening hedge, this is a much more positive position on atomism than the one Bacon arrives at by 1620. In the *Novum Organum*, he rejects both the "hypothesis of a vacuum and that of the unchangeableness of matter" as "both false assumptions" (Jardine and Silverthorne (2000) book 2, aphorism 8).

[9] Donne (2006). Shakespeare (2002): *King Lear* 1.1.79; *Measure for Measure* 3.1.20–21. Within this edition, citations of *King Lear* refer to the 1608 Quarto text, *The History of King Lear*.

[10] Martin (1945) 176.

[11] Shakespeare (2002) *Romeo and Juliet* 1.4.57.

Donne's library, which contained books that suggest a longer acquaintance with natural philosophy in general and Epicurean materialism in particular? Donne also had close connections to the circle of Henry Percy, Earl of Northumberland, whose coterie of atomist-inspired philosophers and poets cohered in the late 1580s and is currently at the center of a nascent movement to relocate the emergence of English science to a significantly earlier, pre-Baconian period.[12] Northumberland, in turn, was a close friend of Sir Walter Raleigh, a fellow freethinker and mathematician and a dedicatee of Spenser's *The Faerie Queene*, which contains a loose translation of Lucretius's invocation to Venus.[13]

This slippery atomist lineage, with its cryptic, multivalent poetics and shadowy circles of transmission, can quickly come to seem conspiratorial or occult. Indeed, studies of Raleigh's alleged "School of Night" undertaken by M. C. Bradbrook and Francis Yates in the 1930s have something of this dark and tenuous feel, as if the critical studies have absorbed some of the hermeticism explored by their subjects. I would like, however, to suggest a different model for the unsettled, patchy textual history of Epicurus and Lucretius in the period, and for its uncanny effects on contemporary historiography: a Lucretian poetics of reception and dissemination. What is perhaps most remarkable about the afterlife of *De Rerum Natura* is the way that the poem's dynamic treatment of atomism and mutability seems to generate heterodoxy and turbulence in the history of its own reception—a turbulence that still conditions contemporary efforts to articulate its importance for early English humanism. In what follows, I will set out some of the theoretical groundwork for such an approach, then briefly consider two exemplary cases: Erasmus's 1545 dialogue "The Epicure" and Spenser's *The Faerie Queene*. My aim is both to call attention to a still-neglected problem in Renaissance intellectual history and to show how that problem might inflect our account of the way intellectual histories should be mapped.

The notion that *De Rerum Natura* provides a model for the poetics of its own subsequent transmission is neither as tautological nor as new as

---

[12] On Donne's library and his connections to the Northumberland circle, see Hirsch (1991) 72. On the growing sense that the Northumberland circle in general and Thomas Hariot in particular were involved in an early, insufficiently acknowledged advance in the development of the sciences in England, see Fox (2000), and especially Clucas (2000) in that volume.

[13] Harrison (1930) 15.

it might seem: both Michel Serres and Jaques Lezra have offered subtle and compelling bases for this argument, rooted in both cases in Lucretius's own Epicurean treatments of chance, causality, poetics, and translation. Serres, in *The Birth of Physics* and elsewhere, calls attention to the analogy that Lucretius repeatedly sets up between atoms in objects and letters in literature: "the same letters," Lucretius writes in book 2,

> . . . eadem caelum mare terras flumina solem
> significant, eadem fruges arbusta animantis;
> si non omnia sunt, at multo maxima pars est
> consimilis; verum positura discrepitant res.
> sic ipsis in rebus item iam materiai
> concursus motus ordo positura figurae
> cum permutantur, mutari res quoque debent. (*De Rerum Natura* 2.1013–22)

denote sky, sea, earth, rivers, sun, the same denote crops, trees, and animals. If they are not all alike, yet by far the most part are so; but position marks the difference in what results. So also when we turn to real things: when the combinations of matter, when its motions, order, position, shapes are changed, the thing also must be changed.[14]

This principle of recombinatory meaning, supported elsewhere in Lucretius by the applicability of the Latin *elementa* to both physical elements and the letters of the alphabet, leads Serres toward a conditional model of discourse that echoes the concept of the "statement" developed by Foucault in *The Archeology of Knowledge*. "We can say, without too much error," Serres writes, "that for linguistic atoms, as well as for the letters of matter, a given element placed here or located in such and such a vicinity is not the same as the same element elsewhere and in a different context or structure."[15] Unlike Foucault, however, Serres is interested in

---

[14] As Schuler points out, the Lucretian analogy between atoms and letters is a recurring theme in Bacon's treatments of atomism. In the *Cogitationes*, Bacon writes that, "Surely as the words or terms of all languages, in an immense variety, are composed of a few simple letters, so all the actions and powers of things are formed by a few natures and original elements of simple motions. And it were shame that men should have examined so carefully the tinklings of their own voice, and should yet be so ignorant of the voice of nature; and as in the early ages (before letters were invented), should discern only compound sounds and words, not distinguishing the elements and letters" (Schuler (1992) 36).

[15] Serres (2000) 141.

modeling discourse on the kind of fluid turbulence of which he finds Lucretius to be the pioneering expositor. Tropes, he argues, emerge in discourse the way that Lucretius's famous *clinamen* or "swerve" emerges in the straight, laminar flow of atoms through the void: "at no fixed place and at no fixed time" (*nec regione loci certa nec tempore certo*).[16] Sense is always already a slight deviation from sense, a declination from a previous trajectory of meaning; identifiable discourses grow from these sudden swerves of sense as eddies appear in a stream—they are turbulences whose static form is only an emergent effect of a underlying recursive motion. The resulting picture of discursive time is one in which semiotic births, deaths, and rebirths are distributed stochastically, with their constitutive conditions persistently elsewhere and thus never fully resolvable. The "trope" as a fundamental unit of discourse regains, on this model, much of its etymological sense: *tropos*, "turn."

Such an account seems particularly germane to flows of texts and ideas in the Renaissance, both because that period so often constitutes the limit-point past which intellectual historiography must contend with irreducible uncertainties of time and place, and because the Renaissance is self-fashioned as a *rebirth*, an origin with a past, a set of events that are always doubled elsewhere. Here we approach Lezra's concerns in *Unspeakable Subjects: The Genealogy of the Event in Early Modern Europe*. Lezra reminds us of the importance of Lucretius's *clinamen* for Renaissance humanism, which adopted and developed the Epicurean alignment of this uncaused change with the possibility of free will. But Lezra also suggests that the return of Lucretius made the problem of the event newly visible through "the return, in a different sphere, of classical debates between and within Cynic and Epicurean dogmas concerning *tyche* (chance *as well as* destiny), in the form of a profound change in the sense of *events as such*."[17]

It is not simply the singularities of freely willed actions that generate indeterminacy in the orderly progression of things. The Lucretian swerve introduces an irreducible contingency into the world at large, not only through the first *momen mutatum* of originary matter but through atomic movement generally: minimal bodies, Lucretius tells us, are "*apt* to incline," lending an even richer indeterminacy to a causal field that

---

[16] Lucretius *De Rerum Natura* 2.293.
[17] Lezra (1997) 3.

is already in endless motion "far beneath our senses."[18] Lezra argues that the Renaissance rediscovery of this notion of *eventum* ("accident") not just as non-essentiality but also as temporal contingency radically challenges our own writing of Renaissance intellectual history: debates over how to define and periodize the Renaissance "quickly show themselves to be debates about what characteristics or attributes are definitionally proper or accidental (*eventa*) to a thing or a term, in this case the 'Renaissance' or 'early modern period.'"[19] Tracing the impact of Lucretius on the early modern sense of events, Lezra suggests, encourages us to keep open the question of how that sense of events still conditions our own understanding of origins, thresholds, and transformations. Discursive historiography, for Lezra as for Serres, can no longer be a matter simply of tracing steadily branching causal lines from usage to usage

---

[18] The reading of this passage as entailing an extension of the *clinamen* (or its ongoing possibility) to atomic motion generally is controversial. For an opposing view, see Long (2006) 157–77.

[19] Lezra (1997) 4. The precise meaning of *eventum* in Lucretius is subject to some ambiguity, particularly in its relationship to Epicurean and Aristotelian terminology; my (and Lezra's) sense of it here may require some further explanation. Lucretius defines *eventa* as "all . . . which may come and go as the nature of things remains intact"—"slavery," for instance, or "poverty" (Lucretius *De Rerum Natura* 1.455–58). These are distinguished from *coniuncta*, which W. H. D. Rouse and others have translated as "properties"—those qualities "which without destructive dissolution can never be separated or disjoined, as weight is to stone, heat to fire . . . " (1.450–55). The prevailing interpretation of this passage finds *eventa* to be cognate with Epicurus's *sumptōmata* ("symptoms"), designating accidental attributes that are neither essential to a thing nor even necessary to its existence; *coniuncta*, on this reading, map onto Epicurus's *sumbebekota*, "accidents," which may nonetheless be necessary properties; see, for example, Krämer (1971) 92–93. Smith's note to lines 449–50 of book 1 glosses this reading, although Rouse translates *eventa* as "accidents" rather than "symptoms." Yet neither *coniuncta* nor *eventa* are obvious choices for a literal Latin rendering of *sumbebekota* and *sumptōmata*, and both can be read as motivated translations. The choice of *coniuncta* in the passage cited above, for instance, enables a curious but effective slippage: heat is inseparably "conjoined" to fire, but heat is not essential to fire in an absolute, Aristotelian sense because the essence of fire is only a particular conjunction of void and minimal bodies—even the most inseparable *coniuncta* of things and properties are accidents of these more fundamental, literal *coniuncta*. The translation thus pushes us away from a static, categorical understanding of accident and substance and toward an apprehension of the active, processual arising of all things in time. Given this reading, we cannot say that *eventum* simply designates non-substantiality, since *coniuncta* are also non-substantial except in their absolute reducibility to bodies and void. Rather, *eventum*, which can also mean "result" or "outcome," magnifies and extends both the temporality and the fundamental contingency already present in *coniuncta*. In this sense, both "accident" and "event" in their common contemporary usages have strong and legitimate resonances with Lucretius's *eventum*.

through the smooth medium of historical time. Instead, historical time must be seen as immanent to the turbulent material transformations it appears to regulate: "Time . . . exists not in itself," Lucretius writes in book 1, "nor may we admit that anyone has a sense of time by itself separated from the movement of things. . . ."[20] Taking up this shift of focus from static events *in* time to mobile events *as* time can help us do justice to what Lezra, borrowing a phrase from Jaques in Shakespeare's *As You Like It*, calls "strange eventful histor[ies]."[21]

It will be helpful to begin my sketch of the strange, eventful history of Epicurean influence in sixteenth-century England by recalling that, by the early years of that century, Lucretius had already been the subject of a thorough disappearance, an unlikely reappearance, a significant dissemination, and at least one famous re-disappearance. Having been all but lost for centuries, the *De Rerum Natura* returns first through the fortuitous event of Poggio Bracciolini's discovery of a single manuscript in a monastery in 1417; that manuscript is, in turn, now lost, as is the name and location of the monastery. Indeed, Poggio's find itself seems to have been nearly lost again almost immediately: little is made of it until the 1470s, when the first printed edition of Lucretius appears in Venice. After this second rediscovery, there is a modest flourishing of printings and commentaries in Italy and France, culminating in Lambinus's influential Paris edition of 1564. In the late 1400s, we can begin to trace Lucretius's importance for Neoplatonists like Marsilio Ficino and, almost a century later, Giordano Bruno.[22]

Just as the turbulences of Lucretius's rediscovery begin to resolve into what looks like a shaped intellectual lineage, however, that lineage becomes subject to reversals, dissociations, and new descents beneath the threshold of historiographical resolution. Ficino's famous decision to burn his early essays on the *De Rerum Natura* (the re-disappearance mentioned above) in recognition of its impiety already constitutes, for intellectual historians like Ernst Cassirer and Lezra, the crucial appearance of a new turn *away* from Epicurean ideas and back toward a

[20] Lucretius *De Rerum Natura* 1.459–63.

[21] *As You Like It* 2.7.164.

[22] Kraye (1998) offers a precise and erudite synopsis of receptions of Lucretius in France and Italy in the fifteenth and sixteenth centuries. See also Jones (1989) 142–65 ("The Humanist Debate") and D. C. Allen's studies of "Three Italian Atheists" and "Three French Atheists" (Allen (1964)).

reactionary Christian worldview.[23] Elsewhere, uses of Lucretius's poem are marked if not by consignation to the fire then by violent but unstable bifurcations of its constitutive elements. Early editions of the poem were regularly given prefaces that rejected its Epicurean tenets while embracing its Lucretian poetics, thus introducing a highly artificial, precarious distinction between content and form. Aldus Manutius provides an exemplary instance of this tactic in the preface to his 1500 edition of *De Rerum Natura*, where he warns readers against belief in Epicurean philosophy but praises Lucretius for rendering that philosophy into verse. Lambinus continued this practice of "steriliz[ing]" the poem, to use D. C. Allen's term, writing to Charles IX that its philosophy is a threat to religion but its verse "illuminated by the light of genius."[24]

In England, on the other hand, distinctions between Lucretius and Epicurus are virtually unknown in much of the sixteenth century because Epicureanism in general is most visible as the object of sweeping, virulent accusations of intellectual lassitude, sensual decadence, and outrageous heresy. Polemicists could and did attack alleged "Epicures" for the absurdity of a world made of "swarmes of atomies," for the denial of an afterlife, for the assertion of the materiality of the soul, for the importation of degenerative foreign ideas, and, most often, for an emphasis on physical pleasure.[25] This last line of attack was aided by the legend, available in Jerome, that Lucretius composed his Epicurean poem in between bouts of lustful insanity that eventually drove him to suicide.[26] In these early attacks, a new set of dissociations occurs: precisely because there are so many heretical targets available, anti-Epicurean polemic in England has a viral effect, invading and dissolving understandings of "Epicureanism" that, on the Continent, were just beginning to cohere around the central binaries mentioned above. These two sets of dissociations—between Epicurean philosophy and Lucretian poetics and between multiple, overlapping aspects of the heretical Hydra of "Epicureanism"—are foundationally confounding factors for any attempt to construct a contiguous, arboreal picture of how Lucretius traveled through Renaissance Europe. In early modern France and Italy, Lucretius emerges under the

[23] Cassirer (1972) 62–63; Lezra (1997) 3.
[24] Allen (1964) 171.
[25] Mayo (1934) xxii–xxiv.
[26] Rouse-Smith (1992) xviii–xxii.

sign of his severance from the absolutely pervasive matter of his poem; in England, he emerges as an Epicurus seen in heterogeneous denunciations. What we are left with, in the latter case, is a discursive formation defined almost entirely in the negative—a kind of Epicurean strange attractor whose shape we can estimate only by its effects.[27]

Given the range of assaults on "Epicureanism" in English polemics in the 1530s and 1540s, it is remarkable how abbreviated and vitriolic they tend to be. Jones is able to argue that Epicurus and Lucretius are essentially absent from English discourse in these years because he is searching for straightforward, sympathetic philosophical assessments, and if this is indeed our aim, we are bound to come up empty. But part of my argument is that a Lucretian poetics of discursive history teaches us how to reread Lucretius's own reception: in this case, for instance, there is evidence to suggest that what Jones dismisses as purely polemical can be understood more precisely as the surface effect of a more complex, manifold circulation of tropes that had not yet cohered as public discourse.

This possibility is clearest in the 1545 English translation of Erasmus of Rotterdam's 1519 dialogue *The Epicure*. Erasmus's argument takes the form of a dialogue between two friends, Spudeus and Hedonius, about the relative merits of the various ancient schools that deal with "the endes of goodnes."[28] The dialogue and its translation are remarkable in their placement of a positive assessment of Epicurus at the center of mid-sixteenth-century humanism as it was available to English readers. Yet this assessment is conditioned throughout by a complex irony of assertion and disavowal typical of humanism in the period.[29] Spudeus opens by expressing a respectable, reserved confusion: he holds in his hand a Ciceronian dialogue and is trying to decide whether the Stoics or the Peripatetics have "erred the lest." In reply, Hedonius sets up what most readers would immediately have recognized as some version of a familiar

---

[27] Elton (1998) performs something like this negative argument for the prevalence of Epicurean skepticism in the sixteenth century, but the specific place of Epicurean thought within his much broader concern with "evidence of Elizabethan disbelief in a just providence" (which extends, for instance, to receptions of Aristotle) is never entirely clear (22).

[28] Erasmus (1545) B4.

[29] One of the most intricate instances of this kind of ironic play infuses and surrounds Thomas More's *Utopia*, published only a few years before "The Epicure" first saw print. As D. C. Allen points out, *Utopia* also contains a theory of "natural pleasure" that closely follows Erasmus's dialogue (Allen (1944) 11).

straw man, ready to be knocked down in defense of all that is holy and true: "Yet I like none of their opinions," Hedonius says, "so well as I do the Epicures." Spudeus, indignant, quickly counters as we might expect: "Amongst all the sects, the Epicure's judgment is most reproved and condemned *with the whole consent and arbitrement of all men*" (my emphasis). Spudeus goes on to reiterate the popular charge that Epicurus's emphasis on pleasure and the senses means that he erases distinctions between men and animals: "Yea, but all men wonder and cry out on [Epicureanism], and say: it is the voice of a brute beast, and not of man."[30] But this easy rehearsal of the most damning commonplace rejections of "Epicures" is, of course, a set-up: the rest of the dialogue is devoted to a defense of Epicureanism on the grounds that it advocates only pleasure that does not bring greater pain and that therefore "no men be more righter Epicures, than Christian men living reverently towards God and man."[31] Jones is right in identifying this as something far short of an explication of the Epicurean worldview, but by neatly boxing up the dialogue as a clever, empty riposte to Luther's indictment of Erasmus as an Epicurean, he glosses over the layered reversals of Erasmus's intervention.

The moment in which it becomes clear that the dialogue is to be a *defense* of Epicureanism and not simply a screed against it must have been a novel one for English readers in the 1540s, and the force of that novelty itself, coming from one of the most respected and influential humanists in Europe, should not be overlooked. It is also important, however, that Epicurus can make the sudden transition from passing pejorative to substantial dialogue here only by being provocatively disguised as a proto-Christian thinker. The emptying out of Epicurean philosophy in the service of its reconciliation with Christian faith in Erasmus's argument is too transparent, too easy, to be anything but a crafted stratagem that uses the apparent subsumption of Epicureanism in Christianity to open the door to a philosophy that the period rarely hesitated to condemn as "atheism." The dialogue form functions perfectly to call attention to this provocative transparency: since Hedonius's argument succeeds

---

[30] Erasmus (1545) B6. Petrarch seems to have crystallized this ancient line of attack for the Renaissance: *quid enim homini miserius quam humanum bonum bono pecudis, hoc est rationem sensibus, substravisse?* (Rossi and Bosco (1933) 1: 115).

[31] Erasmus (1545) B7.

simply by repeatedly positing the rewards of Christianity as the highest form of pleasure, every exchange between Hedonius and Spudeus has the counterintuitive feel of an interrogation of Spudeus's commitment to Christian truth rather than a Christian interrogation of Epicurean pleasure-seeking. The Epicure argues for greater blind faith in salvation, while the anti-Epicure is put in the uncomfortable position of suggesting that the Christian ideal of "fasting, bewail[ing], and lament[ing]" is linked to pleasure of any kind only by a route that is impossible to trace—in short, that it is, on any kind of human scale, "farthest from all pleasures."[32] This inversion, in which Erasmus constructs an almost unrecognizably Christian Epicurus, results in an emptying-out of *both* Epicureanism and Christian belief and a clearing of the ground for a more substantial examination of both.

Such a project is surely more elaborate than the briefer, primarily polemical uses of Epicurus as a "rhetorical shuttlecock," yet it is precisely because Erasmus's dialogue is most immediately legible as merely an erudite move in that game that he manages to put its rules in question. Epicurus's arrival in print in mid-sixteenth-century England, then, is an entrance in double or triple layers of discursive camouflage that continue, even now, to make that arrival all but invisible. The event is all the more difficult to put in sharp focus because we are dealing with a translation made more than two decades after the Latin original and with a degree of declination from it that has not been precisely measured.[33] If new attention to *The Epicure* may challenge Jones's sense that Epicurean discourse actually arrives (at least) a century later, in a much more stable form and, as it were, *ex nihilo*, this challenge is made possible only by the kind of acknowledgement of discursive turbulence suggested by a Lucretian poetics of transmission.

Equally complex issues attend the abrupt and similarly deemphasized appearance of a specifically Lucretian Epicurus in English letters, when Spenser translates and reworks the first twenty-three lines of the *De Rerum Natura*—the opening invocation to Venus—in book 4 of *The*

---

[32] Ibid.

[33] Philip Gerrard, the translator of this edition, notes at the end of his preface that he "do[es] not folow [the] latin, word for word," but sometimes "omits it of a certain set purpose" (Erasmus (1545) B3). Despite this oblique disclaimer, Gerrard produces what Craig R. Thompson describes as "for the most part a fairly close, indeed often literal rendering of Erasmus's Latin" (Thompson (1971) 375).

Faerie Queene. This part of the poem was composed in the early 1590s, but it is preceded by another strongly Lucretian passage: the first half of the poem, composed in the 1580s, contains a description of Venus's "Garden of Adonis" that seems to follow closely Lucretius's account of degeneration and regeneration in books 1 and 2 of the *De Rerum Natura*. The relation of the early Garden episode to Lucretius's poem was the subject of intense debate in the 1920s and 1930s, with Edwin Greenlaw developing the catalogue of similarities in a 1920 article on "Spenser and Lucretius" and other critics vehemently resisting his suggestions. Greenlaw focused on four stanzas in Spenser's account of the Garden that describe the endless transformation and fundamental conservation of matter. The third of these stanzas reads:

> All things from [*Chaos*] doe their first being fetch,
> And borrow matter, whereof they are made,
> Which when as forme and feature it does ketch,
> Becomes a bodie, and doth then invade
> The state of life, out of the griefly shade.
> That substance is eterne, and bideth so,
> Ne when the life decayes, and forme does fade,
> Doth it consume, and into nothing go,
> But chaunged is, and often altered to and fro.[34]

In its exposition of the indestructible nature of matter and its endless, recombinatory cycling between sentient form and formless death, this is an excellent synopsis of one of Lucretius's distinct and central themes, addressed, for instance, late in book 2:

> nec sic interemit mors res ut materiai
> corpora conficiat, sed coetum dissupat ollis;
> inde aliis aliud coniungit, et efficit omnes
> res ita convertant formas mutentque colores
> et capiant sensus et puncto tempore reddant. (*De Rerum Natura* 2.1002–1006)

Nor does death so destroy things as to annihilate the bodies of matter, but it disperses their combination abroad; then it conjoins others with

---

[34] Spenser (1596) 488 (3.35–37).

others, and brings it about that thus all things alter their shapes and change their colours and receive sensation and in a moment of time yield it up again. . . .

Despite this close weave, however, and despite the obvious translation of Lucretius's invocation to Venus in the following book of *The Faerie Queene*, the critical reaction to Greenlaw's alignment of Spenser and Lucretius in the Garden of Adonis episode was to attack it in order to preserve Spenser from the specter of a base materialism. For Brints Sterling, Ronald Levinson, and other Spenserians at the time, proving the absence of any real commitment to Lucretian precepts in any part of Spenser's poem took the form of a rescue mission with strong religious and nationalist overtones. Levinson saw himself as "saving" a fundamentally "spiritualistic," Neoplatonist Spenser from "a charge of inconsistency too gross even for poetic license to condone," a charge that "he is guilty of what at best must be called an appalling incongruity."[35] It is almost as if Spenser stands accused of a heresy that must be explained away as wholly congruent with the true faith. In Sterling's view, Greenlaw's observations put Spenser in mortal danger of being reduced to "a catalogue of fallacies"; he must be rescued from shipwreck on "the shores of simple Lucretian materialism and . . . returned to native English shores."[36] These responses are remarkable in echoing of some of the same widespread rejections of Epicurus and Lucretius that Spenser must have purposely put aside in writing his Lucretian passages. Roger Ascham's 1570 pedagogical treatise *The Schoolemaster*, for instance, offers the typical lament that Epicureanism is a "develish opinion out of Italie" and that it has resulted in "Englishe men Italianated."[37] The initial attempt to establish a resolvable Lucretian influence in sixteenth-century English literature, then, resulted less in a major rediscovery of that influence than in a reproduction of some of its initial conditions of turbulence and obscuration.[38]

[35] Levinson (1928) 676–77.

[36] Stirling (1934) 501.

[37] Ascham (1570) 28.

[38] Traces of this heritage still turn up in even the most judicious and thorough readers of *The Faerie Queene*. In *Spenser's Supreme Fiction*, his magisterial 2001 study of the intellectual backgrounds of the poem, Jon Quitslund allows that Lucretius was "probably on Spenser's mind" while he was writing the Garden episode, and that Bruno's Lucretian ideas concerning motion and change "stimulated and provoked" Spenser, albeit "in ways we cannot hope to recover" (187, 290). Yet there is a lingering sense that Spenser is in

The objections to Greenlaw's work have a further uncanny effect in that their attempts to de-Lucretianize Spenser through an insistence on his poem's conceptual coherence and stability target passages concerned precisely with chaotic multiplicity and impermanence. Read in the context of this debate, Spenser's account of the cycle of dissolution and resolution in the Garden of Adonis passages suggests a reflexive *poetics* of mutability, in which the claim that "formes are variable and decay, / by course of kind, and by occasion" functions in direct resistance to the notion that poetic language can be fully mapped by the lineaments of any philosophical system, let alone one rooted in Neoplatonic "formes." Such a poetics of mutability is important to Lucretius, who, as we have seen, describes the endless recombinations of atoms by analogy with the literary elements of that very description. In fact, the lines from Lucretius quoted above as one of the closest parallels to Spenser's stanza on matter "altered to and fro" lead, only eight lines later, to the first analogy between atomic and linguistic recombination:

> quin etiam refert nostris in versibus ipsis
> cum quibus et quali sint ordine quaeque locata;
> namque eadem caelum mare terras flumina solem
> significant. . . . (*De Rerum Natura* 2.1013–16)

> Moreover, it is important in my own verses
> with what and in what order the various elements are
> placed. For the same letters denote sky, sea, earth, rivers,
> sun. . . .

The notion of poetic form as a recombinatory epiphenomenon gains additional resonance when we consider Spenser's more direct renewal of Lucretian language in his treatment of the invocation to Venus. Here, in translation, Spenser's poetic project is animated throughout by the declinations and recursions that emerge from the reappearance of the same elements in new states of "motion, order, position, [and] shape."

---

danger of being polluted by these associations: "a committed Spenserian cannot read Bruno without some queasiness" at the proximity of Spenser's "plenitude" to Bruno's "excess"; the relationship is, somehow, "mostly ironic" (290). This language is all the more remarkable considering Quitslund's praise of increasing interest in the more "esoteric" Florentine mode of Neoplatonism as an important influence in Spenser, which he explicitly opposes to Stirling (Quitslund 120–21).

I will present the opening of the original text and the corresponding two stanzas of Spenser's loose translation:

> Aeneadum genetrix, hominum divomque voluptas,
> alma Venus, caeli subter labentia signa
> quae mare navigerum, quae terras frugiferentis
> concelebras, per te quoniam genus omne animantum
> concipitur visitque exortum lumina solis:
> te, dea, te fugiunt venti, te nubila caeli
> adventumque tuum, tibi suavis daedala tellus
> summittit flores, tibi rident aequora ponti
> placatumque nitet diffuso lumine caelum.
> nam simul ac species patefactast verna diei
> et reserata viget genitabilis aura fauoni,
> aeriae primum volucres te, diva, tuumque
> significant initum perculsae corda tua vi. (*De Rerum Natura* 1.1–13)

> Great *Venus*, Queene of beautie and of grace,
> The ioy of Gods and men, that vnder skie
> Doest fayrest shine, and most adorne thy place,
> That with thy smyling looke doest pacifie
> The raging seas, and makst the stormes to flie;
> Thee goddesse, thee the winds, the clouds doe feare,
> And when thou spredst thy mantle forth on hie,
> The waters play and pleasant lands appeare,
> And heauens laugh, & all the world shews ioyous cheare.

> Then doth the dædale earth throw forth to thee
> Out of her fruitfull lap aboundant flowres,
> And then all liuing wights, soone as they see
> The spring breake forth out of his lusty bowres,
> They all doe learne to play the Paramours;
> First doe the merry birds, thy prety pages
> Priuily pricked with thy lustfull powres,
> Chirpe loud to thee out of their leauy cages,
> And thee their mother call to coole their kindly rages.
> (4.10.44–45)

Anthony Esolen, in one of the first relatively sustained engagements with Spenser's uses of Lucretius since what he calls the "small war" sparked by Greenlaw some seventy years earlier, has provided an initial look at Spenser's translation practice here.[39] He argues convincingly that "at virtually every opportunity Spenser overgoes Lucretius in celebrating the wildness of love's power": *mare navigerum*, the "ship-bearing sea," becomes "the raging seas"; the west wind *reserata* ("set free") in Lucretius "breake[s] forth out of his lusty bowres" in Spenser.[40] For our purposes here, this amplification represents a provocative inversion of the most popular sixteenth-century indictment of Epicurus and Lucretius, transforming the "lustiness" of a poet thought to have composed his masterwork in between fits of erotic insanity from a principle of condemnation into a principle of natural generation and poetic inspiration. The poetry of turbulent mutability is the matter and the method of the translation; its purpose is to animate and reanimate, eddying into form what has fallen back into a formless dormancy.

In this sense, what is most striking about Spenser's translation is its unprecedented *fidelity* to Lucretius, not through precise reproduction but through what Walter Benjamin, in "The Task of the Translator," described as the translator's "special mission of watching over the maturing process of the original language and the birth pangs of [his] own."[41] For Benjamin, this doubled fidelity positions translation as a rebirth, a renaissance in which "the original can only be raised . . . anew and at other points in time."[42] This describes both Spenser's uses of Lucretius and his larger project in *The Faerie Queene* quite precisely. Those uses do not shipwreck the poem on the rocks of un-English "fallacies," as Sterling feared, but neither do they return it to "native English shores." A translated Lucretius contributes instead to Spenser's efforts to fashion a vitally new English language in a *remade past*. Thus, a hymn to perpetual renewal becomes the occasion for Spenser's closest adherence to a classical source. As in the rest of *The Faerie Queene*, the hymn to Venus develops a vocabulary that sounded elaborately archaic even in Spenser's time, a vocabulary through which he hoped to retroactively remake the English language.

---

[39] As Quitslund (2001) argues, the antiquated line of defense mounted against Greenlaw and Lucretian influences in Spenser has continued to have significant effects in the field for almost seventy years. Further, as Ramachandran (2006) has observed, "the tricky question of how an ardent Neoplatonic poet could draw on Lucretius remains to be addressed." Esolen (1994) is an important exception to this assessment.

[40] Esolen (1994) 38–44.

[41] Benjamin (1968) 73.

[42] Ibid., 75.

To take the clearest example from the passage above, the earth is described as "daedale," a word so nearly unchanged from Lucretius's Latin that Esolen sets it aside as a particular exception to his case for Spenser's departures from the original. This term, a new coinage in English by virtue of its closeness to the ancient original, invokes the ingenious Daedalus in order to evoke a fertility of invention both wholly archaic and wholly modern.[43]

There is no clear trace of how Spenser came by the *De Rerum Natura* to accompany the certainty that he read and engaged it—we have only the trenchant performance of the poetics of translation and transmission discussed above. The Lucretian paths connecting Spenser to Shakespeare, on the other hand, are marked with intriguing traces, but they wind through a historiographical thicket that few critics since Bradbrook, in the 1930s, have been willing to navigate with any confidence.[44] First, we are pointed along from Spenser to Raleigh, the influential patron to whom Spenser presented his epic poem. Raleigh's circle was clearly involved in the kind of provocative balancing of natural philosophy and scripture for which, I have suggested, Erasmus's *Epicure* helped lay the humanist groundwork. The circle's "master" in these pursuits seems to have been Thomas Hariot, whose extraordinary work in optics and mathematics depended significantly on a thoroughgoing atomism. This "school," headed by Spenser's agnostic patron and taught by a dedicated atomist, included Christopher Marlowe, who dominated the London theater when Shakespeare entered it. It also included Lord Strange, the patron of the acting troupe known as Strange's Men, where Shakespeare very likely began his career as an actor and playwright. Shakespeare's *Love's Labor's Lost*, first performed in 1594 at the height of Raleigh's notoriety, appears to be a pointed satire on Raleigh's school; in the play, Shakespeare coins the name Bradbrook uses for Ralegh's circle: the "School of Night."

What is remarkable about this nest of patronage, philosophy, poetry, and theater in the 1590s is the way it projects a holographic but irresistible picture of Epicurean and Lucretian influence without ever

---

[43] For an extensive treatment of the term in Lucretius, see Holmes (2005).

[44] For the connections I sketch here, see Bradbrook (1936); G. B. Harrison's introductory essays to *Advice to His Son* (Harrison (1930)) and *Willobie his Avisa* (Harrison (1966)); Kargon (1966); and Shirley (1983).

giving that picture a comprehensive and solid form. Early modern scholarship keeps its distance from "School of Night" theorists, even as a
Lucretian influence in Shakespeare remains a casual commonplace in
companions to *Measure for Measure* and *King Lear*. The consequences of
this ambivalence for scholarship on *King Lear* are especially strange.
Jonathan Crewe, for instance, acknowledges without further comment
what he calls the "thoroughgoing Lucretianism" of the play, but in the
next sentence writes off the story of an actual Lucretian field of influence
as a myth "at home among other great, mind-blowing humanist fables"[45]
The difficulty with this formulation is not so much that it acknowledges
an intellectual history that is both clearly manifest and in some sense
fabulist—as I have been arguing, Lucretian histories of transmission
may only ever fully cohere in an epiphenomenal or virtual form. The
problem, rather, is that the ambiguity reflected in Crewe's assessment has
so far discouraged nascent readings of a Lucretian *Lear* from moving
beyond the play's engagement with atheism and with the concept of
"nothing," of void. This is indeed a helpful reference point, but it is only
one element in the elaborate interplay of Lucretian themes that *Lear*
develops as the culmination of Shakespeare's ongoing interest in atomism, degeneration, mutability, and suffering in the face of disinterested
gods. Until we can develop a suitably mobile and complex account
of discursive fluidity, *Lear* criticism that mentions Lucretius may only
underline again and again the lesson it has not yet learned from him:
"nothing comes of nothing."

There are a number of ways in which Epicurean materialism, particularly in Lucretius's imbrication of its arguments in a poetics of emergent
form, provides the seeds for an approach to reception histories that have
tended to remain "beneath the senses" of intellectual historiography.
First, it urges us to foreground the imperfect and epiphenomenal character of discursive formations, such that thresholds for what counts as the
cohesion of a given discourse take more careful account of the traces of
its processual emergence. The aim here is to begin to stake out some
of the middle ground between, for instance, Jones's acknowledgement
of the scattered uses of Epicurus in early-sixteenth-century England
and his sense that none of these uses are significant, or between Crewe's

[45] Crewe (1991) 264.

acknowledgement of the "thoroughgoing Lucretianism" of *Lear* and his sense that Lucretian influence in the play is part of a "fable." Second, a Lucretian poetics of reception demands attention to the complex recursive effects that condition discursive emergence, as the work of both Serres and Lezra suggests. If treatments of Epicurus and Lucretius in the Renaissance often involve the lag-times and retroactive contextualizations of renunciation (as in Ficino's burnt commentary), translation (as in Erasmus's dialogue), and delayed publication (as in Bacon's work on atomism), then Lucretius himself can help us model those effects. At issue here as well are the temporal doublings and reversals produced by the recombination of tropological *elementa* into forms that signify anew: Spenser's poetics of generative mutability in the Garden of Adonis episode and in the invocation to Venus, as we have seen, presents us with both the clearest rebirth of *De Rerum Natura* into English letters and a lively resistance to straightforward notions of literary rebirth.

Finally, Epicurus's and Lucretius's turbulent Renaissance reception histories call us to account, as critics, for the aftereffects of that turbulence in the twentieth-century scholarly archive. How is it that critics of a Lucretian Spenser came to rearticulate, at a distance of nearly four hundred years, some of the same anti-materialist and nationalist attacks on Epicureanism that ensured its widespread occlusion in Spenser's day? How is it that this brief critical battle was followed by such a long near-silence on the subject? These are questions that can be put back on the table as that silence is broken, anew and again, by emerging forms of critical engagement with an Epicurean and Lucretian early English Renaissance.

5

Engendering Modernity: Epicurean Women from Lucretius to Rousseau

Natania Meeker

In the preface to *La femme au dix-huitième siècle* (1862), critics Edmond and Jules de Goncourt begin by insisting on the indebtedness of their own century to the one preceding it. They write:

> Un siècle est tout près de nous. Ce siècle a engendré le nôtre. Il l'a porté et l'a formé. Ses traditions circulent, ses idées vivent, ses aspirations s'agitent, son génie lutte dans le monde contemporain. Toutes nos origines et nos caractères sont en lui: l'âge moderne est sorti de lui et date de lui. Il est une ère humaine, il est le siècle français par excellence.[1]

> One century is very close to us. This century produced our own, begetting it and giving it shape. Throughout the contemporary world, its traditions circulate, its ideas live, its aspirations seethe. All of our origins and our characters are contained within it: the modern age springs from it and begins with it. It is a humane era, it is the French century par excellence.[2]

---

[1] Goncourt and Goncourt (1862) i. In her article on the Goncourt brothers, Jennifer Forrest emphasizes "the Goncourts' historical and aesthetic idealization of the eighteenth century, an idealization in which the nineteenth-century [sic] could only represent a fall from grace" (Forrest (2005–2006) 44). The Goncourts' nineteenth century, in its failure to build on the aesthetic and cultural promise of the eighteenth, emerges as a "bourgeois travesty," in Forrest's words, of the very era that engendered it.

[2] All translations are my own unless otherwise indicated.

The eighteenth century—crucible of a particularly French modernity—is marked, for the brothers, by the supremacy of women. "She is the universal and fatal cause, the origin of events, the source of things," they affirm later in the book, in a chapter recounting "the domination and intelligence of woman" (*Elle est la cause universelle et fatale, l'origine des évènements, la source des choses*).[3] With this assertion the Goncourts echo a critical commonplace of the very period that is the object of their study. Their fascination with the status of women within *ancien régime* culture coincides neatly with Enlightenment narratives of the rise of specifically feminine forms of authority, narratives that assign responsibility to women for everything from the spread of political corruption to an increased national dependence on luxury commerce.[4] This understanding of the eighteenth century as peculiarly feminized is a powerful one: it lingers on not only in Revolutionary critiques of a decadent and effeminate aristocracy, but in today's pop renderings of the era—from the libertine fashions of Vivienne Westwood to the persistent interest in Marie Antoinette as an emblem of modern femininity—that trade in the decadent cachet acquired by the period in its rococo guise as preeminently an age of pleasure (fig. 5.1).[5]

Yet the Goncourts' iteration of this "vast myth of female control"[6] tends to outstrip even its more hyperbolic eighteenth-century manifestations, growing ever larger as the brothers' analysis develops, only to emerge as the primary governing force of state, culture, and hearth. Unlike many of their predecessors, the Goncourts celebrate rather than deplore the supposed reign of women over the French Enlightenment.

---

[3] Goncourt and Goncourt (1862) 321.

[4] The pervasive influence of aristocratic women on elite culture and absolutist politics is depicted by authors from Montesquieu to Rousseau as a typically French social phenomenon. See in particular Montesquieu's *Lettres persanes*, originally published in 1721. In Letter 107, Montesquieu's Persian correspondent Rica writes: "The thing is that, for every man who has any post at court, in Paris, or in the country, there is a woman through whose hands pass all the favors and sometimes the injustices that he does" (*Mais c'est qu'il n'y a personne qui ait quelque emploi à la Cour, dans Paris ou dans les provinces, qui n'ait une femme par les mains de laquelle passent toutes les grâces et quelquefois les injustices qu'il peut faire*) (Montesquieu (1946) 173).

[5] For an account of the eighteenth century's commitment to pleasure as a practice and an ideal, see Porter and Roberts (1997). Gutwirth (1992) takes up at length the problem of the critique (and idealization) of women's power in the eighteenth century. Landes (2001) investigates in detail representations of a feminized aristocracy.

[6] Gutwirth (1992) 85.

Figure 5.1: This portrait by Charles-André (Carle) Van Loo (engraved by Basan) appears as the first plate in the 1887 edition of *La femme au dix-huitième siècle*. Reproduction courtesy of the University of Southern California, on behalf of the USC Libraries Special Collections.

They depict women's exaggerated influence on the period as the happy product of a refined female intelligence that manages to be both feminine *and* manly (so that French women are portrayed as reuniting the best qualities of both sexes). As a result, in *La femme*, women's privileged position within the elite culture of the *ancien régime* becomes not just a sign of an eighteenth-century obsession with hedonism or a residual manifestation of innate female charm, but the historical effect of "the determination and spark of a virile idea, a profundity even in riotous coquetry, something thoughtful and piercing, this mix of man and woman of state" (*la résolution et l'éclair d'une idée virile, une profondeur dans la mutinerie même, je ne sais quoi de pensant et de perçant, ce mélange de l'homme et de la femme d'État*)—qualities with which the women of the period were, according to the brothers, regularly and spectacularly endowed.[7] Feminine power, here, has not just cultural and aesthetic but intellectual consequences; it is the manifestation of a *mentalité* that transforms the experiences of men and women alike.

This feminine attitude is, for the Goncourts, an Epicurean one. Eighteenth-century women, who elegantly oversee the epochal transition into modernity, are the purveyors of a "sagesse épicurienne" most perfectly realized in "the firm belief that there is nothing else to do in this world but be happy" (*la ferme persuasion qu'il n'y a rien autre chose* [sic] *à faire en ce monde qu'à être heureux*).[8] In an echo of the Epicurean *tetrapharmakos*, the guiding tenets of this feminine philosophy are described by the Goncourts as fourfold and unconsecrated by religion: as a doctrine, they write, "this rule" is "absolutely and entirely human" (*absolument et entièrement humaine*).[9] With the concluding chapter of their history, a feminized Epicureanism gradually appears to emerge as one of the structuring principles of the age; the inner logic of the period—the moment's "intimate law"—seems to culminate in the development of an enlightened Epicurean *mode d'être* that is seductively embodied by certain exemplary women, free thinkers who are "liberated from all dogma and from every system" (*affranchies de tout dogme et de tout système*).[10] For the Goncourts, the figure of the Epicurean woman thus ultimately stands as the repressed point of origin not just of modern France, but of modernity itself. As the privileged sign of their attachment to an aristocratic past, this figure is both venerated and reified by the brothers; they transform her, through their nostalgia and their hyperbole, into an idealized image of Woman in all her lost perfection. Yet in the midst of their reactionary glorification of the bygone cultures of the *ancien régime*, the Goncourts' insistence on the feminine avatars of a *sagesse épicurienne* once again rehearses a preoccupation with the feminization of Epicurean ideals that, like their fascination with women's dominance within French culture, finds its origins not in the nineteenth century but in the eighteenth.[11]

---

[7] Goncourt and Goncourt (1862) 326.

[8] Ibid., 451.

[9] Ibid., 450.

[10] Ibid., 454.

[11] In *Epicureanism at the Origins of Modernity*, Catherine Wilson argues that a characteristically Epicurean attention to and respect for human pleasures and human happiness is

As I will argue in this essay, the story that the Goncourts tell about the Epicurean origins of modern French womanhood is an overdetermined one. The eighteenth-century reception of Epicureanism and, most specifically, of Lucretius's *De Rerum Natura* does tend to evolve in France in conjunction with a reimagining of femininity within an Epicurean framework. In this respect, the portrait drawn by the Goncourts, disproportionate and reactive as it may be, is not without its insight. But whereas the Goncourts persistently link women's *sagesse épicurienne* to an increasing feminine influence, eighteenth-century renderings of a newly Epicurean femininity often problematize this very connection, exploring women's Epicurean bent as the source both of women's authority *and* of women's submission to men. The debates around women's Epicurean attitudes and practices are interwoven with discussions of women's "place" in eighteenth-century society, and the extent to which their condition could be described as naturally derived. Accordingly, in stressing the Epicurean turn that theories of femininity can take in the eighteenth century, my argument necessarily intervenes in the long-running discussions of the role played by ideas about women's nature in the grand narratives of the Enlightenment. Feminist critics have debated at length the extent to which the great eighteenth-century theorists of modernity—Rousseau most notably—were invested in naturalizing gender difference as a means of excluding women from participation in an enlightened public sphere, and from there in an enlightened politics.[12] More recently, critical histories of the period have once again brought to the fore the emancipatory potential of the period's many revolutions—for both genders.[13] But the image of the Epicurean

---

connected to the increased prominence of women in early modern philosophy. She writes, "The power of women to produce and tend new life is a visible manifestation of the power of nature to create form and value, and the female is the necessary condition of the only eternity that is thinkable in an atomic universe. Her beauty and attractive power are the means by which she accomplishes her generative work. Not only does the female have, in Lucretian metaphysics, a genuine role to play, her role is dominant" ((2008) 256). Wilson also mentions the attraction of seventeenth-century women intellectuals (including Margaret Cavendish, Lucy Hutchinson, and Aphra Behn) to Epicureanism.

[12] See the essays appearing in Lange (2002).

[13] In *Inventing Human Rights: A History*, Lynn Hunt writes of the eighteenth-century novel: "The magical spell cast by the novel thus turned out to be far-reaching in its effects. . . . Readers learned to appreciate the emotional intensity of the ordinary and the capacity of people like themselves to create on their own a moral world. Human rights grew out of the seedbed sowed by these feelings" ((2007) 58). Literary heroines play an important

woman, whose attachment to pleasure is both autonomous and compulsory, does not fit comfortably into either vision of the age. Instead, she demonstrates how seemingly spontaneous feelings of delight are produced from within the cultivation of femininity as a state of privation. Pleasure becomes a discipline in which women, in particular, excel. The classical Epicurean inheritance takes on, here, an erotic cast; the Lucretian investment in a voluptuous nature, vexed as it is, takes precedence over a more sober (and sobering) emphasis on the static pleasures of *ataraxia*. Yet, while the eighteenth-century reading of Lucretius is a sensual one, it is far from ending in a thoughtless hedonism. Instead, sensuality becomes a product of the very restrictions placed upon its expression.

A closer look at the various forms of Epicurean womanhood that circulate through eighteenth-century philosophy and literature reveals how eighteenth-century Epicureanism becomes something other than a return to nature or a liberatory insistence on the primacy of pleasure. To see women as Epicurean subjects entails a recognition of the ways in which what might appear to be the purely physiological experience of voluptuous enjoyment is always dynamically produced in relationship to forms of subjection that are both naturally and socially imposed. Epicurean *voluptas*, I will argue, comes about, on the one hand, as a result of the constraints that necessarily bind all animate beings and, on the other, as a momentary evasion of these constraints: in other words, it emerges from within an intimate experience of subjection. Crucially, these constraints are not only—or even, in eighteenth-century contexts, primarily—natural ones. Indeed, too much dependence on the modern logic of nature against culture tends to hinder this understanding, rather than helping us make sense either of changing eighteenth-century ideas about femininity or of Epicurean philosophies of embodiment. In fact, Epicurean notions of womanhood—and theories of the feminine as Epicurean—make much of the capacity of what would now be called the

---

role in this process. "Readers empathizing with the heroines learned that all people— even women—aspired to greater autonomy, and they imaginatively experienced the psychological effort that struggle entailed" (59–60). Hunt is careful to point out, however, that this learned empathy certainly did not guarantee political changes in women's condition. "Learning to empathize opened the path to human rights, but it did not ensure that everyone would be able to take that path right away" (68). See also Hesse (2001) and Offen (2000).

cultural construction of femininity to reproduce and heighten the natural effects of constraint on human bodies. One of these effects is, ineluctably, pleasure itself. This means that voluptuous delight can never serve as a straightforward expression of human autonomy. Yet it is also inevitably something more than an involuntary physiological response to stimulation. Ultimately, the eighteenth-century production of modes of femininity along Epicurean lines neither affirms women's right to moral self-determination nor carves out a space of anatomical difference from which women can only struggle to emerge. Rather, it makes of women the keepers of an Epicurean knowledge that must remain concealed in its inner workings from men, whose authority women vitiate even as they submit to it.

In what follows, I emphasize the ways in which Jean-Jacques Rousseau, as one of the most prominent eighteenth-century interpreters of Lucretius *and* one of the period's most significant theorists of femininity (for better or worse), gradually develops a concept of feminine identity out of what I will present as a characteristically Lucretian reading of the necessary relationship between delight and constraint.[14] Rousseau makes of human nature itself a poetic response to the false idols of civilization, and then of femininity a libertine recognition of the fictions of masculine freedom. First, in his *Discours sur l'origine et les fondements de l'inégalité parmi les hommes* (1755), Rousseau not only rewrites Lucretian anthropology for an emergent modernity but remains faithful to the Lucretian interest in nature as an object that is revealed to humans not nakedly, in its pre-social state, but through the lens of acculturation. In this sense, the *Discourse on Inequality*, like the *De Rerum Natura*, is addressed not to natural man as he once was but to man as he is: suffering from the bondage of the culture that he has made. And, like Lucretius, Rousseau wrings from the poetic invocation of a nature that is no longer fully accessible to human perception an invitation to imagine ourselves otherwise, to find a more sustaining pleasure in the midst of the constraints that continue to bind us. This cultivation of pleasure in the very throes of

---

[14] This focus on constraint, together with the human capacity to find voluptuous pleasure in the midst of it, is crucial not just to Rousseau's reading of the feminine but to a longer tradition of libertine philosophy more generally. Rousseau ends up breaking dramatically with this tradition, even as he depends upon it to articulate his famous critique of the decadence of his era—a decadence most visible within the period's obsessive pursuit of what we would now call progress.

privation is an art of which Rousseau will go on to make women the privileged practitioners, not because they are more embodied or somehow more natural than men, but because they are historically more subjected than their male counterparts. Rousseau reads Lucretius as a preeminent thinker not of autonomy, but of subjection—or rather, of a form of autonomy that must be cultivated and nurtured *within* the experience of subjection (an experience that notably includes, for Lucretius, the "groveling" of humanity beneath the weight of religion prior to the entrance of Epicurus onto the stage set by the *De Rerum Natura*).[15] In the end, for Rousseau, it is this Epicurean capacity to find pleasure in constraint that becomes coded as feminine, even as it also provides what the Goncourts might call the "intimate law" that brings femininity itself into being. As Claire remarks to Julie in *La nouvelle Héloïse*, "to abstain in order to enjoy (*jouir*) is your philosophy; it is the Epicureanism of reason" (*s'abstenir pour jouir c'est ta philosophie; c'est l'épicuréisme de la raison*).[16] In its guise as a theory of femininity, then, eighteenth-century Epicureanism becomes not a retreat back to biology and away from acculturation but a practice of self-management within the obligations imposed upon women in contexts both natural and social. This practice is eroticized, by virtue of its associations with the feminine, but its consequences extend far beyond the domain of the boudoir: these Epicurean women become, for Rousseau as for the Goncourts, both the heralds and the arbiters of modernity.

1. LUCRETIAN FEMININITIES: DESIRING ARTIFICE

While the detractors of Epicurus have sometimes read his emphasis on pleasure as an endorsement of sensual license, Epicureanism as a whole is consistently attentive to the limits that structure our perceptions, our interactions with nature, and our experiences as embodied beings. In the *De Rerum Natura*, Lucretius both lauds the freedom from fear that

---

[15] Lucretius *De Rerum Natura* 1.62. On Rousseau's Epicureanism, and his kinship with a certain materialist tradition, see Gourevitch (2001). See also Baker (2007) for a discussion of Lucretius's influence on the *Second Discourse*.

[16] Rousseau (1964) 662. For a reading of Julie, heroine of *Julie, ou la nouvelle Héloïse*, as a "sage épicurien," see Fernandez (2006).

Epicurean doctrine enables us to experience (as if for the first time) and insists upon the regularity and continuity of the natural world. As A. A. Long has written:

Our world originated from structures formed by the completely aimless motions and aggregations of atoms, and, according to Lucretius, at least one spontaneous motion or swerve was a necessary precursor of world formation. Yet, within our world, as we know it, law-like regularities hold good and will continue to do so as long as the world's basic structure remains intact.[17]

Long sees Lucretius as particularly interested in what he refers to as "the determinate order of nature."[18] And it is, in fact, the existence of this order that renders moments of divergence from it both perceptible and thinkable. The kinetic tension between, on the one hand, a form of liberation specifically envisioned as a product of materialist philosophy and, on the other, a constraint collectively experienced in the here-and-now plays itself out in the rules that govern the composition of the material universe, including the depiction of atomic movement as it is interrupted by the infinitesimal "tilt" of the *clinamen*. As Lucretius writes, "While the first bodies are being carried downwards by their own weight in a straight line through the void, at times quite uncertain and uncertain places, they swerve a little from their course, just so much as you might call a change of motion" (*De Rerum Natura* 2.217–20). Famously, this swerve serves as the basis for the Epicurean formulation of free will as a kind of deviation of its own, one that, crucially, would "break the decrees of fate" (*quod fati foedera rumpat*, 2.254). *Voluntas* is here articulated as a form of resistance—yet a resistance that opens the way for pleasure, so that free will ("by which we proceed whither pleasure leads each, swerving also our motions not at fixed times and fixed places, but just where our mind has taken us," 2.258–60) generates the voluptuous freedom to follow our desires. Still, the *clinamen*, while it calls into existence worlds of marvelous diversity and variety and engenders voluptuous possibilities, is not a wild shift away from the norm, but a small movement made possible (or, rather, palpable) by the existence of the constraints against which it may be read.

[17] Long (2006) 176.
[18] Ibid., 171.

The Lucretian depiction of sexual need, appearing at the end of the fourth book of the *De Rerum Natura*, itself negotiates between the necessary limits that we must place on our desires and the pleasures that are made possible as a result of these very restrictions. In this context, Lucretius is preoccupied with the way in which the cultivation of desire by artificial means tends to enflame the passions and thereby engender suffering: we want what we cannot have because we imagine ourselves as other than we are. The remedy for this painful condition is not more freedom but a more acute consciousness of our own limitations and a subsequent embrace of repetition as an ideal (either in the form of promiscuous contact with many bodies or in the context of marriage, where habit eventually produces contentment). The Lucretian account of femininity is set in the framework of this extended and influential meditation on the proper management of erotic longing; it famously includes a series of reflections on feminine artifice (and the effects of such artifice on men), reflections that will be revisited by Jonathan Swift[19] and the Marquis de Sade,[20] among others. Lucretius writes:

For this is what men usually do when blinded with desire, and they attribute to women advantages which they really have not. Thus women that are in many ways crooked and ugly we often see to be thought darlings and to be held in the highest honour. One lover will actually deride another, and bid

[19] Swift takes up the Lucretian theme of odiferous femininity in the poem "Strephon and Chloe": "'Twere better you had lickt her Leavings, / Than from Experience find too late / Your Goddess grown a filthy Mate. / Your Fancy then had always dwelt / On what you saw, and what you smelt" ((2010) 615). For a discussion of excrement in Swift, and the latter's fascination with Lucretius, see Siebert (1985).

[20] For a brutal condemnation of women's "defects," seemingly inspired by the Lucretian example, see Sade's discussion of the abject female body at Sade (1998) 3.636–37. Sade, like Lucretius, focuses on the disgusting odors that emanate from women: "We must bear it ever in mind that the woman who strives to get us the most inextricably into her captivity is certainly concealing flaws which would rapidly disgust us if we knew what they were; do we but set our imagination to envisaging these details, to probing after them, to guessing at them; and this preliminary exercise initiated at the same moment love is born will perhaps succeed in extinguishing it. Be she a girl? She surely exhales some unhealthy odor, if not now then later on; is it worth your while, sir, to pant after a cesspool?" (*Ne perdons jamais de vue que la femme qui essaie de nous captiver le mieux, cache certainement des défauts qui nous dégoûteraient bientôt, si nous pouvions les connaître; que notre imagination les voie, ces détails . . . qu'elle les soupçonne, qu'elle les devine; et cette première opération faite dans le moment où l'amour naît parviendra peut-être à l'éteindre. Est-elle fille? Certainement elle exhale quelque odeur malsaine, si ce n'est dans un temps, c'est dans un autre; est-ce bien la peine de s'enthousiasmer devant un cloaque?*) ((2008) 637).

him propitiate Venus as being the victim of a discreditable love, and often, poor wretch, casts not a glance at his own surpassing misery. . . . But, however, let her be of the supremest dignity of countenance, let the power of Venus radiate from her whole body, the truth is there are others, the truth is we have lived so far without this one; the truth is she does all the same things as the ugly woman does, and we know it, fumigating herself, poor wretch, with rank odours while her maid-servants give her a wide berth and giggle behind her back. But the lover shut out, weeping, often covers the threshold with flowers and wreaths, anoints the proud doorposts with oil of marjoram, presses his love-sick kisses upon the door; but if he is let in, once he gets but one whiff as he comes, he would seek some decent excuse for taking his leave; there would be an end of the complaint so often rehearsed . . . . Our Venuses are quite well aware of this; so they are at greater pains themselves to hide all that is behind the scenes of life from those they wish to detain fast bound in the chains of love . . . . (Lucretius *De Rerum Natura* 4.1153–87)

Taken out of context, this passage can easily be presented in a misogynist vein, as a description of women's pathetic investment in the deceitful masking of their disgusting bodies, so that feminine "dignity" primarily functions as an illusion deliberately cultivated by women in the effort to conceal their inherently abject nature. From this perspective, the adornments that are meant to frame feminine beauty and generate feminine desirability only serve to heighten the gross materiality of the female body, the very materiality that such ornaments seem originally designed to hide. The "power of Venus" is stripped from women in order to render them in their brute and naked form—rank and suffused with unpleasant odors. Feminine difference emerges not from the heightened delicacy or superior attractiveness of women's bodies, but from men's susceptibility to the deceptions practiced by women themselves. Once this ruse is unmasked, the "chains of love" are released, and disgust comes to take the place of affection.

But Lucretius's critique of women's artifice takes place not as part of an attack on feminine manipulation of men but in the larger framework of his portrayal of the miseries wrought on humankind by erotic desire more generally. What is at stake, for Lucretius, in his advice to his reader to beware "the snares of love" is not so much that desire will inevitably butt up against the reality of the body, but the terrifying effectiveness of the snares themselves. Women may indeed seek to inspire romantic longing in their partners because they aim to keep them tangled in the "strong knots of Venus," but love more universally described—including in non-heterosexual partnerships—involves the experience of bondage even where it is most requited.[21] The illusions typically engendered by romantic desire do not so much end in disillusionment as they generate *more* desire ad infinitum: they work not fitfully but too well. As Lucretius points out, love is insistently blind, regardless of others' attempts to educate or enlighten the lover in question, who may well possess an ability to recognize love's ill effects in general without being able to see them in himself. This blindness is problematic because it sustains a form of desire that, in its nature, cannot be sated, and thus produces a miserable quest for satisfaction that is by definition never completed. Erotic ardor is based in a need for another body that cannot be fulfilled because it is a need for possession that another human body is formally unable to meet, without ceasing to be a body altogether. Lucretius writes:

This is the only thing, for which the more we have, the more fierce burns the heart with fell craving. For food and liquid are absorbed into the body, and since these can possess certain fixed parts, thereby the desire of water or bread is easily fulfilled. But from man's aspect and beautiful bloom nothing comes into the body to be enjoyed except thin images; and this poor hope is often snatched away by the wind. (4.1089–96)

When we love, whether the object of our desire be male or female, what most enflames us is an image that we cannot possess, both because this image is not substantial enough to grasp, physically, and because the body from which this image emanates resists our attempts to master it. In seeking to throw off the chains of Venus, the lover only succeeds in tightening their grip on him. Where he thinks he is free, he discovers instead, to his surprise and displeasure, a profound subjection. His autonomy in love is revealed to him as a fiction: the beloved object resists the act of possession upon which the subject's need insists.

Lucretius's lists of the various unpleasant forms that the female body may assume—and the various unpleasant smells that it may emit— function in this context more as evidence of the power of romantic love to shape perceptions of what is real than as proof of the disgusting nature of women in and of themselves. If anything, the abject female body

---

[21] Lucretius *De Rerum Natura* 4.1148.

becomes the *product* of a cultural emphasis on feminine beauty, rather than the remedy for the desire that images of it may inspire. It is in the context of a collective focus on divine feminine loveliness—a focus that stimulates the urge to manipulate, possess, and consume this loveliness—that the sheer physicality of femininity takes on its power to shock in the first place. If Lucretius reads erotic passion as galvanized and sustained through artifice, it is because such passion is fundamentally a desire *for* artifice. The fires of this need are thus stoked by the ability of women to adorn and to conceal their bodies artfully, so that feminine ornamentation reanimates rather than satisfies desire. "From this first trickled into the heart that dewdrop of Venus's sweetness," Lucretius writes, "and then came up freezing care" (4.1059–60). Erotic love is neither natural—"For here lies the hope that the fire may be extinguished from the same body that was the origin of the burning, which nature contrariwise denies out and out to be possible" (4.1086–88)—nor liberating to those who experience it: it has no transgressive role to play, culturally speaking. On the contrary, the condition of being in love generates an illusion of enslavement to the beloved—an illusion that is heightened by her presence and enhanced in social contexts, rather than dissipated or somehow "repressed" by them. Love, carefully cultivated through artificial means, produces only a desire from which there can be no respite.

How does Lucretius alleviate this particular form of pain? He responds neither by recommending that the objects of erotic desire be avoided nor by counseling a return to a more natural form of sexuality. Even animals, Lucretius suggests, can fall prey to the violent effects of passion, so that it becomes difficult to determine whether they are joined by "mutual pleasure" or by "chains." (In fact, it is "these joys which were enough to lure them into the trap and to hold them enchained," 4.1205–1206.) The secret to erotic satisfaction, Lucretius suggests, is not to aim to escape the constraints that bind us or to attempt to master the elusive images that fascinate us. Instead, he reimagines sensual pleasure as the product of the very limitations that emerge from within the erotic relationship. Lucretius contends that we might find a more perfect delight in multiple encounters with many bodies—or, conversely, in habituating ourselves to multiple contacts with one body—than we do in our efforts to free ourselves completely from the snares in which Venus entangles us. We can, he intimates, take pleasure in our constraints, rather than despite them: hence, his famous recommendation of promiscuity, "to cast the collected liquid into any body," as a cure for love's wounds (4.1065). This emphasis on repetition, wherein unrequited ardor is assuaged in its very amplification, also informs his discussion of marriage at the end of the fourth book.[22] "Moreover, it is habit that breeds love," he proclaims in the concluding lines. "For that which is frequently struck by a blow, however light, still yields in the long run and is ready to fall" (4.1283–85). Here, the constraints of monogamy ultimately give rise to a form of satisfaction; pleasure is taken in the midst of the bonds forged by convention. In the end, it seems, both marriage *and* promiscuity may be brought to serve the same Epicurean purpose, not because they are both intrinsically delightful, but because of the capacity of repetition to temper our needs by moderating our urges to possess those whom we desire. Indeed, both generate scenes of figurative dissipation, wherein the desiring subject seems to lose himself: "Do you not see that even drops of water falling upon a stone in the long run beat a way through the stone?" (4.1286–87). With this question, that makes of marriage a space of dissolution, book 4 concludes.

2. ROUSSEAUIST FEMININITIES: MAKING THE MODERN WOMAN

Two crucial aspects of the Lucretian critique of erotic desire are taken up and developed in the eighteenth century. During this period, the delicate equilibrium between compulsion and voluptuous freedom, which

---

[22] The Epicurean perspective on marriage is, generally speaking, vexed. In Diogenes Laërtius's *Lives of Eminent Philosophers*, we read that "No one was ever the better for sexual indulgence, and it is well if he be not the worse. Nor, again, will the wise man marry and rear a family: so Epicurus says in the *Problems* and in the *De Natura*. Occasionally he may marry owing to special circumstances in his life" (10.118–19, trans. Hicks (1925)). In her discussion from *The Therapy of Desire* of the Epicurean relationship to love, which includes a lengthy treatment of Lucretius, Martha Nussbaum contends that "Toward erotic love, or *erōs*, Epicurus is unremittingly hostile" ((1994), 149). Lucretius, for Nussbaum, can nonetheless be read in a proto-feminist vein. She writes, "It is one more advantage of Lucretian therapy that it clears the way for men and women to see something true about the bodies and responses of women, something that would not have been seen had therapy not prepared readers to see women, and men as well, in the perspective of nature" (184). For a discussion of Lucretius on marriage, see also R. D. Brown (1987).

informs not only the movement of the Epicurean atom but the actions of the Lucretian lover, finds itself again regularly subject to renegotiation. On the one hand, writers from Mandeville to Rousseau return to the idea that the passions that animate us do so from within social and political contexts, rather than from some point outside of or prior to sociability per se.[23] As in the *Discourse on Inequality*, the Lucretianism of the eighteenth century tends to be based not upon a genuine return to nature—but upon the (more or less) belated reconstruction of the natural as a response to the artifices that characterize our experience of the present moment. In this sense, the Enlightenment struggle over the nature of nature can be said to take place in the realm, if not of fiction *tout court*, at least of poetic hypothesis—as Rousseau so compellingly maintains that it must. Second, the Epicurean insight that Lucretius articulates in his presentation of the miseries of erotic passion—namely, that pleasure must come *in* constraint, rather than in perfect freedom *from* constraint—is central not only to the materialist (and libertine) reception of Lucretius but to the sentimental and Rousseauist reaction to this reception (a reaction that will reverberate through modern political philosophy and structure post-Enlightenment ideas about women's role in social life). Femininity has a crucial part to play in this context, precisely because of the exceptional social constraints under which eighteenth-century women could be said (and shown) to operate. As Rousseau puts it in *Émile* (1762), "if woman is made to please and to be subjugated, she ought to make herself agreeable to man instead of arousing him" (*Si la femme est faite pour plaire et pour être subjuguée, elle doit se rendre agréable à l'homme au lieu de le provoquer*).[24] Yet, if women are designed to be subjugated, this subjugation has a perverse effect (albeit one that Lucretius might have predicted): it intensifies in women themselves the very passions that are thought to be typical of femininity. While we might expect

---

[23] Rousseau, as we know in part thanks to Adam Smith, was a canny and focused reader of Mandeville's *The Fable of the Bees*, without, however, subscribing to this work's "libertine" conclusions regarding the ordering of human social life. Most famously, of course, Rousseau rejects Mandeville's contention that opulent and excessive forms of consumption in fact enable societies to flourish, rather than inexorably degrading and corrupting their members. As Pierre Force has written, "*As far as the civilized state is concerned, Rousseau subscribes entirely to the analyses of Hobbes and Mandeville*" ((2003) 41, emphasis original).

[24] Rousseau (1969) 5.529–30. Trans. Bloom in Rousseau (1979) 5.358.

the discipline to which women are subject to result in meekness, in fact, women become in this context creatures of unlimited desires—desires, contained only by modesty, that easily outstrip those of men. Rousseau's sentimental heroines, virtuous as they may be, share in the longings of their more libertine (and philosophically inclined) sisters. Women in this sense resemble the lovers described by Lucretius prior to their conversion to Epicureanism: constraint serves only to heighten their sense of passionate need, even while preventing this need from being satisfied. The secret to proper femininity then becomes a kind of Epicurean transformation, wherein delight can be taken as a result of the limitations that structure desire, rather than in spite of those limitations.

Improper femininity, on the other hand, with its dependence on forms of artifice and its tendency to stimulate the passions, becomes the driving engine of a modern culture of enforced consumption, as much for Rousseau (who is deeply troubled by this phenomenon) as for a thinker like Mandeville (who promotes it). Rousseau moves away from Mandeville—and ultimately from Epicurean materialism—in attempting to preserve for men alone the fantasy of a fully autonomous subjectivity. First, in extending the Lucretian diagnosis of the effects of feminine artifice to take in the whole of modernity, Rousseau tends to read, in both the first and second discourses, the condition of being modern as the condition of being *like a woman*.[25] The generalized human attachment to a culture driven by forms of display is liable to produce, for all of us, ever-increasing desires, as well as to limit our most enduring pleasures to those that can be taken only in a Lucretian fashion: namely, in subjection. Rousseau accordingly presents what might otherwise be

---

[25] In this way, Rousseau heightens and sexualizes an emphasis originally found in Lucretius on the "softening" and "mellowing" effects of culture. In his discussion in book 5 of the formation of households by early humans, Lucretius writes: "Next, when they had got themselves huts and skins and fire, and woman mated with man moved into one [home, and the laws of wedlock] became known, and they saw offspring born of them, then first the human race began to grow soft [*genus humanum primum mollescere coepit*]" (5.1011–14). Gordon Campbell has remarked of this passage that "the process would seem . . . to be one of the feminization of these early humans, especially given the context of Venus as the principal active in the change" ((2003) 267). For Rousseau, culture feminizes both because it weakens us physically and because it relies on superfluous forms of consumption in order to perpetuate itself. It thus speaks to the "natural" impulses of women, rather than of men, as Rousseau delineates them in *Émile*. Modernity is a narrative written in the feminine: modern social life is organized around the interests and desires of women, which (increasingly effeminate) men are subsequently obliged to share.

called acculturation as, in fact, a process of feminization: in the *Discourse on Inequality*, he writes of man, "As he becomes sociable and a slave, he becomes weak, timid, and servile; his soft and effeminate manner of living completely exhausts both his strength and his courage" (*En devenant sociable et esclave, il devient faible, craintif, rampant, et sa manière de vivre molle et efféminée achève d'énerver à la fois sa force et son courage*).[26] But whereas Rousseau applies to women the Lucretian solution to this dilemma—pleasure in constraint—he denies it to men, who must remain committed to the illusion of a manly autonomy if sexual difference (in a sense *the* enabling fiction of social life, for Rousseau) is to persist.[27] Women internalize the Epicurean capacity to find their delight in an invisible deviation from the laws that bind them, even as men strive to emerge from their unwilled subjection to the passions—and to forge a new mode of subjectivity in an attempt to recuperate the transcendent force of human aspiration that Lucretius himself renounces as yet another metaphysical illusion. If Rousseau's men might be said to move toward the embrace of a Stoic virtue, transforming their suffering into a mode of valor, his women remain Epicurean hedonists, capable of (and seeking) voluptuous self-gratification even in the midst of privation. Meanwhile, Epicureanism as a feminine doctrine takes on an erotic coloring, despite the ancient Epicurean ambivalence toward sexual desire, so that the rendering of Lucretian *voluptas* as a way of being a woman coincides with a revision of the Epicurean legacy as a way of thinking pleasure. Sex, in both cases, takes center stage.

In the *Discourse on Inequality*, Rousseau's concern with the destructive force of erotic desire echoes the Lucretian fascination with the beguiling power of feminine artifice, even as Rousseau's presentation of the

---

[26] Rousseau (1971) 181. Trans. Bondanella in Rousseau (1988) 14.

[27] See Von Mücke (1991) for an exemplary reading of *Émile* that emphasizes the role of women in shoring up both masculine virtue and the authority of the law. Von Mücke writes, "It will be through his attachment to his imaginary beloved that Emile will learn to differentiate between the false discourse of the world and the truth of morally righteous principles of conduct. Thus the tutor proceeds to engrave the portrait of the ideal woman, whom he will call Sophie, into Emile's heart" (52). Von Mücke foregrounds the importance of female chastity for ensuring the stability of the sex/gender system envisioned by Rousseau. I am interested in the way in which Rousseau reads even (or especially) chastity according to a Lucretian logic, wherein restriction can heighten rather than impede enjoyment.

genealogy of human civilization rehearses Lucretius's account of human development from book 5 of the *De Rerum Natura*. Rousseau writes:

Commençons par distinguer le moral du physique dans le sentiment de l'amour. Le physique est ce désir général qui porte un sexe à s'unir à l'autre; le moral est ce qui détermine ce désir et le fixe sur un seul objet exclusivement, ou qui du moins lui donne pour cet objet préféré un plus grand degré d'énergie. Or il est facile de voir que le moral de l'amour est un sentiment factice; né de l'usage de la société, et célébré par les femmes avec beaucoup d'habileté et de soin pour établir leur empire, et rendre dominant le sexe qui devrait obéir. Ce sentiment étant fondé sur certaines notions du mérite ou de la beauté qu'un sauvage n'est point en état d'avoir, et sur des comparaisons qu'il n'est point en état de faire, doit être presque nul pour lui.[28]

Let us begin by distinguishing the moral from the physical in the sentiment of love. The physical is that general desire which leads one sex to unite with the other; the moral is what gives rise to this desire and fixes it exclusively upon a single object, or at least gives it a greater degree of energy for this preferred object. Now, it is easy to see that the moral aspect of love is an artificial sentiment, born of social custom and celebrated by women with much care and cleverness to establish their ascendancy and to make dominant the sex that should obey. This sentiment, being founded on certain notions of merit or beauty that a savage is not in a position to have and upon comparisons that he is not in a position to make, must mean almost nothing to him . . . .[29]

In this passage, as in Lucretius's discussion of desire, erotic love is neither natural nor an expression of human autonomy: it is a constraint that binds us together, even as it drives us apart from one another. It is unnatural, in a profound sense, even as it is a fact of culture, one from which there can be no exit. As Rousseau explains:

C'est donc une chose incontestable que l'amour même, ainsi que toutes les autres passions, n'a acquis que dans la société cette ardeur impétueuse qui le rend si souvent funeste aux hommes, et il est d'autant plus ridicule de

---

[28] Rousseau (1971) 216.
[29] Trans. Bondanella in Rousseau (1988) 30.

représenter les sauvages comme s'entr'égorgeant sans cesse . . . , que cette opinion est directement contraire à l'expérience.[30]

It is, therefore, incontestable that love itself, like all other passions, has acquired only in society that impetuous ardor which often makes it fatal to men, and it is all the more ridiculous to portray savages constantly slaughtering each other . . . , since this opinion is directly contrary to experience . . . .[31]

Unlike Lucretius, though, Rousseau tends to give erotic desire pride of place among the other passions that social life can be said to engender:

Parmi les passions qui agitent le cœur de l'homme, il en est une ardente, impétueuse, qui rend un sexe nécessaire à l'autre, passion terrible qui brave tous les dangers, renverse tous les obstacles, et qui dans ses fureurs semble propre à détruire le genre humain qu'elle est destinée à conserver.[32]

Among the passions that stir the heart of man, there is an ardent, impetuous one which makes one sex necessary to the other, a terrible passion which braves all dangers, overcomes all obstacles, and which, in its fury, seems calculated to destroy the human race, which it is destined to preserve.[33]

The need that men and women have for one another—a need generated within society, rather than by nature acting alone—drives the negative progress of social life toward ever-increasing modes of artificiality and an all-consuming obsession with status. Lucretius would find a remedy for the pain caused by this destructive dynamic in the individual conversion to Epicureanism and, more specifically, in the rejection of ideas of value vested in attempts to transcend or definitively master the voluptuous body. Rousseau eventually comes to a different conclusion, one that, in *Émile*, emerges as bifurcated along gendered lines, so that human *perfectibilité* is eventually salvaged as a masculine rather than a feminine ethos.[34]

---

[30] Rousseau (1971) 216.

[31] Trans. Bondanella in Rousseau (1988) 31.

[32] Rousseau (1971) 215.

[33] Trans. Bondanella in Rousseau (1988) 30.

[34] Here I am following Elizabeth Rose Wingrove's provocative and compelling reading of the relationship between the *Discourse on Inequality* and *Émile*, as she articulates it in *Rousseau's Republican Romance*. She writes, "Rousseau's portraits of men, women and the relationships that sustain them as such respond to and reconstitute the problem of political

Feminine women come to retain the characteristic traits of Epicurean subjectivity—in their softness, their sweetness, and their capacity to transform the subjection under which they labor into a secret source of pleasure (for themselves and for others). Masculine men, on the other hand, rely upon the possibility of women's compliance to their desires in order to solidify their sense of self-mastery.[35]

The *Discourse on Inequality*, which presents both men and women as descending with modernity into a limp and feeble femininity, ends on a deeply pessimistic note. Rousseau writes:

La société n'offre plus aux yeux du sage qu'un assemblage d'hommes artificiels et de passions factices qui sont l'ouvrage de toutes ces nouvelles relations et n'ont aucun vrai fondement dans la nature.[36]

Society offers nothing more to the sage's eyes than an assemblage of unnatural men and artificial passions which are the handiwork of all these new relations and have no real foundation in nature.[37]

The modern citizen takes a perverse pleasure in the state of submission into which he is thrust:

Il fait sa cour aux grands qu'il hait et aux riches qu'il méprise; il n'épargne rien pour obtenir l'honneur de les servir; il se vante orgueilleusement

---

origins outlined in the *Discourse on Inequality*. They respond to that problem inasmuch as they depict difference, interdependence, and desire as aspects of a natural developmental process: the experiences of power and compulsion upon which democratic political agency depend are provided by the experience of sexual maturation. In this way Rousseau's story of bodily and cognitive perfectibility incorporates the imperatives of conventionality: the encounter with dominant and submissive positions is as natural, inevitable, and ultimately irresistible as erotic desire itself" ((2000) 58). I would add to Wingrove's formulation that Rousseau tends to read the problem of dominance and submission through a Lucretian lens.

[35] Perhaps in part because of the inherent fragility of this relationship, Rousseau can often seem preoccupied with the idea of a male femininity; masculinity, which depends upon women to bring it into existence, is an unstable condition. Zerilli (2002) explores this instability in fascinating detail: "For what haunts the writer Rousseau above all else is the similitude of his sexual other, his dread of becoming woman."

[36] Rousseau (1971) 255.

[37] Trans. Bondanella in Rousseau (1988) 56.

de sa bassesse et de leur protection et, fier de son esclavage, il parle avec dédain de ceux qui n'ont pas l'honneur de le partager.[38]

He pays court to the great whom he hates and to the wealthy whom he holds in contempt; he spares nothing to gain the honor of serving them; he proudly boasts of his own baseness and of their protection, and, proud of his slavery, he speaks with disdain of those who do not have the honor of sharing it.[39]

The human capacity for autonomous action and virtuous choice has been erased from the world as *it is*. Men and women remain in thrall to their passions—and to erotic desire in particular—because of these passions' very artificiality, not despite it. To imagine a world in which humans might act differently—in which honor regularly appears in tandem with virtue and happiness—is to imagine a fiction. In *Émile*, Rousseau strives to make this fiction, if not (strictly speaking) real, at least believable, through the enforcement of codes of sexual difference. As it turns out, women retain a Lucretian relationship to erotic pleasure—finding their enjoyment in an unwilled submission to habit and to the external forms of discipline that mark them as feminine in the first place—in order to allow men the fantasy of a more perfect masculine autonomy. This fragile balance provides a modicum of hope for a better future (even if, in the sequel to *Émile*, this dream, too, will eventually be dashed). It is thus thanks to the institutionalization of virtuous femininity as women's *second* nature, one that must be arrived at from within the experience of subjection, that we can resolve the problems that the passions, as the source of both human servitude and human autonomy, pose for society as a whole. What's more, Rousseau's gradual feminization of the Lucretian inheritance will permit some men the luxury of believing themselves to be free, thereby offering a remedy for the forms of suffering that modernity would otherwise tend to perpetuate.

In the fifth book of *Émile*, Rousseau develops a theory of women's subjectivity that not only follows the Lucretian imperative—allowing pleasure to flourish within a heightened awareness of constraint—but makes of this idea the law that perpetually governs the feminine. Here he paints his well-known portrait of Sophie, the young woman who is to

[38] Rousseau (1971) 255–56.
[39] Trans. Bondanella in Rousseau (1988) 56.

become the wife of the eponymous hero. Rousseau's reading of feminine difference in this context is resolutely marked by paradox. In his narrative of the virtuous girl's development, she learns that any autonomy she may enjoy is predicated upon her capacity to embody submission. Women depend upon their ability to conform to social expectations, in other words, in order to free themselves from absolute servitude to masculine authority. This process of submission works to generate forms of feminine pleasure that are both more sustained and more animating than those derived from the more direct exercise of feminine will, which only serves to weaken and feminize men, who are in danger of finding themselves (Rousseau hypothesizes) physically unable to respond to women's ever-increasing demands. Rousseau describes the education of a young girl:

Justifiez toujours les soins que vous imposez aux jeunes filles, mais imposez-leur en toujours. L'oisiveté et l'indocilité sont les deux défauts les plus dangereux pour elles et dont on guérit le moins quand on les a contractés. Les filles doivent être vigilantes et laborieuses; ce n'est pas tout; elles doivent être génées de bonne heure. Ce malheur, si c'en est un pour elles, est inséparable de leur séxe, et jamais elles ne s'en délivrent que pour en souffrir de bien plus crüels. Elles seront toute leur vie asservies à la gêne la plus continüelle et la plus sévére, qui est celle des bienséances: il faut les exercer d'abord à la contrainte, afin qu'elle ne leur coûte jamais rien, à dompter toutes leurs fantaisies pour les soumettre aux volontés d'autrui.[40]

Always justify the cares that you impose on young girls, but always impose cares on them. Idleness and disobedience are the two most dangerous defects for them and the ones least easily cured once contracted. Girls ought to be vigilant and industrious. That is not all. They ought to be constrained very early. This misfortune, if it is one for them, is inseparable from their sex, and they are never delivered from it without suffering far more cruel misfortunes. All their lives they will be enslaved to the most continual and most severe of constraints—that of the proprieties. They must first be exercised in constraint, so that it never costs them anything to tame all their caprices in order to submit them to the wills of others.[41]

---

[40] Rousseau (1969) 5.545.
[41] Trans. Bloom in Rousseau (1979) 5.369.

The virtuous girl's course of study appears here as an education in the relative pleasures of feminine masochism. Yet in giving in to these "severe" and "continual" restraints, women not only gain access to voluptuous fulfillment, but, along with marriage, end up with a measure of social (and erotic) power.

In Rousseau's reading, feminine subjects are molded and shaped by norms that do not originate with them, and this social fact is not just a consequence of the boundlessness of women's desires but the determining condition of the eventual gratification of their passions. As a result, Rousseau's virtuous woman must master the art of satisfying herself in the midst of seeming to be dedicated to the needs and concerns of others. In an example of this dynamic, Rousseau describes a dinner party where the solicitude of the mistress of the house is seemingly unparalleled: "She has omitted nothing that could interest everyone; she has said nothing to anyone that was not agreeable to him; and without in any way upsetting the order, the least important person among her company is no more forgotten than the most important" (*Elle n'a rien omis de ce qui pouvoit intéresser tout le monde, elle n'a rien dit à chacun qui ne lui fut agréable, et sans rien troubler à l'ordre, le moindre de la compagnie n'est pas plus oublié que le premier*).[42] At the end of the evening, each guest returns home satisfied that the mistress "has thought only of him" (*n'a songé qu'à lui*).[43] This satisfaction appears to have come at the expense of the lady of the house herself, who could not, the guests think, have possibly had time even to eat. In reality, Rousseau contends, "she has eaten more than anyone" (*elle a mangé plus que personne*).[44] From within the practice of a feminine concern that appears as a form of self-sacrifice, women find effective ways to cultivate their pleasures. In fact, these pleasures appear to be constructed by means of the very mechanism that permits their concealment. If the hostess is able to eat more than anyone, it is because she has learned the art of appearing not to eat at all.

Feminine self-gratification remains virtuous to the extent that it is in conformity with both social mores and what Rousseau calls "a rule prior to opinion" (*une régle antérieure à l'opinion*): the famous

[42] Rousseau (1969) 5.568. Trans. Bloom in Rousseau (1979) 5.383.

[43] Rousseau (1969) 5.568. Trans. Bloom in Rousseau (1979) 5.384.

[44] Rousseau (1969) 5.568. Trans. Bloom in Rousseau (1979) 5.384.

sentiment intérieur.[45] Rousseau contends that this feeling—and the attachments that it generates—cannot in and of themselves be socially mandated, since this "rule" serves as the final arbiter of opinion and prejudice. As he writes: "It is to the inflexible direction of this rule that all others ought to be related" (*C'est à l'infléxible direction de cette régle que se doivent rapporter toutes les autres*).[46] Yet women come to this law—the one before which all others bend—after having undergone a rigorous early training in pliability, one that is both lengthier and more consistent than the discipline to which little boys are also subjected. Thus,

Il est bon d'observer que jusqu'à l'age où la raison s'éclaire et où le sentiment naissant fait parler la conscience, ce qui est bien ou mal pour les jeunes personnes est ce que les gens qui les entourent ont décidé tel. Ce qu'on leur commande est bien, ce qu'on leur défend est mal; elles n'en doivent pas savoir d'avantage.[47]

It is well to observe that up to the age when reason is enlightened, and when nascent sentiment makes the conscience speak, what is good or bad for young girls is what the people around them have decided it to be. What is commanded them is good; what is forbidden them is bad. They ought not to know more.[48]

Girls' submission to the law of opinion precedes their turn to the law of sentiment and prepares them for it. While Rousseau does suggest that early attachments cannot be produced under duress—a child cannot be obliged, for instance, to love her mother—these attachments are ultimately nurtured and stimulated through experiences of constraint and dutiful obligation. Where the good mother is concerned,

. . . la gêne même où elle la tient, bien dirigée, loin d'affoiblir cet attachement, ne fera rien que l'augmenter, parce que la dépendance étant un état naturel aux femmes, les filles se sentent faites pour obéir.[49]

---

[45] Rousseau (1969) 5.566. Trans. Bloom in Rousseau (1979) 5.382.
[46] Rousseau (1969) 5.566. Trans. Bloom in Rousseau (1979) 5.382.
[47] Rousseau (1969) 5.566.
[48] Trans. Bloom in Rousseau (1979) 5.381–82.
[49] Rousseau (1969) 5.546.

. . . even the constraint in which she keeps her daughter, if it is well directed, will, far from weakening this attachment, only increase it; for dependence is a condition natural to women, and thus girls feel themselves made to obey.[50]

The girl child becomes feminine not as a result of her love for her mother but thanks to her innate recognition of her own dependence. It is this recognition that first makes room for sentimental attachment to flourish and to ripen, later, into other forms of affection.

Rousseau's most successfully feminine women are born into a state of subjection, one that they gradually come to recognize as the source of whatever (relative) autonomy they may be said to enjoy. While both men and women struggle in *Émile* to balance their responsibilities to the larger social order with their duties to themselves, it is only women whose relationship to this order is most consistently framed as a gesture of submission to that which remains, in one way or another, unwilled by them. Women learn to shape themselves, physically and mentally, in accordance with the figures of femininity that repetitively define them; gradually, they materialize these figures in the very passions that move them most consistently. As Rousseau describes this process, the little girl who delights in adorning her doll will one day grow up to be a doll of her own: "She is entirely in her doll, and she puts all her coquetry into it. She will not always leave it there. She awaits the moment when she will be her own doll" (*Elle est toute dans sa poupée, elle y met toute sa coquéterie, elle ne l'y laissera pas toujours; elle attend le moment d'être sa poupée elle-même*).[51] What is remarkable about this formulation of feminine submission is that women, in learning to become their own dolls, in effect learn to construct out of external constraints—on their appearance, their behavior, their actions, their choices—precisely those desires and appetites that gratify them the most. In this way, they reca- pitulate an Epicurean logic of erotic enjoyment. Rather than forging out of her innermost thoughts and feelings an image of the authentic self—and opposing this, more freely chosen, "law" to those thrust upon her—Rousseau's feminine subject reverses this process: the constraints that bring women into being *as women* are made to work, instead, to

---

[50] Trans. Bloom in Rousseau (1979) 5.369–70.
[51] Rousseau (1969) 5.543. Trans. Bloom in Rousseau (1979) 5.367.

satisfy their most secret inclinations, for it is these very constraints that sustain their most satisfying pleasures. Women know themselves, not by looking "within," but by devoting themselves, first, to that which persistently determines them. Virtue itself becomes a form of passion, while modesty becomes a mode of self-assertion. The split feminine selves that Rousseau envisions are fragmented not as a result of an internal struggle to be free but in the process of reshaping their own bondage into a source of intimate delight.

Yet men persist in writing the fictions of an original and authentic freedom, one that may be chosen or rejected by the individual. As a result, Sophie finds herself confronted by a problem, following her marriage to Émile. Masculine desire, rather than being heightened by the spectacle of women's unwilled submission, turns out to be extinguished by it: where women require discipline in order to make their "natural" weakness more legible, men require resistance in order to display their strength. "Men generally are less constant than women," Rousseau explains, "and grow weary of happy love sooner than they do" (*Les hommes sont moins constans que les femmes et se rebutent plus tôt qu'elles de l'amour heureux*).[52] If men tire easily of conjugal love, it is because they privilege the "free" expression of their desire over the opportunity for domination that marriage brings them; they have failed to learn the Lucretian lesson, in that they continue to seek full possession of their beloved (and thus tire easily of the forms of "assujetissement" [subjection] enabled by marriage). "Constraint and love go ill together," says Émile's tutor, "and pleasure is not to be commanded" (*La contrainte et l'amour vont mal ensemble, et le plaisir ne se commande pas*).[53] Hearing this, Sophie appears to be on the verge of blushing. Why? Is it because she is afraid to be seen to understand too well? Or because, having been trained to take pleasure precisely in obedience, she cannot fully agree? Or, even, perhaps because, by imagining a form of pleasure that is *not* to be had for the asking, she is also obliged to envision, however inchoately, one that *is*?

Both Émile and Sophie recognize that marriage engenders a very specific form of feminine servitude, but, in order to prevent future inconstancy on Émile's part, Sophie is obliged to submit to the necessity

[52] Rousseau (1969) 5.698. Trans. Bloom in Rousseau (1979) 5.476.
[53] Rousseau (1969) 5.698. Trans. Bloom in Rousseau (1979) 5.476.

of convincing him that she remains free not to submit to *him*: "It will cost you some painful privations," says the tutor, "but you will reign over him if you know how to reign over yourself" (*Il vous en coûtera des privations penibles, mais vous regnerez sur lui si vous savez régner sur vous*).[54] In this formulation, Sophie's potential mastery over Émile takes the form of a freedom of action articulated *for her alone* as yet another duty; she cannot consistently yield to Émile, even if she desires him, but must instead make it clear to him that her favors are rendered in exchange for his constancy. While the tutor at first maintains to Sophie that desire must be mutual in order to be truly "sweet," here he recommends that she restrict her advances toward Émile in order that Émile may be induced to regulate his own conduct according to hers. Émile requires the illusion that Sophie's body is freely given up to him, as if he were a lover, and not a husband; he requires her, in effect, to *appear* to will her own subjection, rather than merely to give in to it. But Sophie herself is to experience this requirement not as the possibility of an authentic freedom to resist, but as an additional constraint that sustains her passionate attachment. "You will reign by means of love for a long time if you make your favors rare and precious, if you know how to make them valued" (*Vous régnerez longtems par l'amour si vous rendez vos faveurs rares et précieuses, si vous savez les faire valoir*).[55] Sophie is obliged here to take yet again an Epicurean relation not only to her own pleasures—in that they are the products of a duress that is all the sweeter *for her* for being inculcated rather than chosen—but to those of Émile—who becomes in his turn the object of a manipulation of which he can know nothing. Émile needs the illusion of his freedom in order to experience desire, but he, unlike his wife, must remain ignorant of this deception. He clings more fiercely than she to the fiction of his strength, precisely because he is loath to read the latter *as* a fiction.

If voluptuous pleasure, for Lucretius, comes from a moment of brief resistance (in which a small deviation generated in response to an "intimate law" both brings us into existence and constrains us) it resembles nothing so much as what Rousseau describes, in *Émile*, as the state of being like a woman. Femininity remains an Epicurean condition in which men share only at their peril, linked as it is to the transformation

---

[54] Rousseau (1969) 5.701. Trans. Bloom in Rousseau (1979) 5.478.
[55] Rousseau (1969) 5.701. Trans. Bloom in Rousseau (1979) 5.478–79.

of habit into delight, and to the embrace of unwilled restrictions under which virtuous masculinity could only chafe. Sophie, like the anonymous hostess at her dinner party, dedicates herself to cultivating not just the enjoyment of others, but the appearance of privation on her own part. The hostess must appear to resist her desire for food, just as Sophie must seem to resist a desire for sex. In both cases, though, the performance of subjection to another's will conceals pleasures that are heightened, rather than dampened, by this subjection. And it is within such a performance that truly voluptuous forms of enjoyment spring into being—that women's passions are more perfectly gratified. Rousseau's Epicurean women are neither fully "enlightened" nor, in a modern sense, empowered: on the contrary, they collude with one another to maintain men's ignorance of their own subjugation to forces that are in some sense beyond their control, among them masculine passion itself. Were women to give in "freely" to their urges, the result would be catastrophic for both sexes:

Avec la facilité qu'ont les femmes d'émouvoir les sens des hommes et d'aller réveiller au fond de leurs cœurs les restes d'un temperament presque éteint, s'il étoit quelque malheureux climat sur la terre où la philosophie eut introduit cet usage, . . . , tirannisés par elles ils seroient enfin leurs victimes, et se verroient tous traîner à la mort sans qu'ils pussent jamais s'en deffendre.[56]

For, given the ease with which women arouse men's senses and reawaken in the depths of their hearts the remains of ardors which are almost extinguished, men would finally be their victims and would see themselves dragged to death without ever being able to defend themselves.[57]

Here, men are at the mercy of feminine desire—a desire that is theoretically unlimited but must nonetheless always be held in check. This desire can only be "contained" by modesty; it cannot be regulated from within (unlike the "penchants" of men).

[56] Rousseau (1969) 5.530.
[57] Trans. Bloom in Rousseau (1979) 5.358. The translation here is misleading. Men are not "dragged" to death; instead, the implication is that they are so weakened by their sexual exploits that they finally die. Bloom also leaves out Rousseau's reference to "hot climates" where women are more numerous than men.

Rousseau's virtuous women are both voluptuously inclined and highly docile; they are both masters of the art of enjoyment and suspicious of autonomous thought and action for their own sakes. In this sense, they live out the Epicurean insight that we derive our most sustained pleasures not from the free expression of our urges (whether the latter are base or noble), but from the careful management of our desires. Paradoxically, the more we recognize the extent to which our passions drive us (the first Epicurean lesson), the more capable we are of finding delight in what we otherwise perceive as a constraint on our autonomy. The Goncourts write of Rousseau:

Ce que Voltaire est à l'esprit de l'homme au dix-huitième siècle, Rousseau l'est à l'âme de la femme. . . . Il la trouve vide, et il la laisse pleine d'ivresse. . . . Au souffle de Rousseau, la femme se reveille.[58]

What Voltaire is to the mind [*esprit*] of man in the eighteenth century, Rousseau is to the soul of woman. . . . He finds it empty, and leaves it full of intoxication. . . . Inspired by Rousseau, woman awakens.

If modern woman is indeed "awakened" by Rousseau in the eighteenth century, it is to a condition in which femininity exists as a poetic fiction that women alone are trained to read (and to value) as such. Becoming a woman does not mean returning to a more natural condition of femininity per se, but learning to cultivate sensuous enjoyment in the recognition of the (material) limitations that are imposed upon us, often brutally. Women exchange the collective fantasy of autonomous selfhood for the delights that are inherent in embracing their necessary submission to a law that is never theirs to forge. Epicureans, they aim for pleasure, and they find it, in privation.

---

[58] Goncourt and Goncourt (1862) 380–81.

6

Oscillate and Reflect: La Mettrie,
Materialist Physiology, and the Revival
of the Epicurean Canonic

James A. Steintrager

In 1750, Julien Offray de la Mettrie published as part of his collected philosophical works an aphoristic treatise called *Système d'Épicure* (*The System of Epicurus*). It was an expansion of a self-standing volume that had been published slightly earlier—likely in 1749, although the title page states 1750—as *Réflexions philosophiques sur l'origine des animaux* (Philosophical reflections on the origin of animals). While the title of the later version may suggest an interest in historical assessment, the body of the text reveals a modern partisan of Epicureanism.[1] La Mettrie casts himself as translating, extending, and refining in light of contemporary natural philosophy the ancient school of thought. What justifies this identification? The short answer is that La Mettrie's work provides evidence for all three aspects of the Epicurean system as it is presented in the ancient doxographies: physics, ethics, and canonic. The first two are the most explicitly embraced in La Mettrie's writings. The third or canonic Diogenes Laërtius described as providing "procedures for use in the system."[2] It might thus be thought of as a second-order reflection on

---

[1] On atomism and hedonism in La Mettrie's Epicureanism, with particular attention to the reception of Lucretius, see Meeker (2006) 88–125.

[2] Diogenes Laërtius 10.30. This translation and those of other ancient Epicurean texts, with the exception of Lucretius, follow Inwood and Gerson (1994). Translations of Lucretius follow Rouse-Smith. Seneca in his *Epistulae Morales* 89.11 glosses the division in a slightly different manner: "The Epicureans held that there are two parts of philosophy, physics and ethics; they got rid of logic. Then since they were forced by the very facts to distinguish

the first order of physics, itself subordinate to the end of ethics. While the canonic has generally speaking not been the highlight of Epicurus's reception and is the least immediately evident aspect of La Mettrie's Epicureanism, I will argue that it is the most interesting and important for grasping the depth—fundamental if sometimes unthought—of the author's commitment to the ancient system *and* for understanding the historical particularity and modernity of this reception. Indeed, a careful examination of La Mettrie and the complex genealogy of his positions helps us grasp the emergence of modern philosophy, with its focus on epistemology, as profoundly and increasingly unified by a return to Epicurean positions.

The heart of the matter is La Mettrie's adherence to a model that put forward sense perceptions as the basis for ideas and that treated ideas themselves in fundamentally imagistic terms.[3] In this manner, imagination came to be considered as simply the way the mind works and the capacity from which all other mental operations could be derived. This is a trend that can be traced to the mid-seventeenth century, when the term "imagination," strangely at first glance, took on an enormous weight exactly at the moment that faculty psychology was under attack and in decline. La Mettrie was an inheritor of this trend, and at the same time, linked his understanding of the canonic to both ethics and to physics. With respect to the latter, he adopted and adapted the recent return to motive force in physics proper, promoted an increasingly vitalist thrust in physiology, and tried to show how together they could produce a coherent materialism against the prevailing Cartesian dualism in France. In short, La Mettrie's particular return to the Epicurean canonic was simultaneously networked with what we would call, in retrospect, scientific discourses and practices—anatomy, physics, chemistry, and

---

what was ambiguous and to refute falsities lying hidden under the appearance of truth, they themselves also introduced that topic which they call 'on judgement and the criterion' [i.e., the canonic]; it is [just] logic by another name, but they think that it is an accessory part of physics."

[3] I am here in general agreement with Richard Rorty, who argues that modern philosophy develops a model of the mind guided by the figure and ideal of "the mirror of nature." Where I differ is on the historical details and, importantly, the tenuousness and complexity of its construction. In his introduction to this thesis, Rorty holds out a special place—or perhaps opprobrium is the better term—for Locke and Descartes (see Rorty (1979) 17–69); Epicurus and the latter-day Epicureans so important to my case get no mention.

medicine—that likewise frequently called on an Epicurean inheritance while refashioning the soul as mind and brain.[4]

ATOMISM, TELEOLOGY, AND THE ETHICS OF IMAGINATION

Before turning my full attention to the canonic and its implicit but crucial role in La Mettrie's thought, it will be helpful to adumbrate his commitment to Epicurean ethics and physics. In *Système d'Épicure*, he has us consider the case of a woman born "without sexual organs," "an indefinable animal" who was "completely castrated in her mother's womb" and had "neither mound nor clitoris, nor nipples nor vulva, nor labia majora, nor vagina, nor womb, nor periods."[5] Her simpleton husband made do: "He quite simply believed that the channel of excretion was also for reproduction, and he acted accordingly, loving his wife, who loved him also very much, and he was very upset when his secret was discovered" (MM 94). The legal, political, medical, and surgical authorities in Ghent examined the woman, and a plan was made to "fashion a vulva" for her (MM 94). When this project fell through, her marriage of ten years was annulled. The report included the observation that the woman derived no enjoyment from the ersatz intercourse to which she had submitted and that "however much one stimulated the seat of her absent clitoris, she experienced no pleasant feeling" (MM 94). For La Mettrie, this observation is not merely a matter of salacious curiosity. Rather he understood pleasure to be the impetus for reproduction and the absence of the woman's clitoris just as detrimental as her missing womb to the apparent goals of nature:

If even today nature relaxes her vigilance to such an extent, if she is capable of such a surprising mistake, how much more frequent must similar games have been in the past! Such far-reaching distraction, so to say, such exceptional, extraordinary absent-mindedness, explains all those to which nature

---

[4] On the importance of tracking the hybrid or networked relations of discourses and practices such as physiology and philosophy that we now consider largely differentiated, I am following Latour (1993), especially 1–12. By focusing on the Boyle-Hobbes controversy as the spot where the differentiation of the political from scientific takes place—a differentiation that defines modernity for him—Latour's own account, however, lacks the complexity that he otherwise champions.

[5] MM 94. Here and throughout MM = La Mettrie (1996).

must have been subject in the distant past when reproduction was uncertain, difficult, ill-established and equivalent to trials rather than masterstrokes. (MM 94)

Although nature learns only through experience and mistakes, La Mettrie's explanation may still look teleological. However, his figuring of nature as distracted—her mind not really on the task—belies this: it implies that there is no mind and therefore no purpose at work at all.

La Mettrie renders this implication explicit by clarifying that what we might take for intelligent design is really the collusion of chance and eternity: "Through what an infinite number of combinations must matter have passed before reaching the only combination which could result in a perfect animal, and through how many others before reproduction reached the degree of perfection it enjoys today!"[6] These assertions echo Epicurus in the "Letter to Herodotus," where he describes the chance collision of atoms in the void, their rebound vibration or *palmos*, and ultimately their entanglement or, what we might call—and La Mettrie did describe as—organization.[7] La Mettrie's further gloss that "only those to whom lucky combinations *finally* gave eyes and ears, formed and placed exactly like ours, had the faculty of seeing, hearing, and so on" converts finality from the actualization of a *telos*—which his term "perfection" still suggests—into a simple statement of temporality. It also neatly summarizes the Epicurean critique of teleology. We have this critique in its most elaborated form in the *De Rerum Natura*, where Lucretius writes that one "should not suppose that the clear light of the eyes was made in order that we might be able to see before us" (*lumina ne facias oculorum clara creata, / prospicere ut possimus*), that our legs were so jointed in order that we might walk, or our arms and hands fashioned with the obtainment of life's necessities as their end.[8] Such "perverted reasoning" puts effect before cause, since "nothing is born in us simply in order that we may use it, but that which is born creates the use" (*nil ideo quoniam natumst in corpore ut uti / possemus, sed quod natumst id procreat usum*).[9]

---

[6] Ibid., 95.

[7] See Usener (1887) 8.

[8] Lucretius *De Rerum Natura* 4.825–26. On the anti-finalist stance of Epicurus, see also Simplicius's much later *Commentary on Aristotle's Physics* 198b29.

[9] Lucretius *De Rerum Natura* 4.834–35.

In his most famous work, *L'homme-machine* (*Machine Man*) of 1748, La Mettrie had provided a similar assessment of teleology, this time mentioning Lucretius by name, along with "all past and present Epicureans," and using the Roman's example of the eye (MM 25). But while this work was also published anonymously, the author was somewhat more circumspect than in the later *Système d'Épicure*, coyly yet transparently declaring that, although he would not take sides, nevertheless we *might* listen to "naturalists" and *perhaps* even to "atheists" when they claim that the sun "was not made in order to heat the earth and its inhabitants"— which it sometimes harms after all—any more than the reflective properties of water and certain polished surfaces were created "to enable us to look at ourselves" (MM 25). Further, while it is true that the eye is "a sort of looking-glass in which the soul can contemplate the images of objects as they are presented to it," we should not take this as proof that "this organ was really created on purpose for such contemplation nor placed on purpose in its socket" (MM 25).

His anti-teleological stance and insistence on the chance combination of elements are already enough to make La Mettrie an Epicurean, yet he pushed the affinity further. Thus, when in *Système d'Épicure* he moved from a consideration of "the origin of animals"—the topic of his initial inquiry—to "reflections on death" and finally "others on life and sensuality," La Mettrie insisted that this shift was not illogical but rather what made his enquiry "worthy of crowning an Epicurean *system*" (MM 104; emphasis added). In short, La Mettrie follows his model in linking physics, broadly construed to include biology and physiology, to ethics. The crux of this position is the usefulness of knowledge in removing disturbances. La Mettrie's aphorisms in this regard are certainly redolent of Epicurus and Lucretius, and while they add little new, they neatly indicate his debt. For example, on mortality: "To tremble at death's approach is to be like children who are afraid of ghosts and spirits. The pale spectre can knock on my door when it wants; I shall not be terrified of it. The philosopher alone is brave where most brave men are not brave at all."[10] In *L'homme-machine*, La Mettrie concludes his defense and illustration of materialism with similar assertions concerning death and fear, remarking that one enlightened by natural philosophy and yet aware of the limitations of the

---

[10] MM 104.

human mind will be "untroubled about his fate and consequently happy" and that he will "look forward to death without desiring it" (MM 38).

Elsewhere in *L'homme-machine*, La Mettrie considers other disturbing delusions and takes to task those who would "terrify the imagination of weak minds by hell, ghosts and fiery precipices, which are even more unreal than Pascal's" (MM 21). (Pascal was famously reported to have feared tumbling into a flaming abyss to his left, which he blocked with chairs or people.) We are again reminded of Epicurus and Lucretius, who take errant atomic effluences from solid bodies—*eidola* or *simulacra*—as the explanation for supernatural encounters, which, once explained, should trouble us no longer. As Lucretius puts it:

> . . . there exist what we call images of things [*rerum simulacra*]; which, like films drawn from the outermost surface of things, flit about hither and thither through the air; it is these same that, encountering us in wakeful hours, terrify our minds, as also in sleep, when we often behold wonderful shapes and images of the dead, which have often aroused us in horror while we lay languid in sleep; lest by chance we should think that spirits escape from Acheron or ghosts flit about amongst the living, or that anything of us can be left after death, when body and mind both taken off together have dissolved abroad, each into its own first-beginnings.[11]

Generally speaking, the early modern debunking program that came to be tightly associated in France with *philosophie* as a programmatic enterprise—the removal of superstitions, unraveling of mysteries, and unveiling of priestcraft—was deeply Epicurean in impetus if not in its details. It could have taken as its motto the Epicurean *dictum*: "It is impossible for someone ignorant about the nature of the universe but still suspicious about the subjects of the myths to dissolve his feelings of fear about the most important matters. So it is impossible to receive unmixed pleasures without knowing natural science."[12] Generally speaking, however, *philosophie* preferred to give reason the appearance of a pure good rather than casting it as a merely instrumental value. In contrast, La Mettrie in *L'homme-machine* did not shy from subordinating physics to ethics. Writing in defense of experience, for example, he states that

---

[11] Lucretius *De Rerum Natura* 4.30–41.

[12] Epicurus *Kuriai Doxai* 12. On the reception history of this and other *Kuriai Doxai* (*Master Sayings*) in the second and third centuries CE, see Fletcher (this volume).

while we can and in fact ought to admire "great geniuses" such as Descartes, Malebranche, Leibniz, and Wolff, one should "begin, by seeing not what people have thought, but what they should think for the sake of an untroubled life" (MM 5). But while a statement such as this underlines La Mettrie's Epicurean bona fides, any assessment of his allegiance to the school is incomplete without a consideration of the place of the canonic in his writings.

THE CANONIC AND IMAGINATION IN MODERN PHILOSOPHY

The original function of the canonic was to provide an epistemological ground for inferences about the nature of things. In Epicurus, it is the internalization of atomic effluences that accounts for both sense perceptions and ideas; it also provides a concrete correspondence between objects and ideas meant to forestall skepticism. Only when such effluences go astray do we have troubling encounters with supposed ghosts and other chimeras that disturb our souls because they lead us to infer an afterlife in which we may suffer rather than find ourselves handed over to the inanity of death as atomic dissolution. Otherwise, such effluences are simply the stuff of sense perception and the foundation of knowledge. According to Epicurus's "Letter to Herodotus," we "must believe" that "when something from the external objects enters into us that we see and think about their shapes" ("Letter to Herodotus" 49). The formula of a *necessary opinion* indicates that a mild skepticism lurks within the canonic. Objects "stamp into us the nature of their own colour and shape via the air" and they do so "by means of certain outlines which share the colour and shape of the objects and enter into us from them, entering the vision or the intellect according to the size and fit [of the effluences] and moving very quickly" (49). Epicurus refers to this introjection and internal rendering as "presentation" or *phantasia*, and it preserves the "harmonious set of qualities generated by the external object." Moreover, the generation of these *eidola* or effluences originates in the "vibration [*palseos*] of atoms deep inside the object" (50). By itself, presentation is not liable to error:

. . . whatever presentation [*phantasian*] we receive by a form of application, whether by the intellect or by the sense organs, and whether of a shape or of accidents, this *is* the shape of the solid object, produced by the continuous compacting or residue of the image [*eidolou*].[13]

Nonetheless, the very grasping of the similarity of appearances or *phantasmata* to their objects is an intellectual addition to sense perception. Falsehood and error for Epicurus is in every case not the result of sense perceptions and their *presentation* as ideas but, rather, of such additions and especially of opinions that are not explicitly testified for or against. Only with such testimony can truth arise.

How do La Mettrie's writings put the Epicurean canonic into play? In what might seem an aside in *L'homme-machine*, La Mettrie remarks that being "good natured," he avoids disputation except when he wants to "enliven conversation" (MM 17). What we have here is less an instance of social sensitivity than of barbed wit. The refusal to dispute is really a dismissal of a particular philosophical school as beneath notice. La Mettrie continues: "Cartesians will attack us . . . in vain in the name of innate ideas, but I will not expend a quarter of Mr. Locke's effort in refuting such fantasies [*chimères*]" (MM 17). La Mettrie follows up this remark on Locke's unduly prolix demythification of Cartesian philosophy with the following allusion: "What is the use of writing a long book in order to prove a doctrine which was set up as an axiom three thousand years ago?" (MM 17). La Mettrie never names the person or persons who set up such an axiom, and he leaves the reader a bit in the dark as to what the doctrine itself might be beyond the negative instance. But even if the author did not spell out the ancient reference as Epicurean, this seems the most likely attribution. As Diogenes Laërtius in his doxographical summation says concerning the canonic: "*all ideas are formed by sense-perceptions* by direct experience or by analogy or by similarity or by compounding, with reasoning also making a contribution."[14] In *Traité de l'âme* (*Treatise on the Soul*), La Mettrie had echoed this thought almost exactly, stating that the primacy of sense perceptions might keep us grounded, and he had done so in terms that clearly recall Epicurus: "In fact, our senses never deceive us, except when we make too hasty judgements on their reports; for otherwise they are faithful

---

[13] Epicurus *Letter to Herodotus* 50.
[14] Diogenes Laërtius 10.32.

ministers" (MM 62). To the canonic trust in the primacy of sense perceptions and the need to provide testimony, La Mettrie added a dose of pragmatic expediency: "The soul can count on being securely warned by them
of the traps laid for it; the senses are always on the look out and are always
ready to correct each others' errors" (MM 62).

Another clue that the ancient attack on innate ideas in question is
Epicurean comes in La Mettrie's *Abrégé des systèmes* (Summary of systems), which he appended to *De l'âme*. Consisting of encapsulations of
philosophical and physiological thinkers, it was provided by La Mettrie
as a sort of reader's guide to his most important influences. His précis of
Locke includes an assessment of both the English philosopher's criticism
of innate ideas and the sensorially developed ones he puts in their place:

Locke a été le destructeur des idées innées, comme Newton l'a été du système
Cartésien. Mais il a fait, ce me semble, trop d'honneur à cette ancienne
chimère, de la réfuter par un si grand nombre de solides réflexions. Selon ce
philosophe et la vérité, rien n'est plus certain que cet ancien axiome, mal reçu
autrefois de Platon, de Timée, de Socrate, et de toute l'académie: *Nihil est in
intellectu, quod prius non fuerit in sensu.* Les idées viennent par les sens, les
sensations sont l'unique sources de nos connoissances. Locke explique par
elles toutes les opérations de l'âme.[15]

Locke was the destroyer of innate ideas, just like Newton was of the Cartesian
system [i.e., Descartes's natural philosophy and especially his physics]. But,
it strikes me that he granted too much respect to that ancient chimera by
refuting it with such a large number of solid observations. According to this
philosopher and to the truth, nothing is more certain than that ancient
maxim, poorly received in earlier times by Plato, Timaeus, Socrates, and the
entire Academy: *Nihil est in intellectu, quod prius non fuerit in sensu.* Ideas
come via the senses, the senses are the unique source of our understanding.
Locke explains all the operations of the soul by them (my translation).

While attributed here to the ancients, the exact provenance of the expression *nihil est in intellectu, quod prius non fuerit in sensu*—"Nothing is in
the intellect that was not first given in the senses"—is murky. Sometimes
construed as Aristotelian in origin, it floated around in the early
modern period, cited by many and disparate thinkers (Robert Burton,

---

[15] La Mettrie (1796) 255.

for example, in his *Anatomy of Melancholy* [1621]).[16] What is certain is that it became a sort of unofficial motto for nascent empiricism and showed up prominently in the writings of Pierre Gassendi, from whom Locke was likely borrowing when he cited the expression in book 2 of the *Essay Concerning Human Understanding.*

Gassendi was both an ordained Franciscan and an avowed Epicurean, and he dedicated his prominent philosophical career to the strikingly counterintuitive reconciliation of these doctrines, with a good dose of eclecticism as well. He had translated Diogenes' assessment and presentation of Epicurus as part of his *Animadversiones* (1649) and had provided an extensive overview and commentary on Epicurean thought in his *Syntagma Philosophiae Epicuri*, published posthumously in 1658. And while Gassendi's atomism has received the most scholarly attention, this should not overshadow his rehabilitation of other, equally important aspects of Epicurean doctrine, including the canonic. Gassendi, moreover, had published objections to the *Meditations on First Philosophy* in 1641. He followed these objections with his *Disquisitio Metaphysica* (1644), a lengthy refutation of Descartes's replies. So while Locke has gone on to posterity as the most important refuter of innate ideas—and this reception had clearly already asserted itself by the time La Mettrie was writing—it was actually his contemporary Gassendi who had been among the earliest to critique in detail Descartes and his claims.

Gassendi was an important influence on major philosophers such as Hobbes and Locke and minor ones such as Walter Charleton in his *Physiologia-Epicuro-Gassendo-Charletonia* (1654).[17] As these names suggest, moreover, his immediate impact was great—I would venture to say greatest—across the Channel.[18] It is owing to this reception path that, while La Mettrie openly followed ancient Epicurean doctrines, he appears not to have fully realized the importance of Gassendi in reviving these doctrines in and for modern philosophy (which is not to say that La Mettrie did not know or appreciate his countryman's writings). Those English natural and moral philosophers who understood their

---

[16] Cf. Cranefield (1970) 77.

[17] On Charleton, see Booth (2005); Thomson (2008) 50–51, 72–74.

[18] See Kargon (1964). The first major study of this reception history is Mayo (1934). A more recent account of the relations between Hobbes and Boyle, in particular, will be found in Shapin and Schaffer (1989). The latter is also crucial to Bruno Latour's account of modernity (see Latour (1993) 13–48).

task as dismantling Scholasticism and its Aristotelian underpinnings welcomed Gassendi's work as kindred. Furthermore, while atomism had already made inroads as early as Francis Bacon, it was in part thanks to the contemporary reception of Gassendi that atomism became the standard physical model for close to a century in England under the rubric of "corpuscularian" natural philosophy.[19] Robert Boyle is the key figure in this rehabilitation, and though the model was not accepted without controversy—in part because of the association of Epicureanism with atheism—compromise positions were soon enough worked out. In no less a Christian text than *Paradise Lost*, for example, we come upon the four elements in the realm of Chaos bringing their "embryon atoms" as troops to battle and find that Chance reigns here unless "th' Almighty Maker" ordains these corpuscles—"His dark materials"—"to create more worlds."[20] In France, it was less religious concern about materialism—although that certainly existed, too—than the prominence of Descartes's physics of vortices that would delay acceptance of the corpuscularian hypothesis. As La Mettrie's mention of Newton's destruction of Cartesian natural philosophy makes clear, however, by the 1740s the latter had poorly weathered various controversies and its influence had largely waned.

Physics aside, the Epicurean canonic also enjoyed an important place in the writings of Gassendi. In what has frequently been cast as the founding move in modern epistemology, Descartes famously argued that if knowledge only comes from the senses, certainty will always elude us, given the ample evidence that we can, at the very least, err in our inferences from *percipiens* to truth.[21] Confronted with such a position,

---

[19] In light of the corpuscularian hypothesis, it would appear incorrect—as Deleuze and Guattari claim, drawing on Michel Serres—that atomism was historically a strand of minor science in cryptic competition with major science (Deleuze and Guattari (1987) 361). At least from the mid-seventeenth century in England, corpuscularianism was *major*—albeit free from neither controversies nor complications. On Epicureanism as a significant force in seventeenth-century thought and on Bacon's atomism, see C. Wilson (2008) 2–3 (although her entire book makes this case at length) and 22–23.

[20] Milton (2000) 47–48 (2.900, 915–16). Another example of atomism's early entry into England is the poetry and prose of Margaret Cavendish. In the eighteenth century, Pope would combine atomism with other—often incompatible—strands of physical thought in his "Essay on Man."

[21] On Descartes's attack on skepticism and unwilling acquiescence in the same, see Popkin (2003) 143–73.

one can easily grasp why Epicurus's discussion of sense perceptions might appeal to a Christian philosopher engaged in, among other things, a refutation of Descartes and the thought experiment of the "evil spirit" who falsifies our phenomenological experience. There is room for both theodicy—God is not a deceiver and we are not deceived—and for human error or sin in this account. What I want to dwell on, however, is how Gassendi latches onto Epicurean presentation or *phantasia* and from it builds a peculiarly modern understanding of the relation of imagination to the mind—an understanding that would go on to play a key role in La Mettrie's writings.

The genealogy of Gassendi's thought is complicated in this regard. It can be difficult to tease out which strand in his account of imagination comes from Epicurus or Lucretius and which from Aristotle's *De Anima* (and this in spite of Gassendi's often explicitly anti-Aristotelian stances). The latter was a major text in Scholastic thought and in medieval philosophy (particularly important for Aquinas, for example, and prominent in Dante's *Divine Comedy*). The divisions of the soul found therein laid the groundwork for faculty psychology, which dominated theories of the mind until the mid-seventeenth century and survived in various forms for considerably longer. In this respect, it is precisely Gassendi's hypothesis that all faculties can be reduced to one that tips the scale in favor of a fundamental, albeit modified, Epicureanism. This position is most clearly stated in François Bernier's *Abrégé* (1684) of Gassendi's teaching: "While it may be difficult to determine, nonetheless those who reduce all those internal faculties to Fantasy or Imagination alone seem to follow the most likely opinion" (*Quoy que ce soit une chose tout à fait difficile à determiner, neanmoins ceux qui reduisent toutes ces facultez internes à la seule Phantaisie ou Imagination, semblent suivre l'Opinion la plus probable*).[22] The argument continues explicitly against Aristotle's positing of the *sensus communis* as a distinct faculty unless we understand by this simply the place in the brain in which the nerve endings from the various senses find themselves gathered in close proximity. And while *phantaisie* can be differentiated according to its functions or operations—including sensual apprehension, will, and reason—it is

---

[22] Bernier (1992) 4: 141. My translation. Bernier was a disciple of Gassendi and a member of the medical faculty in Montpellier; he translated Gassendi's writings into French and abridged them to make them more accessible.

incorrect to treat these functions as self-standing faculties. In Gassendi's version of the canonic, imagination displaces all faculties, including intellect (which must now be considered a capacity of imagination itself).[23]

If Gassendi's revival of the canonic stopped here, it would be of passing historical interest; but evidence suggests that it did not. We know that during his French sojourn of 1635, Hobbes was in contact with Gassendi, along with Marin Mersenne and other *libertins érudits*. We also know that he read and commented on Gassendi's writings. Still, the precise nature and extent of Gassendi's influence on seventeenth-century England's preeminent materialist has been a matter of debate in intellectual history.[24] Such debate aside, it is safe to say that the fundamental role that imagination plays in Hobbes at the very least put him in the same modern Epicurean camp with regard to the canonic (even while he remained a committed plenist with regard to physics). Hobbes thus begins *Leviathan* (1651) not with the depiction of the state of nature as a state of war—this will wait until the thirteenth chapter—but rather with the claim that the way that we come to know anything must be traced to the sense perception of things coupled with their representation in the imagination:

Concerning the Thoughts of man, I will consider them first *singly*, and afterwards in *Trayne*, or dependance upon one another. Singly, they are every one a *Representation* or *Apparence* [*sic*], of some quality, or other Accident of a body without us; which is commonly called an Object.

. . . .

The cause of Sense, is the Externall Body, or Object, which presseth the organ proper to each Sense, either immediately, as in the Tast [*sic*] or Touch; or mediately, as in Seeing, Hearing, and Smelling: which pressure, by the mediation of Nerves, and other strings, and membranes of the body, continued inwards to the Brain, and Heart, causeth there a resistance, or counter-pressure,

---

[23] Gassendi is not entirely consistent on this score, at times saving a distinct place for intellect—i.e., one that is irreducible to imagination—which is more in keeping with ancient Epicureanism. Nonetheless, his more radical position helped pave the way for the reduction of all mental faculties to imagination in Hobbes and Locke—and later in Condillac and La Mettrie.

[24] On the impact of Gassendi in England, see Kroll (1991); Paganini (2001) 3–24; C. Wilson (2008).

or endeavour of the heart, to deliver itself: which endeavor because *Outward*, seemeth to be some matter without. And this *seeming*, or *fancy*, is that which men call *Sense*.[25]

Imaginatio was the Latin translation of the Greek *phantasia*, and "fancy," which derived from the latter, was used pretty much interchangeably with "imagination" (in Hobbes they are equivalents). Hobbes, as we readily see, does not speak of atomic effluences in this regard—although such a reduction is still possible—but rather of nerves as the means by which objects, either pressing mediately or immediately, are *represented* internally. We can make out in Hobbes's explanation what might be called a mild epistemological constructivism: apparent access to the world of objects is in fact a construction of these objects in and by the imagination. The move is accompanied by an inevitable epistemo-logical skepticism. This is also of a rather mild variety, for Hobbes is ultimately a pragmatically inclined empiricist. That is, while it may be true that we know only by dint of objects impinging on our senses and that we know them only via our senses—and while we only have mediate access to the world and while we might drift off into ungrounded fantasies—the constant pressure of experiences tends for the most part to rein us in.

That imagination was becoming not so much one faculty among many as the fundamental way in which the mind is thought to work and to know is nowhere clearer than in the philosophy of Locke. And while Locke certainly does not present himself as an Epicurean, the underlying importance of imagination in the *Essay Concerning Human Understanding* suggests that he had thoroughly absorbed the Gassendist revival of the canonic. (As Catherine Wilson in her study of Epicurean reception laconically remarks, while intellectual historians have been unable to gauge the exact sources of Locke's epistemology, he "owned two copies of Diogenes Laertius' *Lives*, three copies of *On the Nature of Things*" and "was associated with well-known Gassendists François Bernier and Gilles de Launay."[26]) Locke if anything extends the place of imagination to thought in general with his insistence on the primacy of *ideas* and the

[25] Hobbes (1996) 13–14.
[26] C. Wilson (2008) 149–50.

mind as a receptacle of them. Thus at the outset of the *Essay Concerning Human Understanding*, Locke writes of a terminological decision:

> But, before I proceed on to what I have thought on this subject [human understanding], I must here in the entrance beg pardon of my reader, for the frequent use of the word idea, which he will find in the following treatise. It being that term, which, I think, serves best to stand for whatsoever is the object of the understanding, when a man thinks, I have used it to express whatever is meant by *phantasm, notion, species*, or whatever it is, which the mind can be employed about in thinking. . . ."[27]

What is presented as an innocent preparatory clarification is, in fact, momentous. Locke hereby rejects the favorite terms of Scholastic philosophy: "phantasm," "notion," and "species." But we should not at all think that his embrace of "idea" in their stead is a return to Platonic intuitionism and essential forms; rather, Locke follows Hobbes and Gassendi in treating ideas in distinctly Epicurean terms as—at their most basic— internal correlates of sense perceptions, images above all. This is to say that, ironically, as imagination takes on a greater and greater role in Locke, *fantasy*—which had been a cognate—becomes increasingly suspect. The problem is clear: the line between the two is hazy, and Locke must carefully separate off imagination as a mirror of the world from fantasy as its distortion. Locke, in certain respects less pragmatic than Hobbes and more apt to seek epistemic *terra firma*, was inclined to ground the relation of *ideas* to things in primary qualities and to claim at least some "correspondence" between ideas and secondary qualities.[28]

Locke's work quickly became the touchstone for epistemological inquiry in England and Scotland for the eighteenth century. In France, while he was certainly known, the most significant moment in Locke's reception would wait until 1746 and the publication of Condillac's *Essai sur l'origine des connaissances humaines* (*Essay on the Origin of Human Knowledge*). In this work, Condillac never mentions Hobbes or Gassendi, let alone Epicurus or Lucretius, but Locke is the constant point of reference. Indeed, Condillac tried to systematically follow the English philosopher's claim that there are no innate ideas and that

---

[27] Locke (1997) 58–59.
[28] "Correspondence" is Locke's term, although what has since been debated under the rubric of the "correspondence theory of truth" was not current parlance.

ideas are generated via the senses by carrying out an extended thought experiment. This experiment involved a statue being brought to life and eventually to thought by the gradual addition of the senses. After sense perception and attention—our ability to fix on an object—Condillac added "imagination," which is initially nothing other than perception re-invoked: that which occurs when "a perception, by the force alone of the link that attention creates between itself and an object, retraces itself at the sight of that object" (*quand une perception, par la seule force de la liaison que l'attention a mise entre elle et un objet, se retrace à la vue de cet objet*).[29] From this initial recursion or retracing that is imagination, Condillac went on to generate all other mental operations. With Condillac, then, we can see that, although the revival of the canonic may have initially taken place on French soil with Gassendi, one hundred years later it reentered France in an occluded but no less important manner via England and Locke.

Given its influence, it is not odd that Locke's *Essay Concerning Human Understanding*, which was initially published in 1688, should be cited as an important point of reference by La Mettrie concerning the debate over innate ideas. What also seems clear is that Condillac's work renewed interest on the part of La Mettrie in Locke's topicality and adaptability to materialism. We can see this renewed interest at work if we compare *De l'âme*, published just prior to Condillac's treatise, with *L'homme-machine*, some three years later. When La Mettrie discusses imagination in *De l'âme*, he does so in terms that recall Lucretius to be sure but also— and above all—Aristotle and his division of the soul. There is something atavistic about La Mettrie's apparent reversion to faculty psychology in the *De l'âme*, which can be laid at the door of his return to Aristotle as an important ancient commentator on his subject. Locke, however, does not get a single mention, although there is sufficient textual evidence to suggest that La Mettrie followed him closely on the primacy of ideas and the building of ideas from simple to complex, as well as on the relation of ideas to sense perceptions (cf. MM 60–62). It is an influence that the

---

[29] Condillac (1973) 121. On Condillac, see Knight (1968); Derrida (1987). In contemporary philosophy of mind, recursion has remained—or returned—as a fundamental way of trying bridge the gap between sensation and consciousness (see, for example, Humphrey (2009)).

appended *Abrégé des systèmes* confirms. Still, La Mettrie at this point does not highlight the role of imagination as thought itself.

   This would abruptly change in *L'homme-machine*. Here, La Mettrie follows Condillac—albeit in compact, narrative form rather than systematically and at length—in generating mind from the senses and imagination and turning the latter into the mind *tout court*. As La Mettrie himself puts it:

I always use the word "imagine" because I believe that everything is imagined and that all the parts of the soul can be properly reduced to imagination alone, which forms them all, and that thus judgement, reason and memory are only parts of the soul which are in no way absolute but are veritable modifications of that sort of *medullary screen* on which the objects are painted in the eye are projected as in a magic lantern.[30]

In this formulation, the soul (*âme*) is reduced to the brain (*cerveau*). The brain itself is depicted as a sort of screen or reflective capacity, the various functions of which are mere changes in the way the internally projected world is handled and are not to be treated as discrete faculties. The brain is thereby unified by its basal operation—reflection—and fully materialized by the same gesture. We can grasp this even more clearly when La Mettrie returns to this question of reflection in his attack on teleology in *Système d'Épicure*, where he elaborates the link between basic physics—elemental units interacting at random—and physiology:

Once the elements of matter, by dint of moving about and mixing together, had managed to create eyes, it was as impossible not to see as it is impossible not to see oneself in a natural or artificial mirror. The eye happened to be the mirror of objects, which in turn often act as a mirror for it. Nature no more thought of making the eye to see, than she thought of making water to act as a mirror for the simple shepherdess. Water happened to be appropriate for sending back images; the shepherdess saw her pretty little face with pleasure. This is how the author of *Machine Man* thinks.[31]

The last sentence is a bit of playful bit of self-reference: the author of one anonymously published text refers to an earlier work, also anonymous,

---

[30] MM 14–15 (emphasis added).
[31] Ibid., 95.

as if it is not his—and thus confirms for the savvy reader the authorship of both the one and the other. But we might also read the sentence as a literal declaration of how thinking itself comes about through reflection and the subsequent reflexivity of imagination. In this respect, we can now see that the example of the eye that La Mettrie borrowed from Lucretius in his attack on finalism in fact plays another role. It is not simply that the eye is a wondrous example of creation preceding use. It is also an example of the reflective capacity of matter itself, much like the surface of water or the brain.

As in Hobbes and to a degree Locke, we find a dose of skepticism in La Mettrie, precisely at the point that we would expect: where imagination must look for a *criterion* to distinguish true from false. In La Mettrie's account, moreover, it is precisely imagination itself that must provide such a criterion and not a separate faculty such as intellect. Thus, after having stated that the soul "finds" similarities between objects that the imagination presents to itself while reasoning, he clarifies his terminological decision:

I have the used the word "find," as earlier I used the epithet "apparent" for the similarities between objects, not because I think that our senses always deceive us, as Father Malebranche claimed, nor that our eyes, naturally slightly inebriated, do not see objects as they really are—although microscopes prove this every day—but in order not to have any argument with the Pyrrhonians, the most outstanding of whom was Bayle.[32]

With this nod to ancient skepticism and to one of its preeminent modern practitioners, La Mettrie promotes what I would call a weak correspondence theory of truth or constructivist compromise: he does not deny the reality or the consistency of the environment, as in Malebranche's extension of the Cartesian demon to a general epistemological principle. Rather, he respects, while not fully endorsing, the position that empirical evidence can be deceptive but is the most sure footing we have.[33]

---

[32] Ibid., 16.

[33] La Mettrie's position here is similar to Hume's. Hume balanced, that is, his strong epistemological skepticism about any a priori truths and his skeptical critiques of causality and personal identity with an empirical pragmatism. In a largely complementary vein, Meeker (2006) 97–125 provides an incisive, deconstructive account of La Mettrie's skepticism as tied up with figural language.

Along with the reduction of parts of soul or faculties to imagination alone, what we also see in La Mettrie is an organization and ultimately emergent order that La Mettrie tends to designate as "mind" (*esprit*). But if organization is necessary to produce a mind, it is not sufficient: instruction is also required. Instruction itself, while it sounds Locke's interest in education and the need to carefully guide the etching of the *tabula rasa*, is described in terms that suggest Epicurus and the primacy of sense perceptions for the formation of ideas. To explain the process of instruction, La Mettrie uses the example with which I began: the sexless woman from Ghent. Here, however, she provides an analogy that helps us grasp what would happen if our minds were closed off from the senses and thus foreclosed from ideas:

> If organization is an asset, the first asset, and the source of all the others, then instruction is the second. Without it, the best constructed brain would be wasted, in the same way as without manners the most handsome man would simply be a crude peasant. But also what fruit would the most excellent school produce without a womb perfectly open to the admission or the conception of ideas? It is as impossible to give a single idea to a man deprived of all the senses as to give a child to a woman in whom nature was absent-minded enough to forget to make a vulva, as I have seen in one who had neither opening nor vagina nor womb. . . .[34]

Or, as La Mettrie explains in positive terms:

> But if the brain is both well organised and well educated, it is like perfectly sown, fertile earth which produces a hundred-fold what it has received; or (to abandon the figurative style which is often necessary in order to express better what is felt and to add grace to truth itself) imagination, raised by art to the splendid, rare dignity of genius, seizes exactly all the relations of ideas it has conceived, embraces easily an amazing mass of objects and deduces from them a long chain of consequences, which are simply new relationships born from a comparison with the first ones, with which the soul finds a perfect similarity. Such is, in my opinion, the generation of the mind.[35]

---

[34] MM 16.
[35] Ibid.

The metaphor of the fertile field allows La Mettrie to vividly express the notion that a "well organised" and "well educated" brain takes up the impress of experiences rather than containing innate ideas (just as a field must receive seeds, and preferably those that are purposefully sown). But he also makes a crucial distinction between what we might call system and environment: whatever is out there in the world to be experienced is made available only in the form of ideas that the imagination both produces and reflexively observes. This is to say that imagination describes both the basal function of the *brain* as the production of ideas and the emergent order of *mind.* In a telling slippage of terms, moreover, La Mettrie in the same sentence begins with "imagination" and then ends with what appears an equivalent: "the soul." That is, what we used to think of as the latter can best be grasped in terms of the former and its operations.

Indeed, although La Mettrie continues to use the word "soul" in *L'homme-machine,* he also claims that we must be very careful to specify the reference: "*the soul is merely a vain term of which we have no idea* and which a good mind should use only to *refer to* that part of us which thinks" (MM 26; emphasis added). The mode of criticism here is a common enough one in modern philosophy, and it is particularly associated with the rejection of Scholastic jargon and its misleading tendency to suggest entities where there are in fact none. We find Hobbes and Locke consistently and frequently complaining about the emptiness of terminology and the danger that such emptiness poses for thinking. As for the soul, La Mettrie suggests that we might simply put the term to the test: we cannot produce an *idea* of it—we cannot, that is, *imagine* it. It is somewhat strange, then, that La Mettrie also refers to the soul-idea as a product of our imagination and one that, once conjured, causes just the type of disturbance that good Epicureans hoped to avoid: "The one who knows the most about the physics or mechanics of the human body and who, forgetting the soul and all the worries which this figment of the imagination causes in fools and ignoramuses, concentrates on pure naturalism."[36] What is the so-called "soul" as figment of the imagination once the former soul has been reduced to the imagination? It is not the product of atomic effluences—*eidola* or *simulacra*—nor is it even an

---

[36] Ibid., 34.

image at all. Rather, language itself is granted the power to produce misconceptions that La Mettrie wants to call the misconceptions of the imagination but that, in the final analysis, cannot be: they are simply *unimaginable*. We are reminded of Wittgenstein's comment about the confusions that arise from the philosophical tendency to approach language "like an engine idling" rather than in use and so to misapprehend and misconstrue its object.[37] The major difference, of course, is that while Wittgenstein's comment was linked to his celebrated eschewal of language as adequate representation, the revival of the canonic helped usher in precisely such a model.

THE PHYSIOLOGY AND PSYCHOLOGY OF OSCILLATION

In order to fully appreciate La Mettrie's adherence to the Epicurean canonic—and also where he departed from the ancient model—we must now return to physics and consider the specific form that his materialism took. Hobbes had cryptically endorsed materialism. Out of prudence or sincerity, Locke pleaded a necessary agnosticism on whether matter might be endued with thought.[38] Bishop Berkeley, rejecting the distinction between primary and secondary qualities as specious, pushed in the direction of a thoroughgoing idealism: if ideas produced via the senses are the only access that we have to the world, then there is really no need to posit a material world at all (one might think of this, proleptically, as a critique of Kant's *Ding-an-sich* as an unnecessary multiplication of entities). Condillac might have gone in the opposite direction, but he remained true to the dualist impulse of the Cartesian position in spite of his thought experiment about the endowment of matter with sensation. In the 1740s and beyond, however, there was an increasingly radical tendency in French *philosophie* that did endorse an unqualified materialism. Diderot, to take a major example, advocated for such in his *Lettre sur les aveugles* (Letter on the blind) of 1749. This was dangerous territory,

[37] Wittgenstein (2001) 44 (§ 132).

[38] "We have the ideas of *matter* and *thinking*, but possibly shall never be able to know, whether any mere material being thinks, or no; it being impossible for us, by the contemplation of our own ideas, without revelation, to discover, whether Omnipotency has not given to some systems of matter, fitly disposed, a power to perceive and think, or else joined and fixed to matter so disposed, a thinking immaterial substance" (Locke (1997) 480).

considered subversive of religious and political authority. In the case of the *Lettre sur les aveugles*, Diderot's claim that morality is dependent on sense perceptions and his defense of atheism—albeit placed in the mouth of the blind English natural philosopher and mathematician Nicolas Saunderson—led to a three-month stay in Vincennes prison. As the anonymity of his publications suggest, La Mettrie was hardly unaware of the dangers, yet he was consistent and dogged in his advocacy of the materialist cause.

For La Mettrie, moreover, the research strands of practicing chemists, anatomists, and physicists were profoundly enmeshed with issues that we might like to label epistemological—and ultimately ethical and political.[39] It was these strands that allowed La Mettrie to shift from imagination in the soul to reflection in the brain and, ultimately, to the mere quivering of matter. Nevertheless, his positions on the details of such materialism evolved from one work to the next. In *De l'âme*, the principal dualists whom La Mettrie cites as having twisted their minds—and ironically, therefore, their bodies—in an attempt to wed the corporeal to the non-corporeal are Aristotle, Plato, Descartes, Malebranche, Leibniz, and Georg Ernst Stahl. The least familiar name on the list is Stahl, an anatomist and physiologist who upheld a mechanist understanding of the body wed to animism. The ordering above is La Mettrie's, and it is not, I think, incidental. Of the two ancient dualists, Aristotle comes first, mainly because the *De Anima* is the most important ancient point of reference for La Mettrie's treatise, the title of which echoes its predecessor. (In fact, at this point La Mettrie has just cited Aristotle on the conjunction of the soul and body as implicit confirmation that the soul must have extension.)[40] Descartes and Malebranche come next as the two most

---

[39] Thomson (2008) similarly explores the importance of medical and related discourses in La Mettrie's thought. The reception and influence of the Epicurean canonic does not concern her, but I have benefited enormously from her historical research and sensitive readings (see 180–89 in particular).

[40] La Mettrie writes: "The soul's extent constitutes thus, as it were, the body of this sensitive active being, and because of the closeness of the connection, which is such that one would think the two substances to be individually attached and joined together to form a single whole, Aristotle says, that there is no soul without a body and that the soul is not a body" (MM 64). Compare Aristotle: "As we have already said, substance is used in three senses, form, matter, and a compound of the two. Of these matter is potentiality, and form actuality; and since the compound is an animate thing, the body cannot be the actuality of the soul, but the soul is the actuality of the body. For this reason those are right in their view

important modern representatives of dualism for La Mettrie. Leibniz and Stahl point in the right direction but neither is willing—as La Mettrie is—to push his hypotheses to their logical conclusion. For his part, La Mettrie claims in good Epicurean fashion that "if the soul is not material it cannot act on the body" and that therefore "it is in fact material because it touches and moves it [sc. the soul] in so many ways, which can only be appropriate to a body" (MM 64). This is simply a gloss on Lucretius, and were this in doubt, La Mettrie provides an unattributed quotation—"Nothing can touch and be touched if it is not a body"—that directly translates a line from the *De Rerum Natura*: *tangere enim et tangi, nisi corpus, nulla potest res.*[41]

How do we arrive at this embodied, material "soul" and what might constitute its modernity? In both *De l'âme* and *L'homme-machine*, La Mettrie writes of a "principle of motion" or "motive force" that is inherent in matter, or at least in certain types of matter. These terms evoke Leibniz's physics from the late seventeenth century. Along with extension (that which is grasped geometrically; we might say "form") and *moles* (mass or stuff), Leibniz added force to the corporeal world. He called such force by various names, including *vis, primativa motrice, nisus,* and *conatus.*[42] La Mettrie explicitly nods to Leibniz on occasion, but he also seems to have a more proximate source in Émilie du Châtelet's *Institutions physiques* (Principles of physics) of 1740. This is particularly evident in *De l'âme*, where La Mettrie somewhat uncharacteristically delves into physics narrowly construed. Du Châtelet had tried to account for certain aspects of physics that the then-current Newtonian model—popularized by Voltaire and generally accepted in French academic science by then—could not explain. To do so, she rehabilitated Leibniz's notion of an inherent motility of matter—a notion that had generally fallen into desuetude and disrepute.[43] Du Châtelet contrasted what she called *forces vives* with

---

who maintain that the soul cannot exist without the body, but is not itself in any sense a body" (*On the Soul* 414a14–20, trans. from Hett (1936)).

[41] MM 64; Lucretius *De Rerum Natura* 1.304.

[42] For example, see G. W. Leibniz, "A Specimen of Dynamics" (117–38) and "On Nature Itself" (155–67), both in Leibniz (1989).

[43] Although this was not entirely true in German-speaking lands in particular, where the Leibnizian Christian Wolff helped maintain the reputation and influence of his teacher. On Du Châtelet's influence on La Mettrie, as well as her recurrence to Leibniz and Wolff, see MM xv (Thomson's introduction).

forces mortes (adding a sophisticated mathematical model as well). The purported existence of *forces vives* meant to many natural philosophers an unhappy return to Scholastic "virtues" or powers.[44] These suppositions thus engaged Du Châtelet in a polemic with Jean-Jacques Dortous de Mairan, who had just succeeded Fontenelle as perpetual secretary of the *Académie royale des sciences* and was soon to be inducted into the *Académie française*.[45] For La Mettrie, however, *forces vives* were a welcome return to a conception of matter as intrinsically motile.

Nonetheless, while La Mettrie may have drawn from physics, he inevitably conjoined this influence to properly physiological and medical discourses. After all, what he brought to the table rhetorically was not only a philosophical endorsement of empiricism—and the stress that he placed on experience over the hypotheses of great thinkers makes this endorsement clear—but also the knowledge of a practicing physician, immersed in the medical and anatomical science of his day and well versed in its history. In this regard, his writings mark a broader shift from mechanism to vitalism, or—perhaps more true to La Mettrie's understanding and rhetoric—toward a vitalist mechanics.[46] (The term *forces vives* itself, of course, at least metaphorically suggested vitalism.) Descartes's influential dualism already treated the body and physics in mechanical terms and there was also a strong mechanical bent in Harvey's theory of circulation.[47] It was Newton's research and especially his mathematical models, however, that would go on to have the greatest

---

[44] On the *forces vives* controversy, see Zinsser (2006) 185–86. The critique of "virtues" in the Scholastic sense was at this stage taken for granted, although natural philosophers were clearly still on the qui vive for retrograde occurrences. Molière famously mocked them in *Le malade imaginaire* (1673), where a learned physician explains opium's soporific effect thanks to a *virtus dormitiva* ((1979) 479). In spite of his own anti-Scholastic positions, Newton had interestingly reignited the debate insofar as gravity appeared to some as an occult power. As to whether Du Châtelet should be granted the discovery of what would later be called "kinetic energy" depends a good deal on one's understanding of scientific progress and history.

[45] For his contribution, see de Mairan (1741).

[46] On this shift, see Moravia (1978) and Duchesneau (1982). The concept of living matter could certainly be traced further back to William Harvey's work on the circulation of the blood and to ancient precedents (as we shall see). Although in Harvey's case, the vital aspect of the blood was *opposed* by mechanists—Descartes included, as an upholder of a mechanistic view of the body (see Thomson (2008) 67–69). What concerns me here, on the contrary, is the development of vitalist positions as largely sympathetic extensions of mechanist paradigms.

[47] See French (2003) 173–84.

impact in the eighteenth century. This was true not only of the disciplines in which he was directly involved, but of others such as medicine, where the Newtonian models gave rise to so-called iatromechanism or iatrophysicalism.[48] The chief proponents of these positions were Giovanni Alfonso Borelli and Archibald Pitcairne. Borelli, in his best known work *De Motu Animalium* (1680–81), examined and explained animal movement in terms of mechanical statics and dynamics. Pitcairne, a Scot who taught in Leiden before returning to his hometown Edinburgh, similarly applied physics to physiology in his *Dissertationes Medicae* (1701). The Dutch physician Herman Boerhaave would emerge as a hugely influential—albeit nuanced—proponent of iatromechanism. In his dissertation *De Distinctione Mentis a Corpore* (1689) at Leiden, Boerhaave had upheld dualism and attacked Epicurus and his modern sympathizers, such as Hobbes and Spinoza. His early work in medicine clearly incorporated Newtonian method, as in the aptly titled *Het Nut der mechanistische Methode in Geneeskunde* (The use of the mechanical method in medicine), published in 1701. But in spite of reservations and protestations, he would also increasingly call chemical explanations into physiology, a move that was to feed the shift to iatrovitalism in the mid-eighteenth century.[49] We know that La Mettrie consulted and annotated the compendium of Boerhaave's works, the seven-volume *Praelectiones academicae* (1739–44), which was edited by his most renowned pupil, the Swiss physiologist Albrecht von Haller. Moreover, La Mettrie took it upon himself to translate Boerhaave's writings into French.[50]

In *De l'âme*, La Mettrie not only countered Newtonian mechanics with his assertion that matter has the potential to acquire a "motive power" but also referred to this as matter's capacity for "the faculty of feeling" (MM 44). That these two capacities are fundamentally the same is clear, as when he notes "the unknown but obviously sensitive and active principle" in a living being as lowly as a worm (MM 44).[51]

---

[48] On the influence of Newton on medical science, see T. Brown (1987) and French (2003) 212–15.

[49] See Thomson (2008) 178–79.

[50] *Institutiones Rei Medicae* (originally 1708; translation 1743–50) and *Elementa Chemiae* (1724; translation in 1738). Thomson (1991) provides a full account of the French materialist's relation to the Dutch master.

[51] La Mettrie consistently rejects the Cartesian notion that animals are merely mechanical and have no capacity for feeling. La Mettrie even suggests that Descartes was

Of particular importance here was the notion that there could be a material but still "sensitive soul." La Mettrie attributes this term to the ancients. As with his remarks on innate ideas, he once again refrains from saying exactly which ancients he has in mind, although the Epicureans seem implied. That this is so stems in part from an important point of reference for La Mettrie: Guillaume Lamy and his *Explications mécaniques et physiques des fonctions de l'âme sensitive* (1678, Mechanical and physical explanations of the functioning of the sensitive soul). Lamy was a Gassendist who La Mettrie mentions in *L'homme-machine* as being among those "present day" Epicureans who dispute teleological explanation.[52] Lamy steered clear of materialism: he did not consider the "sensitive soul" to be the thinking and immortal part of the human. La Mettrie modified Lamy's thesis, folding it into his materialism, centering all such activity in the brain, and rejecting the notion of a "universally disseminated sensibility" (MM 55). He opposed, that is, the view that the sensitive soul feels "in all parts of the body because they all have nerves" (MM 55), a view that he attributes to the ancient Stoics, as well as to several moderns, including Perrault, who, in his *De la mécanique des animaux* (1680, On the mechanics of animals), had posited a soul spread out through the body.[53] At this point, the nerves may communicate with the sensitive soul, but they remain mechanical in the Newtonian sense. In fact, La Mettrie draws an analogy between the animal spirits within the hollow nerves, which are set in motion by outside impressions and communicate these impressions to the brain (where sensitivity proper is activated), and billiard balls (MM 59).

In *L'homme-machine*, published some three years later than *De l'âme*, La Mettrie approvingly mentions Borelli, the founding figure of iatro-mechanism, as a physician knowing much more than Leibniz. The implication is not that Leibniz was ignorant, for he did understand something

---

a crypto-materialist rather than a dualist because he could not have seriously believed such a counterintuitive hypothesis given all the empirical evidence to the contrary. On the topic of Cartesian dualism and animal sensibility in general, see Rosenfield (1968).

[52] On Lamy, see Kors (1997); Thomson (2008) 86–89.

[53] The other names mentioned are Stuart and Tabor. The author of *Exercitationes Medicae* (1724), John Tabor conjoined mathematics and animism in his research on muscle fibers. He is briefly treated in French (2003) 239–40. I have been unable to trace the reference to Stuart.

about motive force, but rather that he did not have the necessary practical experience. Between the two texts, however, iatromechanism had made great strides in the direction of iatrovitalism. We get an interesting glimpse into the shift and the terminological perturbation it caused in La Mettrie's frequent recurrence to the term "mechanical" and the metaphors of mechanism to explain the body in *L'homme-machine*: *ressorts* or "springs" are a constant. La Mettrie will also mention the clock, that favorite housing for springs and other tiny mechanisms that give movement. La Mettrie remarks, for example, that the specific organizations of the body and the embodied brain are what differentiates humanity and that the organization itself is all that is required to account for this difference: "a few springs more than in the most perfect animals, the brain proportionately closer to the heart and thus receiving more blood" are enough to explain reason and the "delicate conscience," that is, the moral susceptibility, of humans (MM 26). La Mettrie will still call these vital springs mechanical; but what he means by that increasingly comes to differ from the Newtonian sense of the word. Whereas the spring metaphor was originally based on an underlying physical sameness—the body's "springs" *are* mechanical even if they are not exactly coiled wires—the metaphor in La Mettrie has lost this fundamental agreement and is used instead to figure forth vital movement: "Each part contains its own more or less vigorous springs [*des ressorts plus ou moins vifs*], according to the extent that it needs them" (MM 28).[54]

The subtle but crucial development of the notion of mechanism in La Mettre is confirmed and extended in a terminological coinage that is seemingly unique to *L'homme-machine*. That which La Mettrie suddenly proclaimed the existence of in this text and to which there is no reference at all in *De l'âme* is what he calls "natural oscillation" or the "principle of oscillation." What is this principle and how might we explain its abrupt appearance? Ann Thomson in *Bodies of Thought* suggests possible sources in Baglivi's comments on the *vis innata* of muscles or the Jansenist doctor Philippe Héquet's similar notion of inherent muscular movement.[55] Whether or not an exact source can be found, what appears certain is that La Mettrie was deeply influenced by contemporary discussions

---

[54] French text cited from La Mettrie (1796) 76.
[55] Thomson (2008) 185–87.

about the nature of muscle fiber. In this regard, the defining moment of the shift from iatromechanism to iatrovitalism is usually seen as Haller's distinction between "sensibility" and "irritability" in his aptly named *De Partibus Corporis Humani Sensilibus et Irritabilibus*, which had its origin as a series of lectures in 1752 in Berne and was published in 1753.[56] The distinction was from the outset controversial and became increasingly so with the appearance of Haller's *Elementa* (1757–66), where his ideas were further explained and expanded. In brief, Haller considers "sensibility" a specific property of the nervous system and its communicative capacity with the brain. "Irritability" refers to the capacity of muscular and other fibers to react to stimuli. Haller's observations and assertions did not take place in a vacuum, of course: Haller was drawing on the earlier work of Baglivi and Boerhaave concerning muscular contraction, and he was attuned to—and part of—a ferment of activity on the topic in the 1730s and 1740s.[57] La Mettrie does not use the term "irritability" in *L'homme-machine*. The term's absence makes some sense given the date of Haller's groundbreaking contribution on the topic: La Mettrie died just before the publication of *De Partibus Corporis Humani Sensibilis et Irritabilis*. On the other hand, La Mettrie certainly knew of Haller's work—*L'homme-machine* included a controversial dedication to him—and the concept of "irritability" had already escaped into the less formal scientific networks of the day before the publication of Haller's text. La Mettrie does remark that muscle fibers even after death still "contract although they are no longer *irritated* by the blood and spirits" (MM 32; emphasis added). This comment may seem casual enough—surely "irritated" need not be a technical reference to Haller— but La Mettrie here points out precisely the use to which the Berne physiologist dedicated the term: susceptibility to external stimuli.[58] As we shall see, the emphasis on *external* stimuli gives us a clue as to why La Mettrie may well have avoided the term beyond the fact that it was not yet in wide circulation: he was interested in locating a source of *inherent* material motility.

[56] For an early view of Haller's impact and the embrace of vitalism, see M. Bouillet's article "Faculté Vitale" in Diderot's *Encyclopédie* ((1969) 1.1350–1).

[57] See Steinke (2004). Thomson in her preface to *Machine Man* puts forward Haller's "irritability" as the main influence on La Mettrie's "oscillation" (MM, xviii-xix).

[58] At least one of La Mettrie's editors finds in the author a precursor of Haller's conception (see Vartanian (1960) 82–89; compare Thomson (2008) 183–84).

La Mettrie also appears close to the theories of *sensibilité* that were being developed in the same period in Montpellier, which, since the Middle Ages, had been one of the most important centers of medical research in Europe. Of particular importance with respect to nascent iatrovitalism was Théophile de Bordeu, who contributed to Diderot's *Encyclopédie* and ended up a character in Diderot's later materialist dialogue *Le rêve d'Alembert* (1769, *D'Alembert's Dream*).[59] For Bordeu, *sensibilité* is a principle of the fibers of living things and is irreducible to mechanical and—here he is arguing against Boerhaave above all— chemical reactions. He further specified that the living organism as a whole is composed of organs each possessing a specific vitality or form of sensibility.[60] But while La Mettrie does use *l'âme sensitive* to refer to the brain as late as *L'homme-machine*—following the Gassendist Lamy— he only very occasionally uses *sensibilité* and *sensible*. The latter are simply not important terms for him. The omission is particularly striking because, beyond the specific vitalist direction that *sensibilité* was then beginning to receive in Montpellier, nervous sensibility more generally had established itself as part of the physiological vocabulary and was enjoying a wide cultural influence (especially in English literature and later in France, too).[61]

When La Mettrie writes in *L'homme-machine* of a "motive force" inherent in fibers as a "principle of oscillation," his terminology is thus both idiosyncratic and of a piece with what had become the cutting edge of physiology in the wake of the recent rehabilitation of Leibnizian notions of matter in physics. The lack of a consistent set of descriptive terms is less of a problem—or even simply a confirmation of La Mettrie's eclecticism—than a clear indication of the shifting terrain that La Mettrie occupies. The principle of oscillation describes inherent motility at its most fundamental. It is what drives the brain as an organized body, as

---

[59] On Bordeu and Diderot, see Audidière, Bourdin, and Duflo (2003).

[60] Bordeu's particular take on sensibility would be developed by Menuret de Chambaud, another vitalist who studied in Montpellier. On his influence on Diderot and his contributions to the *Encyclopédie*, see Duflo (2003). Menuret de Chambaud, born in 1739, was not an influence on La Mettrie; his work, however, confirms the vitalist trend that takes off in the 1740s and continues throughout the century.

[61] The secondary literature on sensibility and its impact on literature is vast. Among others, see G. S. Rousseau (1976); Todd (1986); Van Sant (1993); and Barker-Benfield (1996). For the reception and development of sensibility in France—both in medicine and literature—see Vila (1998).

well as the individual organs. Crucially, it is also present in *disorganized* bodies. Muscle fibers, for example, have a force that is independent of the brain and its sensitivity—and one that continues for a while after the death of the organism as a whole, suggesting a lingering vitality in the parts and the elements of these parts. The ultimate explanation for how this can be may well remain mysterious. That it is so is easily demonstrable not through Cartesian introspection but through empirical evidence: the criminal's heart is torn out and yet leaps into the air through muscular contractions; the dead eel continues to undulate even when chopped into pieces; the headless turkey rushes about. While suggesting both medical experimentation and common experience, these examples and others echo Lucretius's discussion of how the body and the soul are necessarily conjoined and his claim that the latter is dispersed throughout the former. Lucretius notes, for example, that a "scythed chariot" may shear off a limb, which will "quiver on the ground" while the soldier in a battle frenzy does not even realize his loss at first; he also suggests cutting up a snake to witness the animate parts writhing for a period.[62] For Lucretius, the examples suggest both the dispersion of the soul and its inability to exist outside of a corporeal substrate: the death of the body, soon enough, entails the end of animation.

La Mettrie's observations confirm that there is no need—in fact that it is wrong—to posit the soul-like capacities of the body as merely seated in the head. The "principle of oscillation" once organized gives bodily organs, including the mind, a certain autonomy. Indeed, by the time that we arrive at *L'homme-machine*, La Mettrie's criticisms of Stoic and modern animism have been both sharpened and inverted: sharpened, because La Mettrie is even more reluctant to posit a soul at all, let alone one that is spread throughout the body; inverted, because he now attributes a degree of sensitivity to all organized bodies, which include organs insofar as they are autonomous vis-à-vis the mind, as well as to matter itself.

Against the physician Stahl, La Mettrie attacks the notion that "the soul alone" is the cause of "all our movements" (MM 31). He does so by simply pointing out obvious counterexamples, such as musicians whose muscle movements are so rapid as to defy voluntarist explanation.

---

[62] Lucretius *De Rerum Natura* 3.642–47; cf. 3.657–63.

Other examples include "the heart's movement" and "the erection of the penis," both of which confirm that matter can move of its own accord. The heart as an example of what we call involuntary muscle contraction underlines the break between the will and motion. While the erection of the penis does involve muscles, La Mettrie recognizes that tumescence has more properly to do with the blood (although the exact nature of the mechanism remains somewhat hazy). The important point is still that erection is not normally subject to intrusions of the will. There is a frankly satirical edge to La Mettrie's attack on Stahl, where he imagines the doctor—whose "machine" in fact "broke down so soon"—as presumably "immortal," so godlike would his abilities have been had his hypothesis proved correct. Unlike mere humans, Stahl with "such a sovereign soul" could have "held without difficulty the reins of all the body's movements and could suspend, calm or arouse them at will!" (MM 32). Moreover, for Stahl there would be "no fever, no pain, no repining and no shameful impotence or embarrassing uncontrollable erections" (MM 32).[63] For La Mettrie, the relative autonomy of the penis is striking evidence not only *against* voluntarism but *for* "the principle of the oscillation of organised bodies" (MM 32). Boerhaave should have realized in his work on the heart that the "laborious and attractive systems" that he was forced to construct in order to defend the soul and its function as the center of all bodily movement required instead Occam's razor and a simple principle. Perhaps if he had spent less effort

---

[63] La Mettrie does not cite John Wilmot, Earl of Rochester at this point, but the libertine poet's "Imperfect Enjoyment," which describes premature ejaculation as a frustrating—for both parties—example of the mind's lack of control over the body would fit perfectly here:

> Her nimble tongue, Love's lesser lightning, played
> Within my mouth, and to my thoughts conveyed
> Swift orders that I should prepare to throw
> The all-dissolving thunderbolt below.
> My fluttering soul, sprung with the pointed kiss,
> Hangs hovering o'er her balmy brinks of bliss.
> But whilst her busy hand would guide that part
> Which should convey my soul up to her heart,
> In liquid raptures I dissolve all o'er,
> Melt into sperm, and spend at every pore.
> A touch from any part of her had done't:
> Her hand, her foot, her very look's a cunt (Rochester (1962) 38).

on the heart and more on "the erection of the penis," he would have arrived at the necessary conclusion.

At this point, La Mettrie switches his target from the Stoics—whom he always seems to have distrusted—to the school of thought and its founder that were usually his favored points of reference: Epicurus and Epicureans. The criticism arises from a development in La Mettrie's thinking: the more he embraced vitalism, the more emphatically he opposed animism. Certainly Epicurus had committed to animism of some sort when he stated, with affirmation of the canonic reliance on the senses, that "[n]ext, one must see, by making reference to our sense-perceptions and feeling (for these will provide the most secure conviction), that the soul is a body [made up of] fine parts distributed throughout the entire aggregate, and most closely resembling breath with a certain admixture of heat."[64] This *pneuma*-like soul was apparently too close to dualism for La Mettrie, and it led him to take his distance from Epicurus.[65] As for the moderns, in *L'homme-machine*, La Mettrie attributes such animism to Perrault and to the English physiologist Willis. The latter was a declared Epicurean who had written of the "fiery soul" disseminated throughout the animal or "brute" body, much in the manner of Lamy (whom he certainly influenced). While neither Perrault nor Willis might have had the great mind of a Boerhaave, their "careful observations" led them in the right direction; nevertheless, they ultimately went astray, incorrectly positing "a soul generally spread throughout the body" (MM 32). According to La Mettrie:

Their hypothesis—which was Virgil's and that of all the Epicureans, and which the history of the polyp seems at first sight to support—the movements which survive after the death of the subject in which they are found

---

[64] Epicurus *Letter to Herodotus* 63.

[65] Lucretius appears to have maintained a more consistent materialism on this score, and one that clearly appealed to La Mettrie: ". . . if anyone denies that the body can feel, and believes that it is the spirit mingled throughout with the body that takes on that motion which we name feeling, he fights against those things that are quite manifest and true. For who will ever explain what it is for the body to feel, unless it be what experience has openly shown and taught us?" (Lucretius *De Rerum Natura* 3.350–55). Still, Lucretius did make a basic distinction between body and mind or soul—he seems to use *mens* and *anima* interchangeably—and subscribed an animism that La Mettrie ultimately rejected (see *De Rerum Natura* 3.546–641).

come from a remnant of the soul, preserved in the parts which contract although they are no longer irritated by the blood and spirits.[66]

In this passage, which I have already cited in relation to Haller, we can see that oscillation is not only akin to irritability but that it also differs from it. It names not a mere reaction to stimuli but a movement originating in the parts themselves.

Similarly, La Mettrie might still retain the brain as the place where sensitivity or sensibility as a specific organization of oscillation is located while preserving the autonomy of other organs. The physicians Perrault and Willis *saw* this principle of oscillation—the evidence of the senses was there for them—but they were misled by philosophy and its terminology and simply misstated their actual findings:

> . . . these writers, whose solid works easily eclipse all the fables of philosophy, were only mistaken in the same way as those who accorded matter to the faculty of thought; I mean that they expressed themselves badly, using obscure and meaningless terms. For what is this remnant of the soul but the Leibnizians' motive force, badly conveyed by such an expression, but which Perrault in particular really had an idea of.[67]

Recalling his endorsement of language as adequate representation—and his distrust of vain and misleading terminology—La Mettrie here decries a concatenation of bad terms: Willis and Perrault use "soul" to indicate Leibniz's "motive force," which should ultimately be resolved into La Mettrie's own "principle of oscillation." (Of course, the irony is that such oscillation cannot be grasped as such but must be inferred—just as Epicureans inferred atomism without being able to point to any atoms per se.) In spite of his allegiance, then, to Epicureanism in its doxographical division into ethics, physics, and, implicitly, the canonic—not to mention his allegiance to what he rightly saw as an Epicurean thread in modern physiological explanations—La Mettrie nonetheless rejected the tradition on this one local but important point: the *apparent* evidence for the soul being spread throughout the body is *in fact* evidence that matter is oscillatory rather than animate.

---

[66] MM 32.
[67] Ibid.

This rejection aside, we might still see in La Mettrie's apparently idiosyncratic term "oscillation" the place where he forged a linkage of the physical and the anatomical that remained deeply indebted to Epicurus. "Oscillation," after all, is not so much a trace of the famous swerve or *clinamen*—the chance deviation of atoms in their downward trajectory— as that internal quivering, *palmos* or *palseos*, that Epicurus describes as a feature of atoms and that Gassendi had translated with *agitatio* and *palpitatio intestina*.[68] La Mettrie's adaptation of Epicureanism is thus Epicurean in its own way: it rests on the melding of an idea from Epicurean physics, inherent motion, to the canonic, even if the result is at odds with some of classical doctrine. As he puts it in *L'homme-machine*: "Given the slightest principle of movement, animate bodies will have everything they need to move, feel, think, repent, and, in a word, behave in the physical sphere and in the moral sphere that depends on it" (MM 26). This "slightest principle of movement" can be nothing other than the tremulous nature of matter itself. All the rest follows as in Condillac, but without the need for dualism. We can see this linkage most clearly in a comparison of the two organized bodies that seem to have most fascinated La Mettrie: the brain and the penis. The gap between them is both as small—and as large—as between humans and animals. For the penis may have what La Mettrie calls a "singular spring," irreducible to voluntary control, but the penis, along with the heart, the sphincters of the bladder and the rectum, and other muscles and systems are only "little minor springs" compared to the "subtle and wonderful one" within the brain: "that instigating and impetuous principle which Hippocrates calls ἐνορμων (the soul)" (MM 28).[69] The main distinction must simply

---

[68] Gassendi (1658) *Opera Omnia* 3.18.

[69] According to Thomson (MM 28n), La Mettrie's reference to the Hippocratic soul— *enormon* or *impetum faciens*—may be borrowed from Gaub (1745). See further Thomson (2008) 178, 183–84, which addresses Boerhaave's own use of *impetum faciens* and the Gaub connection. In the works of Josephus Thomas Rosetti we find both *enormon* and the Latin translation taken up from Hippocrates—*divinus Senex*—and theorized at length as part of the author's critical rejection of certain aspects of mechanical physiology as insufficiently explanatory and of his advocacy of an *energetic* model (see French (2003) 240–44). On the nature and function of the *enormon*, see Rosetti (1735) 10–17 in particular. In the reception of Hippocratic theory, the concept was associated with the vital or impulsive force of breath or spirit (*pneuma*), as Castellus (1721) 320 (a well-known medical dictionary) makes clear: ἐνορμων, *impetum faciens. Dicitur et simpliciter* ὸρμων. *Epitheton spirituum aptissimum, & rei naturam exprimens, videlicet summam levitatem, tenuitatem,*

be that the penis may move of its own accord but it does not imagine. It has not developed the reflective capacity of matter that allows the brain to present ideas and to treat them recursively—that is, to think.

Moreover, it is imagination that guarantees that the mind can communicate with the penis even though the penis is nonetheless relatively autonomous and not subject to voluntary control:

> Why does the sight, or mere idea, of a beautiful woman cause singular movements and desires in us? Does what happens then in certain organs come from the very nature of those organs? Not at all, but from the intercourse and sort of sympathy of those muscles with the imagination. All we have here is one spring, excited by the Ancients' "beneplacitum" or by the sight of beauty, exciting another one, which was very drowsy when the imagination awoke it. And what can cause this except the riot and tumult of the blood and spirits, which gallop with extraordinary rapidity and swell the hollowed-out organs?[70]

We glimpse in this otherwise lascivious example of visual stimulation an opening onto La Mettrie's modified Epicureanism with respect to ethics. La Mettrie rejected Stoicism, which might be seen to share the Epicurean position on fear and death, as precisely a misguided corruption of our "innate taste for life" (MM 109). In contrast, La Mettrie was an open apologist for pleasures in his treatise *De la voupté* (On sensual pleasure), first published in 1745 and republished in expanded form with the even more pointed title *L'art de jouir* (The art of enjoyment) in 1751 (the year of his death at just shy of forty-two). With regard to ancient ethics, La Mettrie's defense of sensual and frankly sexual indulgence more than anything else looks Cyreniac, that is, indebted to the sectarians of Aristippus, who upheld so-called kinetic pleasures and denied the katastematic pleasures—those of withdrawal and lack of disturbance— that Epicurus asserted and generally emphasized.[71] In short, La Mettrie's

---

& activitatem. We are, of course, much more familiar with early twentieth-century revival of the term as "hormone."

[70] MM 29. La Mettrie's use of *beneplacitum* appears unorthodox. It was one Vulgate translation of *eudokia*, and will be found in Ephesians 1:9 and 1 Corinthians 10:5. In these contexts it refers to God's good will. I can find no pagan reference or sense in which it means "sight of beauty."

[71] See, for example, his pointedly titled *Anti-Séneque* or *Anti-Seneca* (cf. MM 117–43). La Mettrie wrote approvingly of the Cyreniacs' derivation of justice from convention and

free thinking and open interest in the physiology of sexual response would seem ill-equipped to dispel the charges of hedonism long laid at the doorstep of Epicurus in Christian Europe—a hedonism that was considered of a piece with materialism, itself deemed tantamount to atheism.

But although La Mettrie certainly did not try to circumscribe happiness by limiting it to katastematic pleasures, his avowed sensualism did not run entirely counter to the injunctions of Epicurus and the more stringent Lucretius, who suggested avoiding love—and the images or *simulacra* associated with it—as a disturbance and believed that at most we ought to treat sexual intercourse as a way to safely drain off love's troubling influence.[72] For La Mettrie also looked to moderation and balance, wishing only to relive the existence he has known: "in the midst of good food, good company, joyfulness, study and seduction, dividing my time between women—that charming school of the Graces— Hippocrates and the Muses, always both hostile to debauchery and favorable to sensuality. . . ." (MM 111). And while he allows that among the organs of touch are the "reproductive organs, whose vivid feeling penetrates and transports the soul into the sweetest and happiest moments of our existence," there is a place for more sophisticated, educated enjoyments, such as good company, intellectual pursuits, and beauty, too (MM 58). What we see in La Mettrie is the sort of libertinage that developed as an intellectual position and ethical stance in France in the 1740s: a philosophically informed and moderated license. As a literary genre, the best example of this trend is *Thérèse philosophe*, now usually attributed to Jean-Baptiste Boyer, Marquis d'Argens, and published in 1748. This tale of initiation combines lessons in materialist science and ethics with pedagogy in sexual pleasure.[73] But while assuredly licentious

---

advantage alone: "How much proof of judgement was given by the Cyreniacs, when they realised that laws and customs alone had created the distinction between the just and the unjust, and that in order to weigh up and appreciate vices and virtues legitimately, all scales were inaccurate except those in which only the advantages for a society were taken into account" (MM 130).

[72] "But it is fitting to flee from images [*simulacra*], to scare away what feeds love, to turn the mind in other directions, to cast the collected liquid into any body, and not to retain it, being wrapped up once and for all in the love of one, nor to cherish care and certain pain for yourself" (Lucretius *De Rerum Natura* 4.1063–67).

[73] On *Thérèse Philosophe*, see Jacob (1993) 180–85, 201–202; Darnton (1995), esp. 89–115; and Meeker (2006) 126–54.

and frankly pornographic in its representations, this work still cautions against deleterious excess. Like the author of *Thérèse philosophe*, La Mettrie is thus surprisingly true to Epicureanism even when he swerves toward an area considered suspect in by the orthodox classical sources. It would be wrong, however, to think of mental enjoyment as somehow fundamentally distinct from that of other bodily organs, such as the penis or clitoris: for La Mettrie, the pleasures produced by imagination and in the brain may be "subtle and wonderful" but they are for that no less material.

7

Sensual Idealism: The Spirit of Epicurus and the Politics of Finitude in Kant and Hölderlin

Anthony Curtis Adler

I. EPICUREANISM'S PECULIAR FATE

If the reception of a school of philosophy or system of beliefs involved only the explicit philosophical appropriation of *doctrine*, we could hardly speak of a reception of Epicureanism in German philosophy during the late eighteenth century. Explicitly Epicurean ideas played a vital role in the early German Enlightenment, and were advanced by none less than Frederick the Great, the king of Prussia, who, as Reid Barbour suggests, "gave Lucretius his best chance at hegemony in eighteenth-century Europe."[1] Yet the centrality of Kant's critical turn for subsequent German philosophy would seem to have rendered Epicureanism irrelevant shortly thereafter. So, at least, it must appear if, following a still common interpretive tendency, we consider the absolute idealism of Hegel as the culmination of the philosophical revolution initiated by the *Critique of Pure Reason*. While we find sporadic, curious references to Epicureanism

I would like to thank Brooke Holmes and Wilson Shearin for their helpful comments and support during the process of revision. The following abbreviations will be used in citing Kant and Hölderlin: Kant (1900–) = KA; Hölderlin (1995–2008) = SW. Unless otherwise noted, all translations are my own.

[1] Barbour (2007) 163. Regarding the reception of Epicureanism in the early German Enlightenment, see Kimmich (1993).

in the texts of idealist philosophers after Kant, Epicureanism for the most part no longer appears as a doctrine to which any true philosopher could ascribe, but rather as a way of thinking that is not only false, but fundamentally unphilosophical: the antithesis of the spirit of German idealism, with its revolutionary attempt to regard every immediate experience of reality and seemingly self-evident philosophical truth as a mere moment in the process through which absolute spirit realizes itself and discloses its essence. It is thus that Hegel treats Epicureanism in his *Lectures on the History of Philosophy*.[2] Even more tellingly, in the *Phenomenology of Spirit*, which considers historical phenomena only insofar as they are exemplary for the "history of spirit," Hegel neglects Epicureanism altogether: Stoicism and Skepticism are followed immediately by the unhappy consciousness of medieval Christianity.[3]

The fate of Epicureanism, moreover, seems already sealed in Kant's own philosophical development. In his precritical writings, where he struggles with the conflict between the rationalism of the Leibniz-Wolff school and the empiricism of Newtonian natural science, one occasionally encounters a more or less direct, and explicitly affirmative, appropriation of Epicurean doctrine. In the *Universal Natural History and Theory of the Heavens* (1755), Kant calls attention to the similarity between his own doctrine and that of Lucretius, and indeed his theory could be seen to reproduce, in only somewhat veiled fashion, the most central tenets of Epicurean natural and moral philosophy, despite rejecting Epicurean "chance" in favor of the regularity and order of a strict determinism.[4] And Kant's *Observations on the Feelings of the Beautiful and Sublime* (1764) presents a Lucretian counterargument to Burke's own anti-Lucretianism.[5] Yet the texts that lay the foundations for Kant's critical philosophy—the *Critique of Pure Reason* (first published in 1781) and the *Critique of Practical Reason* (1788)—challenge the main tenets of Epicureanism: its atomistic conception of physical reality and its hedonistic conception of the good.

It is not hard to explain Kant's rejection of Epicurean doctrine. By insisting that there can be no theoretical knowledge of things as they

---

[2] Inwood (1992) 262.
[3] Ibid.
[4] Fenves (2003) 11–12; see also Baker (2007) 285 and Aubenque (1969) 293–303.
[5] Baker (2007) 284. See also Baker (2001).

are *in themselves,* but only in their relation to the knowing subject, Kant's critical turn excludes not only the atomistic materialism at the foundation of Epicurean natural philosophy but any philosophical system based on fundamental claims about the nature of things as such.[6] Thus, in the transcendental dialectic of the first critique, Epicureanism represents the pure, dogmatic form of empiricism, which, in contrast to the skeptical, protocritical empiricism of Hume, does not merely affirm that there is no knowledge that is not empirical, but—passing from epistemology to ontology—asserts dogmatically that whatever cannot be known empirically does not exist (KA 3: 327–28).[7]

From a theoretical perspective, both dogmatic empiricism and dogmatic rationalism (e.g., Platonism) are at once justified by the perfectly consistent operations of natural reason, and yet ultimately involve a similarly illegitimate overstepping of reason's proper limits. From the perspective of practical philosophy, however, the "dogmatic empiricism" of Epicureanism is subject to a special critique. Whereas the dogmatic assertion of the existence of a transcendent principle, however theoretically misguided, supports true morality and religion, its dogmatic denial undermines the very possibility of moral action.[8] Kant expands on this critique of Epicurean ethics in the second critique, the *Critique of Practical Reason.* An action, if it is to be truly ethical, must be motivated only by obedience to a principle formulated by pure reason. Sensual interests, such as the pleasure of the Epicureans, cannot play any role in the motivation of action (KA 5: 21–22). Moreover, as in the case of theoretical philosophy and metaphysics, the rejection of Epicurean moral doctrine also reflects a more general critique of the approach taken by ancient philosophy. Thus, in the lectures on ethics given while he was working on the first critique, Kant distinguishes between ancient ethics, which presents an *ideal* of the "best kind of person," and modern ethics, which, oriented toward the principles of ethical action, involves claims about

---

[6] Neither Kantian nor post-Kantian idealism should be confused with Berkeley's claim that reality is exclusively mental. Denying neither the existence of reality outside the mind nor the objective validity of knowledge, Kant claims, rather, that we cannot know things as they are in themselves, but only in relation to the knowing subject. For further discussion of this point, see Allison (1986).

[7] See Aubenque (1969) 295.

[8] Ibid.

"what to do and why to do it."[9] Whereas ancient ethics tells us how we should ideally be, modern ethics tells us how we should act.

The very fact that Kant's rejection of Epicurean doctrine rests on a more general rejection of doctrinal, dogmatic presentations of philosophy, all of which either involve an overstepping of the rightful limits of reason (as in the case of theoretical philosophy) or a fundamental misconception of the nature of ethics, suggests that Kant does not reject Epicureanism so much as its presentation as *doctrine*. In this respect, his rejection of Epicureanism would be no different than his rejection of the other philosophical schools of antiquity and their modern descendants. Moreover, it would be wrong to think that Epicurus disappears altogether from Kant's work or that the anti-Epicureanism of post-Kantian idealism was inevitable. In a footnote to the *Critique of Pure Reason*, Kant, after doubting whether Epicurus presented his own principles dogmatically as objective assertions about reality, states that "if these were nothing more than maxims of the speculative use of reason, then he showed in so doing a more authentically philosophical spirit than any other of the philosophers of antiquity" (KA 3: 327). This strange formulation suggests a remarkable possibility: if the "spirit of Epicurus" anticipated critical philosophy, then Kant's explicit rejection, in the name of critique, of Epicurean doctrine is itself an Epicurean gesture. The spirit of Epicurus—of restricting philosophical speculation to the evidence of the senses—is itself what demands a rejection, or at least a marginalization, of Epicurus's doctrinal "letter."

Once we grant that Kant distinguishes the Epicurean spirit from the Epicurean letter, then, in addressing his reception of Epicureanism, we must allow that an "Epicurean spirit" is at work in his thought even where there is little direct evidence of Epicurean doctrine.[10] From this new perspective, things look very different. Indeed, as Peter Fenves has argued, Kant's thought remains engaged, from beginning to end, with

---

[9] Wood (2005) 9.

[10] The distinction between the spirit and the letter plays a critical role in Fichte's Kant-reception and the early development of German idealism. But it is also present in Kant. *Reflexion* 778 (KA 15.1: 340–41), for example, distinguishes between imitating the spirit and the mere letter of genius. Regarding this passage in its historical context, see Gammon (1997) 563–92.

"the spirit of Epicurus."[11] Yet even allowing this, if we consider the German idealist philosophers who followed Kant, it might still seem that his enduring respect for Epicurus remains a fluke, without consequence for the subsequent development of German philosophy. As Hegel's treatment of Epicureanism suggests, it is no longer just the doctrines of Epicurus that will be rejected, but the Epicurean spirit.

This conclusion, though, fails to recognize the complex philosophical development that takes place between Kant's first critique and Hegel's mature system. Recent decades, indeed, have seen a flourishing interest in the formative years of German idealism. Scholars have precisely charted the path leading from Kant's critical philosophy to Hegel, paying more attention to mediating figures such as Salomon Maimon, Karl Leonhard Reinhold, and Friedrich Immanuel Niethammer, as well as to marginal textual moments—to a letter that resists, or even contradicts, the spirit of idealism.[12] And they have also begun to take seriously other intellectual tendencies that emerged from the same context as German idealism and even followed the same path up until a certain point, but that, insofar as they broke from it in decisive ways, cannot be reduced, as Hegel would have had it, to mere sterile and pathological aberrations from the true destiny of spirit.

The works of Friedrich Schlegel, Friedrich Hölderlin, and Friedrich Wilhelm Joseph Schelling represent the most significant of these other paths. Their projects are vastly different, and yet all three demonstrate, at certain crucial junctures in their early intellectual development, a striking interest in and affinity with Epicureanism. With Schelling and Schlegel there is a remarkable testament to this engagement: the poem "Heinz Widerporst's Epicurean Confession of Faith," which Schelling composed around 1800.[13] Written as a satirical response to the new religiosity that Novalis and Schleiermacher introduced into the romantic movement, Schelling, at the time still closely associated with Schlegel's Jena circle, suggests the fidelity of both Schlegel's ideas and his own to an

---

[11] Fenves (2003) 10. Epicureanism is a major theme of the first chapter of Peter Fenves's study of Kant's late writings.

[12] Notable in this regard is the work of Dieter Henrich, Manfred Frank, Frederick Beiser, Philippe Lacoue-Labarthe, and Jean-Luc Nancy. Pinkard (2002) offers an accessible survey of these developments, while Beiser (2008) provides a more detailed account of the formative stages of German idealism.

[13] Schelling (1869) 1: 282–92.

Epicurean sensualism.[14] The poem's Epicureanism, as simplistic as it seems in its rejection of all that transcends the senses, is hardly peripheral to Schelling's philosophical project. Indeed, it is linked not only to the intentions of his philosophy of nature but also, as Lacoue-Labarthe and Nancy argue, represents the failed attempt at a poetic presentation (*Darstellung*) of philosophy: an attempt that, paradoxically, is at once heroic and satirical.

The explicit evidence of Hölderlin's Epicureanism is even more slight and has attracted almost no critical attention. This certainly has to do with the elliptical and fragmentary fashion in which Hölderlin develops his philosophical insights. Yet once we recognize how Kant transforms the question of the reception of Epicureanism, we can appreciate the extent of Hölderlin's own engagement with the Epicurean tradition, and interpret the few scattered references to Epicureanism in the proper light.

Such, at least, is the aim of this chapter. More concretely, I hope to show how Kant comes to conceive Epicureanism not as a system of philosophical doctrine but in terms of an "Epicurean spirit" at work in both the history of philosophy and human rationality. This Epicurean spirit, I further argue, comes to exert a powerful, even guiding influence on the development of Hölderlin's thought. This influence, in turn, results in a philosophy of "sensual idealism" that not only challenges the intellectualism of the dominant forms of post-Kantian idealism but suggests the limits of the theoretical attitude, insisting on *poetic language* and *political engagement* as principle ways of "doing philosophy."

The first part of this essay (sections II, III, and IV) focuses on Kant's critical philosophy. In section II, I explore Kant's invocation of *prolēpsis* in the *Critique of Pure Reason*, arguing that his idiosyncratic interpretation of *prolēpsis* as a nonempirical form of knowledge suggests that he draws a distinction between two different concepts of Epicureanism. Whereas the transcendental dialectic conceives of Epicureanism as the exemplification of "dogmatic empiricism," in "The Anticipations of Perception," Epicureanism appears, instead, as a philosophical sensualism. In this way, Kant gives a more concrete sense to the distinction between the doctrine of Epicureanism and its spirit. The discussion of the

---

[14] Lacoue-Labarthe and Nancy (1988) 79–80.

anticipations of perception, moreover, suggests what is at stake in this "spirit of Epicureanism": nothing less than the difficult, even paradoxical idea of an a priori knowledge and experience of the constitutive passivity and finitude of the subject. Thus we can begin to identify a sublimated, spiritualized Epicureanism as a guiding force in Kant's critical philosophy.

In section III, I turn to the preface of the second edition of the *Critique of Pure Reason* and the concluding section on "The History of Pure Reason." Both texts concern the way in which pure reason, which by definition exists independent of empirical experience, is nevertheless experienced in historical time. To explain this peculiar kind of historical experience, Kant invokes Epicureanism, which he conceives of not as a system of dogmatic claims about the nature of reality but as an essential tendency of reason, originating in the ineradicable a priori presence of sensibility (*Sinnlichkeit*) within pure reason. In this way, Epicureanism, far from being banished from philosophy by Kant's critique, assumes a central importance. The history of pure reason comes to be understood as a battle between two opposing tendencies: one sensualist and Epicurean, the other intellectualist and Platonic. Kant's discussion of the historical character of the experience of reason might nevertheless seem rather peripheral to the critical project as a whole, which is often conceived of as antihistorical in its intention. Against this conception, I argue that the "critical turn" itself involves reason reflecting upon its own operations and thus recognizing the tendencies that operate within it. Since these tendencies (sensualism and intellectualism) are manifest in the futile struggles that unfold in the course of reason's history, Kant's "Copernican revolution" in philosophy involves nothing else than reason becoming aware of its historical character. This historical character, moreover, is marked by futility. Thus, the critical turn consists above all in reason recognizing its own tendency toward failure; the impossibility of realizing the very success—systematic closure—that it demands of itself.

Section III concludes by suggesting that this understanding of Epicureanism as a "philosophical tendency"—a spirit animating reason—rather than a dogma requires a very different interpretation of the problem of reception. Section IV expands on this point by arguing that Kant, in the *Critique of Judgment*, explicitly transforms Epicurean sensualism into a theory of reception, reading, and history. Crucial to this theory of reception is the analysis of the aesthetic judgment of the beautiful as the ability to feel and judge that we belong to a community of finite rational subjects who share not merely a common rational nature but a common sensibility, a common capacity for feeling. The aesthetic experience of the beautiful, I further suggest, resembles Epicurean *ataraxia*. Like *ataraxia*, aesthetic pleasure is a feeling of restful self-sufficiency. In this way, Kant restores what he recognizes as the basic ethical problematic of ancient thought: the question of "how we should be" rather than "what we should do." Yet he proposes, in place of the *ataraxia* of the Epicurean sage, a "modern" ethics of being, privileging vital activity, an openness to experience and to the vicissitudes of social existence over a static, secluded freedom from mental disturbances and pain.

It is precisely this "modern" ethics of being, I argue in the second part of the chapter (sections V and VI), that Hölderlin, inheriting the "Epicurean spirit" of Kant's critical philosophy, develops into an original, philosophically penetrating account of politics, poetry, and historical existence. Section V begins by arguing that Hölderlin's early fragments on punishment and suffering revise Kantian ethics by insisting on the primacy of sensibility over the intellect. The full consequences of this revision appear in later philosophical fragments such as "Being Judgment Possibility" and "The Declining Fatherland," where Hölderlin argues that the absolute does not reveal itself directly to human reason but exhibits itself through a fundamentally temporal *feeling* of the dissolution of reality. This dissolution of reality constitutes a "sensual idealism" and is explicitly identified with Epicureanism.

In the final section (VI), I turn to Hölderlin's tragedy, *The Death of Empedocles*. The *Empedocles* tragedy, I claim, represents an attempt to present through poetic language the "real dissolution" of sensual idealism. But it also subjects Epicureanism, as an ethical ideal—a "way of being"—to a powerful critique. The result of this critique, however, is not to reject Epicurean sensualism but to transform it into the demand that we exist politically and historically, remaining open to, and even embracing, the turbulence and dissonance that comes from commerce with our fellow human beings. Thus Hölderlin develops Kant's Epicurean insights regarding the sensibility and finitude of human reason and the role of feeling in historical experience. History demonstrates our failure as human beings to realize the highest ethical ideal, transcending our human limitations and becoming like the gods. While Hölderlin decisively rejects the ethical goal of Epicureanism, he does so in the name of an even more fundamental, political rather than ethical, materialism, which he will identify in his tragedy with Empedocles.

II. KANT'S FIRST CRITIQUE: THE ANTICIPATION OF PERCEPTION

Perhaps the most striking indication both of Kant's philosophical debt to Epicureanism and of the curious manner in which an Epicurean spirit informs the critical project is the treatment of the anticipations of perception (*Antizipationen der Wahrnehmung*) in the *Critique of Pure Reason*. Anticipation, for Kant, refers to "all knowledge [*Erkenntnis*] through which I am able to recognize [*erkennen*] and determine a priori that which belongs to empirical cognition" (KA 3: 152). It is, in other words, the knowledge of that which forms empirical cognition in advance: of the a priori basis without which no empirical experience is possible. Kant then refers this concept of anticipation back to Epicurus: "and without doubt that is the meaning in which Epicurus used the expression πρόληψις."

This definition of *prolēpsis* seems unusual. The evidence of Epicurus's teachings recorded in Diogenes Laërtius suggests that *prolēpsis* does not involve notions given prior to empirical experience but rather universal notions, derived from frequently repeated sensations, about what a certain thing—such as a "man" or "truth"—is. These are invoked whenever we use the name of the thing in forming a judgment (10.33).[15] When I judge that "this certain thing (that I see before me) is a man," I must not only be sure of the truthfulness of my sensations, but I must also already know what a man in general is. *Prolēpsis*, so conceived, is a priori in a relative rather than absolute sense: preconceptions are given in advance of specific empirical judgments but not of empirical experience *as such*. But precisely this is what Kant, in his *Logic*, understands by an "empirical concept."[16]

Kant's interpretation of *prolēpsis* as a fundamentally nonempirical form of knowledge is less strange if we consider that his understanding of Epicureanism most likely drew on Lucretius and Cicero rather than

---

[15] Regarding *prolēpsis* in Epicureanism, see Long and Sedley (1987) 1: 87–89.
[16] Kant (1801) 130–31.

Diogenes Laërtius.[17] In Cicero's *De Natura Deorum*, the Epicurean Velleius, defending his school's understanding of the gods, conflates Epicurus's *prolēpsis* with a notion of innate ideas imprinted in the soul. Epicurus's *prolēpsis*, he explains, "is what we may call a delineation of a thing, preconceived by the mind, without which understanding, inquiry and discussion are impossible" (*De Natura Deorum* 1.43b).[18] Yet while Cicero's rather idiosyncratic reading of Greek philosophy explains Kant's interpretation of *prolēpsis* in "The Anticipations of Perception," it is hard to reconcile this interpretation with Kant's own understanding of Epicureanism. How is it that Epicurus, the archetype of the dogmatic empiricist, could have anticipated, in the very concept of anticipation, the principle of Kant's own critical revolution?

This statement is no mere confusion, I propose, but rather suggests that Kant, in the first critique, doubles the figure of Epicureanism, drawing an implicit distinction between the two forms it may take: one involving a dogmatic empiricism and materialism, the other a form of sensualism. The difference between empiricism and sensualism, while subtle, allows precise formulation within a Kantian framework. Empiricism—dogmatic or otherwise—maintains that all legitimate knowledge derives from empirical experience, in which objects impact our senses and give rise to sensations (*Empfindungen*). Sensualism, by contrast, maintains that knowledge begins with the senses rather than reason. But it leaves open the possibility that sensibility (*Sinnlichkeit*) can produce knowledge a priori. Empiricism, so understood, implies sensualism, since all empirical experience is sensate, but sensualism does not necessarily imply empiricism.

The potential scope of Kant's concept of anticipation is immense. It seems to coincide with the a priori itself, for a priori knowledge is, by definition, the anticipation of the formal aspect of the a posteriori. It is perhaps surprising, then, that Kant does not deploy the concept of anticipation more systematically in the first critique. Why is the more general notion of anticipation introduced first of all with respect to a certain species of anticipation: the anticipation of perception? A possible answer emerges if we consider more closely the nature of the anticipation

---

[17] See Aubenque (1969) 302.
[18] Trans. Long and Sedley (1987).

of perception itself. This consideration involves a sort of limit case of the a priori. In the anticipation of perception, it is not the formal qualities of empirical experience, as with a priori intuitions of space and time, that constitute the anticipations of appearance (*Erscheinung*), but, rather, the anticipation of precisely that which, at first glance, seems incapable of anticipation: sensation itself (*Empfindung*) as the material of perception. The anticipation of perception, in other words, involves a priori knowledge of that which constitutes empirical experience as empirical experience: the very fact of the subject being affected through sensations that are irreducible to the spontaneous and productive faculties of the subject. It is the a priori knowledge and experience of the constitutive passivity and finitude of the subject.

For Kant, the possibility of a priori knowledge rests on the spontaneity of the subject. The anticipation of perception is thus something quite odd: the spontaneous, active production of a pure, constitutive passivity—the anticipation of the very capacity to have experiences that cannot be fully anticipated.

The anticipation of perception ultimately suggests the "mixed" nature of a subject that is at once *rational* and *finite*. The entire critical project thus depends on *prolēpsis*. Yet the fact that critical philosophy rests on this ostensibly Epicurean ground indicates a potentially contradictory aspect of the critical project—one that would challenge Kant's own systematic optimism and the Enlightenment faith in reason. If critical philosophy depends on a transcendental sensibility and materiality, then perhaps the critique of pure reason must lead reason to the realization of its own irreducible irrationality.

In the next section, I consider the problem of history in Kant's *Critique of Pure Reason*. Here Kant presents his most sustained reflections on the finitude, irreducible sensuality, and even irrationality of human reason. Here, too, the spirit of Epicureanism comes to play a more extensive role in his thought.

III. KANT'S FIRST CRITIQUE: THE RUINS OF REASON

Despite the attention devoted in recent decades to Kant's philosophy of history, there remains a perception that the project announced in the *Critique of Pure Reason* is either indifferent to history or even virulently anti-historical.[19] Yet while Kant's search for the transcendental, a priori conditions of human knowledge and experience challenges any attempt to make the operation of reason subject to historical change, the problem of the history of metaphysics nevertheless frames the *Critique of Pure Reason*. It is the subject of the prefaces to both the first and second editions, as well as the preface of the final section.

In contrast to Lessing, Herder, and later Hegel, who all conceive of history as a progressive realization of human rationality, and even in contrast to the ostensive intention of his own writings on the history of humanity, Kant seems to regard the existing history of metaphysics as a series of failures. Comparing the ongoing history of metaphysics with the state of mathematics and physics before they set upon the "royal road of science," he claims that true progress occurs only when this history of failure is brought to an end through an act of institution, creating the secure and lasting foundation upon which an edifice of "scientific knowledge" can be built (KA 3: 7–12). The origination of a scientific discipline involves a moment of rupture: a decisive break with its past history.

It is from this perspective that Kant understands the specific problem posed by the history of metaphysics. As he explains in the preface to the second edition of the *Critique of Pure Reason*, the other main a priori disciplines—logic, mathematics, and physics—have all already achieved this foundation and made lasting contributions to our knowledge.[20] Metaphysics, in contrast, remains a "field of combat" for a sort of play-fighting (*Spielgefechte*), "upon which not a single swordsman [*Fechter*] has ever achieved through fighting the least bit of land and been able to found an enduring possession upon his victory" (KA 3: 11). The aim of the "Copernican revolution" of Kant's critical philosophy, indeed, is nothing less than to provide metaphysics with a secure foundation, thereby instituting a break with its own (pre)history (KA 3: 11–13).

The notion of this prescientific development is more complicated and curious than may first seem to be the case, since it can neither be

---

[19] Traditionally neglected, the problem of history in Kant has recently become the subject of much interesting research. Most notable in this regard is Fenves (1991). Focusing on "incidental" texts in Kant's work, Fenves shows how the question of world-history, emerging from the exposition of metaphysics, comes to call metaphysics into question.

[20] For Kant, physics was not purely empirical, but had an a priori foundation.

teleological in any clear sense nor absolutely senseless and random. If it involved a progressive development toward the moment of foundation, then it would already be proceeding along the "secure path of a science." Yet while the prehistorical development of metaphysics does not yet clearly *envision* the goal toward which it works, nevertheless, over the course of time, if only accidently and without a clear linear progress, it comes closer to the goal. Kant speaks of this development as a groping (*Herumtappen*), a word that suggests the searching of a blind person who is neither capable of recognizing the clues that would lead him closer to his goal nor even has a clear idea of what he is looking for. The full meaning of this carefully chosen image emerges only if we consider that what the "blind" prescientific discipline is "tapping around" for in the dark is nothing other than the principle of reason and illumination, nothing other than the principle of vision itself.

The concluding section of the *Critique of Pure Reason*, "The History of Pure Reason," again tries to conceptualize the shape of the history of metaphysics. The aim of these remarks, Kant notes, is to provide a preliminary sketch of a part of the system that still remains to be "filled out" in the future. He continues:

I will content myself with casting a fleeting glance, from a merely transcendental point of view [*Gesichtspunkt*], namely that of the nature of pure reason, on the whole of the ways in which pure reason has been treated in the past. This glance, to be sure, presents buildings to my eyes, but only in ruins. (KA 3: 550)

The striking contrast between the earlier image of blindness and the metaphors of vision ("point of view," "glance," "eyes") in the above passage suggests no inconsistency on Kant's part. It merely signals the fact that *now*, with the revolutionary gesture of the *Critique of Pure Reason* behind him, it is possible to envision what reason was doing before it discovered its own principle of vision. From the transcendental perspective attained through a revolutionary moment of foundation, reason will reflect on the sequence of events leading to this revolution. What this perspective reveals is not something objectively true, but something subjective, as the use of the possessive pronoun before "eyes" suggests. This, moreover, is also expressed with a metaphor: "Buildings, but only in ruins."

This metaphor is again suggestive. That Kant sees buildings only in *ruins* suggests a nonteleological, materialistic conception of history, in which history consists merely of a procession of chance combinations of elements: a creation and destruction of new formations of the elementary and eternal constituents of reality that would end, if at all, with the mere chance emergence of a lasting formation. Nevertheless, he does not see only ruins, but *buildings* in ruins.

With this image of "buildings in ruins," Kant invokes a tension between two contrasting conceptions of the nature of history that can be described, respectively, as "Epicurean" and "anti-Epicurean." The idea that the history of the universe involves a ruinous sequence of chance collisions and formations is a familiar motif of the Epicurean tradition, if not of Epicurus's own extant writings, and is eloquently formulated in Lucretius's *De Rerum Natura*.[21] Moreover, it is precisely this conception of history that Kant, in his *Idea for a Universal History from a Cosmopolitan Point-of-View*, explicitly identifies with Epicureanism, referring to an "*Epicurean* convergence of efficient causes" in which "the states, like the little particles of material, attempt all sorts of formations through their chance collisions" (KA 8: 25). That the history of philosophy imitates the chance movements and formations of atoms is expressed even more explicitly in the penultimate chapter of the *Critique of Pure Reason*, "The Architectonic of Pure Reason": "The systems appear, like heaps of worms, to have formed—at first in a stunted way but in time reaching perfection—through a *generatio aequivoca* from the mere confluence of concepts that have been picked up along the way" (KA 3: 540). This notion of spontaneous generation, which goes back to the Presocratics and Aristotle, assumes critical importance within the Epicurean tradition. Lucretius, for example, repeatedly invokes the spontaneous generation of worms from the soil as palpable evidence for his doctrine of nature, while also claiming that the first animals were stunted failures, incapable of sexual reproduction.[22]

Whereas these two passages refer only to "formations" and "forming" (*Bildungen* and *bilden*), the word "building" (*Gebäude*) suggests a human (or divine) artifact—created "architectonically" according to a

---

[21] See Lucretius *De Rerum Natura* 5.187–94, 243–6, 258–61, 376–79, 419–31.

[22] See Lucretius *De Rerum Natura* 2.871–73, 898–901, 926–30; 3.717–36; 5.797–98, and esp. 837–54, where he discusses the earth's early monstrous experiments.

preexisting, already-envisioned plan—rather than a "blind" product of nature. If the ruins suggest an ateleological cycle of creation and destruction, they are comprehensible as ruins only in so far as they refer back to an *artifact* rather than to a mere natural formation, and thus to something that was built for a specific purpose.

In the *Idea for a Universal History from a Cosmopolitan Point-of-View*, Kant posits the "idea of universal history" as the guiding thread by which to discover the natural purpose hidden in the seeming chaos of historical events. Significantly, however, the "purposiveness" he discovers in the history of metaphysics is quite different from this. The history of metaphysics does not involve the progressive realization of a "germ of enlightenment" passed down through history despite its cataclysms, but instead its purposes appear at cross-purposes. Kant's fleeting glance at the history of metaphysics does not reveal a single hidden plan but only a seemingly futile conflict between competing principles (KA 3: 11).

I suggested earlier that the final section of the *Critique of Pure Reason* seeks to illuminate the blindly groping precritical history of reason through the power of vision that Kant's critical revolution institutes. Whereas before it was possible to see only destruction and futility, now one can glimpse, in the movement of history, the tension between Epicurean and anti-Epicurean tendencies. This tension, in other words, is the optic through which the seemingly senseless history of metaphysics becomes comprehensible. Turning now to the continuation of "The History of Pure Reason"—up to this point I have considered only the first paragraph—it becomes clear that the problem of Epicureanism is even more intimately bound up with the history of metaphysics. The tension between Epicurean and anti-Epicurean tendencies not only describes the overall shape of this history—its "edifying ruination"— but also constitutes the fundamental tension that animates it, gives it shape, and ultimately accounts for its futility.

In the remarks that follow, Kant makes no attempt to "differentiate the times when this or that change of metaphysics took place," but rather seeks only to describe the ideas that occasioned the most important revolutions, going on to identify, in this vein, "three ends in respect to which the most notable changes have been instituted on this stage of conflict" (KA 3: 550). These three perspectives involve, in order, the "object of all our rational cognition," "the origin of our rational cognition," and, finally, the method through which rational cognition is achieved (KA 3: 550–51). Under the first heading, Kant introduces Epicurus as the preeminent representative of a sensualistic philosophical tradition stretching from the most distant past to the present in an uninterrupted chain (KA 3: 551). Whereas the intellectualists (*Intellektualphilosophen*)—represented above all by Plato—maintain that "in the senses there is nothing but deception [*Schein*], and only the understanding recognizes the true [*das Wahre*]," the sensualists (*Sensualphilosophen*) argue "that all reality [*Wirklichkeit*] is to be found in the objects of the senses, and everything else is merely fantasy [*Einbildung*]" (KA 3: 551).

Under the second and third heading, Kant goes on to identify two further oppositions animating the "history of reason": between empiricists and rationalists, and between commonsense and theory-driven methods of scientific inquiry. We may suppose, though it is never explicitly stated, that these latter two develop out of the first, which would be not only historically but logically prior. The very "revolutionary" nature of Kant's "Copernican revolution" presupposes that the more natural, original, if ultimately errant, attitude of philosophy involves an orientation toward objects. The conflicts in the "origin of rational cognition" and "method" develop out of a more fundamental opposition in the nature of the object of rational cognition. So, for example, the empiricist belief that knowledge originates with experience would develop out of a prior orientation toward a sensual rather than an intellectual object of knowledge.

The history of reason, this account in turn suggests, begins with the opposition between sensualism (and hence Epicureanism) and intellectualism and remains determined by this opposition throughout, even as philosophy itself turns further and further away from its original objective orientation.

Even though these reflections on the history of pure reason seem peripheral to the project of the *Critique of Pure Reason*, I would argue that recognizing the underlying tendencies of reason's history is necessary for the "Copernican revolution" that will bring this ruinous history to a close. In the preface to the second edition of the *Critique of Pure Reason*, Kant contrasts the fate of logic, mathematics, and physics with that of metaphysics, providing an account of the increasing degree of difficulty each must encounter in becoming a science. The less abstract the relation between the faculty of knowing and the object of cognition, the harder it is to achieve the revolution that will turn it into a science. This principle is due to the nature of the revolution in question, which in each case consists in *discovering* that the object of cognition is determined by the knowing subject—in finding within the subject the constitutive principles for the knowledge of an object (KA 3: 8–10). Because logic concerns the mere form of understanding in abstraction from the object, it easily became scientific, and soon exhausted its store of knowledge (KA 3: 7–8). With mathematics and physics, the scientific revolution requires much more effort. In each instance, it is necessary to overcome the "natural attitude," which conceives of our knowledge of the object as determined by the object, and discover within the subject the a priori determinations of the object (KA 3: 9–10).

Kant conceives of the "Copernican revolution" of metaphysics through an analogy with the revolutions of science and mathematics (KA 3: 11–12). But what has stood in the way of philosophical revolution? Kant does not address this question explicitly, but the answer seems clear. In the case of metaphysics, the subject and the object are even less abstractly, even more intimately, related to one another, and perhaps even thoroughly intertwined. With mathematics and physics, the scientific revolution involves recognizing the a priori determination by the subject of an objective, spatiotemporally structured reality. It is not a matter of denying the objective validity of mathematical or physical reality, but only of recognizing the a priori determination of objective reality through the subject. The true objects of metaphysics, in contrast, transcend empirical and pure spatiotemporal experience. The revolutionary discovery of the *Critique of Pure Reason* is that the purely metaphysical objects that dogmatic metaphysics had sought to represent are mere "objectifications" of the a priori cognitive powers of the subject. In truth, however, the object and the subject of metaphysical knowledge are one and the same.[23] Metaphysics can become scientific only when it recognizes this unity.

---

[23] Metaphysics concerns the productive powers of the subject involved in the constitution of an objective reality (and not just the knowledge of an object that has already been subjectively constituted). The founding revolution of mathematics implicitly recognized that mathematical objects are "constructed" a priori and not empirically deduced, but it did not grant explicit insight into the constitutive powers of the subject as such.

For Kant, the a priori powers of the theoretical subject consist fundamentally in sensibility (*Sinnlichkeit*) and understanding (*Verstand*). As he explains in the first section of the first critique:

In whatever manner and through whatever means [*Mittel*] a cognition may relate itself to objects [*Gegenstände*], it is through the intuition [*Anschauung*] that it does so immediately. Thinking is directed toward the intuition as means. Yet intuition only takes place in so far as the object is given to us: and this in turn is only possible, at least for *us human beings*, when the object affects [*affeziere*] the mind [*Gemüt*] in a certain way. The capacity (receptivity) to receive representations through the manner that we are affected by objects is called sensibility [*Sinnlichkeit*]. By means of sensibility objects are thus given to us, and it alone conveys intuitions to us: through the understanding, however, objects are thought, and from it arise concepts [*Begriffe*]. All thinking, however, must ultimately relate itself—either directly or indirectly—*by means of certain characteristics* to intuitions, and hence, in our case, to sensibility, because no object can be given to us in any other way. (KA 3: 49)

The entire critical project depends on this distinction between intuitions (*Anschauungen*) and concepts (*Begriffe*). Whereas intuitions involve an *immediate* relation to the object of knowledge—the simple presentation of an object to our cognitive faculties—concepts, which derive from the faculty of judgment, relate to their object mediately: a concept is a "representation of a representation" (KA 3: 85). Having distinguished between concepts and intuitions in this way, Kant goes on to assert that, *at least* for a human mind, intuitions are only possible through sensibility (*Sinnlichkeit*), a faculty of "receptivity" through which we are affected by objects.

While the intuitions given to us immediately through sensibility always involve receptivity, not all the intuitions of sensibility are empirical—they do not necessarily involve a sensation (*Empfindung*) in which an object affects us (KA 3: 50). There are also pure intuitions, which present not the material but the pure form of sensibility (KA 3: 50). These pure intuitions, which belong to the mind a priori independent of sensation, include the intuitions of space and time, the subject of the "Transcendental Aesthetic" (KA 3: 50–51).

If the essence of Epicureanism consists of privileging sensibility over the intellect, then this notion of an a priori, nonempirical receptivity suggests that Epicureanism, far from being banished, has in fact come to reside at the very heart of Kant's critical system. Moreover, the a priori structure of subjectivity involves nothing else than the conflicting relation between sensibility and understanding, the very powers that determine the history of reason. On this analysis, the "Copernican revolution" in metaphysics involves the recognition that the tendencies determining philosophical history as a battle between different conceptions of the nature of things merely express the inner nature of the subject. The *Critique of Pure Reason* would thus return to the original rift in the history of philosophy—the opposition of sensualism and intellectualism—attempting to "heal it" not by eliminating it, but rather by conceiving of both tendencies and their conflict with one another as essential to reason. The answer to the chaotic, futile history of philosophy—its history of failures—is to discover the principle of this failure within reason itself.

By conceiving of the sensible (intuitions) and the intellectual (concepts) as the two equally original sources of cognition, Kant preserves in the center of his critical project the spirit of Epicureanism and its conflicts with other philosophical schools such as Platonism and Stoicism. Whereas dogmatic rationalists and empiricists both believed they could eliminate these conflicts by refuting their opponents' positions, for Kant the conflict between sensualism and intellectualism, and thus between Epicurus and Plato, becomes inextricably bound up with human reason. Yet the moment that the spirits of Epicurus and Plato are recognized by philosophy as essential to the operation of human reason, they lose their doctrinal aspect. Hence, the "Copernican revolution" of the *Critique of Pure Reason* marks a break in the uninterrupted chain of doctrinal transmission that formed its own prehistory. It dissolves the letter of Epicurus and Plato into their pure philosophical spirit. If we take seriously the philosophical revolution that Kant announces, recognizing in it a fundamental transformation of the destiny of human reason, then we must acknowledge that, with Kant's revolution, the conflict between Epicurean sensualism and Platonic intellectualism assumes a different shape than before.

This transformation poses significant challenges to the traditional narrative of the post-Kantian reception of Epicureanism. In discovering the pure spirit of both sensualism and intellectualism and thus breaking with the doctrinal continuity of each tradition, Kant's revolution at the same time undermines the possibility of representing either principle in its purity. Neither sensibility nor intellect can be conceived in abstract isolation. Whereas the doctrinal expressions of sensualism and intellectualism insisted on the existence of a single, original principle—each represents a fundamentally one-sided perspective on the nature of things—Kant's critical project tied them together in such a way that each must be understood in its agonistic relation to the other. Moreover, it is doubtful whether they can be *conceived* at all. Critical philosophy, for Kant, consists fundamentally in an act of philosophical self-reflection. It is not clear, however, how this specifically philosophical, self-reflective "experience"—in which reason reflects back on its own operations—can translate into a communicable philosophical discourse. Theoretical cognition itself is mediated through the categories of the understanding, and yet these categories apply only to sensible objects presented through the intuitions of space and time. Yet subjectivity, the object of philosophical introspection, is not itself something given in space and time.

I have tried to show thus far that for Kant, the history of metaphysics, prior to the revolution of critical philosophy, is the history of the failure and futility generated by the coexistence of opposing sensualist and intellectualist principles. The critical revolution itself consists in recognizing that this conflict belongs to the essence of human reason. Perhaps, then, the only philosophical style suitable to the representation of human reason is one marked by failure. Perhaps the only way to represent the accomplishments of critical philosophy is by *explicitly* inscribing into philosophical discourse the very signs of the futility that had before blindly governed the fate of metaphysics. While this inscription stands at odds with Kant's optimism that his "Copernican revolution" will finally secure for metaphysics a foundation upon which to construct its system, it also explains his own resistance to his successors' attempts to overcome the dualisms of critical philosophy by deriving their systems from a single principle.

Before continuing, let us review the argument to this point. Our discussion of the anticipations of perception has shown that for Kant, the spirit of Epicureanism involves the philosophical inquiry into how sensibility, as the irreducible finitude of human reason, presents itself a priori. The problem of the Epicurean spirit reemerges in the treatment of the historical character of reason framing the first critique. Kant conceives of

Epicurean sensualism and Platonic intellectualism as the two most fundamental tendencies guiding reason's development—tendencies that are reflected in, but not exhausted by, the philosophical systems that have emerged throughout history. These details already suggest that Epicureanism, far from being banished, comes to assume a central place in Kant's critical philosophy. But here we can make an even stronger argument for Epicureanism's importance. On the one hand, pure reason could not be thought to exist *historically* were reason, or at least human reason, not finite in a way that is essential and a priori rather than merely contingent and a posteriori. Thus one can only think the historical character of pure reason from the perspective that the spirit of Epicureanism reveals—which is to say, in terms of an a priori sensualism. On the other hand, the "Copernican revolution" of critical philosophy involves reason reflecting back on itself and recognizing, in its operation, the tendencies that determine its historical development. To engage in critical philosophy is thus to recognize an Epicurean tendency at work in reason. This Epicurean tendency, moreover, is not just the principle of the finitude of (human) reason but of its fallibility, its inherent tendency toward error.

In the next section, I consider how Kant's *Critique of Judgment* develops this idea of the inherent fallibility of reason into an account of history as the history of the reception of feelings, and specifically of those feelings that reflect our ability to belong to a community of finite beings who are at once rational and conditioned by sensibility, sharing not only the same reason but a certain disposition of their senses. This consideration uncovers, in turn, a thoroughgoing transformation of Epicurean ethics. Kant, with his celebrated notion of aesthetic pleasure, re-envisions Epicurean *ataraxia* as a quiet, self-sufficient, yet nevertheless active experience of the harmonious interactions of the different faculties of the mind.

IV. KANT'S THIRD CRITIQUE: HISTORY AND THE COMMUNITY OF FEELING

Within the *Critique of Pure Reason*, Kant's optimism that a metaphysical system might be built on the foundation of critique is given its most powerful formulation in the chapter on "The Architectonic of Pure

Reason," which directly precedes "The History of Pure Reason." The passage from this section cited above, in which Kant compares the genesis of philosophical systems with the spontaneous generation of worms, segues into the affirmation of a hidden plan:

The systems appear, like heaps of worms, to have formed—at first in a stunted way but in time reaching perfection—through a *generatio aequivoca* from the mere flowing together of concepts that have been picked up along the way, even though they all contained their schema, as the original seed, in the mere self-development of reason, and therefore not only are all these systems articulated for themselves according to an idea, but in addition, considered in relation to one another, they are all purposively united in a system of human cognition as members of a whole, and hence allow an architectonic of all human knowledge, which, in the present time, since so much material has been gathered together, or can be extracted from the ruins of old, collapsed buildings, is not only possible, but would not even be very difficult. (KA 3: 540)

While these systems appear as the result of mere chance, they contain a "schema" that can be discovered in view of the self-production of reason that Kant's critique has itself brought into view. And thus it is now possible, even easy, to build a new philosophical edifice from the debris of past ruins. The architectonic of reason, in turn, is the plan for this systematic edifice.

I would suggest, though, that Kant, without in any way renouncing the need for a philosophical system, deliberately undermines his own optimism about its finality. While it may be easy to build a new edifice and while the new edifice may be built according to a plan that reason has revealed to itself through critique, the very ease with which this new construction can be "thrown together" from the ruins of the old buildings suggests that reason has once again gotten ahead of itself. It seems too easy, and perhaps the new edifice is also fated to become another ruin. And if one must erect a new system, it is perhaps only, as Kant mentions later in the chapter, because

human reason, which is already dialectical through the very direction of its nature, would never be able to dispense with such a science, which restrains it, and, through a scientific and thoroughly illuminating self-knowledge, keeps at bay the devastating consequences that an anarchic speculative reason would inevitably cause in both ethics and religion. (KA 3: 549)

Systematic metaphysics, though it may never achieve anything that could stand the test of time, is needed to rein in the anarchic powers of reason.

Kant's use of the term "schema" suggests, moreover, that the systematic intention might not be so easily realized after all. Kant's invocation of this term points back to the second book of the "Transcendental Logic" of the first critique, where it plays a crucial role in the deduction of the categories. The transcendental schema (the schema of the pure concepts of understanding) mediates between intuitions and concepts by producing, as an immediate representation, a concrete, intuitive presentation of general concepts in their generality (KA 3: 133–39). Because it involves the creation of a nonempirical image (for example: of a triangle *as* such), it is attributed to the power of imagination. Through this mediation, the transcendental schema makes it possible to subsume the representation of an object under a concept. Yet the schema itself, far from being luminously clear to reason, is itself "a hidden art in the depths of the human soul"—it is the mysterious core of finite human reason's self-productivity. While the schema hidden in the ruined systems of philosophy suggests the plan for the construction of the new metaphysical system, this plan remains shrouded in obscurity.

The fundamental problem of the schema—of the unity of the a priori faculties of human reason—is taken up again in the *Critique of Judgment* in the analytic of the judgment of beauty. The purported aim of the third critique is to reconcile the clashing perspectives of theoretical and practical reason, of nature and freedom (KA 5: 176–77). Contradicting the systematic intentions of the architectonic of reason, Kant conceives of the "historicity of reason" in the third critique in terms of the irreducible and essential hiddenness of reason to itself.

In "The Analytic of the Beautiful," Kant argues that the judgment of beauty has a unique structure setting it apart from both the theoretical judgments of cognition and the practical judgments of moral action.[24] The act of judging the beautiful, rather than resulting in a cognitive knowledge of the object that it judges, at once presupposes and confirms

---

[24] Porter (2007) offers an alternative account of the Epicureanism of the *Critique of Judgment*, arguing that the "aesthetic subject" of the sublime rather than the subject of the beautiful is Epicurean.

a restful, harmonious, and playful interaction between the different faculties of the mind. Rather than culminating in either knowledge or action, it is contemplative: it continues indefinitely in time, with the subjective condition of judgment producing a feeling of aesthetic pleasure that in turn encourages the subject to tarry longer with its object (KA 5: 209, 222).[25] Such aesthetic judgments make a claim to necessity and universal assent, yet of a very different kind than the necessity and universality involved in theoretical and practical judgment. Unlike either theoretical or practical judgment, aesthetic judgment involves neither a determination of the cognizable properties of an object nor a universal and objectively binding principle issuing from the moral law (KA 5: 236–37). Rather, the basis of aesthetic judgment is a subjective principle that nevertheless determines the judgment universally, although through feelings and not through concepts (KA 5: 236–37). When we judge that an object is beautiful, what we are really saying is that it produces a harmonious relation between our powers of understanding (a discursive reasoning involving concepts) and our imagination, and that, nevertheless, because we feel motivated to this judgment not by the particular way in which the object affects our senses but only by its pure form, we believe that everyone else should agree with our judgment, since it seems to express an aspect of the power of imagination that, while rooted in sensibility, is common to all (KA 5: 237–44). The judgment of beauty thus provides no knowledge of the object as such but only registers the relation of the different mental faculties in the mind of the judging subject.

Kant's account of the unique nature of the aesthetic judgment of the beautiful depends on his analysis of the special kind of enjoyment (*Wohlgefallen*) involved in this judgment. Whereas the pleasant (*Angenehm*) and the good (*Gute*) both entail a relation to the faculty of desire, demanding the representation not merely of an object but of its existence, aesthetic enjoyment is free of either moral or sensual interest (KA 5: 209–11). Aesthetic contemplation tarries with the object, deriving an enjoyment from this tarrying that is neither increased if we represent the object as existing nor diminished if we represent it as absent.

[25] For a lucid account of this aspect of the judgment of beauty, see Wicks (2007) 38–45.

Perhaps the most important sign of the revived sensualism of the third critique, this suggests, is the centrality of feeling.[26] And one might draw an even more specific connection between aesthetic pleasure and the Epicurean concepts of *aponia* and *ataraxia*. Aesthetic pleasure, arising independent of sensual and ethical interest, allows the mind to experience a contemplative, playful enjoyment of its own capacities. Thus it would momentarily free us, or at least distract us, not only from actual physical sensations of pain but also from such mental sensations as the desiring of what we do not have or the fearing of some future suffering. Not surprisingly, Kant describes aesthetic contemplation as "tranquil" (*ruhig*). Yet the contemplation of beauty, unlike *ataraxia*, is not simply an experience of absolute tranquility and calm, but involves a ruleless order, a controlled chaos: it is a dynamic movement that seems compatible with our faculty of understanding, yet cannot actually be understood and articulated through concepts. While this seems to suggest an unbridgeable distance from the Epicurean tradition, it might make more sense to say that Kant, by reconceiving *ataraxia* as aesthetic pleasure, endows it with the content and internal coherence that it previously lacked. By transcendentalizing Epicureanism and transforming the Epicurean subject from the merely passive victim of experiences to an active creator of her own reality, Kant makes it possible to think the freedom from all externally conditioned pain and pleasure not as an empty and abstract calm but as an active experience of the faculties of the mind in their own immanent nature.

Aesthetic pleasure, however, is not merely a private and individual experience but has an inherent reference to a community. This aspect of aesthetic pleasure, and thus of sensibility, appears most clearly in Kant's discussion of the *sensus communis*.[27] Rejecting the commonplace and misleading identification of the *sensus communis* with mere common understanding, Kant conceives of it instead as the capacity of judgment that

in its reflection pays regard to the mode of representation [*Vorstellungsart*] of everyone else in thought (*a priori*), in order as it were to pass judgment on

---

[26] For a short and insightful discussion of feeling in the *Critique of Judgment*, see Deleuze (1984) 46–54. Wieland (2001) offers a more thorough treatment, stressing the tension between the discursive (conceptually articulated) structure of judgment and the role of feeling in the aesthetic judgment of the beautiful.

[27] For one of the most suggestive readings of the political dimension of Kant's *sensus communis*, see Arendt (1982) 72.

the entire human reason [*an die gesammte Menschenvernunft*] and therefore escape the illusion that, issuing from subjective private conditions that could easily be considered as objective, would have a disadvantageous influence on judgment. (KA 5: 293)

Common sense, in other words, is the ability to escape from the limitations of one's own perspective and enter into the perspectives of others. Kant goes on to argue that the *sensus communis*, thus understood, is nothing other than the faculty of taste (*Geschmack*), the capacity of aesthetic experience and judgment (KA 5: 296)—the capacity to judge the existence of the conditions under which it would be possible to communicate universally the feelings that are produced by a given mental representation without the mediation of concepts. What the communicated feelings involve, in particular, is "the inner feeling of a purposive condition of the subject [*Gemüt*]" (KA 5: 295–96).

What we thus feel when contemplating an object is an anarchic harmony between imagination and understanding. At stake in this feeling of harmony, and indeed in the harmony itself, is a dimension of human sensibility common to all. When the faculty of taste judges that a feeling can be communicated universally without the mediation of a concept, it judges in effect that a "universal community" exists among human beings that is based not on universal concepts but on a common sensible nature: a common power of imagination. What we feel and judge, as it were, is that we belong to a community of feeling and communication. What is common to the community is something that cannot be grasped and communicated through general concepts, but only felt. Moreover, what is felt in this way is not just the present state of the community, but its changing existence over time. The changes in taste not only reflect its historical development, but involve the self-reflective awareness of the historical existence of the community. Taste itself is an a priori capacity for experiencing both community and history as an essential part of human existence.

We saw earlier that the Kant of the first critique not only praises the relative coherence and consequence of Epicurean doctrine despite its ultimate illegitimacy but indeed identifies the Epicurean spirit with his own attempt to conceive of sensibility as the a priori source of reason's finitude. Epicureanism, in this sense, comes to play a vital role in Kant's theoretical philosophy: not only does an Epicurean spirit characterize the historical unfolding of reason but the "Copernican revolution" in metaphysics demands recognizing that reason itself exists as the never-ending conflict between two tendencies—one Epicurean-sensualist and the other Platonic-intellectualist.

It nevertheless seems that, for Kant, Platonism and intellectualism ultimately win out over the "spirit of Epicurus." The *Critique of Practical Reason*, in a devastating critique of Epicureanism's hedonistic ethics, argues that a truly moral action cannot be motivated by "sensual" principles such as pleasure, pain, or happiness. Yet without contradicting the position of the second critique, the *Critique of Judgment*, as we have seen, nevertheless offers a different account of how to live based on the primacy of sensuality and feeling over the purely intellectual. Kant's notion of aesthetic pleasure, moreover, can be seen not only as vaguely Epicurean in spirit but as recasting the Epicurean notion of *ataraxia*.

One might recall Kant's distinction between ancient and modern concepts of ethics. Whereas modern ethics tells us what to do, ancient ethics tells us how to be. This suggests an intriguing possibility: even if Kant for the most part reserves the vocabulary of ethics for the *Critique of Practical Reason*, the third critique is perhaps no less concerned with ethics than the second. It is just that it involves an ethics of being rather than doing. Nor is there any reason to suppose that an intellectualist ethics of doing and a sensualist ethics of being could not be compatible.

The sensualist ethics of aesthetic pleasure diverges in crucial respects from Epicurean hedonism as ordinarily conceived. Aesthetic pleasure is positive rather than negative—characterized by the positive presence of a harmonious interaction of the faculties rather than the mere absence of pain and disturbances. Moreover, it involves community, sociability, and a specifically historical form of existence. Yet rather than undermining its affinities with an Epicurean "ethics of being," these features suggest what is at stake for Kant in resuming the ancient inquiry into how we should exist. Aesthetic judgment involves a new—even specifically modern—form of an ancient ethics of being: open to the world and the danger of experience, vital, social, and willing to face our finitude rather than flee from it. Taking up the problematic of Kant's second and third critiques, Hölderlin, as I now demonstrate, elaborates precisely such a "modern" ethics of being.

V. PUNISHMENT AND SUFFERING IN HÖLDERLIN'S
EARLY PHILOSOPHICAL FRAGMENTS

Kant's critical philosophy had an extraordinary impact on intellectual life in Germany. Within a decade of the publication of the first edition of the *Critique of Pure Reason*, a voluminous secondary literature had already emerged.[28] By the last decade of the eighteenth century, however, it was no longer enough to try to explain what Kant was doing or refute him from a more traditional philosophical outlook. Philosophers such as Salomon Maimon, Karl Leonhard Reinhold, and Johann Gottlieb Fichte sought, instead, to develop Kant's most profound insights further than he himself was able to do. It is this attempt that led to German idealism and romanticism. Although Friedrich Hölderlin is not nearly as well known in Anglo-American scholarship as Schelling, Hegel, and Fichte, he played a crucial role in these developments. Nor is he merely a transitional figure. Rather Hölderlin's thought offers a powerful alternative to the dominant tendencies of German idealism, and, above all, to its privileging of intellect over sensibility.[29]

This last point suggests, I argue, that Hölderlin receives and further develops the "Epicurean spirit" of Kant's critical philosophy. This claim may seem odd, since Hölderlin's writings refer to Epicureanism by name only once. Yet the significance of Epicureanism for Hölderlin's thought far exceeds its explicit textual presence. More than any of his contemporaries, Hölderlin implicitly recognized how an Epicurean sensualism was knotted into the heart of Kant's critical system. Rather than trying to overcome the Kantian dualism between concepts and intuitions—and thus between intellectualism and sensualism—by instituting a higher philosophical perspective, Hölderlin seeks instead to think through the paradoxical presence of sensibility within human reason. Indeed, it is not the dominant idealist tradition of German philosophy nor even the romantics (whom Hegel would associate with a cult of feeling) but rather Friedrich Hölderlin who will receive, transform, and develop the

---

[28] For a concise account of the extraordinary impact of Kant's *Critique of Pure Reason*, see Pinkard (2002) 19–21.

[29] The claim that German idealism privileges intellect over sensibility is made by Heidegger in *Kant and the Problem of Metaphysics*. For an accessible survey of Heidegger's argument, see Cutrofello (2005) 20–23.

implications of Kant's insights into the historical character of feeling and the *felt* character of history.[30]

We can trace Hölderlin's concern with the "Epicurean" moment in Kant back to two thematically related philosophical fragments: "There is a natural condition . . ." and "On the Concept of Punishment." These were written in the early fall and winter of 1794, during which time Hölderlin, who was intensively engaged with Kant's philosophy, moved to Jena, where Fichte was giving his immensely influential lectures on the *Doctrine of Science*.[31] A close look at these fragments suggests the significance that Hölderlin attaches to Kant's treatment of sensualism.

The argument of these fragments starts out from the distinction between an intellectualist and sensualist ethics. Whereas in the former the moral law (the law of freedom) issues commands in absolute independence from nature, in the latter the feelings of pleasure and pain provide the only motivation for moral action. Kant draws a similar opposition. And yet whereas Kant's second critique argues that ethical action is truly ethical *only* when purely intellectual, motivated exclusively by the self-imposed commands of the moral law, Hölderlin suggests that the two forms of ethics are inextricably bound together. Thus the first of the two fragments suggests that there is an ethical "natural condition" of the faculty of imagination involving a harmony between the moral faculties (the *Begehrungsvermögen*) analogous to the harmony of the cognitive faculties treated in the third critique. This aspect of the empirical faculty of desire—Hölderlin refers to it as a "natural innocence" or even a "morality of instinct"—is most apparent when "the necessary and freedom, the conditioned and unconditional, the sensual and the holy, seem to join one another as brothers" (SW 17: 134). This state of "natural innocence"—a morality of instinct accompanied by a "heavenly" fantasy—results purely from natural causes: it is "a mere happy chance [*ein bloses Glük*] to be determined in this way" (SW 17: 134).

---

[30] While Hegel, following Reinhold and Schelling, attaches the greatest significance to the historical character of reason and while feelings also play an important role in his philosophy, he nevertheless regards feelings as merely subjective, not yet fully articulated expressions of a content that still awaits objective, rational articulation. Thus in the penultimate paragraph of the *Phenomenology of Spirit*, Hegel contrasts the "lofty feeling of the eternal, sacred, infinite" with the "labor of the concept" that alone grants true thoughts and scientific insight ((1980) 9: 48).

[31] The dating of Hölderlin's manuscripts follows Hölderlin (2004).

Hölderlin recognizes the threat this contingency poses to ethics, insisting in response on an ethical and even aesthetic intellectualism, in which both the faculties of desire and fantasy are subject to the law of freedom. Here, in turn, as if to resolve the contradiction that emerges between ethical autonomy and heteronomy, Hölderlin introduces the concept of punishment. The law of freedom presupposes a resistance in nature, since otherwise it could not issue commands to us. "The first time the law of freedom expresses itself to [*an*] us, it appears *punishing*. The beginning of all our virtue happens with [*geschieht vom*] evil" (SW 17: 135).

Hölderlin has not yet said anything directly contradicting Kant: one need only distinguish between efficient causality and the causality of freedom to eliminate the seeming paradox of the claim that the good, while originating in the autonomy of the will, is nevertheless *occasioned* by evil. Yet while the first fragment can still be made to accord with Kant's *Critique of Practical Reason*, the second fragment, "On the Concept of Punishment," suggests an extraordinary reversal of Kant's ethical intellectualism: moral law, however purely intellectual in its origins, does not reveal itself in the "propositional form" of the categorical imperative but is only able to exhibit and realize itself through a sensual ethics focused on the feelings of suffering that we passively undergo. Even though the commandments of the moral law, originating in a principle of autonomy, allow reason to dominate nature, this moral law, precisely because it is infinite, can only announce itself negatively—not through a positive finite determination but only through the continual negation of every finite determination (SW 17: 147). It cannot reveal itself in its abstract and formal purity as law, but only through the opposition of two finitely determined active wills. Thus the ethical law first announces itself as punishment, destroying the blissful state of natural innocence: we must at once will something that is contrary to the law, and suffer resistance as a result of this will (SW 17: 147). It is only the contradiction between two wills—one radically good and the other radically evil—that gives us knowledge of the moral law. Thus morality, rather than issuing purely from absolute autonomy, necessarily involves the experience of heteronomy.

This conclusion unsettles Hölderlin. To escape from its most disturbing implications, he reminds himself that "there is however a difference between the ground of knowledge and the real ground," as if he could thus salvage as "real ground" the purity of the moral law despite the necessity of its manifestation through opposing wills (SW 7: 148). Yet this reassurance is short-lived, and Hölderlin's fragment breaks off with him doubting whether punishment is even able to make the moral law known. For Kant, the practical sphere of morality allows for the disclosure, forbidden to theoretical cognition, of the thing-in-itself. Theoretical cognition allows knowledge of objects only insofar as they are conditioned by sensibility. Practical reason, in contrast, *determines* its object, transcending the finitude imposed by human sensibility. This formulation suggests all that is at stake in Hölderlin's revision of Kantian ethics. By challenging the possibility of a direct, practical revelation of human freedom, Hölderlin attacks the last reserve of the absolute in Kant's critical philosophy. In this way, moreover, Hölderlin also parts ways with German idealism. Whereas Fichte attempts to overcome the Kantian dualisms by deducing theoretical philosophy from a practical first principle (the *Tathandlung* or deed in which the "I" posits itself), Hölderlin's first fragmentary confrontations with Kant initiate a more general critique of every attempt to ground philosophy in an absolute principle.

In the short piece "Being Judgment Possibility," written in April 1795, Hölderlin, responding to Fichte's (and Schelling's) attempts to conceive of the "I" as an absolute principle uniting both subject and object, argues that the very form of judgment implies an original rupture in the absolute unity between subject and object. No proposition, not even "I=I," can express the unity of Being presented in intellectual intuition (SW 17: 156). Kant rejected this notion of intellectual intuition (of an intuition capable of producing both its form and its material or content), yet it plays a central role in early idealism.[32] But whereas Fichte and Schelling conceive of intellectual intuition as the ground of both the Being and the direct, conceptually articulated knowledge of the absolute, Hölderlin suggests, in contrast, that the intellectual intuition of the absolute is cut off from the possibility of knowledge.

---

[32] Intellectual intuition has a rich past in the history of philosophy, going back through Spinoza to Plotinus and Plato. It is impossible in the context of this paper to do justice to the complex range of meanings and functions that intellectual intuition assumes in Fichte and Schelling.

Hölderlin's fragment "The Declining Fatherland," written in 1800, goes even further in confronting the thought of the impossibility of the absolute presenting itself directly and fully to human reason. Hölderlin argues that the absolute exhibits itself through the never-ending, non-teleological transition from one historical world to the next rather than through a teleological progress toward a final and perfect state (SW 14: 174). The world of all worlds, the absolute principle behind history, never appears through a single world, and not even the last. Nor is it manifest through a finite succession of different worlds. Rather it exhibits itself only *in time*, and, indeed, in time's very transience—in the moment when one world dissolves and passes over into another.

This transience, moreover, is likened to language:

and this decline [*Untergang*] and beginning is like language, [the] expression[,] sign, [or] exhibition [*Darstellung*] of a living but particular whole, which is again present in all its effects, and indeed in such a way that in it, as in language, there seems to be in one respect little or nothing that would vitally subsist, and yet in another respect everything. (SW 14: 174)

Here, moreover, Hölderlin invokes the concept of feeling: the moment of transition is felt in "all the limbs of the existing world," and what is felt is nothing else than the "possible." Indeed, it is the possible itself, the absolute as the totality of possibilities, that feels itself in these moments of transition, since it is precisely in transition that the "possibility of all relations," rather than a determinate set of relations, prevails.

With "The Declining Fatherland" Hölderlin returns, even more explicitly than before, to the understanding of history as a history of failure. In returning to this Kantian motif, moreover, he also draws on two very crucial moments of Epicureanism, both of which play a role in the *Critique of Judgment*. Lucretius, in the *De Rerum Natura*, draws an analogy between the combinatorial potency of the letters of the alphabet and the atoms that make up the universe.[33] When Hölderlin claims that the linguistic sign contains, on the one hand, "little or nothing vitally existing" and, on the other hand, "everything," he makes a similar point.[34]

___

[33] See Lucretius *De Rerum Natura* 1.820–29.

[34] Friedrich Schlegel's concept of "wit" involves a similar sense of the "literality" of thought. Schlegel's "wit," moreover, invokes the curious discussion of laughter in the second critique, where Kant again invokes Epicurus, suggesting that he "might not have been

Yet he also goes further: linguistic signs not only come together to form all the different possible words but they would seem to signify—in and through their very nothingness—the absolute. This signification, moreover, takes place as *feeling* and, more specifically, the feeling that happens with the dissolution of the specific configuration of a world. Feeling, as it were, is the moment in which the sign, becoming nothing, attains its fullest significance. It is only when we decompose a word into letters that we sense the possibilities these letters contain.

"The Declining Fatherland" contains the one explicit reference to Epicureanism in Hölderlin's writings. The moment of "real [*wirklich*] dissolution," in its opposition to the "ideal dissolution," is "sensual idealism, Epicureanism" (SW 14: 176). Having pursued Hölderlin's engagement with the themes of sensibility and history, we can now recognize in this passage more than just a passing, casual reference to Epicureanism. The notion of a "sensual idealism" indeed suggests nothing less than an alternative to the "intellectual idealism" that Fichte, Schelling, and Hegel—albeit in very different forms—would pursue. This "sensual idealism," however, demands for its explication not the abstract and discursive language of philosophy but the concrete and sensual language of poetry.

VI. *THE DEATH OF EMPEDOCLES*: POLITICS AND THE FAILURE OF PHILOSOPHY

"The Declining Fatherland" indicates how the language of poetry can serve to present a sensual, as opposed to intellectual, idealism. What is truly original and enduringly creative about the "authentically tragic language," Hölderlin explains, is its ability to effect (*bewirken*), or indeed perform, the moment of dissolution and becoming. It is able to present this dissolution as an effective reality, as something *wirklich* (SW 14: 174). Hölderlin composed "The Declining Fatherland" right after working on the final version of the *The Death of Empedocles*. The tragedy, which consists of three very different unfinished versions, can thus be understood as an attempt to realize the "authentically tragic language" of an "Epicurean" sensual idealism. In order to present the "real dissolution"

---

wrong" to regard all pleasure (*Vergnügen*) as corporeal sensation (KA 5: 330–36). For an extensive treatment of this passage, see Fenves (2003) 24–31.

of a historical "world," the suffering of the tragic hero must be historical rather than simply individual in nature. His individual suffering must represent the pain felt in all the limbs of the fatherland. Thus Empedocles himself, as Hölderlin explains in his "Foundation of Empedocles," is "a son of his heaven and his period, of his fatherland, a son of the violent oppositions of nature and art in which the world appeared before his eyes" (SW 13: 872).

Judged by conventional criteria, even the first, relatively complete version of Hölderlin's *Death of Empedocles* must strike us as a dramatic failure: bogged down in dialogue, with little action, the play is seldom performed on stage. The source of the tragedy, indeed, rests not with Empedocles' actions but with the form of existence that he exemplifies. Accordingly, the ethical problematic in *Empedocles* does not have to do with duty and action but with an ideal form of existence; it is a problematic, then, reminiscent of Kant's treatment of aesthetic pleasure. This observation does not mean, however, that Hölderlin simply wishes to restore the perspective of ancient ethics. Rather the "authentically tragic language" of *The Death of Empedocles* not only presents an Epicurean "sensual idealism" but, at the same time, subjects the specific ethical ideal of ancient philosophy, and Epicureanism in particular, to a transformative critique, proposing, in its place, a very different sort of ideal.

Empedocles, of course, is hardly a figure of indifference for the Epicurean tradition. Lucretius, while rejecting Empedocles' doctrine of the four elements, nevertheless lavishes him with praise, taking his philosophical poem as his model (Lucretius *De Rerum Natura* 1.705–33). Central to the critique of Epicureanism that emerges in *The Death of Empedocles* is a problem that, as already suggested, is of paramount importance for Hölderlin's appropriation of Kant's Epicurean sensualism: the moral status of sin, suffering, and punishment. This same problem is no less important for Lucretius. The greatest threat to the mind's tranquility comes not from mere physical pain but from the fear of death and of the endless punishments we imagine to follow it. Enlightenment requires, above all, the realization that "whatsoever things are fabled to exist in deep Acheron, these all exist for us in this life" (Lucretius *De Rerum Natura* 3.978–79)—that they are nothing but the punishments we inflict on ourselves, not only through our desires for bodily pleasures, love, or power, but above all else through our very fear of punishments in this world and the next (3.980–1023).[35] We punish ourselves by entering into a relation through fear and desire, both of which are mediated by imagination, to that which is beyond our immediate power, belonging not to the present but to an as-yet-unrealized future. The only way to achieve tranquility, in turn, is to expel from the mind all these desires and fears. But, above all, one must no longer believe that the gods concern themselves with mortals and have any interest in punishing them. When we do achieve mental calm, expelling the images of gods convulsed by storms of passion, the images of the true gods in their serenity will flow from the heavens into our minds (Lucretius *De Rerum Natura* 6.68–79).

But the Epicurean sage, having achieved this tranquility of mind, is not only filled with the images of the gods but himself becomes like a god, experiencing divine joy. "For the very nature of divinity," Lucretius explains, "must necessarily enjoy immortal life in the deepest peace, far removed and separated from our affairs; for without any pain, without danger, itself mighty by its own resources, needing us not all, it is neither propitiated with services nor touched by wrath" (*De Rerum Natura* 2.646–51).

It is precisely this "higher divine joy"—for Friedrich Schlegel, the essence of Epicureanism—that Empedocles experiences: he is "the needless one [*der Unbedürftge*]" who "wanders [*wandelt*] in his own world," walking "in the gentle tranquility of the gods" (SW 13: 699; Schlegel (1964) 12: 67). He feels like a god (SW 13: 699), and he is one of the "overhappy spoiled sons of heaven who feels nothing but their souls" (SW 13: 821). Likewise, both the Epicurean sage and Empedocles look down upon human affairs from calm heights. Thus Empedocles explains to Pausanius:

and when I often sat on the still mountain summit and contemplated [*übersann*] the alternating and erring ways of men, too deeply seized by your transformations, and felt that my own wilting was near, then the healing aether breathed for me, as for you, around the love-sore breast, and, like a cloud of flame, my cares dissolved in the high blue. (SW 13: 829)

---

[35] Translations of Lucretius are from Rouse-Smith (1992).

This directly echoes the memorable lines from Lucretius:

But nothing is more delightful than to possess lofty sanctuaries serene, well fortified by the teachings of the wise, whence you may look down upon others and behold them all astray, wandering abroad and seeking the path of life:—the strife of wits, the fight for precedence, all labouring night and day with surpassing toil to mount upon the pinnacle of riches and to lay hold on power. (Lucretius *De Rerum Natura* 2.7–14)

Yet these two passages, despite their striking resemblance, diverge in a crucial way. For Lucretius, the state of tranquility is fortified and strengthened by his wisdom. It is the product of a doctrine and even a technique that can be learned and mastered. And thus the sage experiences a blissful joy untarnished by any fear or apprehension. Yet while Empedocles experiences something very much like the divine calm of the ideal Epicurean sage, he is in no way secure in its possession. Since his very tranquility and feeling of unity with nature are themselves gifts of nature over which he has no control, he is seized by a sort of vertigo as he looks down at the confusion of human affairs from the heights, and, as if pulled into their flux and alternation, begins to anticipate, not without dread, his own demise. And if Empedocles' calm is no longer calm but disturbed, rather, by a second order of anxiety, the punishment and suffering that interrupts this calm is of a very different nature than the self-inflicted torture that the author of the *De Rerum Natura* hoped to banish from the minds of human beings. Whereas for Lucretius, punishment results from confusing the gods with mortals, Empedocles is punished for forgetting his own mortality. The gods took Empedocles' power away from him, Hermocrates explains, on the day when "the drunken man called himself a god before all the people . . . [b]ecause he too much forgot the difference in his excessive happiness, and only felt himself; thus it happened to him, he is now punished with limitless desolation" (SW 13: 702–703).

The punishment Empedocles endures is nothing else than the suffering that must always interrupt the Epicurean sage's godlike, but ultimately self-satisfied, bliss.[36] The source of this punishment is the absolute, which,

---

[36] Eric Baker suggestively observes that "the 'Epicurean sublime of equipoise' is the archenemy of the Stoic sublime, for such equipoise is premised on a radical critique of the

as we saw in "The Declining Fatherland," demands of all human beings that they exist historically. But if Empedocles' fall is the punishment for a transgression and not just the result of a natural fallibility, his fate suggests a critique of the very aim, however difficult it might be to achieve, of attaining a godlike inner tranquility. For Hölderlin, this end is itself hubristic, since it involves "forgetting the difference" between human beings and the gods. Whereas Aristotle recommends that the protagonist of a tragedy should not be perfectly virtuous, the protagonist of *The Death of Empedocles* is a true sage who has actually achieved a godlike state. The theme of his tragedy, accordingly, is not the fragility of human, political virtue but the hubris that necessarily comes with the divine tranquility of the philosopher.[37]

There is no reason to associate this hubris with Epicureanism in particular. For Hölderlin, no doubt, Empedocles' hubris is characteristic of the hubris of ancient philosophy as a whole.[38] The target of this critique, moreover, is not just the sage of ancient philosophy but the attempts of other post-Kantian idealists, such as Fichte and Schelling, to overcome the Kantian divide between sensibility and intellect by grounding philosophy in intellectual intuition.

What Hölderlin ultimately seeks to show, by having Empedocles echo Lucretius, is that Epicureanism misunderstood Presocratic materialism when it used it to justify an "apolitical" existence.[39] While Empedocles at

---

tragic *agon* that is central to Longinus and to most eighteenth-century theories of the sublime" (Baker (2001) 26). By presenting the "Epicurean sage" as a tragic hero, Hölderlin suggests the ultimate impossibility of the very equipoise that promises escape from the tragic logic of fate.

[37] Hölderlin's concept of hubris is closely related to Schelling's *Philosophical Letters* (1795), which itself explicitly treats Epicureanism. While Schelling identifies Stoicism and Epicureanism—the "two most contradictory systems of morality"—with the fundamental philosophical tendencies of "criticism" and "dogmatism," he goes on to claim that both seek "absolute blessedness," and they differ only in how they seek this. Whereas the Stoic strives to become independent from the power of objects, the Epicurean "throws himself into the arms of the world." (Schelling (1982) 3: 99) Yet this final goal is itself the essence of *Schwärmerei*—a derogatory word for religious fanaticism and enthusiasm (85–86). The contradictory logic of Greek tragedy ultimately offers a higher perspective than either dogmatism or criticism, since it allows the conflict between the conflicting principles of human reason to appear *as* a conflict (106).

[38] Hölderlin indeed first intended to write a tragedy about Socrates.

[39] Regarding the difficult and contested question of the relation of Epicurus and the Epicurean tradition to politics, see E. Brown (2009). Epicureanism, Brown argues, did not reject all forms of political association, but, in fact, advocated living in a relatively

first will have nothing to do with human beings, his hubris takes on a decisively political character, reaching its height when, exposed to the people (*Volk*), he not only identifies himself with a god but, proclaiming his divinity before the people, tries to rule over them as a tyrant. His self-chosen death thus closes the "age of kings" and, breaking with tradition and the very continuity of historical time, initiates a new democratic age (SW 13: 742). Thus he exhorts the people of Agrigento: "So dare it! What you have inherited, what you have acquired, what the fathers' mouth told and taught to you, law and customs, the names of the old gods, boldly forget it, and raise, like newborns, your eyes up to divine nature" (SW 13: 745). For Hölderlin's Empedocles, in other words, the materialist postulate of a unity with nature leads to a series of political conclusions: first, the desire to be a philosopher-king, and then his support for a radical democracy that would be instituted through his own renunciation of kingship. Epicureanism, in contrast, arose during the Hellenistic period, with the decline of Athenian democracy and the autonomous city-states, and it is in crucial ways post-political in its outlook.[40] The Epicurean sage, far from being tempted to philosophical kingship, retreats altogether from the political sphere, concerning himself only with the "care of the self." If Empedocles' hubris was to identify himself with the divine kings of the Saturnine age, the Epicurean hubris was, rather, to believe that one could retreat from the political realm entirely and escape from the claims it makes on us as human beings.

In this way, I would argue, Hölderlin contrasts the apolitical materialism of Epicurus with the political, radically democratic materialism

---

small community of friends. And it also recognized the need to engage in politics when emergency conditions threaten the security upon which the practice of Epicureanism depends. Still, Epicureans remain opposed to politics insofar as they "discourage starting a family and engaging in politics, and they deny that justice exists by nature" (E. Brown (2009) 179).

[40] The claim that Hellenistic philosophy favored a "quiet life" over "active, public citizenship," misleading as it may be, is, as Eric Brown argues, a common claim since Hegel ((2008) 79–89). A reading of the novel *Hyperion*, moreover, suggests that it is not anachronistic to attribute such a critique of the "apolitical" quality of Hellenistic philosophy to Hölderlin. *Hyperion*, as I have argued elsewhere, involves a complex attempt to reconsider political philosophy in light of the impossibility of returning to an Athenian model of politics: see Adler (2005).

that the Empedocles of his play institutes after his tragic fall from grace. This other, and more historically original, materialism originates with the experience of the impossibility of any human being, and even the wise man, being "secure in the security" of his godlike status. For Hölderlin, Epicureanism is not Epicurean enough: it shirks the most extreme consequences of materialism by replacing a politics of human finitude and danger with an escapist ethics of divine tranquility.

While Hölderlin's reinterpretation of the life of Empedocles culminates in a far-reaching critique of Epicureanism, this very critique is made possible only by reading and receiving Empedocles through an Epicurean lens. Receiving Epicureanism in this way means at once rejecting it as an ethical doctrine in the strict sense (even while preserving its sensualism) and receiving it as a theory of reception, history, and politics. Empedocles' final words to the archon in the last version of Hölderlin's tragedy give a hint both of what such a theory of reception will involve and of its relation to poetry and politics. The experience of mortality emerges as the condition not only of truth—"it was the word of a mortal / and those who do not return speak the truth" (SW 13: 746)—but also of his word passing on to, and being received into, the future:

Go now and greet the city you call home and its fields! on the beautiful day when, to free the eye from the work of the day, you will go out to the holy grove, and as it receives you from out of the merry heights with friendly songs, then a tone of mine will blow like the sound of harp in song. Then you will lovingly hear again the word of the friend, concealed in the love-chorus of the beautiful world, and it is more marvelous this way. (SW 13: 751)

With death the word becomes a poetic word. This Epicurean theory of reception is the theory of a practice of poetry that, originating with the painful failure of mortals to abide in the absolute, passes the memory of this failure to future generations. Poetry is sensual or receptive in a double sense: for what it receives is nothing less than the memory of receptivity—of finitude and sensuality—as the essential limitation imposed on human beings. Developing and expanding on Kant's own conception of a history of feelings, Hölderlin maintains that it is historical experience alone that allows us to remember the irreducible sensualism that Kant discovered at the heart of human reason, just as it is this sensualism, in turn, that allows us to remember, through suffering, our origin in the absolute. What is ultimately at stake in remembering human finitude is an affirmation of politics. If none of us can become gods for more than an instant, then we must live as human beings. While a life of divine tranquility might still be the best life, it is not for us.

8

The Sublime, Today?

Glenn W. Most

Histories of the sublime tend to follow what I shall call here the "standard account." In structure, it resembles a two-stage motor, like a diesel engine or a thermonuclear device: first a small, relatively limited explosion, which in itself need not be especially consequential but which is required as a premise in order to allow another, much vaster deflagration to occur at some later time. It is worth considering that account briefly in its basic outlines before subjecting it to criticism and revision.

According to its terms, there is a first moment in which the slowly revolving starry vault of ancient rhetorical theory is enlivened, suddenly and briefly, by a single brilliant but enigmatic comet, the treatise on the sublime ascribed (probably mistakenly) to Longinus, a text whose exact date, cultural context, and author's identity are quite unknown.[1] No later ancient writer ever quotes this text or refers to it, or even seems aware of its existence; after the brief flash in which it appeared, it seems to have languished in total obscurity for the rest of antiquity, and to have survived the Middle Ages only in a single incomplete manuscript, dating from the tenth century and conserved in Paris. There is no evidence that anyone ever read or even knew about this manuscript until the middle of the fifteenth century, when it was first copied. And even after these copies began to circulate, the dissemination of the treatise was at first quite

An earlier version of this article was published in Italian as Most (2007). My thanks for their advice and suggestions to James Chandler (Chicago), Stephen Halliwell (St. Andrews), and the editors of the present volume.

[1] If I refer to the author as Longinus henceforth, it is only for the sake of convenience, not because I am sure that that really is his name.

modest: about a dozen surviving manuscripts were copied from the Paris manuscript during the fifteenth century; by 1600 the Greek text had been printed, but not more than three times (though it had also been translated into Latin and Italian).

All this was changed almost overnight by the extraordinary impact of the translation (more exactly, the explanatory paraphrase) of Longinus's treatise that Nicolas Boileau-Despréaux published in 1674. Throughout the next century and a half, the treatise on the sublime went on to become one of the most familiar ancient texts not only within the narrow confines of Greek philology and rhetoric but also within the wider circles of cultivated taste throughout Europe; and the concept of the sublime became pivotal for all forms of imaginative literature, art, and aesthetic theory, and also encroached deeply upon moral philosophy, psychology, and numerous other more or less closely related disciplines. During the course of the eighteenth century, at least fourteen full editions of the Greek text were published, while by the end of that century, Boileau's version had been reprinted at least eighteen times in France and had been translated into English three separate times. And yet by the middle of the nineteenth century, the steam seems to have run out of the second phase too of the engine of the sublime. The pictorial arts turned away from scenes of mountain avalanches and storms at sea; the idea of the sublime ceased to play a central role within aesthetic theory; poets like Heinrich Heine invoked the sublime, if at all, only so as to ridicule it or to dismiss it ironically; even the word seemed to go into retreat, so that it could scarcely be used without quotation marks.

Here, then, we would have the two phases of the sublime, according to the standard account: first a sudden spark limited to a single, remarkable instant; and then a much broader second conflagration that lasted somewhat less than two centuries before it, too, eventually ground to a halt. With slight variations, this account is to be found in countless modern studies in historical aesthetics. There is much to be said for it, and several of my own contributions to the subject over the past years have been indebted to it, at least to a certain extent.[2] But if I have chosen to call this interpretative model the standard account it is because it now appears to me to be defective in certain key regards, and in this article I shall

---

[2] Especially Most (1984) and Most (2002).

propose a significant modification of it. I will be suggesting here that the restrictive identification of the sublime with the text of Longinus, which has hitherto tended unquestioningly to dominate discussions of the topic, in fact neglects a theoretically and historically crucial alternative to the Longinian conception, one that can be identified with Lucretius, his reception of Epicurus, and the reception of his own text in later times; and that broadening our notion of the sublime to include this Lucretian alternative protects the standard model against a number of potentially fatal objections. For the standard model is, in fact, open to serious question in a number of aspects, but here I concentrate on one problem in particular, the disturbing historical paradox that it entails—namely, that this model makes it very difficult, indeed impossible, to understand the robust survival of one version of the sublime into our own modern world.

For is it indeed the case that the sublime dies out once and for all in the middle of the nineteenth century? On the one hand, there can be no doubt whatsoever that a certain kind of sublime does indeed go out of fashion, perhaps irrevocably, sometime during that period in a number of domains of European culture (in America, the fashion seems both to start and to peter out somewhat later). In aesthetic theory, the last philosophers for whom the sublime is a central category are Hegel and his immediate pupils like Solger and Vischer; in lyric poetry, the great season of the Romantic sublime, in Wordsworth, Shelley, Coleridge, Hölderlin, and Leopardi, yields by mid-century to tones that are either more domestic, or more ironic, or both; in fiction, ex-Romantics like Stendhal and Flaubert analyze compassionately and yet dispassionately the self-destructive errors that are produced by the attempt to transcend the given world of everyday social reality in favor of some mirage of the sublime, while the great nineteenth-century comic novelists, such as Balzac and Dickens, devote themselves precisely to the meticulous investigation of that social world; in art, the high and dramatic ambitions of Delacroix, Friedrich, and Turner yield to the tamer world of Biedermeier, Victorianism, and, eventually, Impressionism. Only in the field of symphonic and operatic music does the sublime continue to reign even into the beginning of the twentieth century—evidently music forms an exception among the arts, and we may suspect that its very non-discursiveness gave a broad scope within its domain to the public expression of sublime emotions that could not long survive such exposure elsewhere. We may of course disagree about the moment in each of these domains at which the sublime becomes passé, but it seems impossible to deny that by the second half of the nineteenth century, European culture as a whole had taken the single step that, according to Napoleon, separated the sublime from the ridiculous.

And yet, on the other hand, it seems equally impossible to deny that in a number of fields the sublime has been enjoying a remarkable renaissance since the second half of the twentieth century. In art, Barnett Newman and Mark Rothko produced large-scale nonrepresentational paintings, such as Newman's 2.4 meters high and 5.4 meters wide *Vir Heroicus Sublimis* of 1950–51 (fig. 8.1; see color insert) and numerous celebrated monumental artworks by Rothko: vast canvases of bold yet subtle coloration that were designed to produce, and succeeded in producing, feelings of oceanic unease and anxious exaltation in viewers who were expected to stand as close to them in order to experience them as the artists had stood to paint them. Indeed, in one essay entitled "The Sublime is Now," Newman theorized a contemporary American attempt to revive the tradition of the sublime against what he saw as the European fashion of the small, beautiful, fastidiously representational artwork.[3] In aesthetic and psychological theory, since the last quarter of the twentieth century the sublime has celebrated a remarkable return in the works of such writers as Harold Bloom, Jean-François Lyotard, and Slavoj Žižek[4]; whatever doubts one may have about the philosophical cogency of their attempts to use the category of the sublime for exploring the dimensions of the unrepresentable in thought and art, there can be no doubt at all about the extraordinary popularity and influence of these writers, and hence about the existence and urgency of the widespread cultural need to which they are responding. In literature, Don DeLillo and many other American and Anglophone novelists have been remarkably successful in excavating elements of the sublime even in our seemingly technological and pragmatic world, while in cinema the peculiar combination of extreme dread and consolatory exhilaration that in past centuries had been the special preserve of the sublime has become one of the staples of whole genres of films—terror, thriller, horror, and so on—which

---

[3] Newman (1992) 170–73.
[4] Bloom (1976) and (1989) and (2011); Lyotard (1983) and (1991); Žižek (1989).

evidently succeed in exciting and satisfying the emotions of many millions of people.

The evident death of the sublime in the nineteenth century and the evident vitality of the sublime in the twentieth century are a problem for the theory of the sublime whose importance and difficulty may not yet have been adequately recognized. Is the sublime alive or dead, or both? It is not clear how best to set about theorizing its self-survival. Surely it is not historically accurate to deny the precipitous decline of the sublime in the nineteenth century; but by the same token it is no longer possible, as it might still have seemed to be some decades ago, to dismiss its boisterous return in the twentieth century as nothing more than a flash in the pan. The intimate link between rapture and rupture that constitutes the sublime is back: what are we to do?

The most promising way to resolve this difficulty is to drive a wedge between the text of Longinus, on the one hand, and the idea of the sublime, on the other, in the hope that the version of the sublime enshrined in the treatise will turn out to be only one of the possible varieties of the concept, so that different periods can witness the flowering of different varieties of it. It may be that the standard model will turn out upon reflection to have been generated in part by a simple methodological mistake— namely, the restrictive identification of the concept of the sublime with the treatise of Longinus, as though there could not be a valid notion of the sublime that was not directly derived from his text. After all, Longinus himself ceased to be a household name long before the middle of the nineteenth century—indeed, already by the time of Burke the sublime had begun to emancipate itself from Longinus's treatise, and in the following centuries, numerous writers discussed the concept enthusiastically and competently, writers who had surely never even read Longinus. So let us reconsider the traditional Longinian sublime and ask to what extent that version had characteristics that might mark it as only one idiosyncratic variant of the sublime rather than as its sole possible representative; and let us focus for this purpose not upon the terror of the sublime, its grandeur, or its emotional appeal, but rather upon the degree to which it is intrinsically bound up with an idealistic view of the world as being governed by some form of divine providence.

It is easy enough to allow the discomfort, indeed the terrors, of Longinus's version of the sublime to distract us from its fundamental theological component and mislead us into thinking that the sublime tells the story of the annihilation of humankind in the face of a pitiless universe. But that is very far from being the case. For the story that the Longinian sublime tells is one not only of endangerment even to the point of physical destruction but also of spiritual, moral, and intellectual elevation above the pettinesses of the human body and its daily needs. Those who are in the grip of the sublime are raised up toward a higher level from which they can look down upon human limitations from a distance, and can thereby overcome them, at least in thought, identifying themselves with the divine plan that is ultimately responsible for the world and for their place in it. The Longinian sublime, after all, produces not only terror but also and above all a thrill of elevation; and that elevation is due to a cognitive leap by which we abandon temporarily our usual human smallness and, for an instant, and even if necessary at the cost of forfeiting our human life, manage to adopt a god's eye view of the world. As Longinus puts it,

Τί ποτ'οὖν εἶδον οἱ ἰσόθεοι ἐκεῖνοι καὶ τῶν μεγίστων ἐπορεξάμενοι τῆς συγγραφῆς, τῆς δ'ἐν ἅπασιν ἀκριβείας ὑπερφρονήσαντες; πρὸς πολλοῖς ἄλλοις ἐκεῖνο, ὅτι ἡ φύσις οὐ ταπεινὸν ἡμᾶς ζῷον οὐδ'ἀγεννὲς †ἔ.κρινε τὸν ἄνθρωπον, ἀλλ'ὡς εἰς μεγάλην τινὰ πανήγυριν εἰς τὸν βίον καὶ εἰς τὸν σύμπαντα κόσμον ἐπάγουσα, θεατάς τινας τῶν ἄθλων αὐτῆς ἐσομένους καὶ φιλοτιμοτάτους ἀγωνιστάς, εὐθὺς ἄμαχον ἔρωτα ἐνέφυσεν ἡμῶν ταῖς ψυχαῖς παντὸς ἀεὶ τοῦ μεγάλου καὶ ὡς πρὸς ἡμᾶς δαιμονιωτέρου. διόπερ τῇ θεωρίας καὶ διανοίας τῆς ἀνθρωπίνης ἐπιβολῇ οὐδ'ὁ σύμπας κόσμος ἀρκεῖ, ἀλλὰ καὶ τοὺς τοῦ περιέχοντος πολλάκις ὅρους ἐκβαίνουσιν αἱ ἐπίνοιαι, καὶ εἴ τις περιβλέψαιτο ἐν κύκλῳ τὸν βίον, ὅσῳ πλέον ἔχει τὸ περιττὸν ἐν πᾶσι καὶ μέγα καὶ καλόν, ταχέως εἴσεται πρὸς ἃ γεγόναμεν. (35.2–3)

What then was the vision which inspired those divine writers who disdained exactness of detail and aimed at the greatest prizes in literature? Above all else, it was the understanding that nature made man to be no humble or lowly creature, but brought him into life and into the universe as into a great festival, to be both a spectator and an enthusiastic contestant in its competitions. She implanted in our minds from the start an irresistible desire for anything which is great and, in relation to ourselves, supernatural. The universe therefore is not wide enough for the range of human speculation and intellect. Our thoughts often travel beyond the boundaries of our surroundings. If anyone wants to know what we were born for, let him look round at life and contemplate the splendor, grandeur, and beauty in which it everywhere abounds.[5]

The sublime is for Longinus not merely a literary or rhetorical category: his analysis of its effect upon us when we read the great works of classical Greek literature is founded upon a deep anthropological and cosmological construct that aims to naturalize the sublime by allowing us to interpret our very ordinary dissatisfaction with our very ordinary lives as the proof that we were really intended for a different, extraordinary form of reality, a higher and more noble one. To feel and understand the sublime is not quite to become a god, for no mortal can, but it is to approach the gods' own plan for us as close as any human possibly can, if only for a moment. This idealistic dimension remains a constant in theorizations of the Longinian sublime throughout its long career, and indeed is one of the markers that helps to differentiate the sublime from such related concepts as the ugly, the dreadful, or the terrifying. Even Kant, to be sure, though he allows the external object and its divine maker to be swallowed up within the grandeur of the human subject who feels himself to be sublime and is therefore its sole true locus,[6] insists that the feeling of the sublime reminds us that our authentic habitation is in a spiritual domain which cannot be affected in any way by the painful vicissitudes to which our bodies may be exposed; and Schiller's transformation of the Kantian theory further reinforces this idealistic, optimistic, ultimately teleological interpretation of the concept.[7]

Thus the Longinian sublime depends upon the premise of the divine, providential administration of the world. We suffer because we have bodies, but our spirit is capable of elevating us above the condition of animals to our more proper place near if not quite among the gods, endowed with knowledge and bliss like theirs—even if, sometimes, at the cost of our life itself. Seen in this light, it becomes easier to understand

---

[5] Trans. Russell and Winterbottom (1972) 494. The Greek text is that printed in Russell (1964).
[6] Kant (1974) § 28 (A103–104=B104–105) 100–101.
[7] Schiller (1993) 22–44 ("On the Sublime"), 70–85 ("Concerning the Sublime").

why such a version of the sublime had trouble surviving the nineteenth century. One superficial reason for its decline is obvious: the category of the sublime never quite succeeded in emancipating itself adequately from its original source in the tradition of Greco-Roman rhetoric, and hence was doomed to suffer the same eclipse that the rest of that tradition underwent once Romanticism, with its contempt for rhetorical recipes and its infatuation with spontaneous original genius, arrived on the scene. But more importantly, the general decline of a sense of religious transcendence in secular Western societies since the mid-nineteenth century must inevitably have made it very difficult for this version of the theological sublime to be able to assert itself successfully. Where the limits of the real are taken to coincide with the limits of the human—if not, yet, of what humans can actually do, then at least of what humans can know now and can hope to do someday—then it is not clear what room could possibly be left for a genuine experience of the Longinian sublime. Once the technical manipulation of nature had proceeded to the point that it has reached for many inhabitants of Western societies during the past generations, the raging oceans and lofty mountain peaks that so moved the imaginations of earlier tourists and readers could come to seem, instead, a matter for civil engineering, marine meteorology, hydroelectric power, or Club Méditerrané. In a world in which technical progress, the disasters of war, and the ideology of secular humanism could make the very idea of divine providence seem more and more remote, the power of the Longinian sublime not only to terrify but also to elevate and to delight must inevitably have been attenuated, and any authors and artists who might still have sought to emulate its powerful effects would have run increasingly the risk of being accused of producing not great art, but kitsch.

It might be tempting to suppose that the very possibility of elevation intrinsic to the sublime depends upon the premise of the benevolent divine ordering of the world. After all, without providence would the experience of the sublime not be bound to finish simply as an unredeemable catastrophe? And yet the fact that this is not the case is proven by the work of at least one ancient author who is deeply imbued with the rhetoric and ethos of the sublime but who has not the slightest trace of a theological optimism or indeed of any belief whatsoever in divine providence. This is Lucretius, whose Epicurean didactic poem, *De Rerum Natura*, seems almost an anthology of purple passages conveying impressive instances of the sublime.[8] Consider, for example, the celebrated opening of book 2:

> Suave, mari magno turbantibus aequora ventis,
> e terra magnum alterius spectare laborem;
> non quia vexari quemquamst iucunda voluptas,
> sed quibus ipse malis careas quia cernere suave est.
> suave etiam belli certamina magna tueri
> per campos instructa tua sine parte pericli.
> sed nil dulcius est bene quam munita tenere
> edita doctrina sapientum templa serena,
> despicere unde queas alios passimque videre
> errare atque viam palantis quaerere vitae,
> certare ingenio, contendere nobilitate,
> noctes atque dies niti praestante labore
> ad summa emergere opes rerumque potiri.
> o miseras hominum mentes, o pectora caeca!
> qualibus in tenebris vitae quantisque periclis
> degitur hoc aevi quodcumquest! (*De Rerum Natura*
> 2.1–16)

Pleasant it is, when on the great sea the winds trouble the waters, to gaze from shore upon another's great tribulation: not because any man's troubles are a delectable joy, but because to perceive what ills you are free from yourself is pleasant. Pleasant is it also to behold great encounters of warfare arrayed over the plains, with no part of yours in the peril. But nothing is more delightful than to possess lofty sanctuaries serene, well fortified by the teachings of the wise, whence you may look down upon others and behold them all astray, wandering abroad and seeking the path of life:—the strife of wits, the fight for precedence, all laboring night and day with surpassing toil to mount upon to the pinnacle of riches and to lay hold on power. O pitiable minds of men, O blind intelligences! In what gloom of life, in how great perils is passed all your poor span of time! (trans. Rouse-Smith)

These lines read like a catalogue raisonné of an exhibition of eighteenth-century paintings of the sublime: a storm-tossed ship at sea, a battlefield

---

[8] This has been demonstrated in an important article by Gian Biagio Conte: "Instructions for a Sublime Reader: Form of the Text and Form of the Addressee in Lucretius' *De rerum natura*," in Conte (1994) 1–34. See now also Porter (2007) and (2010); Hardie (2009); and Bloom (2011) 133–93.

filled with troops and strewn with carnage. The pleasure that they describe is achieved not by the sadistic satisfaction in seeing the sufferings of others—at least, that is the claim—but by the height and distance with which the philosophical spectator looks down and from afar upon the errors to which almost all other people are subject. This cognitive elevation withdraws Epicureans from human ignorance and approximates them to a divine wisdom.

Lucretius's world is one made up entirely and exclusively of atoms and void which interact with one another according to no principle other than that of sheer chance; the gods exist, to be sure, but they are far too busy enjoying their interplanetary leisure to be bothered with the causal or moral ordering of our world or of any other one. Thus the gods certainly exist, but there is no divine providence and no providential ordering of the world: the world is as it is not because the gods wanted it to be that way, but only because of the random collisions of atoms with one another. To recognize the truth of Epicurus's doctrine of the absolute irrelevance of the gods in any regard except as moral paradigms provides men with the specific combination of the two incompatible but interdependent emotions that have always been the hallmark of the sublime, divine delight (*divina voluptas*) and shuddering terror (*horror*):

> nam simul ac ratio tua coepit vociferari
> naturam rerum, divina mente coortam,
> diffugiunt animi terrores, moenia mundi
> discedunt, totum video per inane geri res.
> apparet divum numen sedesque quietae
> quas neque concutiunt venti nec nubila nimbis
> aspergunt neque nix acri concreta pruina
> cana cadens violat semperque innubilus aether
> integit, et large diffuso lumine ridet.
> omnia suppeditat porro natura neque ulla
> res animi pacem delibat tempore in ullo.
> at contra nusquam apparent Acherusia templa,
> nec tellus obstat quin omnia dispiciantur,
> sud pedibus quaecumque infra per inane geruntur.
> his ibi me rebus quaedam **divina voluptas**
> percipit atque **horror**, quod sic natura tua vi
> tam manifesta patens ex omni parte retecta est.
> (*De Rerum Natura* 3.14–30)

For as soon as your reasoning begins to proclaim the nature of things revealed by your divine mind, away flee the mind's terrors, the walls of the world open out, I see action going on throughout the whole void: before me appear the gods in their majesty, and their peaceful abodes, which no winds ever shake nor clouds besprinkle with rain, which no snow congealed by the bitter frost mars with its white fall, but the air ever cloudless encompasses them and laughs with its light spread wide abroad. There moreover nature supplies everything, and nothing at any time impairs their peace of mind. But contrariwise nowhere appear the regions of Acheron; yet the earth is no hindrance to all being clearly seen, whatsoever goes on below under our feet throughout the void. Thereupon from all these things a sort of **divine delight** gets hold upon me and a **shuddering**, because nature thus by your power has been so manifestly laid open and uncovered in every part.

So the absence of providence does not lead in Lucretius to an absence of the sublime. On the contrary, Lucretius's passionate conviction of the truth of Epicurus's doctrines allows him to see that Greek philosopher as a sublime and heroic warrior who rescues cowering humankind from the oppression of superstitious error and delivers us to the light of truth and freedom (1.62–71); and his poem is filled with memorable passages describing in majestic language the sublimity of such overwhelming large-scale spectacles as the celestial bodies (5.1204–10) or earthquakes (6.577–84).

To be sure, Lucretius does not express anywhere an explicit theory of the sublime, but instead merely deploys the language and rhetoric of the sublime; correspondingly, he never uses the substantive and only uses forms of the adjective four times in his poem.[9] And yet it is not at all difficult to identify a characteristically Lucretian sublime and to distinguish it from the more familiar Longinian sublime. Whereas the Longinian sublime is fundamentally a form of theodicy, justifying human suffering by appeal to the superior logic of divine wisdom, the Lucretian sublime venerates a form of human heroism possible within a universe that has been left by the gods to its own devices. The Longinian sublime presupposes the gods' benevolence within an ultimate teleological framework for human existence and provides a compensatory meaning for suffering and loss in the form of the understanding of divine providence; the Lucretian sublime posits the irrelevance of the gods and the fundamental

[9] *Sublima*: 1.340; *sublime*: 2.206, 4.133, 6.97.

randomness and meaninglessness of the universe and identifies the sublime as a gesture of courageous defiance in which humans compensate
for the absence of divine providence by giving themselves some form
of meaning nonetheless. The Longinian sublime magnifies God, whose
power and benevolence we come to understand even through suffering,
thereby overcoming our pettiness albeit at the cost of our destruction;
the Lucretian sublime magnifies humans, who achieve greatness precisely
in the absence of any effective divinity and thereby become themselves
gods of a kind within a world devoid of ultimate meaning, indeed of
any meaning whatsoever beyond what they themselves can manage to
impose.

Given that Lucretius did not theorize the sublime himself and that
Longinus did do so but remained unread in antiquity, it would obviously
be somewhat of an exaggeration to claim that they represented two
rival ancient traditions of the sublime. Instead, we will do better to speak
of them as offering us two differently conceived ancient models of the
sublime, which have generated two differently articulated varieties in
modern times. Lucretius is important for my argument not because
I want to claim that he was a frequent point of reference for those who
wished to theorize the sublime in a way different from the Longinian
tradition (though in fact he often was),[10] but only because his very existence proves that one did not have to believe in Longinus's optimistic
theology in order to be fascinated by sublimity. To be sure, Longinus is
the one who has attracted the attention of historians—after all, he was the
one who wrote a book on the subject that is still extant and that bears the
word "sublime" in its title, and it was Boileau's translation of that book
that detonated a European fashion. But it would be mistaken to think that
the Lucretian sublime did not accompany the Longinian one throughout
the period of its greatest prominence and compete with it to define the
theological terms that were really at stake. In the last several decades,
a number of scholars of eighteenth-century English literature have come
to recognize the importance of a skeptical or comic sublime in such
authors as Pope and Sterne, whereby the Lucretian sublime perspective

---

[10] For example, Rothko does not seem ever to refer in his writings to Lucretius or to
the sublime. But his discussions of beauty repeatedly invoke classic features of the sublime like exaltation, terror, pain, and death: Breslin (1993) 390; Rothko (2004) 63, 69–71;
(2006) 125.

downward upon the follies of deluded humankind serves to elevate the enlightened speaker, but without committing him to a determinate view of moral order.[11] We would do well to attend not only to Longinus's traces, but to Lucretius's as well.

Even at the height of the Longinian sublime, its Lucretian rival insists upon manifesting itself sporadically as a threatening countercurrent capable of suggesting, even at the moments of greatest theological optimism, that in fact the gods abandoned us long ago and that there is nothing left any longer in this whole meaningless universe except for human grandeur and human presumption. Consider, for example, Mont Blanc, a key reference point for the whole Romantic discourse of the sublime. A series of five texts composed over a period of only twenty-seven years shows how what began as a figure designed to demonstrate incontrovertibly the glory of God becomes in the end a monument to the godless arrogance of man. The series begins with a lyric hymn composed in 1791 by Friderike Brun and addressed, typically, to the most sublime of all German poets of the day, Friedrich Gottlieb Klopstock.[12] Brun dwells upon the superhuman, forbidding grandeur of the mountain as it comes clearly into view at dawn. To her question, who could possibly have possessed the power to frame that awesome immensity, she can find only one answer: all of nature shouts, roars, and whispers, "Jehovah! Jehovah!" (17, 19). A little more than a decade later, Coleridge translates and expands Brun's short hymn (without acknowledgment) and thereby creates one of the great lyric poems of English Romanticism.[13] Here, too, he repeats her gesture of asking who could possibly have been mighty enough to create the mighty mountain, and can find no other answer than the one that nature itself seems to cry out, "God!" (60). And yet this time it is not enough for Coleridge simply to describe nature and listen to its supposed voice. He looks down in tears and only then lifts his gaze up once again to the mountain, which he invokes: "Rise, mighty form,

---

[11] Lamb (1981); Noggle (2001); Fanning (2005). In his doctoral dissertation, Baker (2001) applies their findings to such theorists of the sublime as Burke, Kant, and Schiller; the author plans a forthcoming book on this subject. On the Lucretian sublime especially in nineteenth century English poets, see now Bloom (2011) 133–93.

[12] "Chamouny beym Sonnenaufgange. An Klopstock. (Im Mai 1791)," in Brun (1806) 1–2.

[13] "Hymn Before Sun-Rise, in the Vale of Chamouni" (1802), in Coleridge (1924) 165–67.

even as thou *seem'st* to rise" (66)—the mountain must perform in reality the very same action that the poet's imagination attributes to it if the poet is to be capable of hearing what he takes to be its voice. About the same time or slightly later, this gradual encroachment of the poet's imagination upon the prerogatives of God is taken a significant step further, in the celebrated passage on the crossing of the Alps in book 6 of the *Prelude* written by Coleridge's friend Wordsworth.[14] Here, the encounter with the sublime is broken up into a narrative of repeated disappointments and frustrations, in which disillusionment with the natural world is compensated for by the discovery of the internal resources of the poet's own creative imagination. The first sight of the real mountain of Mont Blanc, so far from thrilling the travelers, disappoints them by imposing a mere lifeless vision of nature upon the soul's fantasy, suffocating it; then their hope to experience the majestic feeling of crossing the Alps is thwarted by the fact that, lost and confused, they have already done so. Wordsworth does indeed invoke the full Miltonic register of the sublime language of divine providence, the book of nature, the apocalypse, "The types and symbols of Eternity, / Of first, and last, and midst, and without end" (6.571–72). But the infinitude that he identifies as humankind's authentic destiny, nature, and home is, in fact, not God but his own imagination, which rises up at the moment in which experience of the outer world has been stymied in a crisis—it is to his own soul, not to its divine maker, that Wordsworth cries out climactically, "I recognize thy glory" (6.527). Another decade later, Shelley repeats and intensifies the tendency in his own poem to Mont Blanc.[15] Shelley looks at the mountain, but what he really sees is his very own faculty of imagination, and he is capable of welcoming the sublime sight only because it is one of the products of his own poetic creativity. In the poem's final lines, Shelley does indeed assert that there is some secret power which inhabits the mountain. And yet, he concludes by suggesting that such objects have no genuine existence on their own, but that it is nothing other than the human mind's ability to project meaning onto the meaninglessness of nonhuman nature that can give them a life and permit them to enter into fruitful intercourse with us. Two years later,

---

[14] 6.452–572 (Wordsworth (1926) 198–206). I cite from the 1805–1806 version.
[15] "Mont Blanc. Lines Written in the Vale of Chamouni" (1816), in P. B. Shelley (1968) 532–35.

Shelley's wife, Mary Wollstonecraft Shelley, took the final step in chapter 10 of her novel *Frankenstein*.[16] Mary Shelley's novel takes the form of a series of letters surrounding the central chapters, in which the monster delivers an autobiographical narrative to the fascinated and horrified man who created him. As the setting for that central narrative, Mary Shelley chose, precisely, Mont Blanc. The sublime mountain that only a few decades earlier had seemed the perfect symbol of God's benevolent omnipotence now suggested itself to her as the most appropriate possible backdrop for an account of what happens when humans try to substitute themselves for God by arrogating to themselves the divine power to create life. Thus, within a few decades, what had begun as the sublime of divine providence had turned into the sublime of human presumption in a world emptied of the gods; and even if the Romantics are still criticizing godless human hubris, it is evident that at the same time they are fascinated by its possibilities and are experimenting with their limits. Underneath the consoling mask of the Longinian sublime, we can recognize ever more clearly the cheerless grimace of the Lucretian sublime.

In fact, when we look upon the countenance of the sublime as it is manifested most significantly in the second half of the twentieth century, what we really see are the lineaments of the Lucretian version. This is not to say that artists like Newman and Rothko actually studied the *De Rerum Natura*, but that is not the point. Our world is no longer, at least for many of us, one that is filled throughout with the unmistakable traces of divine providence: and yet even for those who can no longer accept the idea of an overarching divinely engineered master plan and who incline instead to attribute the history of the universe ultimately to atoms, void, and chance, there remains a kind of sublimity that can be recognized, if not in the benevolence of God, then in the defiant courage of humankind. Where once humans had admired in astonishment the well-meaning might of a superhuman power that could have crushed them but had preferred, for the time being, not to do so, they have now learned to admire in astonishment their very own capabilities for good and for evil, for knowledge and for annihilation, for better and for worse. The Lucretian sublime, particularly in its contemporary expressions, uses

---

[16] See now M. W. Shelley (2008).

the majesty of external nature, if it uses it at all, only as a mirror, or as a pretext, to show men their own grandeur as a creative and destructive force.

My argument can be clarified by appeal to illustrations drawn from painting, for these have a greater visceral immediacy than textual examples do and they may serve to make these abstract categories somewhat less rebarbative. After all, if what is at stake in the sublime is ultimately a representation of our ineluctable embodiedness within the material world we see around us, then it is easy to understand that visual artifacts will often succeed in communicating the emotions involved with greater immediacy, specificity, and poignancy than linguistic ones can.

The classic painting of the Longinian sublime, as it flourished from the second half of the eighteenth to about the middle of the nineteenth century, tended to follow the same general pattern for over a hundred years (fig. 8.2). The paintings are most often set in a horizontal format, and they are usually quite large. Within this horizontal picture frame, they emphasize both broad vistas and sharp vertical differences in height, thereby inviting us to survey a vast domain from a position of relative motionlessness, in which the verticality of our own bodies is not invoked or endangered: we are reduced to a rotating, all-seeing eye that can easily move up and down and penetrate toward distant vistas but above all scans left and right. If the panorama is shown from a low viewpoint, we are being invited to marvel at the force that threatens to crush us; if from above, then we gaze from a position of power, like a hovering eagle. The objects shown are natural scenes of the most inhospitable, inhuman kind: places not to live in, but to admire from a safe distance, barren tracts that separate more hospitable settlements from one another and present barriers to human communication that are insuperable, or almost so: mountains, waterfalls, oceans. And yet they are bathed in a majestic light by the sun, which, whatever the time of day, creates palettes of color and plays of light and shadow that may well reveal dissonances of hue and treatment but always end up remaining quite harmonious. Very often our own viewpoint as spectators of the painting is introjected into the painting itself in the form of small human observers depicted from behind, usually along the bottom margin. These serve by their puniness to give an idea of the immense dimensions of the natural scene they witness together with us, yet they also demonstrate that this region, too, forbidding as it is, has in the end become opened up to the penetrating

Figure 8.2.   William Turner, *Fall of the Rhine at Schaffhausen* (ca. 1805–1806). Oil on canvas, 148.6 × 2.39.7 cm. Museum of Fine Arts, Boston. Bequest of Alice Marian Curtis, and Special Picture Fund, 13.2723. Photograph © 2012, Museum of Fine Arts, Boston.

gaze and activity of travelers. The scenery, though it remains inhuman, is thereby somewhat humanized; it reminds us that for all its apparent hostility to humanity, it has been made by the very same Creator who made humans to be the lords of his creation.

This underlying theological optimism is sometimes made clear in these paintings by a cross, accompanied or unaccompanied by a human worshipper, set into the middle of nowhere, not for any pragmatic reason one can possibly imagine but simply as a symbolic indication of a profound natural religiosity anchored in a time before human institutions and detectable in places devoid of any other sign of human passage (figs. 8.3 and 8.4). Alien as it is and remains, the sublime landscape is thereby by implication transformed somewhat into a church, a vast Gothic cathedral in which the columns return to their origin as trees and the spires to mountains that point us upward toward our Maker. To be sure, not always does the artist manage (or even really try) to maintain the delicate balance between the dominance of the object and the puniness of the spectator. Instead, sometimes the focus is much more upon the represented viewer than upon what is viewed (fig. 8.5), and in such cases we are doubtless entitled to suspect that the true subject of the painting is the grandeur within the spectators' soul, for which the outward grandeur they view is only a stimulus or even a pretext; at other times the spectators are entirely suppressed explicitly (fig. 8.6). And yet even where, as here, what is shown is so inhuman that no explicit spectator could easily be supplied, the implicit eye that has managed to invent and inspect so forbidding a scene becomes even more impressive than in those paintings that seem to emphasize the spectators' body.

Thus, for all its evident emphasis upon the natural object, the classic Longinian sublime painting can sometimes be at least as much about the viewers as it is about what they see. Just as we noted that the Longinian literary theme of Mont Blanc's theodicy could gradually slip into a Lucretian version of human hubris, so too paintings of the sublime can sometimes exploit the outside world as little more than an excuse for the play of the artist's sense of color and rhythm. Indeed, few paintings before the twentieth century come as close to pure abstraction as do some of Turner's studies of light in the mountains (figs. 8.7 and 8.8; see color insert).

Suppose we take one of the more abstract traditional depictions of a sublime landscape, such as Casper David Friedrich's *Monk by the*

Figure 8.3. Casper David Friedrich, *Morning in the Riesengebirge* (1810–11). Oil on canvas, 108 × 170 cm. BPK, Berlin / Neuer (Schinkel) Pavillon, Charlottenburg Castle, Stiftung Preussische Schlösser & Gärten Berlin-Brandenburg, Berlin. Photo: Joerg P. Anders / Art Resource, NY.

Figure 8.4. Frederic Edwin Church, *Cross in the Wilderness* (1857). Oil on canvas, 41.3 × 61.5 cm. © Museo Thyssen-Bornemisza, Madrid.

Figure 8.5. Casper David Friedrich, *Wanderer Above a Sea of Fog* (ca. 1818). Oil on canvas. 94.8 × 74.8 cm. BPK, Berlin / Hamburger Kunsthalle, Hamburg, Germany. Photo: Elke Walford / Art Resource, NY.

Figure 8.6. Casper David Friedrich, *The Polar Sea* (1823–24). Oil on canvas. 96.7 × 126.9 cm. BPK, Berlin / Hamburger Kunsthalle, Hamburg, Germany. Photo: Elke Walford / Art Resource, NY.

Figure 8.1. Barnett Newman, *Vir Heroicus Sublimis* (1950–51). Oil on canvas. 242.2 × 541.7 cm. Gift of Mr. and Mrs. Ben Heller, The Museum of Modern Art, New York. © The Museum of Modern Art/Licensed by SCALA/Art Resource, NY.

Figure 8.7. Joseph Mallord William Turner, *Sunset From the Top of the Rigi* (c. 1844). Oil on canvas. 71.1 × 96.5 cm. © Tate, London 2011.

Figure 8.8. Joseph Mallord William Turner, *Sun Setting over a Lake* (c. 1840). Oil on canvas. 91.1 × 112.6 cm. © Tate, London 2011.

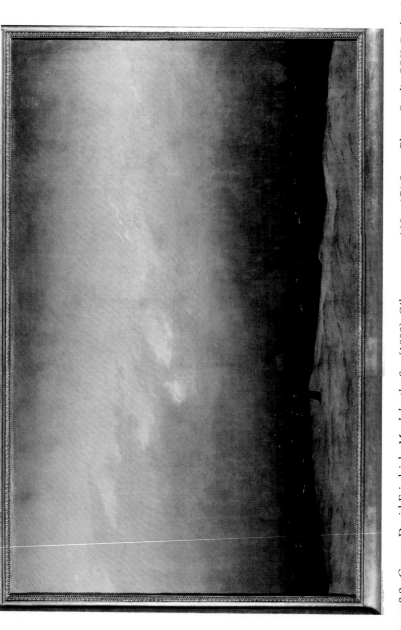

Figure 8.9. Caspar David Friedrich, *Monk by the Sea* (1809). Oil on canvas. 110 × 171.5 cm. Photo Credit: BPK, Berlin / Nationalgalerie, Staatliche Museen, Berlin. Photo: Joerg P. Anders / Art Resource, NY.

Figure 8.10. Mark Rothko, *Untitled* (1969). 266.1 × 289.6 cm. Coll. Kate Rothko Prizel. © ARS, NY. Photo Credit: Art Resource, NY.

Figure 8.11. Joseph Mallord William Turner. *The Scarlet Sunset* (c. 1830–40). Watercolour and gouache on paper, unique. 13.4 × 18.9 cm. Accepted by the nation as part of the Turner Bequest 1856, © Tate, London 2011.

Figure 8.12. Mark Rothko, *No. 10.* (1952). Oil on canvas. 207.65 × 107.95 cm. Seattle Art Museum, partial and promised gift of Bagley and Virginia Wright, 91.98.

Sea (fig. 8.9), in which the vast panorama of the barren sea, viewed by a solitary monk on the beach in the foreground, might almost seem to serve as little more than a pretext for a purely painterly exploration of the relations of various large blocks of different color to one another. This painting is already at the very edge of representationality; one slight nudge, and it will fall over that edge into pure abstraction. What if the viewer is not blessed with perfect eyesight but is so myopic that without glasses all he could see would be one big blur? This was the condition of Mark Rothko, for example,[17] and one wonders what exactly he would have seen if he had stood in front of Friedrich's painting of the monk on the shore and taken off his glasses. Perhaps what he would have seen would have looked something like figure 8.10 (see color insert).

Of course, I am not suggesting seriously that the development of twentieth-century painting was largely determined by one painter's relative nearsightedness. Instead, this striking juxtaposition serves to indicate by a kind of visual shorthand that Rothko's art achieves its extraordinary novelty by reason of his radical rethinking and transformation of the classical tradition of Longinian sublime painting that had preceded his work but had been separated from it by an interruption of almost a century. Rothko invents a new, Lucretian mode of sublime painting by means of three ingenious strategic choices. The most obvious, and conventional, of these is his refusal to represent any identifiable objects, be they mountains or oceans or spectators, and his consequent refocusing of the viewer's attention not upon specific individual external realities perceived, as it were, through the window of a transparent canvas, but instead upon the painterly qualities of the surface of the canvas itself, the broad brilliance of its intense but nuanced hues together with the extraordinarily fine detail of the small-scale brushwork. Two other innovations are less immediately evident but no less significant. Above all, Rothko verticalizes the canvas, thereby forcing viewers to become aware of their own body as they stand upright before the painting: instead of simply rotating their eyes or head from left to right, they must shift their vision up and down, thereby entering far more dynamically and corporeally into the viewing process. Moreover, Rothko insisted that his paintings ought to be viewed from very close up, indeed from the very

---

[17] Large, thick-lensed glasses are a feature of almost all the photographs of Rothko from his high school days until the end of his life.

same distance from which he himself had painted them. In this way, viewers are surrounded by large fields of color that stretch in all directions out of their immediate visual field to the furthest limit, the blurry border of what they can see. All three strategies result in annulling the distance between the viewer and the painting, indeed in a certain sense they put the viewer into the very painting. Whatever else these sublime paintings are about, they are also really about their sublime painter, Mark Rothko, and insofar as we are invited to identify ourselves with him they are also about us. In this world without God, the only sublime that is left is that of the heroic, or hubristic, human individual.

Yet at the same time, Rothko's paintings are also sophisticated comments upon the painting traditions that preceded him. We discover that, at least in Rothko's implicit interpretation, Friedrich's painting was not really about a monk on the shore, but about blocks of color in their interrelation with one another. Indeed, a number of Rothko's most extraordinary works can be interpreted as his implicit variation upon the standard traditional landscape painting, in which two or three broad bands of color correspond to the sky, the sea or distant landscape, and the shore or nearer land. So for example in the two paintings shown in figures 8.11 and 8.12 (see color insert).[18] This is not, of course, to say that painters like Friedrich and Turner had really been consciously interested in nothing other than in bars of contrasting colors and luminosities—but from the point of view of Rothko's Lucretian sublime, whatever else these earlier artists had depicted had been at best only a pretext for experiments in color, or at worst a misunderstanding of the true possibilities of art. If the locus of the sublime was indeed the human mind, and not the mountain

---

[18] Other pairs of paintings that lend themselves to such comparison include the following: Casper David Friedrich, *Winterlandschaft mit Kirche* (1811, Dortmund, Museum für Kunst und Kulturgeschichte) and Mark Rothko, *Untitled* (1969, acrylic on paper mounted on canvas, 183.4 × 98 cm, Estate no. 2062.69, coll. Christopher Rothko); or Friedrich, *Neubrandenburg* (ca. 1817, Kiel, Stiftung Pommern) and Rothko, *Violet Bar* (1957, 175.5 × 167.5 cm, private collection); or Friedrich, *Mondaufgang am Meer* (1822, Berlin, Alte Nationalgallerie) and Rothko, *No. 5 (Siena, Orange and Black on Dark Brown)* (1962, 193 × 175 cm, Teheran Museum of Contemporary Art); or Friedrich, *Meeresküste bei Mondschein* (ca. 1830, Berlin, Alte Nationalgallerie) and Rothko, *Untitled* (1949, 142.5 × 83 cm, New York, The Metropolitan Museum of Art); or William Turner, *Sailing Near the Promontory of East Cowes* (1827, London, Tate Gallery) and Rothko, *Untitled* (1950, 230 × 129 cm, coll. Kate Rothko Prizel).

or ocean, as Kant had already insisted in his *Critique of Judgment*,[19] then what point was there in representing an external object at all, what did one need beyond the play of color in which human subjects could vary, enlarge, almost lose, and then rediscover themselves?

Mark Rothko shows one direction that the Longinian artistic sublime was able to follow as it was transformed into a Lucretian version. By taking the tendency toward abstraction in painters like Turner one step further and finally going on to abstract from representation altogether, focusing instead upon the purely painterly qualities of color, hue, and luminosity, Rothko managed to wrench spectators free from their safe position outside the painting and to push them instead as far as possible right into it. This is harder to do with photography, obviously, than it is with painting, for it has proved much harder to shake off the dominance of the represented object in the photographic medium. Yet the Swiss photographer Jean-Pascal Imsand has shown how a similar transformation can be achieved within the medium of photography as well. Consider his extraordinary photograph *Switzerland* (fig. 8.13).[20] What does it represent? Traditionally, painters of the sublime liked to represent mountains or the ocean and they had little difficulty in representing either one (figs. 8.14 and 8.15); even when they played, as they sometimes did, on the obvious metaphorical and visual similarities between the crests of mountains and the crests of waves, they usually took pains to keep the two realms clearly apart, so as not to confuse and unsettle the viewer. In his *Prelude*, to be sure, Wordsworth could speak of "dumb cataracts and streams of ice, / A motionless array of mighty waves" (6.458–59)—but that was poetry, and painters by contrast tended not to conflate the two realms. But Imsand's photograph enacts the metaphorical identity of the wave-crest and mountain-crest by means of a subtle and brilliant montage that manages to blur the distinction between them so thoroughly that we can be sure where there is water, on the one hand, and where there are mountains, on the other, but cannot possibly tell for certain where, precisely, the water ends and the mountains begin. The result is an image that is perfectly intelligible to our minds but that corresponds to nothing that could possibly exist in

---

[19] Kant (1974) § 26 (A94=B95), p. 95.
[20] Fondation Jean-Pascal Imsand (2004) 42.

Figure 8.13. Pascal Imsand, *Switzerland* (1990). © 2000 Fondation Jean-Pascal Imsand / Pro Litteris.

the real world outside of the photographer's darkroom and of his and our creative imagination. Here, too, the sublime is located not in mere lifeless external objects but only within human creativity: the external objects are indeed shown, but only so that their factitiousness can be recognized and the human subject can thereby transcend them. Lucretius would have been proud.

But it would be disingenuous to conclude without at least a word about the dangers of the Lucretian sublime. A world without God offers ample scope to human artists who wish to take his place: there is less competition for the top spot. Yet it is not easy to found one's life as a whole upon nothing other than atoms, the void, and chance, and to know

Figure 8.14. Joseph Mallord William Turner, *Morning amongst the Coniston Fells, Cumberland* (1798). Oil on canvas. 122.9 × 89.9 cm. © Tate, London 2011.

that one's greatest achievements are no more solid than the random collisions of submicroscopic particles. Having no other God to have to deal with may well leave more room for one's own ambitions, but at the same time the resulting arbitrariness and solitude might come in the end to seem to deprive them of any lasting value whatsoever. As they say in America, life at the top is lonely.

Melancholy and depression seem to be the inevitable professional illnesses of the practitioner of the Lucretian sublime. At least according to the probably unreliable testimony of Jerome, Lucretius himself is said to have gone mad because of his abuse of a love potion and to have written his poem during brief intervals of lucidity before he eventually committed suicide. About more recent artists we are better informed.

Figure 8.15. Joseph Mallord William Turner, *The Shipwreck* (1805). Oil on canvas. 170.5 × 241.6 cm. © Tate, London 2011.

Mark Rothko killed himself by cutting his wrists in his New York studio on February 25, 1970.[21] Jean-Pascal Imsand committed suicide by throwing himself under a train on March 29, 1994.[22]

---

[21] See Breslin (1993) 521–43.

[22] The choice of the specific means of suicide is usually determined only partly by immediate circumstances, but also partly by long-term psychological structures and obsessions. Rothko, surrounded by a six-foot by eight-foot large red patch of blood on the floor of his studio, becomes one of his own paintings, his last one. Imsand's fascination with trains and train tracks is clear throughout his oeuvre.

9

From Heresy to Nature: Leo Strauss's History of Modern Epicureanism

Benjamin Aldes Wurgaft

INTRODUCTION

The political philosopher Leo Strauss is seldom associated with Epicurean thought, and for good reasons: he is usually thought of as a follower of Plato who advocated a return to "natural right" thinking in political philosophy, and who valorized the pursuit of human excellence over the pursuit of human happiness.[1] On the face of it, the Epicurean question of happiness or well-being seems not just distant from, but even inimical to, Strauss's concerns. Epicureanism is rather too *therapeutic*—too preoccupied with the relief of pain and insufficiently concerned with the aspiration toward virtue—to fit comfortably with Strauss's mature political philosophy. Furthermore, Epicureanism seems to counsel retreat from, rather than theoretically informed engagement with, the political community.[2] Indeed, when Strauss does mention Epicureanism explicitly in his writings, it is usually to criticize it as a baleful influence on modern

---

[1] By "natural right," Strauss meant the existence of an ideal political order, one in which humanity would naturally flourish. Strauss understood "natural" to imply universality, and distinguished natural right from merely conventional systems of rights that could hold only within a given culture or polity. The concept of "natural right," then, rested upon an implicit division between the natural and the merely cultural and historically contingent. For one classic account of nature in political thought, see Collingwood (1949).

[2] For a review of Epicureanism's reception as an apolitical philosophy, see Nichols (1976). Nichols offers a sustained reading of Lucretius's *De Rerum Natura* in order to argue that, despite Epicureanism's apparent counsel of retreat, it is still politically minded: its argument

political thought. While Strauss's attitude toward Epicureanism may seem dismissive, however, careful examination reveals that Strauss harbored a deep interest in that form of philosophy throughout his career. Furthermore, and as this essay seeks to demonstrate, investigating Strauss's meditations on Epicureanism can explain much about his views on religion, atheism, and modern political theory.[3]

Strauss called Epicureanism "the classical form of the critique of religion," and his interest in it was natural, given his preoccupation with what he called, after Carl Schmitt, the "theologico-political" predicament of the modern subject.[4] From his student days on, Strauss harbored a deep interest in the political and philosophical implications of religion, and despite his own atheism he frequently expressed admiration for those versions of monotheism that conceive of religion as a source of law guiding human life. Paradoxically, while Strauss was critical of Epicureanism understood as the atheistic critique of religion, there is reason to think that he also harbored a deep sympathy for the skepticism at the core of the Epicurean project. If there were real tensions and incompatibilities between a religious and a philosophical life—as Strauss thought there were—then all philosophers would have to take the Epicurean position seriously and could perhaps feel implicated in it themselves. Epicureanism, for Strauss, thus represented the "radicalization" of a potential all philosophies contain within them.

The Epicurean critique of religion thus became, in Strauss's hands, one instance of what he saw as the eternal conflict between philosophy and society, a conflict driven by philosophy's inherent skepticism. To Strauss, this skeptical attitude included a tendency to suspend judgment and maintain doubt about any theoretical or practical issue—including social and cultural institutions, and even when skepticism might shake them

---

for human happiness is intended to help those living within the human realm rather than sequestered from it.

[3] Among Strauss's readers and critics, the political theorist Shadia Drury holds that Strauss understands Epicureanism as a variant of conventionalism. This essay implicitly argues that Drury's account is too constrained, missing some of the other meanings Strauss sees in Epicureanism. See Drury (1987).

[4] One irony in Strauss's characterization of Epicureanism as a critique of religion is that Epicurus himself was at one point venerated as the central figure of a cult, and his disciple Lucretius considered him a god. For an account of Epicureanism that attends to the cultic aspects of its tradition, see Clay (1999), a collection of papers that spans the previous thirty years.

to their very foundations. In his volumes on the history of political philosophy, Strauss returned again and again to the theme of the essential difference between philosophers and their non-philosophical neighbors. Ever since the trial and death of Socrates, philosophers had understood that their skeptical critiques of religious, social, and political mores could incur the hostility of their fellow citizens. Indeed, because Strauss understood religion as a political phenomenon—viewing it, as he did, according to the model of traditional Jewish law—he suggested that philosophy and religion would always come into conflict. Strauss's conviction that philosophy and society were naturally at odds would find its most famous articulation in the essay "Persecution and the Art of Writing," in which Strauss claimed that throughout Western history the philosophical elite had always had to mask their teachings whenever those teachings seemed to threaten the established political order. This led philosophers to produce polysemic texts with "exoteric" levels, available to a general reader, and "esoteric" levels that only a philosophically trained reader could assess.

Strauss began to write on Epicureanism in the 1920s, and it was among the central concepts treated in his first book, *Spinoza's Critique of Religion* (1930), which staged a conflict between Spinoza and the medieval Jewish philosopher Maimonides in order to judge whether the Enlightenment critique of religion had been successful.[5] Further developed in the 1935 *Philosophy and Law* and the 1936 *The Political Science of Thomas Hobbes*, as well as in the unpublished *Hobbes's Critique of Religion*, Strauss's treatment of Epicureanism reached its fullest form in the 1949 *Natural Right and History*, in which he interpreted the Enlightenment philosophy of Hobbes and Rousseau as an adaptation of key Epicurean concepts.[6] A review of these studies of Hobbes suggests, in fact, that we will never fully understand Strauss on Hobbes without attending to his view that Hobbes was himself an Epicurean of a sort. However, Strauss's use of the term "Epicurean" to describe Hobbes in *Natural Right and History* is strikingly different than his earlier uses of the term. Whereas the early Strauss focused on Epicureanism as the classic form of the critique of religion, in his later incarnation he interpreted Epicureanism as a version of materialism that Hobbes transformed to create what Strauss called

---

[5] Strauss (1965). Hereafter I will cite this work as SCR.
[6] Strauss (1950). Hereafter I will cite this work as NRH.

"political hedonism": a mindset that made human comfort and pleasure (as opposed to virtue) the central goal of political progress. Political hedonism was, in fact, a code-term for bourgeois liberalism, which Strauss always saw as denigrating the pursuit of excellence in favor of material comfort. Strauss's persistent but protean interest in Epicureanism and his critiques thereof are thus the subjects of this essay.

It seems curious that Epicureanism has remained one of the few terms in Strauss's thought that his assiduous readers—both loyal and critical— have not yet subjected to their full scrutiny.[7] After all, Epicureanism directly relates to two themes that remained central for Strauss throughout his career: first, the conflict between skeptical philosophy and revealed religion; and second, the political meaning of the term "nature." The conflict between philosophy and religion had an ultimately political significance for Strauss, representing a struggle to determine whether the authority regulating human life derives from the human subject itself or from an external and possibly divine force. The question of nature was essentially about the teleological or non-teleological connotations of the term "nature": did that word mean a measure toward which "Man" aspires, or did it refer to mere matter in motion, without ultimate purpose? It was on Epicurean impulses, if not on Epicurus himself, that Strauss sometimes blamed the major missteps of modern thought: a misunderstanding of the role of religion in political life, an unhealthy optimism regarding reason's power to reshape the political world, and

---

[7] The genealogy of Leo Strauss's political philosophy has been traced many times by scholars both friendly and hostile to his thought and with increasing frequency since the mid-1990s, when his *Gesammelte Schriften* appeared under the editorial supervision of Heinrich Meier. Given Strauss's own conservatism and the political influence of a handful of his students and his students' students, it is unsurprising that his reception has been a politicized one. If it is understandable that we tend to see Strauss's attacks on modern liberalism as stemming from his conservatism, it is unfortunate when our readings skip over the details of those attacks. Strauss's engagement with Epicurean thought is precisely such a detail, readily lost when we attend only to the larger contours of his arguments. Returning to Strauss's reading of Epicureanism follows naturally from the recent return to the historical roots of Strauss's thought, seen in the recent intellectual biographies by Eugene Sheppard and Daniel Tanguay, and in a philosophical-theological study by Leora Batnitzky. He first used the term "Epicurean," after all, in the politically and intellectually fraught climate of Weimar Germany. Caught by his own admission in a "theologico-political predicament," Strauss began his career-long effort to think his way out of such predicaments in *Spinoza's Critique of Religion*. There he would read Spinoza as the first in a long line of modern Epicureans, stating "Epicurus is truly the classic of the critique of religion." See Batnitzky (2005); Sheppard (2006); Tanguay (2007).

liberal democracy's tendency to water down the political virtues that it was intended to promote and defend.

The intellectual historians who have chronicled Strauss's career tend to divide his work into phases, each linked to a major "turn" in his meditations on philosophy and society. Each turn is then associated with Strauss's discovery of a particular key text or method of reading: his reading of the medieval Islamic philosopher Alfarabi in the late 1930s, for example; his exchange with Alexandre Kojève in the 1940s; or his late essays on Plato.[8] Though this approach has its merits, there was no "Epicurean" or "anti-Epicurean turn." Rather, I suggest that Strauss developed his critique of Epicureanism gradually throughout his career. If we require a schematic model to understand Strauss's interest in Epicureanism, we might see it as an arc beginning with Strauss's early work on Spinoza, Hobbes, and the problem of heresy and concluding with his later work on Hobbes, Lucretius's *De Rerum Natura*, and the idea of nature. Strauss's use of the term "Epicurean" would always carry the moral charge suggested by "heresy," but he gradually came to apply it just as readily to those modern thinkers who not only imagined studying the natural world but also dreamt of mastering it so as to improve "Man's" estate on earth. Strauss began by presenting Epicureanism as an affront against the idea of God, and ended by presenting it as an affront against the idea of nature. The problem of Epicureanism thus underwent a kind of "secularization" in the course of Strauss's career, while maintaining its associations with heresy, even when nature became its point of reference. Importantly, Strauss usually avoided writing directly on Epicurus or his disciples, and instead tended to treat Epicureanism in more abstract terms. Indeed, Epicureanism took on an abstract and symbolic function for Strauss early in his career, and it seems justifiable to say that it served him as a "screen" onto which he could project different heretical ideas.

---

[8] Strauss's work with Kojève and his interest in Plato are well known. Tanguay (2007) provides the most complete treatment of Strauss's interest in Alfarabi. Alfarabi's reading of Plato's *Laws* was especially important for Strauss, offering a politicized understanding of the relationship between philosophy and religion that helped Strauss develop ideas he had been entertaining ever since his work on Spinoza and Maimonides during the 1920s and early 1930s. Michael Zank, in an introductory essay for Zank (2002) offers an intriguing critique of the idea of the motif of the "turn" deployed by intellectual historians in order to understand their subjects of inquiry.

EPICUREANISM AND THE CRITIQUE OF RELIGION

In 1925, not long after finishing his doctorate, the young Leo Strauss was offered a research fellowship at the Berlin *Akademie für die Wissenschaft des Judentums.* The *Akademie,* founded in 1917 by the Jewish philosophers Franz Rosenzweig and Hermann Cohen, was intended not only to foster research in Jewish studies but also to apply the skills of its researchers to projects in Jewish adult education, one of Rosenzweig's special interests.[9] At the time Strauss entered the *Akademie,* it was directed by the rabbi, theologian, and philosopher Julius Guttmann, who had been strongly influenced both by Cohen's neo-Kantian philosophy and by Cohen's vision of Judaism's compatibility with the Western philosophical tradition. It was under Guttmann's direction that Strauss completed his first brief treatment of Epicureanism, contained within *Spinoza's Critique of Religion,* which he wrote between 1924 and 1928 and published in 1930. Guttmann had charged Strauss with the task of writing on Spinoza's Bible science, a topic of great interest to many scholars in Jewish studies who, like Guttmann himself, were interested in the genealogy of their own basically historicist treatment of Jewish texts.[10] The central methodological assumption of their historicism was that one could understand a religious text by simply reconstructing its original chronological horizon—it need have no "timeless" significance. Strauss, who, unlike Guttmann, was skeptical about the merits of Spinoza's Bible science, turned instead toward the larger and more controversial question of whether the Enlightenment critique of religion begun by Spinoza had successfully made its arguments against the authority of

---

[9] For a detailed account of the *Akademie's* history, see Myers (1992).

[10] In 1924, Strauss had published an essay contesting the reading of Spinoza's Bible science put forward by Hermann Cohen, Guttmann's own teacher. In the essay, "Cohen's Analysis of Spinoza's Bible Science," Strauss attacked Cohen's treatment of Spinoza without actually defending Spinoza. It seems, rather, that Strauss was eager to have a stronger foundation from which to defeat the Spinozist project of biblical criticism than that which Cohen provides. Strauss's criticisms of Cohen's treatment of Spinoza are too complex for easy summary here, but it suffices to say that while Strauss agreed with Cohen that Spinoza's philosophy ignored the political interests of the Jewish people, he disagreed with Cohen on the question of whether or not rationalist philosophy and the interests of the Jewish people could ever be harmonized. Despite Strauss's disagreements with Guttmann's own mentor, the essay impressed Guttmann sufficiently that he invited Strauss to join the *Akademie* as a researcher. See also Wurgaft (2009).

religious revelation. *Spinoza's Critique of Religion* stages a confrontation between two of the most important figures in Jewish intellectual history, Spinoza and the medieval philosopher Moses Maimonides. This in turn staged a conflict between two different historical epochs—the premodern and the modern—as well as between two very different attitudes toward the compatibility of Judaism and philosophy.[11]

At every point in the work, Strauss refrains from taking one side or the other, but expresses his doubts regarding whether the Enlightenment's critiques of religion had truly found their mark. More specifically, he doubts whether Spinoza's critique of miracles had defeated Maimonides' philosophically grounded defense of the belief in miracles. In 1930, the work was published, bearing Strauss's dedication to the recently departed Franz Rosenzweig, whose work had marked for Strauss, as for so many others, a return to Judaism within philosophy.[12] The irony of this dedication is that while, for Strauss, Rosenzweig's work represented the possibility of a harmonious relationship between philosophy and Judaism, Strauss hoped to reopen the question of whether such harmony was possible.

As Strauss later reflected in a preface written for the 1962 English edition of *Spinoza's Critique of Religion*, in this work he identifies the heretical Spinoza—who was expelled from Amsterdam's Jewish community for his views—as a modern Epicurean and identifies Epicureanism as the "classic form" of the critique of religion:

---

[11] The comparison Strauss struck between the medieval and the modern naturally stood in a particular relation to the later juxtaposition he struck between ancient and modern thought. Medieval thinkers such as Maimonides, for Strauss, were the inheritors of classical thought rather than philosophical innovators in their own right. Moreover, they inherited and developed ancient thought at a very specific historical juncture where circumstances of political persecution constrained the direct verbal and written expressions available for philosophers. Thus, while Maimonides was not himself an "ancient" thinker, he became, for Strauss, a mouthpiece for a modified classical attitude. It is important to note here that Strauss was also part of a running debate among interpreters of Maimonides regarding whether the "great eagle" (as he was sometimes called) was an Aristotelian or a Platonist. In 1908, Hermann Cohen had published an important study, the "Ethics of Maimonides," in which he argued for the Platonist view (recently translated into English as Cohen (2004)). Strauss, despite his criticisms of Cohen on other issues, would be deeply indebted to Cohen's view.

[12] See Gibbs (1992); Batnitzky (2000); Gordon (2004).

For the understanding of [the antagonism between Spinoza and Judaism] the Jewish designation of the unbeliever as Epicurean seemed to be helpful, especially since from every point of view Epicureanism may be said to be the classic form of the critique of religion and the basic stratum of the tradition of the critique of religion. Epicureanism is hedonism, and traditional Judaism always suspects that all theoretical and practical revolts against the Torah are inspired by the desire to throw off the yoke of the stern and exacting duties so that one can indulge in a life of pleasure. Epicureanism can lead only to a mercenary morality whereas traditional Jewish morality is not mercenary.[13]

"Mercenary" or self-serving morality would be no morality at all according to Strauss's interpretation of Judaism as holding standards for moral action beyond the mere satisfaction of human appetites. Strauss's later appreciation of the centrality of Epicureanism in a text he had authored decades earlier does not merely reflect the clarity of hindsight. The link between Epicureanism, the "classic" form of the critique of religion, and the modern Spinozist variant is established explicitly in the original 1930 text: "Epicurus's criticism of religion is one source, and the most important one, of seventeenth-century criticism of religion."[14] Strauss goes on to describe the Epicurean doctrine as he understands it. The aim of philosophy is to cultivate a condition of *eudaimonia* (happiness or well-being), which provides all the justification necessary for the scientific enterprise. Insofar as *eudaimonia* can follow only from the elimination of the fear of the gods, the critique of religion is central to the Epicurean project.[15] All superhuman standards are stripped away; "the only standard is pleasure."[16] The elimination of pain is a necessary part of the project because pain limits pleasure and, thus, "the security of pleasure is for Epicurus only the more general form of the achievement of pure pleasure."[17] Science has a crucial role to play in securing pleasure because

---

[13] SCR 19.

[14] Ibid., 38.

[15] Interestingly, Strauss did not place much emphasis on the distinction between the Greek terms *eudaimonia*, or "happiness," and *ataraxia*, "freedom from disturbance." As we will see later in this essay, when Strauss turned to the subject of Lucretius he used the term *ataraxia* in such a way that he could as easily have used *eudaimonia*, suggesting that he may have seen this as a distinction without a difference, at least where the Epicureans were concerned.

[16] SCR 38.

[17] Ibid., 39.

the discoveries of science will "bring us tranquility of mind and not still greater anxiety."[18]

Notably, Strauss offers a critique of the arbitrary relationship between Epicurus's eudaimonic ends and his proposed means: skeptical scientific inquiry, writing that, "the connection between Epicurus's motive and the science corresponding with that motive is . . . important for understanding the criticism of religion in the seventeenth century."[19] In other words, Strauss wishes to understand whether any necessary opposition exists between the scientific and the religious impulses and to determine if any opposition between the two inheres in a purified or "archetypal" form of the Epicurean impulse.[20] If there is no such necessary opposition, he believes, we might need to look to historically emergent factors in search of explanations. Strauss's critique of Epicurus's account of the relation between scientific means and eudaimonic ends is, quite simply, that no necessary relationship exists between the two. For evidence, he cites the report of Diogenes Laërtius, according to whom Epicurus himself thought that the belief in gods might not be inherently bad, provided that one believes in benign rather than malicious deities.[21] However, Epicurus seemed unable to integrate his own opinion—namely, that religion is not fundamentally opposed to human happiness—with his philosophical practice. This failed integration, for Strauss, provides grounds for viewing Epicurus as the expression of a "universal" human motive to oppose religion. It thus becomes possible to divide Epicurus's critical analysis of religion from the motive underlying that criticism.

From this assessment of Epicurus's writings, Strauss catapults his reader into the future. In the age of "revealed religion"—that is, the age in which Judaism and then Christianity flourished in the Near East— Epicureanism remained a force, even though the increasing social power wielded by religious institutions tended to drive religion's critics

---

[18] Ibid., 40.

[19] Ibid., 41.

[20] It is important to add that skepticism would go on to be an abiding concern for Strauss throughout his career. Several of his readers, most notably Stephen P. Smith, have described Strauss's own philosophy as fundamentally skeptical. See S. P. Smith (2006).

[21] Diogenes Laërtius 10.134: "It were better, indeed, to accept the legends of the gods than to bow beneath that yoke of destiny which the natural philosophers have imposed. The one holds out some faint hope that we may escape if we honour the gods, while the necessity of the naturalists is deaf to all entreaties" (trans. Hicks).

underground. Strauss argues that in a world governed by the Law, the
followers of *eudaimonia* would have to maintain their solidarity in secret
against the believing multitude: "Special precautions are needed for the
guidance of the ignorant many, for the sake of social law and order."[22]
One important shift from the classical period to the period of revealed
religion concerns the ultimate purpose of the critique of religion: whereas
for Epicurus, the critique "by the means of theory" has the ultimate goal
of human happiness, for the philosophers working under the prosecuto-
rial eye of monotheism, the critique of religion is meant to defend philosophy itself. The import of that defense is simple: only philosophy can
secure the state of *eudaimonia* itself, and even if that state is only available
to a few, its possibility still has to be preserved.[23]

Strauss then moves quickly from the age of revealed religion to
Spinoza's native seventeenth century, tracing Spinoza's critique of religion
back to three main sources. In addition to "Epicureanism," the Averroist
and Machiavellian critiques were also available to Spinoza. Strauss's
reason for viewing Epicureanism as the most important is based on a
transparently anti-historicist premise: "We have preferred the name of
Epicurus for the reason that of the three motives which brought forth
that criticism—ataraxia, theory, virtue—the first is the least mediate,
in the sense of not having been called forth under the pressure from a
particular historical situation."[24] Strauss wanted to understand the
Epicurean motive as a universal human impulse. For him, its move away
from the religious fear of gods and toward the study of the natural world
seemed part of human nature.

---

[22] SCR 47. Given the resemblance between this line and many of Strauss's later
statements regarding the differences between the intellectual elite and the masses, it is
important to point out that at this juncture in his career, he had not yet fully formulated
those later views. However, his understanding of the social function of religion, which he
certainly had developed by the late 1920s, did stand in an indirect relation with those
views.

[23] It is important to note that Strauss, at this early point in his career, had not yet
reached his mature understanding of the divide between philosophers and other men.
However, it seems clear that the miniature history of Epicureanism's development presented
in *Spinoza's Critique of Religion* contained some of the seeds that later produced Strauss's
ultimate view of the divide existing between theoreticians and the rest of society.

[24] SCR 49. It is perhaps telling that Strauss did not justify his choice to explore
Epicureanism over Averroism and Machiavellianism on the grounds that *Spinoza* himself
understood himself as an Epicurean. That is, his very grounds for the choice signified his
opposition to treating Spinoza as Spinoza treated the Bible—namely, historically.

Strauss is also concerned in this brief history of Epicureanism
with underscoring the major change between the doctrine of Epicurus
himself and the "Epicureanism" of Spinoza. Whereas classical "hedonistic" Epicureanism understood its goal of human happiness in terms of
serenity of mind—a goal located within the individual human subject—
the "hedonistic" Epicureanism of the Enlightenment cast its gaze beyond
the subject. The modern Epicurean tried to transform not only the individual but the entire social world as well in order to secure tranquility
of mind for man: to accomplish that goal, the Epicurean endowed himself with activist initiatives and powers. Far from a "therapeutic" philosophy that heals the human from within, it healed through preventative
measures, hoping to change the world until all threats from without
(for example, all opportunities for a violent death) were eradicated.
However, as I note later in this essay, Strauss associates Spinoza only with
the beginnings of such an activist stance. It is Hobbes whom he associates
with the full flowering of a modern philosophy that aspires not only
to understand but also to shape both the natural and the social world.

Strauss then traces the universal impulse toward pleasure and
away from pain that impelled Epicurus himself through several different
incarnations. He deals first with Uriel da Costa (about 1585–1640), the
Portuguese philosopher and Marrano whose critique of certain aspects
of religion illustrates the malleable character of the Epicurean doctrine:
in Strauss's view, da Costa shows that Epicureanism can take on "a charge
of moral content which is not to be accounted for by [the critique of
religion in pursuit of human happiness] itself."[25] Strauss makes similar
remarks in the sections on Isaac de la Peyrère (1596–1676), another
Marrano and a heretic against the Catholicism to which Peyrère himself
converted, and Thomas Hobbes. Although in the late 1920s, Strauss
had not yet begun the Hobbes research that would supply one of the
pillars of his later critique of modernity, he had already begun to view
Hobbes as the agent who transformed the Epicurean critique of religion
during the modern period. It was in Hobbes, in fact, that Strauss saw
a return to "the archetypal originality, the integral breadth and depth,
which characterized that critique in the case of Epicurus and Lucretius."[26]
However, Hobbes broke away from his classical forbearers by equating

[25] SCR 62.
[26] Ibid., 86.

science with the critique of religion, and in the process, Strauss argued, he missed one subtle dimension of Epicurus's critique. Whereas Epicurus saw science and religion as different means toward the same end—human happiness—and criticized religion as an *inadequate* means toward that end, Hobbes established a strict dichotomy between science and religion. For him, the former sought to end man's misery by securing mastery over nature; the latter acted as a mere psychological salve that did nothing to improve the human condition.

In contrast to Hobbes, Spinoza's view of philosophy or "science" was more in keeping with the Epicurean idea that a harmonious mind is achieved through internal transformation. If part of the project of maximizing pleasure and minimizing pain is to reduce the mind's anxieties, especially those that arise from the fear of death, part of Epicurean practice is for the philosopher to ease his own mind, and perhaps to help others to ease their minds. While the comparison around which most of Strauss's work turned was the aforementioned juxtaposition of Spinoza (the critic of religion) and Maimonides (religion's champion), and while that juxtaposition was crucial for Strauss's central inquiry into the success of the Enlightenment's critique of religion, when it came to the question of the ultimate *social implications* of the critique of religion, the most important comparison may have been between Spinoza and Hobbes. Whereas for Hobbes happiness could be secured via technological progress, Spinoza hoped for a perfection of "Man" that would begin within the subject itself.[27] In this regard, Strauss seems justified in saying that Spinoza cleaved more closely to Epicurus's own philosophical project.[28] The meaning of the less developed but clearly important comparison between Spinoza and Hobbes becomes more apparent when we consider that the figure of Hobbes would loom large in Strauss's work for decades to come. A Hobbesian, rather than a Spinozist, version of the Epicurean

---

[27] Ibid., 210.

[28] Although interestingly, Strauss noted that Spinoza's conception of *beatitudo* as "a stable condition complete in itself" (SCR 210) is equally close to the Stoic or Epicurean understanding of such a state. For Strauss both Epicurus and the Stoa agree with Spinoza's essentially pragmatist idea that the ultimate object of philosophical knowledge is, grandly put, the "eternal enjoyment of enduring and supreme joy," or less grandly, an unperturbed mind. One may criticize Strauss to the extent that his discussion ignored the considerable differences between a modest (the pursuit of peace of mind) or ambitious (the pursuit of eternal happiness) Epicurean project. This is particularly interesting because the distinction he drew between Spinoza and Hobbes is based on a very similar difference in intention.

motive would become central for Strauss, despite his greater *philosophical* respect for the Spinozist variant.[29]

Part of Strauss's stake in invoking Epicureanism, however, had less to do with philosophy and more to do with the reputation that "Epicureanism" enjoyed in the other tradition to which he was heir, namely modern Jewish thought. The terms "Epicureanism" and "heresy" have a longstanding connection in Jewish thought, of which Strauss was well aware when he spoke of "the Jewish designation of the unbeliever as Epicurean."[30] While Strauss's depiction of the Jewish view of Epicureanism may seem strained—after all, it rests on a problematic depiction of Jewish culture as legalistic and an equally problematic depiction of Epicureanism as a one-dimensional form of hedonism— there were internal Jewish precedents for Strauss's characterizations. In the late eighteenth century, the Jewish philosopher Solomon Maimon remarked to Moses Mendelssohn "We are all Epicureans" (*Wir sind alle Epikuraer*), playing on the Hebrew term *apiqores*, or heretic. As Abraham Socher points out in his important intellectual biography of Maimon, both interlocutors would certainly have understood this pun.[31] The two men were just then embroiled in a dispute over the compatibility of philosophy with Jewish religious belief, itself a recurring conflict in Jewish thought. By invoking heresy and implying a relation of equivalence between the *apiqores* and the Epicurean, Maimon attacked the religious Mendelssohn and pushed the point that doing philosophy made both of them—in fact, made all philosophical Jews—heretical before the Jewish Law. Maimon may have even been aware of the tradition initiated by his namesake, Moses Maimonides, of giving a precise legal definition of *apikorsut*, or heresy.[32] According to Maimonides, the fundamental types of heresy include the denial of the legitimacy of prophecy, the denial of the revelation made to Moses at Sinai, and the denial of God's knowledge of human deeds.[33] Benjamin Lazier has pointed out that

[29] Strauss would have found grounds to disagree, then, with Jonathan Israel's description of the European Enlightenment as fundamentally Spinozist. See Israel (2001).

[30] SCR 19.

[31] See Socher (2006) 6.

[32] If Maimon had indeed been making such a reference, it would have to have been with a sense of irony: Maimonides himself was well known for holding the view that philosophy and Judaism were entirely compatible with one another.

[33] See "Apikorus," *Encyclopedia Judaica* (1972) 177.

Maimonides might not have applied the term *apiqores* to apostates such as converts to Christianity, and by that reasoning, his use of "Epicurean" would have been intended to suggest a different type of unbeliever, someone who has left Judaism but not yet entered the fold of its monotheistic relative.[34] Thus, in associating Spinoza with Epicureanism, Strauss was effectively making the same rhetorical gesture Maimon had made—far more than a pun, in both cases. Strauss was suggesting that philosophizing opened up an alternative between the abandonment of the Jewish religion and the acceptance of other gods. The eighteenth-century Maimon thus stood as a worthy inheritor of Spinoza's lasting contribution to modern Jewish identity, namely, the idea that one could leave the Jewish fold without going to the Cross. It is important to note that neither in 1930 nor later in 1965 did Strauss *explicitly* endorse the Jewish demonization of Epicureanism as heresy. Such an endorsement would have meant breaking with his stated intention of simply investigating the validity of Spinoza's critique of religion.

However, Strauss's scholarly prevarications and stated goal of objectivity aside, an understanding of the broader context of his political and religious concerns in the late 1920s can help us understand why the tension between Epicureanism and Judaism was a pressing concern for him and why the category of the Jewish heretic was, to say the least, intellectually galvanizing. From the age of seventeen, when Strauss "converted" (as he put it) to Zionism, he was involved with a number of Zionist youth groups. During the 1920s, he wrote brief articles for several Zionist journals, including the mouthpiece of the influential organization *Blau-Weiss,* which sponsored a wide range of activities for young Jewish people, from the intellectual to the social to the athletic.[35] It was during this period—approximately the same period in which he began his research on Spinoza's Bible science—that Strauss became intensely aware of the conflicts between certain Zionists and certain members of the Orthodox and neo-Orthodox Jewish communities, whose variety of religious practice had attracted his intellectual curiosity.

In a 1925 essay entitled "Ecclesia Militans," Strauss focuses on the tensions between Zionists and a community of neo-Orthodox Jews

---

[34] See Lazier (2008).

[35] These essays have been translated and published in a single volume: see Zank (2002).

based in Frankfurt and investigated the views of that community's intellectual leader Isaac Breuer. As David Myers has shown, Breuer and Strauss shared a number of concerns, including a resistance to historicism as applied to Judaism and Jewish thought.[36] However, the most influential aspect of Breuer's work for Strauss was, undoubtedly, his insistence on the primacy of biblical law.[37] While the observant Breuer and the atheist Strauss would have been divided on the issue of actual belief, for both of them the simple existence of Orthodoxy meant that Jews had to confront the question that Breuer had phrased so elegantly: whether "God and the Torah are primary over the Jewish nation or if the historical relation is primary."[38] By his phrase "the historical relation," Breuer meant to invoke the Jewish people's "entrance into history" through modernization and assimilation into European society—he conjured up an opposition familiar to traditional Jewish thought, between the timeless and basically ahistorical condition of the Jewish people in exile and the "historical" experiences of the Gentile nations.[39] Reading Breuer at the same time as he labored over Spinoza and the major works of Maimonides, Strauss developed what could with some justice be called a philo-orthodox attitude.[40] Given his attraction to the idea of Judaism as a religion of revealed law, his use of the devices of Epicureanism and heresy to describe Spinoza can be understood as radicalizing the ongoing conversation concerning the relationship between philosophy

---

[36] See Myers (2003).

[37] Breuer and Strauss also shared an appreciation, more restrained in Strauss's case, for the writings of Franz Rosenzweig. A letter from Breuer to Rosenzweig (March 11, 1924) and Rosenzweig's response (March 28, 1924) testify to the impression that Rosenzweig's *Star of Redemption* made on Breuer, and to the effect which Breuer's tract, *Messiaspuren* (traces of the Messiah) had on Rosenzweig. These letters are stored at the Leo Baeck Institute Archive, Item # MF 579.

[38] Breuer (1925) 353.

[39] The problem of history in Jewish thought is explored in depth in Yerushalmi (1989).

[40] The attractions of Breuer's neo-Orthodox movement for Strauss went deeper than can be explored within this essay. Briefly, Breuer's philosophy of Jewish law served as a counterpoint to the neo-Kantian emphasis on the individual human subject "giving the law to himself." Strauss had encountered that latter view not only in the works of the prominent neo-Kantian Hermann Cohen but also in certain of his followers, like Julius Guttmann. Kantian thought had always offended Strauss with its tendency to dismiss the idea of religion as a source of law beyond the subject—to say nothing of Kant's derisive dismissal of Judaism as a "defunct constitution for an extinct polity." Where Kant derided Judaism as legalistic, Breuer celebrated it precisely for maintaining an external source of law against the modern temptation to characterize law as self-given, by the individual subject.

and religion. Viewed in the context of the Weimar intellectual scene in which Strauss crafted these arguments, the invocation of heresy can be seen as signaling that moderate positions such as those of Hermann Cohen and Julius Guttmann, who, like Maimon's interlocutor Mendelssohn, argued that a harmonious relationship between religion and reason was possible, would have to be abandoned.

A very different internal Jewish debate may have also influenced Strauss's deployment of the language of Epicureanism and heresy at this juncture: while Strauss had begun his study of Spinoza in order to fulfill Julius Guttmann's wish for a study of Spinoza's Bible science, the project became an effort to resist the impact of historicism on the study of Jewish thought. The apparently innocuous question upon which the study was based—namely, whether Spinoza's Enlightenment critique of religion had succeeded—was thus far from innocuous. It was Spinoza's "scientific" treatment of the Bible that had helped inspire the modern project of treating Judaism as a cultural artifact rather than the result of revelation. In German Jewish thought, such a project found influential exponents in the early nineteenth-century *Wissenschaft des Judentums* ("Science of Judaism") school.[41] The intention of many *Wissenschaft* thinkers was to provide Judaism with a degree of dignity as an object of scholarly investigation, but this effort was linked to the more general attempt to apply the tools of Western scholarship to the central texts and traditions of Jewish life: studying them meant depriving them of their power to guide everyday affairs. The choice seemed to be between historical consciousness and living tradition; the cost of modernizing—of entering the modern world as a historical people with equal standing to other peoples—was to give the Jewish tradition "a decent burial."

In Strauss's view, Guttmann was unfortunately complicit with the tendency of modern Jewish thought toward historicism. As he said in a critical review of Guttmann's work, written after he had left the *Akademie*'s employ, "scientific knowledge of Judaism is purchased at the price of belief in the authority of revelation."[42] Treating Judaism as a cultural rather than a legal affair seemed part of the general trend toward

---

[41] There is a very extensive literature covering the *Wissenschaft* movement in Jewish studies, and its early nineteenth-century proponents, in particular. See Glatzer (1964) 27–45; Schorsch (1994).

[42] Strauss (1987).

historicism that Strauss hoped to work against and, more importantly, in following the *wissenschaftlich* (scientific) approach to Jewish thought, Guttmann was following in step with the general trend in German political life during the 1920s: pursuing a liberal hope despite the evidence that liberalism was incapable of resolving the crisis of the present. What Strauss hoped to do, then, was to revive the rhetoric of heresy, whether by the name of Epicureanism or *apiqorsut*, in order to adequately address the climate of crisis in German Jewish life during the 1920s. Not mere concern for the truth but, rather, an attunement toward the political stakes in scholarship guided Strauss toward his designation of heresy as "Epicurean."

Another intriguing document, seldom discussed by Strauss's biographers, is a letter that he sent in 1930 to his friend Gerhard Krüger.[43] Strauss's letter to Krüger reveals that he felt at a loss about how to engage with the phenomenon of "Epicureanism," which is puzzling, given the apparent confidence with which Strauss had labeled Spinoza an Epicurean in a work published that same year. At the very least, the letter suggests that Strauss's understanding of the term was still in flux at the time. Tellingly, Strauss describes what motivated his interest in heresy and atheism, saying, "The next answer is given to me directly from the Jewish tradition, which identifies the heretic absolutely as an Epicurean." He also speaks of his need to "justify himself" before "the forum of Jewish tradition." That latter phrase attests to Strauss's consciousness of the same pun (which was more than a pun) that Solomon Maimon had once used. Strauss does not say whether he himself *shared* the traditional Jewish view of heresy, only that he feels somehow bound to it. To set the letter's message in almost formulaic terms, then, Strauss simultaneously characterizes Epicureanism as a classical impulse that has become part of the non-scientific and "willful" side of modernity and reveals that his own sense of responsibility to *respond* to Epicureanism stems from his Jewish background. While there is little discussion of the Jewish view of

---

[43] Like Strauss, Krüger was a philosopher who had studied with Martin Heidegger and had worked under Paul Natorp and Nicolai Hartmann at the University of Marburg as well. He would make some of his greatest intellectual contributions in the fields of Kantian and Platonic philosophy, and he resembled Strauss in that his interests were divided between ancient and modern sources. He was a thus a natural person for Strauss to seek out at a time when his research led him from the Enlightenment critique of religion to the question of that critique's larger importance for political theory.

Epicureanism in Strauss's later writings, in which Strauss became more interested in the modern adaptation of Epicurean themes and less preoccupied by the critique of religion, his later efforts display the same moral tone that derives from the characterization of Epicureanism as heresy.

HOBBES, EPICUREANISM, AND THE EMERGENCE OF "POLITICAL HEDONISM"

In 1932 Strauss left Germany in order to pursue research on Thomas Hobbes, first in France and then in England, aided by a grant from the Rockefeller Foundation.[44] Out of this research he produced *The Political Philosophy of Hobbes: Its Basis and Its Genesis*, part of his ongoing efforts to locate the origins of modern political thought in the fraught space between "ancient" and "modern" thinking.[45] Strauss at this point considered Hobbes to be the founder of modern political philosophy, and while he would later correct this view and give that laurel to Machiavelli instead, he would continue to see Hobbes's *De Cive* and *Leviathan* as

---

[44] Strauss's departure from Germany in 1932 should not be seen to reflect any presentiments of the National Socialists' coming rise to power. Strauss's degree of foresight into the political situation in Germany, despite his pessimism regarding the fragility of the liberal Weimar government, seems to have been limited. Much has been made of Strauss's correspondence with the National Socialist jurist and political theorist Carl Schmitt, but as Heinrich Meier has demonstrated in his work on that correspondence, Strauss seems neither to have understood the extremity of Schmitt's political views nor to have known about Schmitt's membership in the Nazi party at the time of their last correspondence in 1933. See Meier (1995).

[45] Strauss's interest in Hobbes, naturally enough, had developed out of his earlier work on Spinoza. Daniel Tanguay cites a telling note found in the Strauss archives in which Strauss himself described his research agenda of the early 1930s as an extension of interests he began in his 1920s work on Spinoza and Maimonides. That is, both *Philosophy and Law* and *The Political Philosophy of Hobbes* attempted to answer similar questions. Strauss wrote, "The two paths of research I have just sketched, although quite far apart in the material they treat, are connected by the intention, which has long guided my work, to contribute to the understanding of the history of political theories, in particular of the history of natural right. Both aim to clarify the genesis of the modern understanding of the State in the light of religious and political tradition, especially that of the Middle Ages" (trans. Tanguay). Tanguay cites this as "Unidentified document [1932?], p.4, in *Leo Strauss Papers*, box 3, folder 8." See Tanguay (2007) 226 n.2. The *Leo Strauss Papers* are stored at the Special Collections Department, Regenstein Library, University of Chicago.

crucial texts in the establishment of modern liberal thought.[46] Crucially, the study of Hobbes would also contribute to Strauss's own reorientation away from an explicit consideration of religious themes and toward the motif of nature. Despite the relatively few references to Epicureanism, *The Political Philosophy of Hobbes* continues inquiries that Strauss had begun in *Spinoza's Critique of Religion*, including his comparison of Spinozist and Hobbesian attitudes toward religion and science. Furthermore, there is reason to see the earlier, more extensive treatment of Epicureanism provided in the Spinoza volume as the key to understanding Epicureanism's place in *The Political Philosophy of Hobbes*.[47] Strauss himself noted the continuity between his first two works, writing that in the Hobbes volume he sought to "reopen" "the case of the moderns against the ancients,"[48] much as he had in *Spinoza's Critique of Religion*. Before his later discovery of Machiavelli's importance, Spinoza and Hobbes were, for Strauss, the founders of the modern order.

Intriguingly, the two explicit references to Epicureanism in *The Political Philosophy of Hobbes* present the book's central figure as rejecting all Epicurean tendencies. Criticizing Wilhelm Dilthey for portraying Hobbes as a Stoic—mistaking "residual" elements of ancient thought in Hobbes's writings for evidence of a classical basis for his thought—Strauss writes that Dilthey "did not take Hobbes's express and systematic opposition to the whole tradition—including the Stoa and Epicureanism—seriously enough."[49] Through this criticism of Dilthey, Strauss sought to free scholarship from the trap of rooting Hobbesian philosophy either in classical ideas or in the modern scientific break

---

[46] In *Natural Right and History*, Strauss would write, "It was Machiavelli, that greater Columbus, who had discovered the continent on which Hobbes could erect his structure" (177). When reading Strauss on Hobbes, it is necessary to recall that it is one thing to call Hobbes a founder of liberalism, another to call him a liberal. Strauss was well aware that, as Ryan (1996) points out, the term "liberal" did not enter widespread use in English political life until around the beginning of the nineteenth century.

[47] Strauss alerts his readers to the fact that his ongoing reading of Hobbes had actually begun in the Spinoza volume via subtle means, with a brief footnote in *The Political Philosophy of Hobbes*: "For the fundamental difference between Hobbes's political philosophy and Spinoza's, cf. Strauss, *Die Religionskritik Spinozas*, Berlin 1930, pp. 222–30" ((1936) 28).

[48] Strauss (1936) xv.

[49] See Strauss (1936) 4. Strauss is referring to Dilthey (1914–2006) 2: 452.

with them. As Strauss saw it, Hobbes's relationship with classical sources, including Epicureanism, was more complex than designations of Hobbes as "classical" or "modern" could convey: "a transitional figure, Hobbes . . . . philosophized in the fertile moment when the classical and theological tradition was already shaken, and a tradition of modern science not yet formed and established."[50] In other words, the categorical distinction between modern and premodern thought was not yet operative, with the result that Hobbes's criticisms of classical philosophies such as Stoicism have to be understood carefully. Against those who would underestimate the complexity of Hobbes's relation to both Stoicism and Epicureanism, Strauss hoped that his readers would see Hobbes as bound up in a complex relationship with the classical sources he hoped to employ in untraditional ways.

While much of the Hobbes book is taken up with relatively clear discussions of its subject's central views and his various debts to modern science, humanism, Aristotle, and Plato, Strauss does return to the comparison between Hobbes and Spinoza that he had begun to explore in his previous work. Here he attends to the way in which Hobbes's and Spinoza's respective critiques of religion related to the very modern categories of the public and the private. In his view, Hobbes, like Spinoza, treated and thus encourages us to treat "theologico-political" predicaments. Referring to *De Cive*, *Leviathan*, and *The Elements of the Law*, he writes that "Hobbes's three presentations of political philosophy may with scarcely less justice than Spinoza's expressly so entitled work be called theologico-political treatises."[51] The *Leviathan*, Strauss observes, marks a deepening of Hobbes's criticism of religion, and we may infer that said critique of religion is by extension comparable with those of Spinoza and Epicurus. However, whereas Spinoza sought to deny both Christianity and Judaism—and thus became a heretic and, in the sense conveyed by Maimon's Epicurean/*apiqores* wordplay, a new kind of atheistic person—Hobbes kept his private feelings about religion from influencing his public statements. He was willing to support the church and religion insofar as they contributed to social cohesion and the virtues that make social life harmonious.[52] As Strauss notes, Hobbes understood

[50] Strauss (1936) 5.
[51] Ibid., 71.
[52] Ibid., 75–76.

his own skepticism regarding either positive or natural religion to be dangerous and, accordingly, hid it. If Hobbes was an Epicurean in this regard, he was a distinctive kind of Epicurean, one who constructed his public views according to the dictates of political philosophy rather than natural philosophy or natural science. Hobbes's "Epicureanism" was tempered by his conclusion that "Man" is the highest creation in the universe and that, accordingly, the harmony of "Man's" social life is more important than the truth as it is understood by natural scientists. The public-spirited aspect of Hobbes's concerns was part of a larger shift in focus from the eternal order to "Man," from natural philosophy and its reflection on atoms and *pneuma* to political philosophy. This pattern of interests justifies the observation that, for Strauss, the distinction between Hobbes and Spinoza has less to do with an actual disagreement about the nature of truth and more to do with their disagreement about what account of religion is most beneficial for society.

Some of the ideas regarding Epicureanism developed in *The Political Philosophy of Hobbes* are also presented in slightly different forms in an unpublished text that occupied Strauss during the early 1930s, *Hobbes's Critique of Religion*. As in his published volume, Strauss here argues that Hobbes's connections with Epicureanism had been insufficiently appreciated in the existing scholarly literature.[53] He names Epicurus as the source of Hobbes's critique of religion and also describes Epicureanism as an expression of a fundamental human drive toward pleasure and away from suffering, much as he had in 1930. Interestingly, in this work Strauss cites in passing Hobbes's "Concerning Heresy and The Punishment Thereof," a brief text that surveys the early history of the concept of the heretical and its later development in the Christian church and begins with an epigram from Lucretius.[54] Strauss understood that for Hobbes,

---

[53] Strauss (1996) 315 (my translation): "Hobbes's explicit judgment regarding Epicurean philosophy (see *Opera* III 540, *English Works* IV 387 and VI 98) is nothing other than an explicit, more or less disparaging judgment over ancient philosophy in general (and see the detailed critique of Epicurus and Lucretius in *De Corpore* XXXVI 3). But the point that in truth a tight relationship between Hobbes and Epicureanism exists is never sufficiently understood. It is only on the judgment of J. Fr. Buddeus that Hobbes is characterized as '*Epicurae Philosophie Consectator*.'"

[54] See Hobbes (1939–45) 4: 388–89. The epigram:
nam veluti pueri trepidant atque omnia caecis
in tenebris metuunt, sic nos in luce timemus
interdum nilo quae sunt metuenda magis quam

the relationship between philosophy and heresy was of the utmost importance, much as it had been for Spinoza. In this text, Hobbes gives "opinion" as the original meaning of "heresy," and names a collection of
prominent Greek thinkers—including Epicurus—as "heretics" in the
sense that they were men who made their private opinions known to the
public at large. According to Hobbes, it was from the reception of their
ideas and the mistranslation of these ideas in the hands of lesser thinkers
that the term "heretic" derived the secondary meaning "member of a
sect." Hobbes holds that the concept of heresy entered the Christian
church due to the prominence of philosophers within the early church's
leadership. Then, due to the need to control differing opinions, "heresy"
went from meaning the private opinion of a philosopher and became a
public act of disobedience against the church. Catholic and heretic were
from then on opposed terms. Hobbes then proceeds through a chronicle
of the major heresies in church history, leading up to the charge of heresy
that, presumably, occasioned his essay: the charge against his own
Leviathan. Hobbes defends his work against the charge that it opposed
the ecclesiastical powers-that-be by saying that: "A book called *Leviathan*
was written in defense of the King's power, temporal and spiritual,
without any word against episcopacy, or against any bishop, or against
the public doctrine of the church."[55] It cannot be inferred from Strauss's
discussion that Hobbes's "Heresy" was a key work in shaping Strauss's
view of the relation between Hobbes and Epicureanism. However,
Hobbes's effort to save political philosophy from the charge of heresy
by showing that it was more like the work of philosophers like Epicurus
than a truly antireligious effort may well have served to exemplify the
dangerous associations between philosophy and heresy and to strengthen
the associations that Strauss had drawn between Hobbes, Epicurus, and
Lucretius.

---

quae pueri in tenebris pavitant finguntque futura.
—Lucretius, *De Rerum Natura* 2.55–58

For just as children tremble and fear all things
in blind darkness, so we in the light fear, at times,
things that are no more to be feared than what
children shiver at in the dark and imagine to be at hand.

[55] Hobbes (1939–45) 4: 407

By the late 1940s, Strauss was at work on his strongest statement on the implications of Epicureanism in the modern era, and one that explicitly made Epicureanism into the forerunner to modern materialism: *Natural Right and History*, which began as the Walgreen Lectures, a series presented at the University of Chicago in 1949.[56] Strauss had recently moved to that institution from the New School for Social Research in New York, where he had taught for nearly a decade, and his Walgreen Lectures marked the beginning of a new phase in his career. Between 1935 and 1949, Strauss had published a number of important essays on medieval Jewish thought, political theory, and the relationship between literary style and political life, including the classic "Persecution and the Art of Writing." He had also enjoyed a formative exchange of letters with the influential Hegel scholar Alexandre Kojève, an exchange that produced two competing readings of Xenophon's *Hiero*, published together as *On Tyranny*.[57] Indeed, the period between *Hobbes's Political Science* and *Natural Right and History* was characterized by an increasing politicization of Strauss's view of intellectual history and a deepening sense that a fundamental contradiction existed between classical political philosophy and modern thought.[58] These shifts transformed Strauss's reading of Hobbes and made Strauss far more direct in deploying the category of Epicureanism to explain trends in intellectual life, particularly as it

[56] We know from Strauss's letters to Alexandre Kojève that he was greatly preoccupied with writing the Walgreen Lectures during this time. See, in particular, Strauss's letter to Kojève of September 4, 1949, in Gourevitch and Roth (1991) 243. It is clear that Strauss saw *Natural Right and History* as a major work, the culmination of many of his philosophical efforts up to this point.

[57] In the course of the Kojève-Strauss correspondence, Kojève refers to "Epicureanism," using that term to describe all philosophies based on a withdrawal from the world to a state of reflection. There is no reason to think that this reference left an impression on Strauss. See Kojève's essay "Tyranny and Wisdom," in Gourevitch and Roth (1991).

[58] For differing accounts of Strauss's development between 1935 and 1949, see Sheppard (2006), Tanguay (2007); see also Michael Roth's "Introduction" in Gourevitch and Roth (1991). The different influences acting on Strauss during this time included the obvious weight of his flight from Europe and the need he felt to respond to the Holocaust, a deepened interest in medieval thought that led to several other essays on Maimonides, and an introductory essay written for Pines's translation of Maimonides' *Mishneh Torah*, and his discovery of the reading of Plato offered by the medieval Islamic thinker Alfarabi. The academic climate in which Strauss operated during this time must also be considered: the New School and its journal were markedly liberal establishments, and many of its social scientists held views inimical to Strauss's own. This may well have added to the radicalization of Strauss's views during this time. See Sheppard (2006) 86–92.

developed during the modern age that Spinoza, Hobbes, and Machiavelli had ushered in.

Before examining Strauss's treatment of Epicureanism in *Natural Right and History*, it is useful to understand the larger project of the book. The book is notoriously difficult to summarize, both because its chronological scope ranges from the classical period to the present and because it seems to argue from many perspectives at once. This point is perhaps best illustrated by Strauss's exchange with one of his early reviewers, Helmut Kuhn, who called the text a defense of the idea of natural right against modern liberalism by historical, rather than philosophical, means.[59] There is some justice to Kuhn's claim: the book makes the case that the question of natural right, that is, of the existence of an ideal political order, universal and without the limitations inherent in merely conventional systems of rights and politics, might not have been closed by the rise of historicism and relativism within modernity. Strauss opened his responding letter, however, by saying "I myself regard the book as a preparation to an adequate philosophic discussion rather than as a treatise settling the question."[60] That is, Strauss claimed that his work was intended to reopen the question of natural right, rather than to champion natural right as the proper foundation of political theory. He argued, therefore, that *Natural Right and History* should be read as a work in the tradition of the history of ideas that seeks to provoke a reexamination of questions generally considered closed by philosophers and by academics, especially those in the social sciences. It would, of course, be naïve to suggest that Strauss hoped to reopen the question of natural right solely out of scholarly interest. Any choice of research topic carries with it a polemical thrust, a point illustrated by Strauss's own earlier shift from researching Spinoza's Bible science to researching his critique of religion.[61]

---

[59] See Kuhn (1956).

[60] See Strauss (1978). The main substance of Strauss's dispute with Kuhn in this letter concerns several technical points beyond this essay's scope. The first was not whether *Natural Right and History* defends natural right, but rather whether Strauss's method in the book entangles him in a "negative historicism" of his own (23). Kuhn and Strauss also disagreed over Aristotle's interpretation of natural right (24).

[61] In fact, one criticism of Tanguay on this point is that he affords Strauss a greater degree of "scholarly objectivity" than is perhaps reasonable and that he does not inquire into the polemical aspects of Strauss's interest in reopening the question of natural right.

In *Natural Right and History*, Strauss traces the development of his title's two keywords, "natural" or more properly, "nature," and "history," from the forms they took in classical thought to the way modern discussants, principally Hobbes, Locke, Rousseau, and Burke, understood them. By tracing these ideas, Strauss means to make an intervention in the historiography of the ideas of natural right and natural law. While many historians considered modern natural right to be the result of the secularization of Jewish and Christian natural law, Strauss finds its origins in the birth of political philosophy in the classical period. Natural right was always a concept apart, he insists, rather than part of the idea of revealed legislation standing behind Judeo-Christian practice. Strauss defines the classical idea of natural right as being "identical with the actualization of a human possibility which, at least according to its own interpretation, is trans-historical, trans-social, trans-moral and trans-religious."[62] As another early reader of Strauss's work pointed out, the decision to employ the phrase "natural right" rather than "natural law" was itself important. In a 1954 review, the legal scholar Harold Gil Reuschlein noted,

there is a point to this inasmuch as the word "right" in its abstract sense indicates something that our word "law" does not. "Right" in its abstract sense conveys the idea of ethical correctness. It answers to one meaning of the Latin "jus," serving to indicate law in the abstract, that is, law as the foundation of all rights, the sum total of underlying moral principles which gives the affirmative character of justice to positive law and imparts to it an ethical content.[63]

Viewed in this light, the choice of "right" over "law" becomes an effort to undo the common translation of *jus* as "law." In Strauss's view, the concept of natural right becomes necessary at a point when laws seemed to have only a mere conventional validity, lacking the ethical implications that *jus* might carry.[64]

It is precisely the point of transition from political philosophies relying on the concept of natural law to ones reliant on the concept of natural right that concerns Strauss in *Natural Right and History*. Hobbes becomes

---

[62] NRH 89.
[63] See Reuschlein (1954).
[64] NRH 84.

a crucial figure in Strauss's narrative because he is situated at precisely that historical juncture at which a discourse of *law* was replaced by a discourse of *rights*. Importantly, Strauss disputes the idea that Hobbes himself represented the origin of natural rights discourse. Instead, Strauss's Hobbes takes up the question of natural right—namely, the question of how the regime might best be constituted—that Aristotle and Plato had meditated on before him and changes it fundamentally. Rather than ask how the human political order might reflect a greater cosmic order, he asks how "Man's" immanent and, comparatively speaking, baser needs might be satisfied. These, of course, included the defense of one's bodily health, property, and peace of mind. Without disregarding the importance of these goals, Strauss notes Hobbes's role in a shift from an ethic of virtuous aspiration to an ethic of base instincts and needs. Such an understanding of society based on personal rights rather than duties to the world beyond the self seemed to Strauss to be the basis of modern liberalism.

One of the indirect results of this shift from law to rights is the politicization of philosophy. A fixation on the defense of personal rights and welfare transforms philosophy, as it transformed all sciences and arts, into an instrument for the amelioration of humanity's estate on earth. Moreover, it transforms philosophers into mere "intellectuals" (Strauss's term) less concerned with the pursuit of truth than with applying the techniques of philosophy to merely "local" problems. Against this Epicurean turn, complicit with the politicization of philosophy, Strauss pits Plato, noting at one point that "the whole work of Plato may be described as a critique of the notion of 'the intellectual,'" that is, the sort of person who politicizes philosophy.[65]

The term "history" in Strauss's title, though seemingly polyvalent— referring either to the process of natural right's development or to the version of intellectual history that Strauss employed in order to trace that arc—quickly becomes attached to the premise of historicism as it emerged in the late nineteenth and early twentieth centuries. For Strauss, however, the word does not merely imply *historismus* as the methodological agenda championed by figures in the German academy like Julius Guttmann. It suggests to him a radically relativist attitude toward the possibility of

[65] Ibid., 58.

philosophical or religious truth, with corresponding implications for the validity of different modes of government. Strauss thus spends the opening sections of *Natural Right and History* attacking those historicist thinkers who "deny the significance, if not the existence, of universal norms," and in the process destroy "the only solid basis of all efforts to transcend the actual."[66] While Strauss's attitudes toward historicism were complex, as noted earlier in this essay, in *Natural Right and History* historicism becomes a keyword by which Strauss could refer to a conventionalism that seeks to "make men absolutely at home in 'this world,'" by abandoning all pursuit of the transcendent (as Strauss defined it) in order to make the present world a better one. Historicism is, then, the ideology of the intellectuals and not the philosophers. Strauss was eager, however, to differentiate historicism and skepticism, arguing that while skepticism represents a timeless view that "all assertions are uncertain,"[67] historicism, to be consistent, would have to locate *its* version of uncertainty in a particular historical moment.[68] Because of its inability to do so while retaining any critical purchase, historicism was inevitably self-undermining in Strauss's view.[69]

In an effort to undo the historicist challenge to natural right, Strauss goes on to retell natural right's history. He leads his readers through the rebellious replacement of private meditation on the truth as conveyed by tradition with the public discussion of the truth provided by scientists through their investigation of nature. What differentiates classical natural philosophy from modern science, on Strauss's view, is that, according to classical philosophy, the natural order is greater than "Man" and is owed a special kind of obedience that has the same structure as obedience to the revealed divine Law. The distinction between nature and convention serves to distinguish between the work of philosophers and the immediate political realities that govern men. It is this distinction that the modern Enlightenment sought to efface, seeking as it did to simultaneously mold both nature and convention. The oldest and most influential version of conventionalism that preoccupies Strauss in *Natural Right and History*, unsurprisingly, was Epicureanism.

---

[66] Ibid., 15.
[67] Ibid., 20.
[68] Ibid., 20.
[69] For a more in-depth examination of Strauss's skepticism, see S. P. Smith (2006).

Here Strauss is less explicitly concerned with Epicureanism's critique of religion and more concerned with a different dimension of the Epicurean impulse, namely, the drive to maximize pleasure and minimize suffering, writing that "[t]he most developed form of classical hedonism is Epicureanism." He further associates Epicureanism with both materialism and conventionalism, citing no less an authority than Plato's *Laws* as a precedent for this association.[70] According to Strauss, Hobbes was an Epicurean to the extent that he arrogated to humans the power to change their own world and, in the process, attributed a kind of "messianic potential" to philosophy as a transformative tool. It was Hobbes, moreover, who was responsible for transforming Epicureanism into part of an ideology that went on to have disastrous consequences for political life (and thought) in the modern period: Strauss dubs this ideology "political hedonism." Hobbes had joined the Epicurean tradition by rejecting the assumption of traditional political philosophy that "Man" is "by nature a political or social animal."[71] Hobbes then tried to form a political philosophy out of Epicureanism's apolitical anthropology, or as Strauss writes, "He thus bec[ame] the creator of political hedonism, a doctrine which has revolutionized human life everywhere on a scale never yet approached by any other teaching."[72]

This "political hedonism" combined, in a contradictory manner, the idealistic assumption of the fundamental status of political philosophy with the view that, because of our asocial and animal natures, the good for us is identical with the pleasant. As Strauss writes, Hobbesian political hedonism was "the typically modern combination of political idealism with a materialistic and atheistic view of the whole."[73] Strauss then divides political hedonism from classical Epicureanism and provides an intriguing redefinition of classical Epicureanism itself by comparing the two.[74] According to Strauss, "Hobbes had to oppose Epicurus in two crucial points in order to make possible political

---

[70] NRH 109. Strauss cites Plato's *Laws* 889b–899. It seems certain that, rather than making the anachronistic claim that Plato's *Laws* somehow associated Epicureanism with materialism, Strauss was reading Plato's *Laws,* book 10 as offering a critique of materialism that could be applied to Epicurean thought.

[71] NRH 169.

[72] Ibid.

[73] Ibid., 170.

[74] Ibid., 188.

hedonism."[75] The first point is that, whereas Epicurus had denied that man enjoyed natural rights within a state of nature, Hobbes sees such rights as a minimum requirement for the emergence of civil society. The second is that Hobbes rejects Epicurus's ideal of repose, finding it too ascetic, and replaces it with a more active ideal of pleasure. The "realistic" approach to politics forced Hobbes to lift all restrictions on the striving for unnecessary sensual pleasures or, more precisely, for the *commoda hujus vitae*, or for power, with the exception of those restrictions that are required for the sake of peace.[76]

By means of this contrast with political hedonism, Strauss shows Epicureanism to be nonpolitical. This understanding, while not entirely unprecedented in Strauss's work—for he had always noted the contrast between Epicureanism natural philosophy and Platonist political philosophy—does mark a shift away from his earlier understanding of Epicureanism's theologico-political implications. The "classical form" of the critique of religion always has political consequences because of religion's political character. Despite these differences, Strauss points out, Hobbes and Epicurus still agreed on the equivalence of the good with the pleasant and the consequential unimportance of virtue or the pursuit of excellence. Their primary difference had to do with whether they advocated pursuing their goal of maximizing pleasure in the public sphere or minimizing unhappiness via an ascetic existence in the private.

To Strauss, one of political hedonism's hallmark traits was its typically bourgeois denigration of excellence in favor of comfort. Moreover, the followers of comfort were likely to reinterpret human excellence as a means toward the end of securing greater pleasure and security. Strauss, on the other hand, saw such excellence—for example, in the arts, in government, in science or athletics—as evidence of the existence of natural right: "We admire excellence without any regard to our pleasures or to our benefits. No one understands by a good man or man of excellence a man who leads a pleasant life."[77] Moving from this comparison between the self-indulgent subject of political hedonism and the self-improving, relatively anhedonic subject of natural right to a

[75] Ibid., 189.
[76] Ibid.
[77] Ibid., 128.

comparison between the forms of government with which they are correlated, Strauss took these arguments further. If, as he put it, "Man is so built that he cannot achieve the perfection of his humanity except by keeping down his lower impulses," governments are much harder to perfect.[78] Ideal government requires the kind of restraint represented by the self-improving subject, but it is even harder to impose such control on others than it is to impose it on the self. To rule over the body politic is much harder than to rule over the actual body: "Serious concern for the perfection of a community requires a higher degree of virtue than serious concern for the perfection of an individual. The judge and ruler has larger and nobler opportunities to act justly than the ordinary man."[79] Strauss was fundamentally suspicious of the security and pleasure of the individual as a basis for politics. He thus turned a dubious eye toward the self-gratifying subject of political hedonism. In contrast, within classical natural right the pursuit of excellence—especially in the public field of political life—provided a much sounder basis. The formulation of a theory of happiness rooted in sound political practice rather than the pursuit of pleasure struck Strauss as the sign of the superiority of classical political philosophy over Hobbesian political hedonism. The latter philosophy sought not so much to champion Epicurus over Plato as to completely abandon the plane of philosophical contestation upon which Platonic and Epicurean forces did battle by moving into the political sphere. However, Hobbes's abandonment of any political or natural teleology left his philosophy without a solid foundation.

Thus one of the interesting aspects of Strauss's reading of Hobbesian "political hedonism" is that it condemned, as noted previously, the effects of Epicureanism without condemning the Epicurean impulse itself. Strauss began with the "purer" and more ancient forms of the doctrine, which associate the most pleasurable life with philosophy, and then proceded to the modern period in which Epicureanism was mistranslated or corrupted, in part through the influence of Hobbes and the Enlightenment *philosophes*, into a doctrine that hedonistically satisfies the body rather than the mind. Thus Strauss was able to show that while Epicurus and his school were never Strauss's true opponents, they

[78] Ibid., 133.
[79] Ibid.

were genealogically linked to "political hedonism," which revealed the potential for abuse within the original Epicurean motivation. Yet Strauss also understood that the same motivation prompted other Epicureans, such as the Roman Lucretius, to provide philosophy with an enormously useful rhetorical aid in the form of poetic writing.

READING LUCRETIUS WITH STRAUSS

During the first two-thirds of his career, Strauss conspicuously employed the terms "Epicurean" and "Epicureanism" as if for their symbolic value without meditating on explicitly Epicurean texts themselves. *Natural Right and History* marked the beginning of a shift, with Strauss identifying the *De Rerum Natura* of Lucretius as the greatest document of philosophic conventionalism.[80] Strauss would subsequently continue his treatment of that text with the essay "Notes on Lucretius," published in the later collection *Liberalism Ancient and Modern.*[81] In *Natural Right and History*, Lucretius's work is simply offered as the exemplary text of conventionalism, the category in which Strauss gathers together Rousseau, Hobbes, and the other founders of modern liberalism. Appropriately, given his preoccupation with larger arguments about Hobbes and the modernization of political thought, Strauss provides only a brief account of the work's content and does not treat its formal properties, and he does not go into detail regarding the relationship between Lucretius and Epicurus. It is precisely these aspects of *De Rerum Natura* that preoccupy him in his later essay. It seems justifiable to claim that "Notes on Lucretius," while substantially an elaboration of the extended narrative of the *De Rerum Natura*, is really a meditation on the relation between the philosopher Epicurus and the poet Lucretius and, more specifically, on the peculiar fact that Lucretius wrote an epic poem about a philosophy that resists many of the central themes of the poetic epic, including romantic love, the designs of the gods, and fate.[82]

---

[80] Ibid., 112.

[81] Strauss (1995).

[82] Nichols (1976) 25 describes the peculiar aspects of *De Rerum Natura*, including its status as an epic poem that banishes many of the familiar elements of the epic including gods, fate, and romantic love. See also Godwin (2004) 51: "There is a giant problem for an Epicurean poet to overcome, however, and that is Epicurus's own avowed disapproval

From that latter, potentially inconsequential fact, Strauss extracts a lesson regarding the utility that poetry may hold for the expression of the philosophical truth, especially given the politically hostile conditions in which philosophers often work. The late "Notes on Lucretius" thus bind Strauss's earlier interests in Epicureanism together with his fundamental preoccupation with the political character of philosophy.

At the essay's opening, Strauss describes Lucretius's poem as a gradual introduction to Epicureanism. The poem's reader—perhaps projecting herself or himself into the position of the Roman politician Memmius, to whom the poem is addressed—is to ascend from her or his current temporal position to a greater position as an Epicurean. This helps us to understand the beginning sections of the *De Rerum Natura*, which offer an elaborate genealogical link between the Romans and the Greeks; as Strauss puts it, the Roman politician must be reminded that he has links to the Greek world before he can grasp that world's philosophies. Once he has grasped the Epicurean doctrine and gained access to the state of *ataraxia* that it provides, Memmius will also have been cured of the religious beliefs that cause him fear and suffering because of his expectations for the afterlife.

The pain associated with the knowledge of the Epicurean truth can, however, be counteracted by clothing philosophical material in poetic form. As Strauss writes,

The movement from the untruth to the truth is not simply a movement from unrelieved darkness and terror to pure light and joy. On the contrary, the truth appears at first to be repulsive and depressing. A special effort is needed to counteract the first appearance of the truth. This special effort is beyond the power of philosophy; it is the proper work of poetry.[83]

Even if Strauss refers to Lucretius as Epicurus's "weaker follower," unable to say the truth directly as his master could, poetry makes

---

of poetry as a form of writing. The evidence is scant (as so often), but there is enough of it to suggest that Epicurus—like Plato in many ways—believed that poetry was a bad way to write as it used obfuscating metaphors instead of plain speech and also because poets usually told dangerously false tales about the gods in their poems." If we read Lucretius with Nichols and Godwin in mind, the *De Rerum Natura* becomes an epic poem against the genre of the epic poem, denying the gods, who are honored by most Greek and Roman epics, and at the same time celebrating the mortal lineage of its addressee, Memmius.

[83] Strauss (1995) 83.

Lucretius capable of doing something Epicurus could not. He is the doctor who has bitter medicine to administer and coats it in a sugar pill. Lucretius himself offers an analogy between the use of poetry to sweeten the truth and the doctor's use of honey to sweeten a dose of wormwood before giving it to children.[84] For Strauss, Lucretius's poetry is a politically expeditious adaptation made necessary by the threatening elements inherent in Epicurus's philosophy, which might be depressing for the individual but offered a genuine threat to society at large.

Poetry's powers are not limited to sweetening the truth, however. In addition to its rhetorical advantages, which enable philosophers to tread the very difficult path between the philosophical truth and the necessities of political life, poetry offers the advantage of an ambiguous relationship between worldliness and worldlessness. Strauss writes,

Philosophy which, anticipating the collapse of the walls of the world, breaks through the walls of the world, abandons the attachment to the world; this abandonment is most painful. Poetry on the other hand is, like religion, rooted in that attachment, but unlike religion, it can be put into the service of detachment.[85]

Lest this passage be misunderstood, we have to bear in mind that for Strauss, "religion" was associated here not with a transcendental divine order but rather with a revealed legislation governing the temporal world. Poetry, like religion, is directly concerned with the temporal world. Yet because of its rhetorical qualities, on the one hand, and its attention to transcendental themes, on the other, it readily functions as philosophy's handmaiden. This may make it the best possible medium for those who wish to live both philosophically and politically, or at least a vehicle to bring listeners from the one realm to the other, just as Lucretius seeks to recruit Memmius.

A requirement for poetic mediation may have been built into the fabric of Epicureanism itself. As James Nichols has argued, Epicurean philosophy enjoys a fraught relationship with the category of "the political" due

---

[84] Nichols (1976) 36 offers the following analysis of the language used by Lucretius in his analogy: "When doctors put honey on the rim of a cup containing wormwood, children are fooled (*ludificetur*, I, 939), deceived (*decepta*, I, 941)—not of course, in order to be harmed, but to be made well."

[85] Strauss (1995) 85.

to its origins in natural philosophy.[86] As he points out, "one will search in vain in the works of Epicurus or in the *De Rerum Natura* for a political teaching like what one finds in Plato or in Aristotle."[87] Furthermore, ascetic Epicureanism seems to have counseled retreat from political life into the "garden" where Epicurus taught his students, and furthermore to have urged men to avoid public life altogether.[88] Against the standard view, Nichols argues that there is an Epicurean political philosophy, with the result that Epicureanism presents us with a very curious turn in classical thought. Following arguments laid down by Benjamin Farrington, he sees it as the descendent of the naturalistic philosophical tradition that originated with Thales, but having the aim not of describing the universe and its laws but of explicating a philosophy of "Man" and society. Epicureanism accepted Democritean atomism as a sufficient description of the structure of matter, but inquired into what kind of human life must follow from such a description.[89] As Strauss noted, Epicurean thought contains a kind of political philosophy that is entirely unlike those of Plato and Aristotle: Epicureans like Lucretius were concerned with politics in part because the philosophy they offered had direct implications for the political world, but unlike Platonists or Aristotelians, they had no substantial theory of how the political community should operate. The materialist critique of religion is political because religion is political. Largely because it offers only political critique and analyzes human life in terms of the nature of the universe, Epicureanism requires poetic explication in order to have a less harmful effect on the social order as a whole.

As this essay has endeavored to show, Strauss hardly ever wrote about Epicurus himself but always about how other thinkers received and developed Epicureanism. It was precisely this tendency that enabled him to treat Epicureanism in highly abstract terms—almost as a universal impulse in philosophical life rather than as a historically situated view. In stating that the "classic of the tradition," the *De Rerum Natura*, was written not by a philosopher but, rather, by a poetic ally of the philosophical, Strauss implies that Epicureanism required a poetic agent for

---

[86] Nichols (1976) 36.
[87] Ibid., 14.
[88] Ibid.
[89] Farrington (1965) 20.

its best expression. Throughout his career, Strauss developed the notion that there is an inherent tension between rationalist philosophy and the interests of society at large. This was largely because philosophers can foment doubt regarding the legitimacy of religion and the state, institutions essential to society's stability. Epicureanism, the "classic" of the critique of religion, would naturally be potentially inimical to the interests of society and, as such, it needs to be candy-coated. It is entirely possible that a parallel exists between Hobbes's adaptation of Epicurus into a modern form of political hedonism and Lucretius's poetic adaptation of Epicurus, a parallel of which Strauss was aware. In other words, both writers found a way to make the lessons of Epicurus tame enough so that they would not threaten social stability.[90]

CONCLUSION

The chronological account of Strauss's interest in Epicureanism presented in this essay is intended as a suggestive rather than an exhaustive study, a starting point for further work on the subject. On examining Strauss's treatments of the term "Epicurean," it becomes tempting to summarize the basic conflict he surveyed, throughout all his works, as the struggle between Platonism and Epicureanism, or between idealism and conventionalism. However, this would be unjust due to the range of purposes to which Strauss set the term "Epicureanism." It would be less ambitious but more accurate to call Epicureanism a "bridge" concept that links Strauss's early concern with religion, law, and the relationship between the philosopher and the heretic, and his later concern with the definition and political consequences of the ideas of nature and convention.

However, as I suggested in my discussion of *Spinoza's Critique of Religion*, Strauss's sense of his own proximity to Epicureanism deserves special consideration. Strauss's early reflection on Epicureanism as *apikorsut* was likely driven by an awareness that he himself might be seen as an Epicurean, despite his leanings toward Plato. While he never associated himself, either at that early moment in his career or later, with the materialism or conventionalism that he associated with Epicurus

---

[90] Strauss (1995) 83.

and Lucretius, he believed that any philosopher could be a heretic due to the distance he might take from the political community at large. And while Strauss was not an observant Jew, he frequently expressed the view that philosophers are incapable of the salutary obedience to the law that religion brings. His discourses on heresy seem to implicate him as a heretic in the same spirit as Solomon Maimon. Strauss himself was a creature of paradoxes—an admirer of orthodox religion who once said that he hoped his own soul would "die the death of philosophers." While it is unclear what he meant by that statement, it is possible that it reflects a very Epicurean understanding of the soul as having a material, and thus mortal, nature.

Meditating on Epicureanism was thus a means by which Strauss could meditate on the larger meanings of his own identity as a Jewish philosopher. In continuing to use the term "Epicurean" throughout his career—which, as we have seen, was not really necessary, for Strauss could have used different terms rather than imputing different meanings to the same one—Strauss maintained his attachment to the word's heretical associations. Epicureanism was philosophy red in tooth and claw, at least when it came to maintaining Jewish religious beliefs, and thus dramatized the basic conflict that Strauss—against his teacher Julius Guttmann—saw running between philosophy and religion. Strauss may not have considered himself an Epicurean, but the Epicurean impulse earned his respectful treatment. He always understood its proximity to the skeptical elements in his own thought, which Wittgenstein has taught us to call a "family resemblance."[91]

---

[91] Wittgenstein (2001) 27 (§67).

10

Epicurean Presences in Foucault's
The Hermeneutics of the Subject

Alain Gigandet

"Epicurean presences"—yes, but doubtless we should speak at the same time of "Epicurean absences." Certainly, Epicureanism is present in the text of Foucault, and obviously more here (that is, in *The Hermeneutics of the Subject*) than in his other published works on ancient philosophy, but how is it brought into his discussion and which Epicureanism is under discussion? In short, it is precisely his use of Epicureanism in *The Hermeneutics of the Subject* that is problematic. Does one Epicurus not conceal another? Most often, Foucault seeks in the doctrine of the Garden confirmation of hypotheses developed elsewhere, essentially in Stoic contexts; sometimes he also seeks complements or nuances of these hypotheses. Therefore, on the whole, his attention to Epicurean texts is less precise and his style of reference much more conventional than that which prevails in his analyses dedicated to Stoic texts. For the specialist, then, his reading of Epicureanism can be a bit frustrating, although there are several notable exceptions. For example, the specific nature of the Epicurean treatment of friendship allows Foucault to take into account the delicate link between the salvation of the self and the salvation of others within the doctrines of the Hellenistic period;[1] the organization of the Epicurean school is given an exemplary position

This piece originally appeared in French as Gigandet (2003). It is presented here in English for the first time, with a few added notes and minor modifications. For consistency in exposition, translations of Greek and Latin texts are based upon Gigandet's French originals but have been compared with their Greek and Latin originals.
    [1] Foucault (2005) 192–96.

in understanding the collective practices addressed to the "care of the self";[2] and his study of *parrhēsia* is based in large part upon the treatise of Philodemus devoted to the subject.[3]

In other words, if there is manifestly a "Stoic path" (Roman Stoic, in any case) within *The Hermeneutics of the Subject*, there is nothing similar for the Epicureans. The network of references to the Garden is discontinuous, heterogeneous. How does this network relate to the more general system of Foucault's project? As I suggested above, it appears alongside his primary analyses, either to confirm them or to render them more precise. A brief map of Foucault's Epicurean references, one with no pretense of completeness, will provide an idea:

Confirmation by reference to Epicureanism

(1) In considering the problem of the relation between philosophy and medicine, Foucault presents Epicurus's *ontōs philosophein* as characteristic of the idea of healing in accordance with the truth.[4]

(2) The beginning of the *Letter to Menoeceus* shows how, for the Hellenistic schools of philosophy, the "care of the self" constitutes "an obligation that should last for the whole of one's life."[5]

(3) The organization of the Epicurean schools gives form to Foucault's thoughts on the necessary, mediatory role that the philosopher plays for salvation.[6]

(4) The role of "frank speaking" (*parrhēsia*) as it is discussed in Philodemus's eponymous treatise (*Peri parrhēsias*) allows Foucault to refine the function of truth-telling in these philosophical communities.

(5) The original topic of Epicurean friendship confirms the problematic link between the salvation of the self and the salvation of others.[7]

---

[2] Ibid., 115, 134–38.

[3] Ibid., 372–76.

[4] Ibid., 97, with n. 53.

[5] Ibid., 87; cf. 13.

[6] Ibid., 136–38, where the discussion arises from a critical reference to the reconstructions of the Epicurean school of De Witt (1973).

[7] Foucault (2005) 192–95.

(6) Epicurean *physiologia* provides an exemplary illustration of the "ethopoetic" form given to natural science by Hellenistic philosophies.[8]

Epicurean "exceptions," which allow Foucault to nuance his argument

(1) "Care of the self" and economy: by contrast with the Stoics, in the Epicureans there is a clear tendency to uncouple the demands of the "care of the self" from economic obligations. From here there arises an inquiry into the domain proper to the "care of the self."[9]

(2) The Epicurean opposition to the *praemeditatio malorum* of the Stoics bears witness to a different posture in the ethical manipulation of representations.[10]

***

We can put forward a hypothesis concerning the reasons for this situation: the architecture of Epicurean philosophy, while in a general sense raising the question of the "care of the self," presents—not only in its details but also in some of its fundamental aims—its own distinctive traits, its own noteworthy departures from the structure proposed by Foucault. If this hypothesis is correct, Epicureanism could not have been evoked except for at the margins and in general terms in the course of 1981–82.[11] Taking up the very terms of Foucault's own inquiry, we may ask what type of subject the Epicurean ethical program puts into place. The answer, it seems to me, is a subject that is defined above all by the conquest of a place or a site, and in a defensive manner.

In his course on the seventeenth of February, Foucault comes to underline the political import (in the modern sense of that term) of what he calls the "ethics of the self" in conjunction with his inquiry into the "care

---

[8] Ibid., 236–44.
[9] Ibid., 59.
[10] Ibid., 468.
[11] Translator's note: Gigandet here refers to the fact that the *Hermeneutics of the Subject* represents the edited transcript of a course Foucault gave in 1981–82. The course explored the topic of the "care of the self" that, as Foucault saw it, previously had been overshadowed by an emphasis on self-knowledge. For further information about the course and its intellectual context, see Foucault (2005) 491–550.

of the self" as he deciphers it in texts from the Hellenistic period. After having critiqued the poverty of contemporary "Returns to the Self," Foucault adds:

Although the theory of political power as an institution usually refers to a juridical conception of the subject of right, it seems to me that the analysis of governmentality—that is to say, of power as a set of reversible relationships—must refer to an ethics of the subject defined by the relationship of self to self. Quite simply . . . power relations, governmentality, the government of the self and of others, and the relationship of self to self constitute a chain, a thread, and I think it is around these notions that we should be able to connect together the question of politics and the question of ethics.[12]

We should, of course, locate this comment within the trajectory of the vast consideration of power and power relations that Foucault develops from *Discipline and Punish* onward. I content myself—in order to hold strictly to my topic—with the observation that no reference is made to Epicurus in this particular passage of *The Hermeneutics of the Subject*. Now, it seems to me that the very particular fashion in which Epicurus works out the separation of ethics from politics raises fundamental questions touching upon the significance of philosophical practice and the status of the subject concerned, "taken," in some sense, into this practice.

We owe to Epicurus, or more likely to his student Metrodorus, a remarkable metaphor for the human condition: ". . . from the fact of death, we dwell in a city without walls [*polin ateikhiston oikoumen*]."[13] This statement means several things.

First, this sense: if the final cause, the *telos* of ethics—that is, of the whole of philosophy—is happiness, then we must observe well that this quest for happiness is fashioned upon the basis of absolute precariousness. Not only experience but also natural science, *physiologia*, teaches us this lesson: every sensible body—that is, every composite of atoms and void—is destined for decomposition and death. The determining circumstance for philosophy is thus the urgency created by the overarching reality of death. Curiously, it is this dimension that Foucault leaves

---

[12] Foucault (2005) 252.
[13] Epicurus *Vatican Sayings* 31. All citations of Epicurus refer to Usener (1887) but have been checked against Conche (2009).

to the side when he comments on the opening of Epicurus's *Letter to Menoeceus*.[14] It is nevertheless this urgency that the first utterance of the letter communicates: "it is never too soon nor too late for anyone to practice philosophy." To delay happiness is a luxury that is permitted to no one. And we understand from the same passage why all philosophy converges upon an ethics, the certainty of which is guaranteed by natural science, atomist physics, and the sensualist theory of knowledge—the canonic—that accompanies it. Such a perspective, of course, leads Epicurus to a strict instrumentalization of the truth.

Furthermore, we must understand the metaphor of the city without walls as a way of calling into doubt the classical political model in philosophy. The world—which in no way resembles the common space of gods and men imagined by the Stoics—suspends my existence from an uncertain thread. No more than the "burning walls" of the world (the *flamantia moenia mundi* of Lucretius) can those of the city provide security. This communal place, this place of solidarity, which Greece of the classical period thought proper to justice and happiness, is regarded with defiance by the Epicureans in a gesture fraught with consequences. To practice philosophy demands, in principle, retiring from the political community, its laws, and its power structure, for no law has ever rescued anyone from the fear of death or of the gods. Worse still, it is precisely from within the enclosure of the city that danger arises: ambition takes hold of souls, exacerbating their turmoil; competition weighs upon each as a permanent menace[15] such that "the most pure security arises from a tranquil life, apart from the crowd."[16] We shall therefore find only in ourselves the conditions of happiness, the means to secure ourselves against "the disease of death"—a chief aspect of the "care of the self." Only the criteria for the happy life—once we have succeeded in determining their nature—will allow us to establish the function and the (necessarily relative) value of political life. The "positive" Epicurean conception of justice, as well as the ideal of a community based upon friendship, follows from a single intention to redefine the relationship to others on the basis of the ethical principles for individual salvation.[17]

---

[14] Foucault (2005) 87–88.
[15] Lucretius *De Rerum Natura* 3.59–78.
[16] Epicurus *Kuriai Doxai* 14.
[17] For friendship, see the suggestive analysis of Foucault (2005) 193–95.

If death weighs upon me both because of its inevitability and because of the unforeseeable nature of its circumstances, if the fear of suffering and the anguished uncertainty that results from it prevents me from being happy much more surely than physical pain, the demands to which Epicurus submits the definition of the ethical good can seem exorbitant. This good, in effect, must be such that it assures us of a happiness not subject to the vagaries of chance (the criterion of invulnerability);[18] that the subject can achieve it and enjoy it in total autonomy (the criterion of auto-sufficiency);[19] that it is complete with regard to that which our nature requires (the criterion of perfection).[20] Pure pleasure is the sovereign good only insofar as it proves itself the only good capable of satisfying the totality of these requirements.[21] By what violent paradox does it claim to pass from a situation of extreme precariousness, an expression, it seems, of the very nature of things, to one of inviolable security that makes the condition of the sage equal to that of the gods?

The prelude to the second book of the *De Rerum Natura* allows us to make the nature of this solution more precise: the conquest by the wise man is of *a site*. *Suave mari magno. . . .* The spectacle of unhappy men at the mercy of a storm comes to reinforce the sense of security enjoyed by one who observes it on solid ground, *on the shore*; the sage can also be compared to this observer beyond reach who, from the summit of the mountain, sees armies confront one another in the plain. What is this shore? What are these "lofty places, fortified by the knowledge of the wise men?"[22]

To fortify one's defenses is, on the one hand, to separate oneself, to retreat to a marginal or distant location, which implies *detachment*; it is at the same time to protect oneself against that which threatens this position of retreat, to build a system of defense—walls; it is, finally, to ensure from there an overhang allowing a view from on high, a view which envelops human affairs and puts them in their place. Foucault well describes this practice of viewing from above in the context of the Stoic examination of representations in Seneca and Marcus Aurelius.[23]

---

[18] Epicurus *Letter to Menoeceus* 131.

[19] Epicurus *Letter to Menoeceus* 130; *Vatican Sayings* 44, 77.

[20] Epicurus *Letter to Menoeceus* 131.

[21] This statement of the problem is reconstructed in remarkable fashion by Mitsis (1988).

[22] Lucretius *De Rerum Natura* 2.1–10.

[23] Respectively, Foucault (2005) 280–85 and 306–309.

But to be precise, as Olivier Bloch has definitively shown, the Stoics here are inspired directly by Lucretius.[24] The most significant difference for our study, it seems to me, is that in Lucretius, the idea of a site that directs the metaphor establishes a theoretical ethical system and does not simply participate in one as a particular technique.

But, once again, how does one secure such a place? The Epicurean method is clear and rigorous. Since it is useless to build a fortress against the intrusion of external danger, the solution will proceed by a displacement: it will no longer be a question of acting on things but of acting on their representation and, thereby, on the manner in which they affect us. Salvation will lie in an interior reexamination of the manner in which we conduct ourselves and expose ourselves to danger. As a consequence, the only place able to be secured is *the soul*; it alone can be established in the "fixed point" represented by the "immobile lightning bolt in the plain," one of the keys to Lucretius's delicate articulation of this point.[25] So to evade danger (*se soustraire*) is thus literally to operate by subtraction (*soustraction*): death is universal and necessary, but what is it, in truth, that binds us to it, what sort of paradoxical, imaginary experience? Epicurus's response is found in his celebrated thesis "Death is nothing to us." The first-person experience of death is in itself contradictory, because to feel or undergo anything at all, I precisely must be alive. In sum, death is reduced to the level of an "ill of the imagination," as Alain will say in a happy turn of phrase. To heal us of this disease is the very role of ethics.

The effective practice of this analysis is very much a removal—in this new sense of subtraction: "the proper understanding that death is nothing to us renders happy the mortal condition—not by adding infinite time but by removing the desire for immortality."[26] The sage "has ceased having connection with" all sources of trouble from which he cannot protect himself directly, "and he has separated from his life everything that was advantageous to treat so." Thus, by a remarkable reversal, it is death that takes nothing away from a happy life.[27] The speech of Torquatus, the Epicurean of Cicero's *De Finibus*, puts this framework

---

[24] Bloch (1997) 119–31.
[25] Lucretius *De Rerum Natura* 2.308–32.
[26] Epicurus *Letter to Menoeceus* 124–25.
[27] Epicurus *Kuriai Doxai* 20.

in relief: "it is wisdom, which after having removed fears and strong emotions and having snatched away the imprudence of all false opinion, is given to us as the most certain guide towards pleasure"; "the wise man, who has cut up and diced all that he had in himself of empty opinions and errors, the wise man, who holds himself within the limits of nature, is the only one able to live without chagrin and fear."[28] Significantly, in this last text, the movement of retrenchment to within the limits fixed by nature appears rigorously homologous to the subtraction of empty opinions and desires. The strange subtraction of the empty (or void, *vide*)[29]. . . .

Such a mechanism manifestly puts into play the principles of the Epicurean canonic. As the criterion of every certainty resides, in effect, in sensation, the work of reason does not consist in judging or in correcting this faculty, but, on the contrary, in unburdening it of the opinions and beliefs that cover it over or disturb its manifest content. And therefore the search for the truth very much rests in an operation of subtraction, which has been rightly called the Epicurean "principle of epistemological frugality." Hence, the hedonistic calculus, upon which, in the last instance, the entire ethical system is based. In reality, the positivity of pleasure, the fact that it constitutes the "ultimate goal," is the result of manifest, irrefutable internal evidence, which hangs upon the manifest, epistemological evidence of the external sensations. Like every sensation, however, such a sensation is *alogos*, at once mute and irrational: it cannot, without rational calculation, dictate to us an optimal mode of conduct.

To determine a maximum, linked to assigning a quantitative limit to all pleasure, is the object of this calculus: "The pleasure in the flesh cannot be increased once the pain of need has been suppressed; it is only varied."[30] Hence, once this maximum has been reached—and it is reached quickly—pleasure can only vary by changing its objects or within its objects, but it will gain nothing in quantity, intensity, or quality.

The determination of the relationship between pleasure and pain is closely linked to this theory of the maximum. There is no intermediate state between these two opposing terms. If the maximum of pleasure is quickly reached, it is because it coincides with the cessation of the pain

---

[28] Cicero *De Finibus* 1.43–44, cited from Reynolds (1998).
[29] Translator's note: parenthesis added.
[30] Epicurus *Vatican Sayings* 59; cf. *Kuriai Doxai* 18.

caused by want: "He who knows the limits of life knows that it is easy to obtain for himself what suppresses the pain caused by need and what renders life completely perfect."[31] The restriction of desires thus possesses no trace of asceticism; it fits with the very nature of pleasure, which is provided straightaway in its greatest intensity, but future extension and refinement due to variation always threaten to destroy this pleasure and transform it back to suffering.

The interpretation of the relationship between movement and rest in pleasure is delicate. According to the testimony of Diogenes Laërtius, "the absence of trouble and the absence of pain are static (*katastematikai*) pleasures, whereas joy and happiness are considered—because of their activity (*energeia*)—as kinetic (*kata kinesin*) pleasures." On this point, the Epicureans, our author affirms, distinguish themselves from the Cyrenaics, who allow only kinetic pleasure (10.136). But how do they articulate these two kinds or modalities of pleasure? Speaking schematically, there are two principal paths of interpretation: either (1) we allow that kinetic pleasure, which consists in the movement that accompanies the reduction of need and of pain, reaches and achieves katastematic pleasure, static pleasure (the interpretation of Bignone and Bailey);[32] or (2) we refuse to allow that pure, stable pleasure could have movement as its condition and assimilate kinetic pleasure to *poikilmata*, those variations that are not necessary for the suppression of pain but, on the contrary, presuppose the equilibrium of static pleasure and intervene only from this point, as when we eat sweets after having satisfied our hunger with bread (the commentary of Diano).[33]

Whatever the case, this "minimalism" always depends upon a principle of subtraction: pure pleasure is attained by the methodical elimination of the hedonistic criteria of accumulation, intensification, maximizing by duration, variation. . . . And it is precisely through this aspect that it satisfies the requirements of happiness—by assuring the firm protection of the soul. If pleasure is attained upon the cessation of pain and if it is, from this moment, at its highest intensity, then the Epicurean puts into place a model that—in so far as it comes to govern his thoughts and

---

[31] Epicurus *Kuriai Doxai* 21.

[32] Translator's note: for the positions Gigandet mentions, see Bailey (1947) 1: 61 and Bignone (1973) 1: 363 n. 76.

[33] Translator's note: for Diano's position, see Diano (1974) 40–46.

his acts towards himself—assures him of a continuous state of maximal pleasure coincident with the absence of all trouble. It is thus in limited means, the product of a methodical reduction, that the point of stability and certainty in life is reached; and, as Epicurus recalls, there is never want in limited means.

We have been able to observe along the way, in this summary, a number of major elements of the problem of the ethical subject elaborated in *The Hermeneutics of the Subject*: the link between the question of the "care of the self" and that of salvation; the idea of the privileged ethical status granted to the soul (which is noteworthy for a doctrine that otherwise takes the pleasure of the body as a point of reference); the defensive techniques arising from the *paraskeuē*; the privileged status of work upon representations, and so on. But what of the configuration of the subject at stake in this Epicurean procedure of protection-subtraction?

The urgency that directs philosophical decision, especially the manner in which the Epicureans think about this urgency, seems to me to have as a corollary a very particular conception of salvation and of the process that leads to it.[34] Philosophy rests upon a decision that, it seems to me, accords space to something that is more in the order of a reversal than a true, progressive path of conversion. Certainly, preparations facilitate this reversal; that is the point of the subtractive procedures upon which I have insisted, and—from a more external perspective—that purpose undergirds the functions of exemplarity, emulation, and encouragement attributed to the community of friends. But it is necessary to go quickly, and right to the goal. One aspect of this urgency, in particular, is the Epicurean rejection of *paideia* and the strictly utilitarian connection to the truth (with which this rejection is connected).[35] It is from this perspective that we must consider the use of summaries and maxims for presenting briefly the doctrine of Epicurus within the Garden.[36]

---

[34] Recall the beginning of the *Letter to Menoeceus*: "Let no one, being young, wait to begin the practice of philosophy, nor let anyone, though old, give up philosophy; for it is not, for anyone, either too early or too late to assure the salvation of the soul. He, who says that the time to philosophize has not yet come or that it has passed, is like to one who says that the time for happiness has not yet come or that it exists no longer."

[35] See the comments at Foucault (2005) 239–40 on the opposition between *paideia* and *physiologia*.

[36] On this subject, see the remarks of Brunschwig (2002) xxxv.

Of course, the framework of an ethical reversal is consistent with the thesis of a natural criterion for acting well, one inscribed in each living being—pleasure (and here we are obliged to break with Foucault's methodological commitment in order to remain true to the principles of the doctrine). This pleasure, as we have seen, is experienced immediately in its greatest intensity, on the condition of having understood, with a knowledge both intimate and practical, that qualitative variations augment it in no way—to such an extent that the state of the ethical subject seems to me to flow from the scheme or the model of a *point*. The subject secures himself at the same time as he achieves, in a mental "site," the point of view linked to the judgment of desires (the Lucretian seashore or summit), to which corresponds a point in time (a limit, as Epicurus says) linked to the "subtractive" intensification of pleasure. Foucault seems to me to come close to this idea when he addresses the Epicureans' refusal of the *praemeditatio malorum*, without therefore developing the implications (of this refusal).[37] What is at stake, however, is one of the important models of the analysis of the construction of the self proposed by *The Hermeneutics of the Subject*, that of an ascetic course, of ethical life as a *path*.

In fact, Foucault affirms that the procedures for the constitution of the subject go back to a mode of engagement with existence that he reconceives under the figure of the path, a path understood more precisely as a putting to the test, "life as a form of test of the self."[38] The idea that the self is measured against itself in the field opened by the succession of life events seems to me closely linked to the Stoic or Cynic aim toward virtue and, by contrast, difficult to reconcile with the manner in which the Epicureans determine the conditions and the nature of philosophical *askēsis*, such as I have attempted to summarize very schematically for the moment.[39] And that does not take into account the

---

[37] Foucault (2005) 468. The essential text on this topic is Cicero *Tusculan Disputations* 3.32–33, cited from Pohlenz (1918).

[38] Foucault (2005) 486.

[39] The question of *askēsis* constitutes an essential point of divergence between the Epicureans and the Stoics, a fact that seems poorly recognized by Foucault. In effect, there is a moral "athleticism" of the Stoa, which tends to demonstrate virtue by testing it, by turning the obstacle into a challenge for the "progressing student"—indeed, even for the sage. By contrast, the "mental traffic" characteristic of Epicurean *askēsis* consists in a set of operations, all aimed at neutralizing harmful representations: (a) a technique of destruction (for example, that of the subjective content of the idea of death); (b) a technique of

close link, which Foucault has underlined elsewhere, notably in commenting on Seneca, between Stoic asceticism and a conception of providence completely foreign to Epicurean doctrine. But let us listen instead to Epicurus himself: "He who knows the limits of life knows that it is easy to acquire for himself that which suppresses the pain caused by need and that which renders life completely perfect; such that he has no need, besides, of any of the things which bring struggle."[40] Far from seeming the result of a slow discovery of the self in the form of an examination—an examination inseparable from the patient practice of the subject's transformation of himself—the perfection of life is granted, rather, as the stopping point imposed upon the illusion of desire, the illusion of an infinity of pleasure entailing an anguish of loss, itself infinite. Here there is something rather like a short circuit: the gain of the happy life is immediately counterbalanced by loss. The aim of the supreme good is no longer, from this fact, to extend oneself toward a moment of privileged accomplishment that is old age. On the contrary, we know that—by virtue of philosophical practice—the old man becomes young "out of gratitude for what he has been," and the young, old "from his lack of fear of the future."[41]

Similarly, the Epicurean ethical system shows itself removed from another important axis of the interpretation put forward by Foucault—that of an aesthetic stylization of ethical existence. We shall not tarry here upon this result, but we must note that the ethical putting-into-order of existence, considered as a whole, cannot be regarded by Epicureanism as an object of pleasure in itself. Virtue, repeats Epicurus, is only a means. His interest, that of his "athleticism," if you like, is limited strictly to the assurance that virtue gives us "the ability to look upon everything with a spirit untroubled by anything." This is the formula of piety according to Lucretius.[42]

It is perhaps not inappropriate to return to the question with which I began: after having pursued the question of Foucault's interest in

---

minimizing (like that for objects inciting passions or fear); (c) a technique of turning away, like a mental "zapping," (the case for objects of love or sensations or disagreeable representations dismissed by the memory of past pleasures). We can see that these operations always act in "avoidance" rather than in "confrontation."

[40] Epicurus *Kuriai Doxai* 21.
[41] Epicurus *Letter to Menoeceus* 122.
[42] Lucretius *De Rerum Natura* 5.1203: . . . *pacata posse omnia mente tueri.*

Epicureanism, we may ask what interest Foucault's analysis holds for the reader of Epicurus. I would tend to speak of an indirect, or oblique, interest. These analyses allow us to question the doctrine of the Garden in an unconventional manner, free to glimpse that "the hermeneutics of the Epicurean subject" offers something that cannot be reduced to the totalizing interpretation put forward by Foucault.

11

Deleuze, Lucretius, and the Simulacrum of Naturalism

*Brooke Holmes**

La flèche du simulacra épicurien, filant droit jusqu'à nous,
fait naître, fait renaître, une "fantasmaphysique."

—Michel Foucault, "Theatrum Philosophicum"

The practice of philosophy for Gilles Deleuze was deeply embedded in the history of philosophy. Early in his career, he published a monograph on Hume, which was followed, after nearly a decade, by a series of focused studies on Nietzsche, Kant, Bergson, and Spinoza, before his "own" philosophical masterpieces, *Difference and Repetition* and *Logic of Sense*, appeared in the late 1960s. Deleuze's orientation toward the past owed much to his philosophical education—rigorous, and dominated by a canon of masters. Yet his approach was also studiously subversive. His decision to work on Hume at a time when his contemporaries were involved in the exegesis of the three H's (Hegel, Husserl, Heidegger) was the first step in his creation of a counter-canon in Western philosophy, loosely organized, at least initially, around a project that he called "reversing Platonism." His readings of those he elected to this

* I would like to thank the audience at the ACLA panel in Puebla where an earlier version of this paper was first presented. Will Shearin and Jerry Passannante generously contributed thoughtful feedback on the piece; Bridget Alsdorf, Wendy Belcher, and Janet Downie offered sound advice on the structure of the essay and its argument. Finally, I am grateful to Sam Galson for a stimulating conversation on Deleuze and Lucretius at an important stage in the development of my reading.

anti-Platonic tradition are strategic, unexpected, and, above all, creative.[1] Deleuze himself, in a twist on the philosophical pregnancy described by Socrates in Plato's *Symposium*, famously described his work in the history of philosophy in generative terms:

Mais, surtout, ma manière de m'en tirer à cette époque, c'était, je crois bien, de concevoir l'histoire de la philosophie comme une sorte d'enculage ou, ce qui revient au même, d'immaculée conception. Je m'imaginais arriver dans le dos d'un auteur, et lui faire un enfant, qui serait le sien et qui serait pourtant monstrueux. Que ce soit bien le sien, c'est très important, parce qu'il fallait que l'auteur dise effectivement tout ce que je lui faisais dire. Mais que l'enfant soit monstrueux, c'était nécessaire aussi, parce qu'il fallait passer par toutes sortes de décentrements, glissements, cassements, émissions secrètes qui m'ont fait bien plaisir.[2]

I suppose the main way I coped with it at the time was to see the history of philosophy as a sort of buggery or (it comes to the same thing) immaculate conception. I saw myself as taking an author from behind and giving him a child that would be his own offspring, yet monstrous. It was really important for it to be his own child, because the author had to actually say all I had him saying. But the child was bound to be monstrous too, because it resulted from all sorts of shifting, slipping, dislocations, and hidden emissions that I really enjoyed.[3]

Reception is, on this model, turned on its head: active, rather than passive, and unpredictably productive. The avowed fidelity to the text finds its complement in the slippages that ground the resemblance between the father and his "monstrous" child in difference and deviation. Deleuze's understanding of the history of philosophy as a field of dynamic genesis, together with his commitment to radicalizing philosophy's future through "untimely" interventions that incorporate readings of the past, makes him a promising resource for imagining how Epicureanism can become catalytic in the present.

Epicureanism was, in fact, one of the moments in the Western philosophical tradition that Deleuze returned to repeatedly over the course of

---

[1] On Deleuze as a historian of philosophy, see Hardt (1993), esp. xvii–xxi; Sellars (2007c); Tally (2010).
[2] Deleuze (1990b) 15.
[3] Trans. Joughin in Deleuze (1995) 6.

his career. Indeed, among his earliest essays is an article on Lucretius, published as "Lucrèce et le naturalisme" in *Les études philosophiques* in 1961. He considered the essay important enough to republish, with modifications and further elaboration, as "Lucretius and the Simulacrum" ("Lucrèce et le simulacre") in an appendix to the *Logic of Sense* in 1969 on the subject of the simulacrum in ancient philosophy. It serves there as the companion piece to a revised version of a reading of Plato's *Sophist* that first appeared in 1967 as "Renverser le platonisme," retitled "Plato and the Simulacrum" ("Platon et le simulacre") in the appendix.

The significance of the essay on Lucretius, however, has often been overshadowed by Deleuze's reading of Plato, valued for the perspective that it affords on the larger project of *Difference and Repetition* (1968). The emphasis on Plato has colored, in turn, understandings of the ancient simulacrum. In view of Deleuze's representation of Platonism as committed to "repressing the simulacra, keeping them completely submerged" (*de refouler les simulacres, de les maintenir enchaînés tout au fond*), the ancient simulacrum has come to be seen as a primarily subversive phenomenon, one capable of upsetting the entire project of representation initiated by Platonism from within.[4] Moreover, in the main body of the *Logic of Sense*, Deleuze treats the other great Hellenistic philosophical school, Stoicism, as the most important ancient challenge to Platonism and a strategic point of origin for his counter-canon.[5]

Nevertheless, Deleuze's essay on Lucretius makes large claims on behalf of Epicureanism and its famous Roman spokesman. For Deleuze, Epicurus, followed by Lucretius, is the first to identify naturalism as the object of philosophy, both in speculative and pragmatic terms, to the extent that he creates a philosophical system that embraces a cosmos of the diverse and fashions ethics as the practice of affirmation: it is with

---

[4] Deleuze (1990a) 257 [(1969) 296]. See esp. D. W. Smith (2006) on Deleuze's reading of the Platonic simulacrum; Flaxman (2009) on his reading of Plato more generally. (Plato, of course, does not use the [Latin] word *simulacrum*, which is Deleuze's translation of the Greek word *phantasma*. Lucretius uses *simulacrum*, as well as *imago*, *effigies*, and *figura*, to translate Epicurus's *eidōlon*.)

[5] See esp. the "Eighteenth Series of the Three Images of Philosophers" at Deleuze (1990a) 127–33 [(1969) 152–58] and the "Twentieth Series on the Moral Problem in Stoic Philosophy" at (1990a) 142–53 [(1969) 167–73]. On Deleuze and the Stoics, see the series of articles published by John Sellars ((1999); (2006); (2007a); (2007b)) and Bénatouïl (2003), esp. 20–23. The Stoics briefly resurface at Deleuze and Parnet (1987) 62–66 [(1977) 77–81]) but they are largely in the background of Deleuze's later work.

the Epicureans that "the real noble acts of philosophical pluralism begin" (*commencent les vrais actes de noblesse du pluralisme en philosophie*).[6] Moreover, in the years after the *Logic of Sense*, Lucretius reemerges at decisive points in Deleuze's work as a conceptual ally; his position at the head of a refashioned canon of empiricists was affirmed by Deleuze in interviews and essays throughout his life.[7] Lucretius thus occupies a critical point of reference for Deleuze's conceptualization of philosophical pluralism and an ethics of affirmation. If he is a less prominent figure than thinkers like Spinoza or Nietzsche, he is nevertheless a figure who proved remarkably persistent and polyform within Deleuze's œuvre. By returning to the early essay on Lucretius, we can get a better sense of what Deleuze drew from him.

At the same time, Deleuze's essay participates in an important, albeit relatively unrecognized, development in the history of Lucretius's twentieth-century reception. It has become conventional wisdom, especially in the Anglophone mainstream, that, as the twentieth century wore on, people stopped reading the *De Rerum Natura* for its philosophical or scientific import, effectively delivering it into the hands of poets and philologists.[8] Yet this account of the most recent phase of the poem's reception is misleadingly narrow. If we shift our attention to the rich tradition of French philosophy, and particularly the history and philosophy of science in late nineteenth- and twentieth-century France, a different picture of Lucretius's reception in the modern world emerges. Early in his career, for example, Henri Bergson undertook a translation of the *De Rerum Natura*, while ancient atomism serves as the primary vehicle

---

[6] Deleuze (1990a) 267 [(1969) 308]). It is worth noting that Foucault, in his long laudatory review of *Logic of Sense* and *Difference and Repetition*, makes Epicureanism and, more specifically, the "surface effects in which Epicureans take such pleasure," central to Deleuze's philosophical project in those two works ((1977) 169 [(1970) 888]). For more recent readings of Deleuze on Lucretius, see Berressem (2005); Goldberg (2009).

[7] Lucretius is invoked as a thinker of flux, for example, at Deleuze and Guattari (1987) 361–62, 489–90 [(1980) 446–47, 610–11], where the *clinamen* becomes newly important to the dynamics of the "molecular" level. For Lucretius (or Epicurus) in a canon of empiricists, see, e.g., Deleuze and Parnet (1987) 14–15 [(1977) 21]; Deleuze (2003) 138 [(2002) 191–92]. See further below, n. 69.

[8] This is the story told in Johnson (2000) 127–33 (although Johnson offers his own defense of Lucretius's relevance to science at 135–55). It is reprised in Gillespie and Mackenzie (2007), the twentieth-century coverage of Lucretius for the recent *Cambridge Companion*—although the authors do note the path-breaking Kennedy (2002)—and in reviews of that volume, e.g., Gowers (2008). Cf. Shearin (2009).

for tackling epistemological questions in science in Gaston Bachelard's *Les intuitions atomistiques.*[9] Later in the century, the Epicurean *clinamen* became a potent, if multivalent, figure for a number of French philosophers, including Jacques Lacan, Louis Althusser, and Jacques Derrida.[10] No doubt the most important intervention in this tradition has been Michel Serres' *The Birth of Physics*, a forceful defense of Lucretius's relevance to post-Newtonian physics that was first published in 1977.[11] Deleuze occupies a significant node in this network. His essay on Lucretius may have influenced Serres, as well as Lacan and Derrida, in their readings of the poem; it is Serres' Lucretius, in turn, who is heralded a decade later in *A Thousand Plateaus*, which Deleuze coauthored with Félix Guattari.[12] The essay in which Foucault memorably speculates that the twentieth century will one day be called "Deleuzian" positions Deleuze as the heir to nothing other than the Epicurean simulacrum.[13] The tradition of naturalism that Deleuze first locates in Lucretius has recently been taken up as a promising avenue for developing the critical edge of ecological philosophy.[14] From the vantage point of a Deleuzian Lucretius, the twentieth-century reception of the poem is not fated to serve as a cautionary tale about the entrenchment of "two cultures": the arts and the humanities, on the one hand, and the sciences, on the other. Rather, the *De Rerum Natura* becomes an important resource for reflecting on where physics and ethics intersect.

In this paper, I undertake a close reading of the essay on Lucretius as it appears in the *Logic of Sense*, tracking a Deleuzian-Epicurean-Lucretian naturalism as it emerges through Deleuze's own close reading of the poem.

---

[9] See Bergson (1959), first published in French as Bergson (1884), and Bachelard (1933). The divergent approaches of Bergson and Bachelard to ancient atomism are explored by Power (2006). In the *Cambridge Companion*, Gillespie and Mackenzie do touch on both Bergson's translation and references to Lucretius in *Creative Evolution* ((2007) 308–309, 320–21) without mentioning other French philosophers and historians of science.

[10] On Lacan and Derrida, see Lacan (1977) 63–64 and Derrida (1984), with Berressem (2005) 62–67; on Althusser, see Althusser (2006) 163–207, esp. 167–71. See also Goldberg (2009) 31–62, reviewing the impact of Lucretius and Epicureanism on twentieth-century French critical theory; Gigandet's essay in this volume considers the place of Epicureanism in Foucault's reading of ancient philosophy.

[11] Serres (2000), first published in French as Serres (1977). On Serres' interpretation of Lucretius, see Berressem (2005); Clucas (2005); Webb (2006).

[12] See Berressem (2005) 54–55.

[13] Foucault (1977), first published in French as Foucault (1970).

[14] Hayden (2008).

In the second half of the essay, I focus on the function of the Lucretian simulacrum, taking into consideration how it relates to the claims that Deleuze makes on behalf of the simulacrum in his reading of Plato.[15] Do the films and effluences of objects that bathe our senses at every moment according to the Epicurean doctrine of perception contribute to the larger project of "reversing Platonism"? If Deleuze establishes the autonomy of the simulacrum in Plato in order to trouble a philosophical system founded on a hierarchy of models and copies, what is at stake for him in appropriating the Epicurean simulacrum?

Much like Deleuze's redeployed Platonic simulacrum, the simulacrum described by Lucretius arises from a field of teeming difference. Yet insofar as it cannot itself be seen, it raises questions about how we come to grasp the world of difference and flux in which it participates— the very task we must undertake if we are to affirm this world instead of allowing ourselves to be seduced by myths of Being and the false infinite. Despite the dangers of phantasms, Deleuze does not argue that they must be stripped away. Rather, the reading of Lucretius that he enacts can be seen as a simulation of nature *qua* object of affirmation and pleasure. The essay on Lucretius thus shows Deleuze experimenting with the question of how naturalism and readings of naturalism can be strategically deployed in the service of an ethics driven by the "practical critique of all mystifications" (*la critique pratique de toutes les mystifications*), an ethics that Deleuze continued to develop over the course of his life.[16]

THE PHYSICS OF DIFFERENCE

Lucretius's achievement, Deleuze observes at the outset of "Lucretius and the Simulacrum," is to have identified what he calls "naturalism" as the speculative and pragmatic object of philosophy. These registers correspond to the domains of physics and ethics, respectively. The relationship between them is governed by the Epicurean logic of analogy, on the one hand, and the logic of gradation, on the other, with the latter

---

[15] Deleuze presumably wrote the Lucretius essay (first published in 1961) before the essay on Plato (first published in 1967), but much of the new material in the 1969 version of the Lucretius essay concerns the simulacrum.

[16] Deleuze (1990a) 279 [(1969) 324].

allowing, crucially, passage from one register to the other. By descending into the depths of physics, we discover that the phantasms and images that play across the surface are objects of pleasure rather than catalysts of disturbance and anxiety. Indeed, the practice of going beyond—or "decomposing," to adopt Deleuze's own language—the images that lead us astray in order to understand the conditions of their formation in difference and turbulence occupies a significant place in the didactic-ethical plot of Lucretius's poem. It is also central to Deleuze's own strategic articulation of naturalism's project.

Foremost among the mental obsessions that give rise to false philosophy is belief in the One or the Whole or Being, a trap into which many of the early Greek philosophers, on Epicurus's own assessment, fell. Against the myth of the One and the fears it generates about corruptibility and the encroachment of non-Being on Being, Deleuze places the Epicurean commitment to the diversity of the natural world, expressed at the level of the species, the individual, and the parts of a compound body; that diversity is also the basis for the deduction of the diversity of worlds.[17] The constitutive diversity of nature means that it cannot be understood as a totality—that is, a collection of bodies subject to a final and complete reckoning. It is, rather, a distribution: things exist, Deleuze writes, "one by one" (*une à une*) and not all at once; "nature is not attributive, but rather conjunctive" (*La Nature n'est pas collective, mais distributive*).[18] In place of identity and contradiction, Epicureanism substitutes resemblances and differences, compositions and decompositions. Everything is generated—and here Deleuze is quoting from the first book of the *De Rerum Natura* (1.633–34)—"out of connections, densities, shocks, encounters, concurrences, and motions" (*des connexions, des densités, des chocs, des rencontres, des mouvements*).[19]

Even a short précis gives a sense of the axiom at the heart of Deleuze's reading of Epicureanism: nature is power. The question becomes, then, *how* nature generates diversity and, eventually, how, out of diversity, resemblance develops. For the Epicurean line is not simply that the principle of the diverse is itself diverse, a demand that Deleuze sensibly

---

[17] Deleuze (1990a) 266 [(1969) 307–308]. On the critique of Being in Deleuze more generally, see D. W. Smith (2006) 108–11.

[18] Deleuze (1990a) 267 [(1969) 308–309].

[19] Ibid., 268 [(1969) 309].

dismisses as circular. Rather, naturalism outlines a structured principle of causality that engineers the production of the diverse. Such a principle works *inside* the various compositions and combinations that populate the cosmos. As a result, diversity emerges within a world that is also characterized by pattern and resemblance.[20]

One of the most important ways in which power operates is through the collision of atoms in the void. Such collisions are made possible by the *clinamen* or swerve, in the absence of which there would be nothing but a steady rain of sameness, what Michel Serres calls "laminar flow." From antiquity to the present, the *clinamen* has been read as one of the most tantalizing and yet problematic aspects of Epicureanism. For it seems to carve out a space exempt from physical determinism that has conventionally been allocated either to chance or to free will (the difficulty of conflating the two—why would a random swerve produce agency?—is often used to discount the theory). Deleuze acknowledges the line of interpretation that stresses contingency only to reject it, implicating the *clinamen* instead in a different kind of undecideability. The *clinamen* is not a secondary movement that supervenes on the behavior of the atom in order to divert it from its course: there is nothing accidental about it. Rather, it operates within the atom as its "original determination of the direction of [its] movement" (*la détermination originelle de la direction du mouvement de l'atome*), the differential within matter that ensures the atom's contact with other atoms, enabling the emergence of the diverse array of composite beings that populate the perceptible world.[21]

The swerve occurs, crucially for Deleuze, below the threshold of a moment of continuous time—that is, the smallest amount of time that an atom travels in a unique direction before being diverted through a collision. It happens, then, in a time that is "unassignable" (*inassignable*), Deleuze's translation of *incertus* in Lucretius's phrase *incerto tempore . . . incertisque locis* ("at an unassignable time and in unassignable places," 2.218–19). (It is worth noting that Deleuze drops Lucretius's reference to *loci*, focusing on the *clinamen* as it belongs to time, a decision symptomatic of his emphasis throughout the essay on the different temporalities created by the different speeds of things and the ethical fallout of

[20] Ibid., 268 [(1969) 310].
[21] Ibid., 269 [(1969) 311].

these differences.) The impossible-to-grasp time of the *clinamen* represents what Deleuze calls the *lex atomi*, the "irreducible plurality of causes or of causal series, and the impossibility of bringing causes together into a whole" (*la pluralité irréductible des causes ou des séries causales, l'impossibilité de réunir les causes en un tout*).[22] The causes, in other words, cannot be totalized. It is precisely by insisting on the independence of each causal series—rather than, as in the Stoics, the total unity of causes—that the Epicureans believe they escape the nets of determinism.

Before taking a closer look at the relationship of the *clinamen* to thresholds of time, it is worth stressing that the "unassignable" nature of the *clinamen* does not give rise to chancy, unpredictable, chaotic worlds. Rather, it contributes to the formation of worlds articulated by certain laws. There are limits, first, to the atom itself. The atom cannot be so large, for example, that it crosses a threshold beyond which it becomes sensible; such a requirement generates, in turn, limits on the shape of the atom, insofar as an infinite diversity of shapes would eventually result in the atom becoming sensible.[23] Moreover, atoms are limited by their shapes to certain kinds of combinations, a law that forecloses the possibility of a single infinite combination of atoms while prohibiting, too, the viability of each and every contingent combination.[24] The combinations that succeed in cohering with some stability are identified in Epicureanism as specific seeds or sperms, which serve as the building blocks of compound bodies. The seed, insofar as it underwrites predictability within classes of compounds, plays an important role in guaranteeing what Lucretius calls the "laws of nature" (*foedera naturae*), which Deleuze opposes to the "laws of fate" (*foedera fati*).

Lucretius's own interest in offering an atomist explanation for the regularities in nature responds not only to his desire to make the theory fit with what we can observe through the senses but also to the ethical

---

[22] Ibid., 270 [(1969) 312].

[23] The theoretical limit on the size of the atom was introduced by Epicurus (*Letter to Herodotus* 42, 55).

[24] The viability of compounds is renegotiated at the level of animals during the early phases of species production, to the extent that only those animals capable of feeding themselves and reproducing survive past the first phase of spontaneous generation: see *De Rerum Natura* 5.837–924, where Lucretius offers a long excursus on the laws of nature (*foedera naturae*).

significance of natural laws.[25] It is just such laws, after all, that Epicureanism holds up in order to destabilize the belief in wanton displays of the gods' power and the fears that such a belief generates.[26] Deleuze's interest in regularity appears, at first glance, to lie elsewhere. That is to say, he seems less concerned with ethics and more concerned with how regularity and especially resemblance emerge out of the nature of the diverse and the true infinite, in keeping with his commitment to explicating Epicureanism as a philosophy of Nature fundamentally opposed to the One or the Whole. In his reading, he stresses that the very identity of a compound body in Epicureanism is guaranteed not simply by the nature of a seed but also by the resources available to the ongoing renewal of the compound. These resources are defined first and foremost by their infinite plenitude: whereas the shape of the atom is limited, there is an unlimited number of atoms of a particular shape. The infinite bank of seeds guarantees that a compound body, while finite relative to the atom, endures and resembles itself over time. For at every moment, the compound is losing elements and gaining new ones of the same shape. The infinite number of atoms, besides making it probable that any compound body or world will easily find elements to replace those lost, ensures, too, the probability that such a compound—and compounds similar to it—will take shape in the first place.[27] At the same time, certain worlds are by their own composition particularly hospitable to certain compounds. What this means is that as the body loses its constituent elements, the milieu, like "a mother

---

[25] For references to limits in Lucretius and Epicureanism, see De Lacy (1969), esp. 106–107.

[26] See esp. *De Rerum Natura* 1.146–214.

[27] "The production of any composite entity presupposes that the different elements capable of forming it be themselves infinite in number. They would have no chance of coming together, if each of them, in the void, were the only member of its kind or limited in number. But since each one of them has an infinite number of similar elements, they do not produce a composite entity, without their equivalents having the same chance of renewing their parts, and even of reproducing a similar complex entity" ((1990a) 271) (*C'est que la production d'un composé quelconque suppose que les différents éléments capables de le former soient eux-mêmes en nombre infini; ils n'auraient aucune chance de se rencontrer si chacun d'eux, dans le vide, était seul de son espèce ou limité en nombre. Mais, puisque chacun d'eux à une infinité de pareils, ils ne produisent pas un composé sans que leurs pareils n'aient la même chance d'en renouveler les parties et même de reproduire un composé semblable,* (1969) 313–14). In Deleuze's exposition here we see the kernel of Nietzsche's eternal return, which would become central to his thinking.

suited for [that body's] reproduction" (*une mère apte à le reproduire*), readily supplies new ones. Deleuze's reading of Lucretius's Epicurean physics thus insists on both diversity *and* resemblance; flux *and* identity; infinity *and* finitude: nature is not random but a machine of sorts for producing and *re*-producing difference.[28]

Where do ethics belong in all this? As it turns out, Deleuze's reading of Epicurean physics, far from losing sight of the ethical thrust of Lucretius's poem, lays the groundwork for his interpretation of Epicurean ethics. For it is the task of grasping *how* resemblance emerges from difference and distinguishing what really is infinite from what only seems infinite that, for Deleuze, constitutes the central labor of Epicurean ethics. What are the conditions of possibility for such labor?

It is worth backing up here to Deleuze's most significant observation about the pivot of Epicureanism—namely, the atom itself. The atom, in Deleuze's definition, is "that which must be thought, and that which can only be thought . . . the absolute reality of what is perceived" (*ce qui doit être pensé, ce qui ne peut être que pensé . . . la réalité absolue de ce qui est perçu*).[29] The atom, in other words, cannot be understood apart from its status as an object of thought; thought, in turn, is not a way of looking at the real but is, rather, part of the real itself and its nature. Indeed, whereas Lucretius sometimes seems to relate the invisibility of the atom to the limitations of our vision, casting thought as the necessary supplement to our (flawed) senses,[30] Deleuze is adamant that the atom is essentially hidden on account of its own nature "and not the imperfection of our sensibility" (*et non de l'imperfection de notre sensibilité*).[31] Therefore, what can be seen and what can be thought, as well as what cannot be seen and what cannot be thought, are ontological categories, segmentations of the atomists' cosmos. Even more than the dualism of body and void, the cuts and thresholds that these categories create structure the Epicurean worldview on Deleuze's reading in a manner not unlike the

---

[28] See also Berressem (2005). For Berressem, what makes the Lucretius essay so crucial is that it first proposes a "nonlinear and dynamic philosophy," that is, "a 'chaosmos *avant la letter* [*sic*]'" (54). But Berressem does not sufficiently stress the relationship between limits and dynamism in Deleuze's reading.

[29] Deleuze (1990a) 268 [(1969) 310].

[30] E.g., *De Rerum Natura* 1.320–28 (referring to imperceptible changes at or near the atomic level rather than to the atom itself).

[31] Deleuze (1990a) 268 [(1969) 310].

division of what exists into corporeals and incorporeals within Stoicism (a division that is deeply significant in the *Logic of Sense*).[32] They emphasize discontinuities—creases or folds—within the real itself.

The beauty of the Epicurean method is to have developed strategies for passing between these domains according to the principle of analogy, on the one hand, and gradation, on the other. The principle of analogy lines up what is sensible, its sensible parts, and the minimum of what can be sensed with what can be thought, the parts that can be thought (i.e., the parts of the atom), and the minimum of what can be thought.[33] The minima act as thresholds that establish the domain of what cannot be grasped by the senses and by thought, respectively. The limits they set concern not only matter but also time, as we saw in relationship to the *clinamen*. The principle of analogy facilitates the second aspect of the Epicurean method, the principle of gradation. It is through this second principle that one passes between the different domains established by analogy, from the image of a compound object all the way down to the *clinamen*: "we go from the noetic to the sensible analogue, and conversely, through a series of steps conceived and established according to a process of exhaustion" (*on passe de l'analogue noétique à l'analogue sensible, et inversement, par une série de degrés conçus et établis d'après un procédé d'exhaustion*).[34]

The Epicurean method reaches its limits with the minimum of thinkable matter and, especially, thinkable time. Beyond such limits we are in the domain of the *clinamen*: recall that the differential embedded in every atom, by definition, lies beyond the limits of thought altogether. If we wish to preserve the ontological status of what can and cannot be thought, we must understand the statement that such a differential lies beyond the limits of thought to mean not simply that *we* fail to grasp the differential but that the differential participates in an irreducible plurality of causes. It follows that causes—and Nature more generally—cannot be totalized. This is why the *clinamen* is said to happen at a time that is "unassignable" (*inassignable*).[35]

---

[32] On Deleuze's reading of Stoic incorporeals, see Sellars (2007a) 178–79 n. 4, 204 n. 63.

[33] The schematism is emphasized in the diagram Deleuze offers of the analogy in the first published version of the article on Lucretius: see Deleuze (1961) 21.

[34] Deleuze (1990a) 268 [(1969) 310]. This sentence was added to the 1969 version of the essay.

[35] Deleuze (1990a) 270 [(1969) 312].

Nevertheless, the fact that the *clinamen* lies beyond the reach of thought is not simply an ontological truth. Such a state of affairs has powerful ethical implications, too, insofar as it discredits the belief in the One or the Whole. These ethical implications are unleashed when we move down the scale from sensible to noetic and beyond, passing to the limit. By undertaking this passage, then, we succeed in dissipating the One and the Whole as "obsessions of the mind, speculative forms of belief in the *fatum*, and the theological forms of a false philosophy" (*les manies de l'esprit, les formes spéculatives de la croyance au fatum, les formes théologiques d'une fausse philosophie*).[36] The movement along the scale is an act of thought, where thought is understood not as a domain somehow analogous to sensing, but as the *means* of establishing the limits of different domains. It fulfills, as such, the function of discrimination that we saw is fundamental to Deleuze's interpretation of the Epicurean ethical project. The act of thinking becomes critical in the Greek sense of *krisis*: thought performs a separation, a cut.

Such acts of discrimination do not just entail moving between different strata of the real. They lead, ultimately, to the core labor of Epicurean ethics, that is, the elimination of false beliefs, as Deleuze's mention of "obsessions of the mind" indicates. The work of dissipating such phantoms becomes clearer if we shift our attention to what falls below the threshold of sensible time—namely, the simulacrum.

The simulacrum is introduced by Deleuze rather abruptly to make sense of the most pernicious illusions targeted by Epicurean ethics: the illusion of infinite pleasure and the illusion of infinite punishment (related to the belief in the infinite duration of the body and the soul, respectively). Together these illusions create a suffocating, double fear: "the fear of dying when we are not yet dead, and also . . . the fear of not yet being dead once we already are" (*la peur de mourir quand nous ne sommes pas encore morts, mais aussi . . . la peur de ne pas être encore mort une fois que nous le serons déjà*).[37] Grasping the nature of the simulacrum becomes crucial to eliminating these illusions. What does it mean to conceptualize the simulacrum under these conditions? What is the

---

[36] Ibid., 267 [(1969) 309].

[37] Deleuze (1990a) 273 [(1969) 316]. On both illusions, Deleuze cites *De Rerum Natura* 1.110–19; 3.41–73, 978–1023; 6.12–19. On the illusion of infinite pleasure, see also 2.500–506 and the speech of Nature at 3.931–49.

status of its subversive potential? What is its place in a philosophy of affirmation?

THE LUCRETIAN SIMULACRUM

The simulacrum is the pillar of Lucretius's theory of perception and illusion in the fourth book of the *De Rerum Natura*. He argues there that compound bodies are continuously producing a stream of ephemeral, invisible emanations that he calls simulacra. These emanations, intercepted by our sensory organs, produce smell or hearing or vision, depending on the nature of the simulacrum. They are not perceived in and of themselves, being too fine, but are, rather, compressed together with other identical—or nearly identical—simulacra. The resulting aggregate conveys the nature of the object to the senses. The simulacrum thus facilitates a kind of touch—the unmediated sense par excellence— between the sensory organ and a sensible object in situations where the object in question remains at a distance from the percipient.

The natural terrain of the simulacrum is thus best seen as a space-between, and not only insofar as simulacra travel between compound bodies (*entre les surfaces*, as Foucault says in his *Critique* review). They also hover between the world of atoms and the world of bodies.[38] Deleuze stresses the shared ground of the atom and the simulacrum by pointing out that Epicurus describes them both as moving "as swiftly as thought."[39] But the simulacrum belongs to thought only because it falls below the threshold of the minimum sensible. It is defined not as an object proper to thought but as something that eludes the sensible.

The mediate and mediating position of the simulacrum means that it is no easy task to grasp its nature. To do so requires the mind to negotiate not just the relationship between identity and difference or between stability and flux but also the relationship between surface appearances and events that happen in the depths. The simulacrum is, on the one hand, generated by a compound body *qua* stable configuration of qualities that communicate "the atomic disposition without which it

---

[38] Foucault (1977) 169 [(1970) 888].
[39] Deleuze (1990a) 274 [(1969) 317].

would cease to be what it is" (*la disposition atomique sans laquelle il cesse d'être ce qu'il est*).[40] In fact, it is the very persistence of identity that guarantees the steady stream of simulacra responsible for producing the image, thereby enabling the body's representation to the senses as a discrete object. On the other hand, the simulacrum's relationship to the object is not that of a copy to its model. Indeed, like the simulacrum in Deleuze's reading of Plato's *Sophist*, it challenges the very notion of descent through the Idea and internal resemblance.[41] The Lucretian simulacrum is born, rather, out of the atomic quivering of the object; the emission of simulacra—that is, the body's continual reproduction of itself *qua* representation—is an expenditure of matter that necessitates a renewal of atoms from the infinite bank.[42] The simulacrum is not a degraded copy of a more robust model or an Idea, then, but a symptom of the constant re-production of the "model." The different types of simulacra, moreover, confuse distinctions between a body's surface and its depths: the simulacra of the surface are illuminated by light from the depths; emissions from the body's depths are transformed by passing through the surface.[43]

But perhaps the most significant feature of the simulacrum and its Janus-faced nature for Deleuze is its relationship to time and, more specifically, its remarkable speed. The swiftness of the simulacrum cannot be understood apart from the sometimes vast distances that it travels in bridging the object and the percipient. The simulacrum's transit through space contributes, from one perspective, to its transformation and deformation. If a stream of simulacra undergoes these changes collectively, the image itself is affected, as when a square tower appears round to the percipient standing at a distance, an appearance that results from the edges of the simulacra being worn down by their journey.[44] But we can also imagine an internal heterogeneity to the image,

---

[40] Ibid., 277 [(1969) 320–21].

[41] See esp. Deleuze (1990a) 256–58 [(1969) 295–98].

[42] See Downing (2006), likening the image captured by the camera to a Lucretian simulacrum: "it is . . . not a representation in any traditional sense (or in any Platonic sense of remove), but only in the sense in which the object itself is a representation, existing only insofar as it continuously represents itself in the form of continuously projected images" (24). See also Foucault (1977) 169–70 [(1970) 888]; D. W. Smith (2006) 108.

[43] Deleuze (1990a) 273–74 [(1969) 316–17].

[44] *De Rerum Natura* 4.353–63.

generated out of the particularity of each simulacrum's journey. Such heterogeneity seems inherent in the very language Lucretius uses to describe the simulacrum, as when he likens it to a particle of light or heat:

> Principio persaepe levis res atque minutis
> corporibus factas celeris licet esse videre.
> In quo iam genere est solis lux et vapor eius,
> propterea quia sunt e primis facta minutis
> quae quasi cuduntur perque aeris intervallum
> non dubitant transire sequenti concita plaga;
> suppeditatur enim confestim lumine lumen,
> et quasi protelo stimulatur fulgere fulgur.
> Quapropter simulacra pari ratione necesse est
> inmemorabile per spatium transcurrere posse
> temporis in puncto, primum quod parvola causa
> est procul a tergo quae provehat atque propellat,
> quod superest, ubi tam volucri levitate ferantur. . . .
> (*De Rerum Natura* 4.183–95)

In the first place you may very often see that things light and made of minute elements are rapid. An example of these is the sun's light and his heat, because they are made of minute elements, which are as it were beaten with knocks, and do not hesitate to pass through the intervening air when struck by the blow of that which follows: for instantly light comes up behind light, and flash is pricked on by flash, as if in a long team [of oxen]. Therefore the simulacra in like manner must be able to run through space inexpressible by words in a moment of time, first because there is a very small impulse far behind which carries them on and pushes them on, also because they move with so swift a lightness. . . . (trans. Rouse-Smith)

Consulting the original Latin phrases "light comes up behind light" (*suppeditatur . . . lumine lumen*) and "flash is pricked on by flash" (*stimulatur fulgere fulgur*), we see that the nouns *lumen* ("light") and *fulgur* ("flash") are not only doubled by the verb but also undergo a change of case—and hence, a change of letters (that is, literally, atoms)—as they deviate from the nominative, that is, the *naming*, form. The poem thus enacts the declension of the simulacrum as it is propelled through the air as part of a series of effluences. Lucretius's Latin seems to anticipate Deleuze's rejection of a "naked" model of repetition—the simple repetition of the

Same—in favor of a form of repetition that incorporates perversion, deviation, and displacement.[45]

Nevertheless, for all the accidents of origin and transit, "always, the property of being related to an object subsists" (*toujours subsiste la propriété d'être rapporté à un objet*) in the simulacrum.[46] The minor deviations that we can imagine the individual simulacrum undergoes are not perceived by us. They are, rather, submerged into the single aggregate image. Moreover, given that the simulacrum moves too quickly to be registered within the minimum of continuous sensible time, its aleatory journey between surfaces is swallowed up by the moment it takes the image to arrive. As Lucretius asks, speaking of the reflection of stars in a body of water, "do you not see how, in an instant, the image falls from the borders of heaven to the borders of earth?" (*iamne vides igitur quam puncto tempore imago / aetheris ex oris in terrarum accidat oras?*)[47] All of this is to say that when we see, we are not seeing the simulacrum. We are seeing, rather, *because* of the simulacrum or, to be even more precise, because of the rapid succession of many simulacra, which together produce an effect: the image. The image is not, of course, an image of the simulacrum itself, nor does it communicate the object as a cluster of atoms in flux. It is the nature of the image, rather, to conceal the mechanisms of its own production, as well as the instability of the object to which it belongs—in short, to mask the teeming atomic world in which everything comes into being out of "connections, densities, shocks, encounters, concurrences, and motions." If the simulacrum fully participates in a world between surfaces, its nature leads it to occlude the dynamics of that world.

In "Plato and the Simulacrum," Deleuze casts the simulacrum as the subversive imposter, the sophist whose resemblance to the original is founded on difference, rather than being properly noetic, spiritual, and internal. If the aim of Platonism is to track down the simulacrum and drive it from the domain of representation, the Deleuzian counterinsurgency undertakes the simulacrum's liberation, allowing it to rise to the surface (*monter à la surface*) and exercise its rights among icons and

[45] On a "naked" model of repetition, see D. W. Smith (2006) 111–12.
[46] Deleuze (1990a) 274 [(1969) 317].
[47] *De Rerum Natura* 4.214–15; see also 4.199–202.

copies.[48] In erupting on the scene of representation, the simulacrum destabilizes the very ground of representation, forcing the disclosure of a world in which every cave reveals yet another cave, "the intractability of masks and the impassibility of signs" (*l'inaltérabilité des masques, l'impassibilité des signes*).[49]

Is there an echo of Plato in Deleuze's reading of Lucretius or vice-versa? The simulacrum of Lucretius belongs, of course, to a quite different system. The very coupling of the Platonic "simulacrum" and the Lucretian simulacrum is Deleuze's own ingenious juxtaposition of concepts that do not seem, at first glance, to be closely related, a juxtaposition informed by a twentieth-century French fascination with the simulacrum that was catalyzed in part by the work of Pierre Klossowski.[50] For one thing, in Plato the "simulacrum" (*phantasma*) exists among other images and representations, as opposed to making the image possible, as in Lucretius. Its coordinates are, naturally, Platonic, rather than Epicurean, with the result that it is implicated in a set of problems specific to Platonism (e.g., the Idea and its copies, as opposed to nested times). Finally, the "simulacrum" in Plato bears an unambiguous relationship to the false that Deleuze seizes upon as a point of reversal or, rather subversion. The relationship between the simulacrum and illusion is, however, more complicated in Lucretius, complicating, in turn, Deleuze's appropriation of the Lucretian simulacrum.

Yet certain aspects of the simulacrum persist across Deleuze's readings of Plato and Lucretius: its challenge to a system based on models and copies; its production of resemblance as an effect; its emergence from a field that is characterized in the Plato essay as involving "huge dimensions, depths, and distances that the observer cannot master" (*de grandes dimensions, des profondeurs et des distances que l'observateur ne peut pas dominer*), with that failure of mastery an integral part of the impression of resemblance, much as is the case for the Epicurean simulacrum.[51] Do these resonances suggest that the task in the Lucretius essay is to bring the simulacrum to the surface, as it is in the Plato

---

[48] See Deleuze (1990a) 261–62 [(1969) 301–302].
[49] Ibid., 264 [(1969) 305].
[50] See D. W. Smith (2006) 89–90. Deleuze (1990a) 280–300 [(1969) 325–50] is a reading of Klossowski's simulacrum.
[51] Deleuze (1990a) 258 [(1969) 298].

essay? How is this task transformed by being situated within a philosophy of affirmation, rather than enacting the dismantling of a philosophy of illusions of Being from within?

What makes the simulacrum in Deleuze's reading of Lucretius so intriguing is its ambiguous relationship to illusion and delusion and, more specifically, the fact that it is complicit with illusions that are, as much for Deleuze as for Epicurus, subversive of philosophy's proper end: pleasure. We have seen how the simulacrum, in slipping below the threshold of sensible matter and sensible time, conceals the conditions under which resemblance is produced out of diversity and flux, with the unhappy result that we mistake the stability of the image for the reality of the object. The potentially negative ethical implications of the simulacrum are most acute, however, if we turn to a third class of simulacra (in addition to simulacra of the surface and those of the depths)—namely, phantasms that exist virtually independent of any real object. The danger of these phantasms is that they command and feed psychic attachments that are deeply problematic.

The psychic hold exercised by such phantasms is suggested by their classification into three types: theological, oneiric, and erotic. They arise in various ways. Some are generated of their own accord out of air, rather than issuing from objects; they produce the impression of faces of giants and mountains in the sky.[52] Others are too fine to be perceived by the eyes. These phantasms, becoming entangled upon colliding mid-air, strike the mind (*animus*) directly, creating the illusion of Centaurs and Scyllas and the three-headed dog Cerberus.[53] It is in the context of these last images that Deleuze introduces the very Epicurean problem of desire. Desire invests the fact that we are constantly bathed in and battered

[52] *De Rerum Natura* 4.129–42.

[53] *De Rerum Natura* 4.722–48. Deleuze's account of these two classes ("theological" and "oneiric") draws on different aspects of Lucretius's discussion. Deleuze explains cloud-images in terms of existing simulacra that intersect in the air and discusses dream images that seem to dance and speak (see 4.788–801) in the class of theological (rather than oneiric) simulacra. Deleuze compares Lucretius's account of the origins of religious belief to that offered by Hume ((1990a) 275–76 [(1969) 319]), acknowledging Hume's widely known debt to Lucretius in the domain of theology but also perhaps suggesting a relationship between the Lucretius essay and his book on Hume (Deleuze (1953)), where he studies Hume's analysis of the intersection between the raw data of perception and the organizing forces of the human mind. On Deleuze's reading of Hume, see Bell (2009) and Boundas's introduction to Deleuze (1991).

by emanations with new meaning. For if objects are continuously shedding effluences and if we are, as a result, always immersed in these emanations, seeing becomes a motivated act, rather than a passive experience: we see what we pay attention to, neglecting some simulacra to focus on others. The force of attention is even stronger in the realm of imagination, where the effluences available to the mind are virtually limitless. And it is strongest when it comes to erotic simulacra, which generate images that sustain an impossible-to-satisfy desire.[54] These illusions capture us through our own fears and desires: the more we are governed by the hope of infinite pleasure and the fear of eternal punishment, the more we focus on those phantasms that confirm and strengthen our expectations. Yet these phantasms can only arise because of the nature of simulacra, which, Deleuze concludes, "*produce the mirage of a false infinite in the images which they form*" (*produisent le mirage d'un faux infini dans les images qu'ils forment*).[55] It is because the simulacrum is invisible that we pursue the illusions of infinite pleasure and infinite punishment, embracing the false infinite and all the myths it entails.

Given these conditions, it is hard to believe that the simulacrum functions as an instrument of "demystification" in the service of the overarching aims of naturalism. Indeed, one critic has recently voiced the suspicion that, in tracing the mirage of the false infinite to the simulacrum, Deleuze "allows Plato back in, blaming the simulacra as a false version of the sensible," as if the simulacrum's capacity for subversion loses its appeal when what is at stake is a philosophy that Deleuze wishes to endorse.[56]

But the situation is not so straightforward. In the closing section of the essay, Deleuze circles back to naturalism's contributions to philosophical pluralism while shifting into a hortatory mode. What naturalism offers, he argues, is an ethical strategy that prevents the illusions that sustain bitterness and torment "by means of the rigorous distinction of the true infinite and the correct appreciation of times nested one within

---

[54] Deleuze (1990a) 276 [(1969) 319–20].

[55] Ibid., 277 [(1969) 321], emphasis in original.

[56] Goldberg (2009) 38. Goldberg thus concludes that Deleuze understands Lucretius as rejecting the phantasm. But Deleuze does not reject the phantasm, nor does he see Lucretius as rejecting it, as I argue above.

the other, and of the passages to the limit which they imply" (*par la distinction rigoureuse du véritable infini et la juste appréciation des temps emboîtés les uns dans les autres, avec les passages à la limite qu'ils impliquent*).[57] Such a strategy mobilizes critical thought in order to appropriate it for the project of demystification. What role does the simulacrum play here?

Earlier we saw how critical thought is able to demarcate the various levels that structure Epicurean views of the real and to navigate between them. The Epicurean method uses the critical capacities of thought to compose and decompose the image, moving from the thinkable to the sensible and back. By dismantling the image, thought discloses the vertiginous field of difference, the "profound subsoil," out of which the image—and indeed, every compound body, every world—is generated and, hence, the genuine machine-like workings of resemblance and identity (i.e., the "highly-structured principle of causality" discussed earlier).[58] This profound subsoil is the terrain of the simulacrum. We can thus understand the process of disclosing this underworld as a specifically Epicurean strategy for bringing the simulacrum to the surface. Such a strategy does not so much liberate the simulacrum from the nether regions of Platonism but, rather, frees it from the space-time below the threshold of sensing. For it is precisely because the simulacrum is too rapid and too ephemeral to be captured by the senses that it gives rise to myths and indeed to the most disturbing myths of infinite pleasure and infinite pain. The surfacing of the simulacrum in thought can be seen, accordingly, as integral to Epicurean methods for breaking the myth's hold over us.

These are not, however, exactly the terms in which Deleuze himself expresses the demystification promised by naturalism. The last pages of the essay describe the philosophical project ushered in by Epicurus and Lucretius in terms of a denunciation of "everything that is sadness, everything that is the cause of sadness, and everything that needs sadness to exercise its power" (*tout ce qui est tristesse, tout ce qui est cause de*

---

[57] Deleuze (1990a) 277–78 [(1969) 322]. The exhortation is absent from the earlier version of "Lucrèce et le naturalisme," which begins its closing movement, following the discussion of the simulacra (itself expanded in the 1969 version), thus: "Le faux infini est principe du trouble de l'âme" ((1961) 27; cf. (1969) 322).

[58] On the phrase "profound subsoil," see Deleuze (1990a) 263 [(1969) 304], citing from Nietzsche's *Beyond Good and Evil* (§289).

tristesse, tout ce qui a besoin de la tristesse pour exercer son pouvoir)—in short, the false infinite—and a celebration of nature as a source of joy and value.[59] Deleuze frames the accomplishment of naturalism, then, as the transformation of thought and sensibility into affirmation and the refusal to allow the negative to speak in the name of philosophy.

Yet, how are these denunciations and affirmations effected, if not through a process of discrimination? For it is discrimination that traces the proper cuts in reality, allowing us to apprehend not only the sensible and what falls below it but also what can be thought and what falls below the threshold of thought. In fact, by decomposing the image, we are led to what looks like a change of sensibility.

Alors les phantasmes eux-mêmes deviennent des objets de plaisir, y compris dans l'effet qu'ils produisent et qui apparaît enfin tel qu'il est: un effet de vitesse et de légèreté, qu'on rattache à l'interférence extérieure d'objets très divers, comme un condensé de successions et de simultanéités.[60]

Phantasms then become objects of pleasure, even in the effect which they produce, and which finally appears such as it is: an effect of swiftness or lightness which is attached to the external interference of very diverse objects—as a condensation of successions and simultaneities.[61]

---

[59] Deleuze (1990a) 279 [(1969) 323]. Such an affirmation for Deleuze requires bracketing the tragic account of the plague with which the *De Rerum Natura* closes: see Deleuze (1990a) 363–64 n.30 [(1969) 323]; see also Deleuze and Parnet (1987) 15 [(1977) 22]. Goldberg critiques what he sees as Deleuze's failure to admit death as a refusal to recognize the Epicurean distinction between the infinity of, say, an atom and the infinity of an individual life ((2009) 39–40). Yet is this what Deleuze resists at this moment? At no point does he deny Lucretius's central claim that our lives are finite; indeed, he embraces it. What he seems to resist, rather, for better or for worse, is the image of torment with which the poem closes, preferring to privilege in his own reading the image of the serene Epicurean who has come to affirm the true infinite.

[60] Deleuze (1969) 322.

[61] Trans. Lester in Deleuze (1990a) 278. See also Foucault (1977) 171, who sees in this passage the role of Epicureanism in opening up "a metaphysics freed from its original profundity as well as from a supreme being, but also one that can conceive of the phantasm in its play of surfaces without the aid of models, a metaphysics where it is no longer a question of the One Good, but of the absence of God and the epidermic play of perversity" (. . . *une métaphysique affranchie de la profondeur originaire comme de l'étant suprême, mais capable de penser le fantasme hors de tout modèle et dans le jeu des surfaces; une métaphysique où il n'est plus question de l'Un-Bon, mais de l'absence de Dieu, et des jeux épidermiques de la perversité,* (1970) 889).

Deleuze's claim here is challenging. What does it mean, after all, for an effect to appear "just as it is" (*tel qu'il est*)? It is axiomatic in Epicureanism that the senses never lie. But that is not to say that things appear just as they are (the round tower is not really round, although Epicurus infamously pronounced the sun to be the size it appears to us): to perception we must add reason. Deleuze seems to suggest something similar, insofar as naturalism leads us to grasp the mechanics behind the effect of the phantasm. But he perhaps goes even further in suggesting that naturalism leads us to sense differently, as though the phantasm itself can put us in touch with the physics of the simulacrum, thereby becoming an object of pleasure. Similarly, the rigorous pursuit of the Epicurean method to its limits discloses the *clinamen* as a differential that cannot be thought. The passage to the limits causes us, in turn, to think differently. As Deleuze defines it at the end of the essay, naturalism is simply the "thought of an infinite sum, all of the elements of which are not composed at once" (*la pensée d'une somme infinie dont tous les éléments ne se composent pas à la fois*), as well as "the sensation of finite compounds which are not added up as such with one another" (*la sensation de composés finis qui ne s'additionnent pas comme tels les uns avec les autres*).[62]

What we find, then, is that while thought and sensation have objects that are specific to them—the atom and the image, respectively—there are different modes of relating to these objects. Either one mistakes the image for the representation of a false reality, motivated by desire and fear, or one affirms it as an effect of the simulacrum and the positivity of the finite. In the same way—although Deleuze does not develop this line of thinking very far—one is either led astray by the effects of the *clinamen* to believe in free will or one comes to affirm it as a differential within matter that cannot be thought. In both cases, a selection takes place.

How should we understand this selection? In the essay on Plato, there is also a selection of sorts, at least insofar as when we affirm the rights of the simulacrum, we allow it to topple the system of models and icons and copies from within, endorsing its power at the expense of its rivals. Yet, at the same time, the fundamentally subversive role of the

---

[62] Deleuze (1990a) 279 [(1969) 323].

simulacrum, within the logic of Deleuze's reading, causes it to undermine selection altogether, to the extent that selection is understood as the Platonic project of differentiating true claimants to the Idea from false pretenders.[63] In the Lucretius essay, by contrast, selection has a more positive function, which must be understood within the specific terms of naturalism and its critical method of traversing the real through analogy and gradation. To select *is* to affirm the true infinite, on the one hand, and the finitude of the sensible, on the other; it is, at the same time, to denounce the spirit of the negative and the phantasms that it entails (the One and the Whole, the myths of infinite pain and pleasure).[64] Understood from this perspective, the transformation of sensibility and thought brought about by naturalism always involves an active element. If the simulacrum occupies a privileged position in this process it is because Deleuze follows Epicurus and Lucretius in making the double illusion of infinite pain and pleasure the single greatest threat to pleasure. Yet it is also important to see how the process of demystification that unfolds through selection is, in the end, more ambitious than the summoning up of the simulacrum.

Naturalism, then, is a method of critique. But it is also an image or phantasm of sorts itself.[65] For to counter the illusion of the false infinite, a philosophy of pluralism must hold forth a counter-image to be affirmed by thought in the service of joy and pleasure.[66] In the Lucretius essay,

---

[63] Deleuze (1990a) 262–63 [(1969) 302–303]. See also Flaxman (2009) 22–23.

[64] Goldberg (2009) 39–40 neglects this context when he accuses Deleuze of nearly reintroducing Platonic distinctions between true and false.

[65] See Foucault (1977) 178: "Thinking . . . requires the release of a phantasm in the mime" (*Penser . . . ce serait effectuer le fantasme dans le mime*, (1970) 894). Yet thought is also, as Foucault insists, an event.

[66] The idea of the image or phantom to be held forth recurs in the main text of the *Logic of Sense*: "The logic of sense is inspired in its entirety by empiricism. Only empiricism knows how to transcend the experiential dimensions of the visible without falling into Ideas, and how to track down, invoke, and perhaps produce a phantom at the limit of a lengthened or unfolded experience" ((1990a) 20) (*La logique du sens est tout inspirée d'empirisme; mais précisément il n'y a que l'empiricisme qui sache dépasser les dimensions expérimentales du visible sans tomber dans les Idées, et traquer, invoquer, peut-être produire un fantôme à la limite d'une expérience allongée, dépliée*, (1969) 32). Here, however, the image is put forth in the context of another philosophical legacy that Deleuze saw as critical to the reversal of Platonism—namely, Stoicism. He contrasts Stoicism with Epicureanism several times in the text: see esp. (1990a) 183–84 [(1969) 214–15], 335–36 n. 4 [(1969) 16 n. 4], 363 n. 29 [(1969) 320 n. 29]. The major difference between the two philosophical systems suggested by these references is that the Stoics have a more

Deleuze sees philosophy as useful precisely because it is committed to setting forth "the image of the free man" (*l'image d'un homme libre*).[67] The claim that philosophy has as its aim demystification through critique and the holding-forth of the image of the free man is (re)affirmed by Deleuze in his 1962 book on Nietzsche, where Lucretius is located at the origins of philosophy *qua* art of critical thinking and ethical affirmation and where the idea of affirmation as a form of selecting against the negative is a crucial thread.[68] In *Expressionism in Philosophy: Spinoza*, first published in 1968 (as *Spinoza et la problème de l'expression*), Deleuze locates Spinoza, too, in the tradition of naturalism, recognizing that he is also committed to denouncing all myths and mystifications. Like Lucretius, Spinoza "sets the image of a positive Nature against the uncertainty of the gods" (*dresse l'image d'une Nature positive contre l'incertitude des dieux*) as part of a project of forming an ethics around the image of a free man.[69] Whereas in Epicureanism, the image of the free man is actually a simulacrum that reaches us from the space "between worlds" (*intermundium*) where the gods reside in eternal bliss,[70] for Deleuze such an image is the product of naturalism itself.

It is precisely because the power of such an image to eliminate myth depends on naturalism that naturalism must be systematically renewed. "If philosophy's critical task is not actively taken up in every epoch," Deleuze writes in *Nietzsche and Philosophy*, "philosophy dies

---

developed theory of the event, which climbs to the surface not so much as a phantasm but as the incorporeal limit of all possible ideality ((1990a) 7 [(1969) 17]). The Stoics thus appear more suited to the project of the *Logic of Sense*. The phantasm that dominates the latter series in the book is represented as an event that is only "a little like" Epicurean envelopes and emanations ((1990a) 217 [(1969) 253]). But cf. Foucault (1977) [1970], who reads Epicureanism and Stoicism as fully complementary in the *Logic of Sense*.

[67] Deleuze (1990a) 278 [(1969) 322].

[68] Deleuze (1983) 106–107 [(1962) 121–22].

[69] Deleuze (1992) 270–71 [(1968) 249–50]. See also Deleuze (1995) 6 [(1990b) 14] "I see a secret link between Lucretius, Hume, Spinoza, and Nietzsche, constituted by their critique of negativity, their cultivation of joy, the hatred of interiority, the externality of forces and relations, the denunciation of power . . . and so on" (*et entre Lucrèce, Hume, Spinoza, Nietzsche, il y a pour moi un lien secret constitué par la critique du négatif, la culture de la joie, la haine de l'intériorité, l'extériorité des forces et des relations, la dénonciation du pouvoir . . . , etc.*). On the tradition of Lucretian Naturalism in Deleuze, see also Hayden (2008), 25–29.

[70] See *De Rerum Natura* 6.76–77, where Lucretius suggests that we receive simulacra that emanate from the gods (located in the *intermundium*) as positive images of tranquility that serve as models for the Epicurean sage. See also 3.14–30.

and with it die the images of the philosopher and the free man" (*Si la besogne critique de la philosophie n'est pas activement reprise à chaque époque, la philosophie meurt, et avec elle l'image du philosophe et l'image de l'homme libre*).[71] Deleuze's reading of Lucretius enacts just such a renewal to counter the negative force of myth and the false infinite. In so doing, it mimics the ethical labor of the *De Rerum Natura* itself. For Lucretius knew well that we never simply *see* the true infinite. Indeed, the pressures of culture and our own natures tend to keep us from seeing what we need to see if we are to be happy. If we wish to embrace the image, disentangled from fear and impossible desire, as an object of affirmation and a source of ethical pleasure, we need Epicureanism, which is to say we need articulations and *readings* of Epicureanism. Lucretius thus uses poetry to generate in the mind of his reader "the clear light with which you might gaze into the depths of hidden things."[72] And indeed, the *De Rerum Natura* has persisted as the catalyst of just such ethical transformations, read and reread with ever-renewed urgency in the centuries since its rediscovery, as it is by Deleuze himself.

Readings, of course, are never simply repetitions. In a basic sense, this axiom is illustrated by Deleuze's encounters with Lucretius over the course of his career. While he did not offer another sustained reading of the *De Rerum Natura*—from the late 1960s on, he shifted away from readings of other philosophers—he came back time and again to Lucretius, producing ever shifting images of his philosophical pluralism.[73] The poem thus functions in his writings not as a static object but as a dynamic field of generative potential, catalyzing at each encounter new strategies for conceptualizing the diverse and the multiple.

More important, the images of naturalism that readings of Lucretius produce are never copies of an Epicurean original: Deleuze, that is, does not reproduce Lucretius's poem as the Same. Rather, beneath the threshold of the text of his essay lies a space "between surfaces" that troubles both the notion of an original faithfully reproduced at the moment of

---

[71] Deleuze (1983) 107 [(1962) 122].

[72] *De Rerum Natura* 1.144–45. See Holmes (2005) 575–77.

[73] See above, n. 7, on Lucretius in Deleuze's later work. As D. W. Smith (2006) 116 observes, the simulacrum falls out of Deleuze's philosophical vocabulary after the publication of *Difference and Repetition* in 1968; see also D. W. Smith (2009). But cf. M. Cooper (2002) for the importance of the Epicurean-Lucretian simulacrum to Deleuze's later work on the image.

its reception and the notion of a reading faithful to the original text. What we encounter as readers of Deleuze's reading of Lucretius is an image of thought as the dazzling effect of the dynamics of thought triggered by the Epicurean impulse. In reading the essay, we enact, in turn, transmission as another round of repetition and perversion. Naturalism erupts once again within a present where it remains as necessary as ever.

Bibliography

Editions and Commentaries on Classical Texts

Arnim, J. von, ed. (1893–96) *Dionis Prusaensis Quem Vocant Chrysostomum Quae Extant Omnia*. 2 vols. (Berlin).

Bailey, C., ed. (1947) *Titi Lucreti Cari De Rerum Natura*. 3 vols. (Oxford).

Benner, A. R., and F. H. Fobes, eds. (1949) *Alciphron, Aelian, Philostratus—Letters*. (Cambridge, Mass.).

Beroaldo, F. (1487) *Commentarii in Propertium*. (Bologna).

———. (1493) *Commentationes in Suetonium Tranquillum*. (Bologna).

Boissevain, U., ed. (1895–1901) *Cassii Dionis Cocceiani Historiarum Romarum Quae Supersunt*. 3 vols. (Berlin).

Brown, R. D. (1987) *Lucretius on Love and Sex: A Commentary on* De Rerum Natura IV. (Leiden).

Campbell, G. (2003) *Lucretius on Creation and Evolution: A Commentary on* De Rerum Natura 5.772–1104. (Oxford).

Ciapponi, L., ed. (1995) *Filippo Beroaldo, Annotationes Centum*. (Binghamton).

Conche, M., ed. (2009) *Épicure, Lettres et Maximes*. 8th ed. (Paris).

Dindorf, W., ed. (1829) *Aristides*. 3 vols. (Berlin).

Domingo-Forasté, D., ed. (1994) *Claudius Aelianus, Epistulae et Fragmenta*. (Stuttgart).

Einarson, B., and P. De Lacy, eds., trans. (1967) *Plutarch's Moralia*, vol. 14 (1086c–1147a). (Cambridge, Mass.).

Fotheringham, J. K., ed. (1923) *Eusebii Pamphili Chronici Canones*. (London).

Fowler, D. P. (2002) *Lucretius on Atomic Motion: A Commentary on* De Rerum Natura 2.1-332. (Oxford).

Heck, E., and A. Wlosok, eds. (2007) *Lactantius Divinarum Institutionum Libri Septem*. Fasc. 2: *Libri III et IV*. (Berlin).

Henry, W. Benjamin., ed. and trans. (2009) *Philodemus, On Death*. (Atlanta).

Hett, W. S., trans. (1936) *Aristotle, On the Soul; Parva Naturalia; On the Breath*. (Cambridge, Mass.).

Heubner, H., ed. (1983) *P. Cornelii Taciti Libri Qui Supersunt*. Tom. 1: *Ab Excessu Divi Augusti*. (Stuttgart). [Annales]

Hicks, R. D., trans. (1925) *Diogenes Laertius, Lives of Eminent Philosophers*. 2 vols. (Cambridge, Mass.).

Horsfall, N., ed. and trans. (1989) *Cornelius Nepos: A Selection, Including the Lives of Cato and Atticus*. (Oxford).

Hude, C., ed. (1926) *Herodoti Historiae*. 2 vols. (Oxford).

Indelli, G. (1988) *Filodemo, L'ira*. (Naples). [La scuola di Epicuro 5].

Inwood, B., and L. P. Gerson, trans. and eds. (1994) *The Epicurus Reader: Selected Writings and Testimonia*. (Indianapolis).

Klaerr, R., ed. and trans. (1985) *Préceptes de mariage* in J. Defradas, J. Hani, R. Klaerr, eds. and trans., *Plutarque, Oeuvres Morales, Tome II: Traité 10-14* (Paris), 146–66.

Klingner, F., ed. (1959) *Q. Horati Flacci Opera.* (Leipzig).

Klotz, A., ed. (1927) *C. Iuli Caesaris Commentarii.* Vol. 3. (Leipzig).

Konstan, D. et al., eds. (1998) *Philodemus, On Frank Criticism.* (Atlanta).

Körte, A., ed. (1890) *Metrodori Epicurei Fragmenta.* (Leipzig).

Long, A. A., and D. N. Sedley. (1987) *The Hellenistic Philosophers.* 2 vols. (Cambridge).

Malcovati, E., ed. (1972) *L. Annaei Flori Quae Exstant.* 2nd ed. (Rome).

Marcovich, M., ed. (1999) *Diogenis Laertii Vitae Philosophorum.* (Stuttgart).

Marshall, P. K., ed. (1977) *Cornelius Nepos, Vitae cum Fragmentis.* (Munich).

———, ed. (1968) *A. Gellii Noctes Atticae.* (Oxford).

Marx, F., ed. (1915) *A. Cornelii Celsi Quae Supersunt.* (Leipzig). [Corpus Medicorum Latinorum, vol. 1].

Mayhoff, C., ed. (1892–1909) *C. Plini Secundi Naturalis Historiae Libri XXXVII.* (Leipzig).

Pease, A. S., ed. (1920–23) *M. Tullii Ciceronis De Divinatione.* 2 vols. (Urbana).

———, ed. (1955–58) *M. Tulli Ciceronis De Natura Deorum.* 2 vols. (Cambridge, Mass.).

Pelling, C. B. R., ed. (1988) *Plutarch, Life of Antony.* (Cambridge).

Pio, Giambattista, ed. (1511) *Lucretius, De Rerum Natura.* (Bologna).

———, ed. (1514) *Lucretius, De Rerum Natura,* 2nd ed. (Paris).

Pohlenz, M., and R. Westman, eds. (1959) *Plutarchi Moralia.* Vol. 6.2. (Leipzig).

Reynolds, L. D., ed. (1965) *Ad Lucilium Epistulae Morales.* (Oxford).

———. (1977) *Diologorum Libri Duodecim.* (Oxford).

———. (1998) *M. Tulli Ciceronis De Finibus Bonorum et Malorum Libri Quinque.* (Oxford).

Ribbeck, O., ed. (1897–98) *Scaenicorum Romanorum Poesis Fragmenta.* Vol. 2. 3rd ed. (Leipzig).

Rossbach, O., ed. (1910) *T. Livi Periochae Omnium Librorum.* (Leipzig).

Rouse, W. H. D., ed. and trans., (1992) *Lucretius, De Rerum Natura.* 2nd ed. Revised by M. F. Smith. (Cambridge, Mass).

Russell, D. A., ed. (1964) *"Longinus," On the Sublime.* (Oxford).

Sbordone, F., ed. (1947) *Adversus Sophistas.* (Naples).

Schmidt, M., ed. (1867) *Hesychii Alexandrini Lexicon.* Editio Minor. (Jena).

Shackleton Bailey, D. R., ed. (1990) *M. Valerii Martialis Epigrammata.* (Stuttgart).

———, ed. (1987) *M. Tulli Ciceronis Epistulae Ad Atticum.* 2 vols. (Stuttgart).

———. ed. and trans. (2002) *Cicero, Letters to Quintus and Brutus; Letter Fragments; Letter to Octavian; Invectives; Handbook of Electioneering.* (Cambridge, Mass.).

Sieveking, W., ed. (1929) *Plutarchi Moralia.* Vol. 3. (Leipzig).

Smith, M. F. (1996) *The Philosophical Inscription of Diogenes of Oinoanda.* (Vienna).

Usener, H., ed. (1887) *Epicurea.* (Leipzig). Reprinted 1966.

Viereck, P., ed. (1905) *Appiani Historia Romana.* Vol. 2. (Leipzig).

Wakefield, G., ed. (1796–97) *Lucretius, De Rerum Natura.* Notes by Richard Bentley. 3 vols. (London).

Ziegler, K., ed. (1964) *Plutarchi Vitae Parallelae.* Vol. 2.1. 2nd ed. (Leipzig).

Secondary Sources

Abbas, N., ed. (2005) *Mapping Michel Serres.* (Ann Arbor).

Abraham, N., and M. Torok (1986) *The Wolf Man's Magic Word. A Cryptonomy.* Trans. N. Rand. (Minneapolis).

Adler, A. C. (2005) "The Rule of Nature: Dance, Physiocracy, and Poetic Language in Hölderlin's 'Hyperion,'" PhD diss., Northwestern University.

Algra, K. A. et al., eds. (1999) *The Cambridge History of Hellenistic Philosophy.* (Cambridge).

Allen, D. C. (1944) "The Rehabilitation of Epicurus and His Theory of Pleasure in the Early Renaissance," *Studies in Philology* 41: 1–15.

——. (1964) *Doubt's Boundless Sea.* (Baltimore).

Allen, M. J. B. (1993) "The Soul as Rhapsode: Marsilio Ficino's Interpretation of Plato's *Ion,*" in J. W. O'Malley et al. (eds.), *Humanity and Divinity in Renaissance and Reformation.* (Leiden), 125–48. Reprinted in Allen (1995) ch. 15.

——. (1995) *Plato's Third Eye: Studies in Marsilio Ficino's Metaphysics and Its Sources.* (Aldershot).

Allison, H. (1986) *Kant's Transcendental Idealism: An Interpretation and Defense.* (New Haven).

Althusser, L. (1994) *Sur la philosophie.* (Paris).

——. (2006) *Philosophy of the Encounter: Later Writings, 1978–87.* Trans. G. M. Goshgarian. (London).

Annas, J., ed. (2001) *Cicero: On Moral Ends.* Trans. R. Woolf. (Cambridge).

——. (1993) *The Morality of Happiness.* (Oxford).

Arendt, H. (1982) *Lectures on Kant's Political Philosophy.* Ed. R. Beiner. (Chicago).

Ascham, R. (1570) *The Schoolemaster.* (London).

Aubenque, P. (1969) "Kant et l'épicurisme," in Scherer, 293–303.

Audidière, S., J.-C. Bourdin, and C. Duflo, eds. (2003) *L'Encyclopédie du Rêve d'Alembert de Diderot.* (Paris).

Auerbach, E. (1984) *Scenes from the Drama of European Literature.* (Minneapolis).

Bachelard, G. (1933) *Les intuitions atomistiques.* (Paris).

Bailey, C. (1951) Review of Leslie 1950. *Journal of Roman Studies* 41: 163–64.

Baker, E. (2001) "Atomism and the Sublime: On the Reception of Epicurus and Lucretius in the Aesthetics of Burke, Kant, and Schiller," PhD diss., Johns Hopkins University.

———. (2007) "Lucretius in the European Enlightenment," in Gillespie and Hardie (2007a), 274–88.

Baltussen, H. (2000) *Theophrastus against the Presocratics and Plato: Peripatetic Dialectic in the* De Sensibus. (Leiden).

Barbour, R. (1998) *English Epicures and Stoics.* (Amherst, Mass.).

———. (2007) "Moral and Political Philosophy: Readings of Lucretius from Virgil to Voltaire," in Gillespie and Hardie (2007b), 149–66.

Barker-Benfield, J. G. (1996). *The Culture of Sensibility: Sex and Society in Eighteenth-Century Britain.* (Chicago).

Barthes, R. (1977). *Roland Barthes by Roland Barthes.* Trans. R. Howard. (Berkeley).

Batnitzky, L. (2000) *Idolatry and Representation: The Philosophy of Franz Rosenzweig Reconsidered.* (Princeton).

———. (2005) *Leo Strauss and Emmanuel Levinas: The Politics of Revelation.* (Princeton).

Batstone, W. W. (2006) "Provocation: The Point of Reception Theory," in Martindale and Thomas, 14–20.

Baxandall, M., and E. H. Gombrich. (1962) "Beroaldus on Francia," *Journal of the Warburg and Courtauld Institutes* 25: 113–15.

Beiser, F. (2008) *German Idealism: The Struggle against Subjectivism, 1781–1801.* (Cambridge, Mass.).

Bell, J. A. (2009) "Of the Rise and Progress of Philosophical Concepts: Deleuze's Humean Historiography," in J. A. Bell and C. Colebrook (eds.), *Deleuze and History.* (Edinburgh), 54–71.

Bénatouïl, T. (2003) "Deux usages du stoïcisme: Deleuze, Foucault," in Gros and Lévy, 17–49.

Benjamin, W. (1968) *Illuminations: Essays and Reflections.* Trans. Harry Zohn. (New York).

———. (1977) *Gesammelte Schriften.* Band 2.2. (Frankfurt).

Bennett, J. (2010) *Vibrant Matter: A Political Ecology of Things.* (Durham).

Bergson, H. (1884) *Extraits de Lucrèce avec un commentaire, des notes et une étude sur la poésie, la physique, le texte et la langue de Lucrèce.* (Paris).

———. (1959) *The Philosophy of Poetry: The Genius of Lucretius.* Trans. W. Baskin. (New York).

Bernier, F. (1992) *Abrégé de la philosophie de Gassendi.* 7 vols. (Paris).

Beroaldo, F. (1505) *De terraemotu et pestilentia.* (Bologna).

Berressem, H. (2005) "*Incerto Tempore Incertisque Locis*: The Logic of the Clinamen and the Birth of Physics," in Abbas, 51–71.

Bignone, E. (1973) *L'Aristotele perduto e la formazione filosofica di Epicuro.* 2nd ed. (Florence).

Blanchot, M. (1955) *L'espace littéraire*. (Paris).

———. (1982) *The Space of Literature*. Trans. A. Smock. (Lincoln).

Bloch, O. (1997) "*Anôthen epitheôrein*: Marc-Aurèle entre Lucrèce et Pascal," in *Matière à histoires*. (Paris), 119–31.

Bloom, H. (1976) *Poetry and Repression: Revisionism from Blake to Stevens*. (New Haven).

———. (1989) *Ruin the Sacred Truths: Poetry and Belief from the Bible to the Present*. (Cambridge, Mass.).

———. (1997) *The Anxiety of Influence: A Theory of Poetry*. 2nd ed. (Oxford).

———. (2011) *The Anatomy of Influence: Literature as a Way of Life*. (New Haven).

Booth, E. (2005) "*A Subtle and Mysterious Machine*": *The Medical World of Walter Charleton*. (Dordrecht).

Boulogne, J. (2003) *Plutarque dans le miroir d'Épicure: Analyse d'une critique systématique de l'épicurisme*. (Villeneuve d'Ascq).

Bradbrook, M. C. (1936) *The School of Night: A Study in the Literary Relationships of Walter Raleigh*. (Cambridge).

Breslin, J. E. B. (1993) *Mark Rothko: A Biography*. (Chicago).

Breuer, I. (1925) *The Jewish National Home*. (Frankfurt).

Brooks, P. (1984) *Reading for the Plot*. (New York).

———. (1994) *Psychoanalysis and Storytelling*. (Oxford).

Brown, A. (2010) *The Return of Lucretius to Renaissance Florence*. (Cambridge).

Brown, E. (2008) "Contemplative Withdrawal in the Hellenistic Age," *Philosophical Studies* 137: 79–89.

———. (2009) "Politics and Society," in Warren, 179–96.

Brown, T. (1987) "Medicine in the Shadow of the *Principia*," *Journal of the History of Ideas* 48: 629–48.

Brun, F. (1806) *Gedichte. Vierte vermehrte Auflage*. (Zurich).

Brunschwig, J. (1986) "The Cradle Argument," in M. Schofield and G. Striker (eds.), *The Norms of Nature*. (Cambridge), 113–44.

———. (2002) "Entretien de Jacques Brunschwig," in M. Canto-Sperber and P. Pellegrin (eds.), *Le style de la pensée: Recueil de textes en hommage à Jacques Brunschwig*. (Paris), VII–XLI.

Burton, R. (2001) *The Anatomy of Melancholy*. (New York).

Butler, J. (1997) *Excitable Speech: A Politics of the Performative*. (New York).

Cabisius, G. (1985) "Social Metaphor and the Atomic Cycle in Lucretius," *The Classical Journal* 80: 109–20.

Canfora, L. (1993) *Vita di Lucrezio*. (Palermo).

Casella, M. T. (1975) "Il metodo dei commentari umanistici esemplato sul Beroaldo," *Studi Medievali* 3.16: 627–70.

Cassirer, E. (1972) *The Individual and the Cosmos in Renaissance Philosophy*. Trans. M. Domandi. (Philadelphia).

Castellus, B. (1721) *Lexicon Medicum*. (Padua).

Castner, C. (1988) *Prosopography of Roman Epicureans.* (Frankfurt).

Cixous, H. (1981) "Castration or Decapitation," *Signs: Journal of Women in Culture and Society* 7: 41–55.

Clay, D. (1983) *Lucretius and Epicurus.* (Ithaca).

———. (1990) "The Philosophical Inscription of Diogenes of Oenoanda: New Discoveries, 1969–1983," *Aufstieg und Niedergang der römischen Welt* 11.36.4: 2446–559.

———. (1998) *Paradosis and Survival: Three Chapters in the History of Epicurean Philosophy.* (Ann Arbor).

———. (2009) "The Athenian Garden," in Warren, 9–28.

Clucas, S. (2000) "Thomas Harriot and the Field of Knowledge in the English Renaissance," in R. Fox (ed.), *Thomas Harriot: An Elizabethan Man of Science.* (Burlington), 93–136.

———. (2005) "Liquid History: Serres and Lucretius," in Abbas, 72–83.

Cohen, E. E. (2006) "Free and Unfree Sexual Work: An Economic Analysis of Athenian Prostitution," in C. Farone and L. McClure (eds.), *Prostitutes and Courtesans in the Ancient World.* (Madison), 95–124.

Cohen, H. (2004) *Ethics of Maimonides.* Trans. A. Bruckstein. (Madison).

Coleridge, S. T. (1924) *The Poetical Works.* Ed. J. D. Campbell. (London).

Collingwood, R. (1949) *The Idea of Nature.* (Oxford).

Commager Jr., H. S. (1957) "Lucretius' Interpretation of the Plague," *Harvard Studies in Classical Philology* 62: 105–18.

de Condillac, Étienne Bonnot. (1973) *Essai sur l'origine des connaissances.* (Paris).

Connors, C. (1994) "Famous Last Words: Authorship and Death in the *Satyticon* and Neronian Rome," in J. Elsner and J. Masters (eds.), *Reflections of Nero.* (London), 225–35.

Conte, G. B. (1994) *Genres and Readers: Lucretius, Love Elegy, Pliny's Encyclopedia.* (Baltimore).

Cooper, J. (1999) *Reason and Emotion: Essays on Ancient Moral Psychology and Ethical Theory.* (Princeton).

Cooper, M. (2002) "Vitesses de l'image, puissances de la pensée: la philosophie épicurienne revue par Deleuze et Guattari," *French Studies* 56: 45–60.

Coppini, D. (1998) "L'ispirazione per contagio: 'Furor' e 'Remota Lectio' nella poesia Latina del Poliziano," in V. Fera and M. Martelli (eds.), *Agnolo Poliziano: Poeta Scrittore Filologo.* (Florence), 127–64.

Cranefield, P. F. (1970) "On the Origin of the Phrase *Nihil Est in Intellectu Quod Non Prius Fuerit in Sensu,*" *Journal of the History of Medicine and Allied Sciences* 25: 77–80.

Crewe, J. (1991) Review of *Unspeakable Subjects, Shakespeare Studies* 27: 260–66.

Cutrofello, A. (2005) *Continental Philosophy: A Contemporary Introduction.* (London).

D'Amico, J. (1984) "The Progress of Renaissance Latin Prose: The Case of Apuleianism," *Renaissance Quarterly* 37: 351–92.

Darnton, R. (1995) *The Forbidden Bestsellers of Pre-Revolutionary France.* (New York).

Dean-Jones, L. (1992) "The Politics of Pleasure: Female Sexual Appetite in the Hippocratic Corpus," *Helios* 19: 72–91.

De Lacy, P. (1969) "Limit and Variation in the Epicurean Philosophy," *Phoenix* 23: 104–13.

Deleuze, G. (1953) *Empirisme et subjectivité: Essai sur la nature humaine selon Hume.* (Paris).

———. (1961) "Lucrèce et le naturalisme," *Les études philosophiques* 16: 19–29.

———. (1962) *Nietzsche et la philosophie.* (Paris).

———. (1966) "Renverser le platonisme (*Les simulacres*)," *Revue de métaphysique et de morale* 71: 426–38.

———. (1968) *Spinoza et la problème de l'expression.* (Paris).

———. (1969) *Logique du sens.* (Paris).

———. (1983) *Nietzsche and Philosophy.* Trans. H. Tomlinson. (New York).

———. (1984) *Kant's Critical Philosophy.* Trans. H. Tomlinson and B. Habberjam. (Minneapolis).

———. (1990a) *The Logic of Sense.* Trans. M. Lester with C. Stivale. (New York).

———. (1990b) *Pourparlers: 1972–1990.* (Paris).

———. (1991) *Empiricism and Subjectivity: An Essay on Hume's Theory of Human Nature.* Trans. C. V. Boundas. (New York).

———. (1992) *Expressionism in Philosophy: Spinoza.* Trans. M. Joughin. (New York).

———. (1995) *Negotiations: 1972–1990.* Trans. M. Joughin. (New York).

———. (2002) *L'île déserte et autres textes.* Ed. D. Lapoujade. (Paris).

———. (2003) *Desert Islands and Other Texts (1953–1974).* Trans. M. Taormina. (Los Angeles).

Deleuze, G., and F. Guattari. (1980) *Capitalisme et schizophrénie,* t. 2: *Mille plateaux.* (Paris).

———. (1987). *A Thousand Plateaus: Capitalism and Schizophrenia.* Trans. B. Massumi. (Minneapolis).

Deleuze, G., and C. Parnet. (1977) *Dialogues.* (Paris).

———. (1987) *Dialogues II.* Trans. H. Tomlinson and B. Habberjam. (New York).

Del Nero, V. (1981) "Note sulla vita di Giovan Battista Pio (con alcune lettere inedite)," *Rinascimento* 21: 247–63.

———. (1985) "Filosofia e teologia nel commento di Giovan Battista Pio a Lucrezio," *Interpres* 6: 156–99.

———. (1986) "La sessualità nel commento di Giovanni Battista Pio a Lucrezio," *Rinascimento* 36: 277–95.

———. (1990) "G. B. Pio fra grammatica e filosofia: dai primi scritti al commento lucreziano del 1511," in L. Avellini (ed.), *Sapere e/è potere: Il caso Bolognese a confronto; actes du colloque de Bologne, avril 1989.* Vol. 1: *Forme e oggetti della dispute delle arti.* (Bologna), 243–57.

de Man, P. (1983) *Blindness and Insight: Essays in the Rhetoric of Contemporary Criticism.* 2nd ed. (Minneapolis).

———. (1996) *Aesthetic Ideology.* (Minneapolis).

Derrida, J. (1984) "My Chances/Mes Chances: A Rendezvous with Some Epicurean Stereophonies," in J. H. Smith and W. Kerrigan (eds.), *Taking Chances: Derrida, Psychoanalysis, and Literature.* (Baltimore), 1–32.

———. (1986) "Proverb, 'He that would pun—,'" in J. P. Leavey, *Glassary.* (Lincoln), 17–20.

———. (1987) *The Archeology of the Frivolous: Reading Condillac.* Trans. J. P. Leavey Jr. (Lincoln).

———. (1988) *Limited Inc.* (Evanston).

———. (1994) *Specters of Marx: The State of the Debt, the Work of Mourning, and the New International.* (New York).

———. (2000) "Performative Powerlessness—A Response to Simon Critchley," *Constellations* 7: 466–68.

De Witt, N. W. (1973). *Epicurus and His Philosophy.* (Minneapolis).

Diano, C. (1974) *Scritti epicurei.* (Florence).

Didion, J. (2005) *The Year of Magical Thinking.* (New York).

Dilthey, W. (1914–2006) *Gesammelte Schriften.* 26 vols. (Göttingen).

Dionisotti, C. (1968) *Gli umanisti e il volgare fra Quattro e Cinquecento.* (Florence).

Donne, J. (2006) *John Donne's Poetry.* (New York).

Downing, E. (2006) "Lucretius at the Camera: Ancient Atomism and Early Photographic Theory in Walter Benjamin's *Berliner Chronik,*" *Germanic Review* 81: 21–36.

Drury, S. B. (1987) "Leo Strauss's Classic Natural Right Teaching," *Political Theory* 15: 299–315.

Duchesneau, F. (1982) *La Physiologie des Lumières.* (The Hague).

Duflo, C. (2003) "Diderot et Ménuret de Chambaud," *Recherches sur Diderot et sur l'Encyclopédie* 34: 25–44.

Easterling, P., and B. Knox, eds. (1989) *The Cambridge History of Classical Literature*: Vol. 1, *Greek Literature,* Part 4, *The Hellenistic Period and the Empire.* (Cambridge).

Edwards, C. (1998) "The Suffering Body: Philosophy and Pain in Seneca's *Letters,*" in J. I. Porter (ed.), *Constructions of the Classical Body.* (Ann Arbor), 252–68.

———. (2005). "Archetypally Roman? Representing Seneca's Ageing Body," in A. Hopkins and M. Wyke (eds.), *Roman Bodies: Antiquity to the Eighteenth Century.* (London), 13–22.

———. (2007). *Death in Ancient Rome.* (New Haven).

Elton, W. R. (1998) *King Lear and the Gods.* (Lexington).

Encyclopedia Judaica. (1972) (New York).

Encyclopédie, ou Dictionnaire raisonné des sciences, des arts et des métiers. (1969) 5 vols. (New York).

Englert, W. G. (1987) *Epicurus on the Swerve and Voluntary Action*. (Atlanta).

Erasmus, D. (1545) *A Very Pleasaunt [and] Fruitful Diologe Called the Epicure*. Trans. P. Gerrard. (London).

Erler, M. (1994) "Epikur—Die Schule Epikurs—Lukrez," in H. Flashar (ed.), *Die Philosophie der Antike*. Band 4: *Die Hellenistische Philosophie*. (Basel), 29–490.

———. (2009) "Epicureanism in the Roman Empire," in Warren, 46–64.

———, ed. (2000) *Epikureismus in der spaten Republik und der Kaiserzeit Akten der 2. Tagung der Karl-und-Gertrud-Abel-Stiftung vom 30. September–3. Oktober 1998 in Würzburg*. (Stuttgart).

Erler, M., and M. Schofield. (1999) "Epicurean Ethics," in Algra et al., 642–74.

Esolen, A. (1994) "Spenserian Chaos: Lucretius in *The Faerie Queene*," *Spenser Studies* 11: 31–52.

Faietti, M., and K. Oberhuber, eds. (1988) *Bologna e l'Umanesimo, 1490–1510: Bologna, Pinacoteca nazionale, 6 marzo–24 aprile 1988*. (Bologna).

Fanning, C. (2005) "The Scriblerian Sublime," *Studies in English Literature* 45: 647–67.

Farolfi, B. (1977) *Strutture agrarie e crisi cittadina nel primo Cinquecento Bolognese*. (Bologna).

Farrington, B. (1965) "Form and Purpose in the *De Rerum Natura*," in D. R. Dudley (ed.), *Lucretius*. (London), 35–68.

Fenves, P. (1991) *A Peculiar Fate: Metaphysics and World-History in Kant*. (Ithaca).

———. (2003) *Late Kant: Towards Another Law of the Earth*. (London).

Fernandez, P. (2006) "Plaisir/Volupté," in R. Trousson and F. S. Eigeldinger (eds.), *Dictionnaire de Jean-Jacques Rousseau*. (Paris), 725–28.

Ficino, M. (2001–2006) *Platonic Theology*. Ed. and trans. M. J. B. Allen and J. Hankins. 6 vols. (Cambridge, Mass.).

Fischel, H. A. (1973) *Rabbinic Literature and Greco-Roman Philosophy: A Study of Epicurea and Rhetorica in Early Midrash*. (Leiden).

Fish, S. E. (1989) "Why No One's Afraid of Wolfgang Iser," in S. E. Fish, *Doing What Comes Naturally: Change, Rhetoric, and the Practice of Theory in Literary and Legal Studies*. (Durham), 68–86.

Fitzgibbon, P. M. (2001) "Literary Portraits and Caricatures of Second Century Epicureans," PhD diss., Duke University.

Flaxman, G. (2009) "Plato," in G. Jones and J. Roffe (eds.), *Deleuze's Philosophical Lineage*. (Edinburgh), 8–26.

Fondation Jean-Pascal Imsand. (2004) *Jean-Pascal Imsand Fotografo*. (Baden).

Force, P. (2003) *Self-Interest Before Adam Smith: A Genealogy of Economic Science*. (Cambridge).

Forrest, J. (2005–2006) "Nineteenth-Century Nostalgia for Eighteenth-Century Wit, Style, and Aesthetic Disengagement: The Goncourt Brothers' Histories of Eighteenth-Century Art and Women," *Nineteenth-Century French Studies* 34: 44–62.

Foucault, M. (1970) "Theatrum Philosophicum," *Critique* 282: 885–908.

———. (1977) "Theatrum Philosophicum," in *Language, Counter-Memory, Practice: Selected Essays and Interviews.* Trans. D. F. Bouchard and S. Simon. (Ithaca), 165–96.

———. (1984) *Histoire de la sexualité III: Le souci de soi.* (Paris).

———. (1986) *The History of Sexuality.* Vol. 3: *The Care of the Self.* Trans. R. Hurley. (New York).

———. (2001) *L'Herméneutique du sujet: Cours au Collège de France, 1981–1982.* (Paris).

———. (2005) *The Hermeneutics of the Subject: Lectures at the Collège de France, 1981–82.* Trans. G. Burchell. Ed. F. Gros. (New York).

Fowler, D. P. (1989) "Lucretius and Politics," in M. Griffin and J. Barnes (eds.), *Philosophia Togata: Essays on Philosophy and Roman Society.* (Oxford), 120–50.

Fox, R., ed. (2000) *Thomas Harriot: An Elizabethan Man of Science.* (Burlington).

Foxhall, L. (1998) "Pandora Unbound: A Feminist Critique of Foucault's *History of Sexuality*," in Larmour, Miller, and Platter, 122–37.

Frede, M. (1992) "Doxographie, historiographie philosophique et historiographie historique de la philosophie," *Revue de métaphysique et morale* 97: 311–25.

French, R. (2003) *Medicine Before Science: The Business of Medicine from the Middle Ages to the Enlightenment.* (Cambridge).

Frischer, B. (1982) *The Sculpted Word: Epicureanism and Philosophical Recruitment in Ancient Greece.* (Berkeley).

Funke, M. (2008) "Sexuality and Gender in Alciphron's Letters of Courtesans," MA Thesis, University of British Columbia.

Gadamer, H.-G. (1975) *Truth and Method.* Trans. G. Barden and J. Cumming. (London). [Originally published as *Wahrheit und Methode* (Tübingen, 1960)].

Gaisser, J. Haig (2008) *The Fortunes of Apuleius and the Golden Ass: A Study in Transmission and Reception.* (Princeton).

Gale, M. (2000) *Virgil on the Nature of Things: The Georgics, Lucretius, and the Didactic Tradition.* (Cambridge).

———. (2004) "The Story of Us: A Narratological Analysis of Lucretius' *De Rerum Natura*," in M. Gale (ed.), *Latin Epic and Didactic Poetry: Genre, Tradition and Individuality.* (Swansea), 49–71.

Gambino Longo, S. (2004) *Savoir de la nature et poésie des choses: Lucrèce et Épicure à la Renaissance Italienne.* (Paris).

Gammon, M. (1997) "'Exemplary Originality': Kant on Genius and Imitation," *Journal of the History of Philosophy* 35: 563–92.

Gassendi, P. (1658) *Opera Omnia*. (Lyon).

Gaub, H. (1745) *De Regimine Mentis*. (Leiden).

Geiger, J. (1985) *Cornelius Nepos and Ancient Political Biography*. (Stuttgart).

Gibbs, R. (1992) *Correlations in Rosenzweig and Levinas*. (Princeton).

Gibson, R. K., and C. Kraus, eds. (2002) *The Classical Commentary: Histories, Practices, Theory*. (Leiden).

Gigandet, A. (2003) "Présences d'Épicure," in Gros and Lévy, 137–50.

Gilhuly, K. (2007) "Bronze for Gold: Subjectivity in Lucian's *Dialogues of the Courtesans*," *American Journal of Philology* 128: 59–94.

Gillespie, S., and P. Hardie. (2007a) "Introduction," in Gillespie and Hardie (2007b), 1–15.

Gillespie, S., and P. Hardie, eds. (2007b) *The Cambridge Companion to Lucretius*. (Cambridge).

Gillespie, S., and D. Mackenzie. (2007) "Lucretius and the Moderns," in Gillespie and Hardie (2007b), 306–24.

Glatzer, N. M. (1964) "The Beginnings of Modern Jewish Studies," in A. Altmann (ed.), *Studies in Nineteenth-Century Jewish Intellectual History*. (Cambridge, Mass.), 27–45.

Glidden, D. (1980) "Epicurus and the Pleasure Principle," in D. Depew (ed.), *The Greeks and the Good Life*. (Fullerton), 177–97.

Goddard, C. (1991) "Epicureanism and the Poetry of Lucretius in the Renaissance," PhD diss., University of Cambridge.

Godwin, J. (2004) *Lucretius*. (London).

Goldberg, J. (2009) *The Seeds of Things: Theorizing Sexuality and Materiality in Renaissance Representations*. (New York).

de Goncourt, E., and J. de Goncourt (1862) *La femme au dix-huitième siècle*. (Paris). Reprinted 2006.

Gordon, D. R., and D. B. Suits, eds. (2003) *Epicurus: His Continuing Influence and Contemporary Relevance*. (Rochester).

Gordon, P. (1996) *Epicurus in Lycia: The Second-Century World of Diogenes of Oenoanda*. (Ann Arbor).

———. (2004) "Remembering the Garden: The Trouble with Women in the School of Epicurus," in J. Fitzgerald, G. Holland, and D. Obbink (eds.), *Philodemus and the New Testament World*. (Leiden), 221–44.

Gordon, P. E. (2004) *Heidegger and Rosenzweig: Between Judaism and German Philosophy*. (Berkeley).

Goulet-Cazé, M.-O., trans. (1999) *Diogène Laërce, Vies et doctrines des philosophes illustres*. (Paris).

Gourevitch, V. (2001) "The Religious Thought," in P. Riley (ed.), *The Cambridge Companion to Rousseau*. (Cambridge), 193–246.

———, and M. S. Roth, eds. (1991) *On Tyranny*. (Chicago).

Gowers, E. (2008) "Thoroughly Modern Lucretius," *Times Literary Supplement,* October 1, 2008.

Greenblatt, S. (2011) *The Swerve: How the World Became Modern.* (New York).

Greene, E. (1996) "Sappho, Foucault, and Women's Erotics," *Arethusa* 29: 1–14.

Greenlaw, E. (1920) "Spenser and Lucretius," *Studies in Philology* 17: 439–64.

Griffin, M. (1986a) "Philosophy, Cato, and Roman Suicide: I," *Greece & Rome* 33: 64–77.

———. (1986b) "Philosophy, Cato, and Roman Suicide: II," *Greece & Rome* 33: 192–202.

———. (2007) "Seneca's Pedagogic Strategy: *Letters* and *De Beneficiis*," in R. Sorabji and R. W. Sharples (eds.), *Greek and Roman Philosophy 100BC–200AD,* Vol. 1: 89–114.

Grisé, Y. (1982) *Le suicide dans la Rome antique.* (Montréal).

Gros, F., and C. Lévy, eds. (2003) *Foucault et la philosophie antique.* (Paris).

Gruter, J. ed. (1602–34) *Lampas, sive Fax Artium Liberalium.* 7 vols. (Frankfurt).

Gunderson, E. (2009) *Nox Philologiae: Aulus Gellius and the Fantasy of the Roman Library.* (Madison).

Gurd, S. (2005) *Iphigenias at Aulis: Textual Multiplicity, Radical Philology.* (Ithaca).

Güthenke, C. (2009) "Shop Talk: Reception Studies and Recent Work in the History of Scholarship," *Classical Receptions Journal* 1: 104–15.

Gutwirth, M. (1992) *The Twilight of the Goddesses: Women and Representation in the French Revolutionary Era.* (New Brunswick, N.J.).

Hadot, P. (1987) *Exercises spirituels et philosophie antique.* 2nd ed. (Paris).

Hadzsits, G. D. (1935) *Lucretius and His Influence.* (London).

Hallett, J. (2003) "Centering from the Periphery in the Augustan Roman World: Ovid's Autobiography in *Tristia* 4.10 and Cornelius Nepos's Biography of Atticus," *Arethusa* 36: 345–59.

Hankins, J. (2011) "Monstrous Melancholy: Ficino and the Physiological Causes of Atheism," in S. Clucas, P. J. Forshaw, and V. Rees (eds.), *Laus Platonici Philosophi: Marsilio Ficino and His Influence.* (Leiden), 25–43.

Hardie, P. R. (2009) *Lucretian Receptions: History, the Sublime, Knowledge.* (Cambridge).

Hardt, M. (1993) *Gilles Deleuze: An Apprenticeship in Philosophy.* (Minneapolis).

Harrison, G. B., ed. (1930) *Advice to His Son, by Henry Percy, Earl of Northumberland.* (London).

———, ed. (1966) *Willobie His Avisa, 1594.* (Edinburgh).

Havas, L. (1985) "Geschichtsphilosophische Interpretationsmöglichkeiten bei Cornelius Nepos," *Klio* 67: 502–506.

Hayden, P. (2008) "Gilles Deleuze and Naturalism: A Convergence with Ecological Theory and Politics," in B. Herzogenrath (ed.), *An [Un]likely Alliance: Thinking Environment[s] with Deleuze/Guattari.* (Cambridge), 23–45.

Hegel, G. W. F. (1980) *Gesammelte Werke*. Ed. W. Bonsiepen and R. Heede. (Hamburg).

Heinze, R. (1925) "Auctoritas," *Hermes* 60: 348–66.

Hemelrijk, E. A. (1999) *Matrona Docta: Educated Women in the Roman Elite from Cornelia to Julia Domna*. (London).

Hesse, C. (2001) *The Other Enlightenment: How French Women Became Modern*. (Princeton).

Hirsch, D. A. H. (1991) "Donne's Atomies and Anatomies: Deconstructed Bodies and the Resurrection of Atomic Theory," *Studies in English Literature* 31: 69–94.

Hirzel, R. (1908) "Der Selbstmord," *Archiv für Religionswissenschaft* 11: 75–104; 243–84; 417–76.

Hobbes, T. (1939–45) *The English Works of Thomas Hobbes*. Ed. W. Molesworth. 11 vols. (London).

———. (1996) *Leviathan*. Ed. Robert Tuck. (Cambridge).

Hölderlin, F. (1995–2008) *Sämtliche Werke*. Ed. D. E. Sattler et al. (Basel).

———. (2004) *Sämtliche Werke, Briefe und Dokumente*. Ed. D. E. Sattler. (Munich).

Holford-Strevens, L. (2002) "*Horror Vacui* in Lucretian Biography," *Leeds International Classical Studies* 1: 1–23.

Hollander, R., and J. Hollander, trans. (2000) *Dante, Inferno*. (New York).

Holmes, B. (2005) "*Daedala Lingua*: Crafted Speech in *De Rerum Natura*," *American Journal of Philology* 126: 527–85.

Humphrey, N. (2009) *Seeing Red: A Study in Consciousness*. (Cambridge, Mass.).

Hunt, L. (2007) *Inventing Human Rights: A History*. (New York).

Hutchinson, G. O. (2001) "The Date of *De Rerum Natura*," *Classical Quarterly* 51: 150–62.

Hutchinson, L. (1996) "Letter to Lord Anglesey," in H. de Quehen (ed.), *Lucy Hutchinson's Translation of Lucretius, De Rerum Natura*. (Ann Arbor), 1.

Inwood, B. (2005) *Reading Seneca: Stoic Philosophy at Rome*. (Oxford).

Inwood, M. (1992) *A Hegel Dictionary*. (Oxford).

Iser, W. (1974) *The Implied Reader: Patterns of Communication in Prose Fiction from Bunyan to Beckett*. (Baltimore).

———. (1978) *The Act of Reading: A Theory of Aesthetic Response*. (Baltimore).

———. (2006) *How To Do Theory*. (Oxford).

Israel, J. (2001) *Radical Enlightenment*. (Oxford).

Jacob, M. (1993) "The Materialist World of Eighteenth-Century French Pornography," in L. Hunt (ed.), *The Invention of Pornography*. (New York), 157–202.

Jameson, F. (1991) *Postmodernism, or, The Cultural Logic of Late Capitalism*. (Durham).

Jardine, L., and M. Silverthorne, eds. (2000) *The New Organon*. (Cambridge).
Jauß, H. R. (1982) *Toward an Aesthetic of Reception*. Trans. T. Bahti. (Minneapolis).
Jefferis, J. D. (1943) "The Concept of *Fortuna* in Cornelius Nepos," *Classical Philology* 38: 48–50.
Johnson, W. R. (2000) *Lucretius and the Modern World*. (London).
Jones, H. (1989) *The Epicurean Tradition*. (London).
Jope, J. (1983) "Lucretius' Psychoanalytical Insight," *Phoenix* 37: 224–38.
Joyce, J. (1939) *Finnegan's Wake*. (London).
Kant, I. (1801) *Logik: ein Handbuch zu Vorlesungen*. Ed. G. B. Jäsche. (Königsberg).
———. (1900–) *Gesammelte Schriften*. Ed. Königliche-Preußische [later Deutsche] Akademie der Wissenschaften. (Berlin).
———. (1974) *Critique of Judgment*. Trans. J. H. Bernard. (New York).
Kargon, R. (1964) "Walter Charleton, Robert Boyle, and the Acceptance of Epicurean Atomism in England," *Isis* 55: 184–92.
———. (1966) "Thomas Hariot, the Northumberland Circle and Early Atomism in England," *Journal of the History of Ideas* 27: 128–36.
Kennedy, D. (2002) *Rethinking Reality: Lucretius and the Textualization of Nature*. (Ann Arbor).
———. (2006) "Afterword: The Uses of 'Reception.'" In Martindale and Thomas, 288–93.
Ker, J. (2009) *The Deaths of Seneca*. (Oxford).
Keulen, W. (2009) *Gellius the Satirist: Roman Cultural Authority in Attic Nights*. (Leiden).
Kimmich, D. (1993) *Epikureische Aufklärung: philosophische und poetische Konzepte der Selbstsorge*. (Darmstadt).
King, M. L. (1994) *The Death of the Child Valerio Marcello*. (Chicago).
Kirchner, R. (2001) *Sentenzen im Werk des Tacitus*. (Stuttgart).
Knight, I. F. (1968) *The Geometic Spirit: The Abbé de Condillac and the French Enlightenment Thought*. (New Haven).
Konstan, D. (1987) "Between Courtesan and Wife: A Study of Menander's *Perikeiromene*," *Phoenix* 41: 121–39.
Kors, A. C. (1997) "Monsters and the Problem of Naturalism in French Thought," *Eighteenth-Century Life* 21: 23–47.
Krämer, H. J. (1971) *Platonismus und Hellenistiche Philosophie*. (Berlin).
Krautter, K. (1971) *Philologische Methode und humanistiche Existenz. Filippo Beroaldo und sein Kommentar zum Goldenen Esel des Apuleius*. (Munich).
Kraye, J. (1998) "Moral Philosophy," in Q. Skinner and E. Kessler (eds.), *The Cambridge History of Renaissance Philosophy*. (Cambridge), 376–82.
Kroll, R. (1991) *The Material Word: Literate Culture in Restoration and Early Eighteenth Century*. (Baltimore).

Kuhn, H. (1956) "Naturrecht und Historismus," *Zeitschrift für Politik* 3: 289–304.

Lacan, J. (1977) *The Four Fundamental Concepts of Psychoanalysis: The Seminar of Jacques Lacan, XI.* Trans. A. Sheridan. (New York).

Lacoue-Labarthe, P., and J.-L. Nancy. (1988) *The Literary Absolute: The Theory of Literature in German Romanticism.* Trans. P. Barnard and C. Lester. (Albany).

Lamb, J. (1981) "The Comic Sublime and Sterne's Fiction," *English Literary History* 48: 110–43.

La Mettrie, Julien Offray de. (1796). *Œuvres.* (Berlin).

———. (1996) *Machine Man and Other Writings.* Trans. A. Thomson. (Cambridge).

Landes, J. (2001) *Visualizing the Nation: Gender, Representation, and Revolution in Eighteenth-Century France.* (Ithaca).

Lange, L., ed. (2002) *Feminist Interpretations of Jean-Jacques Rousseau.* (University Park, Pa.).

Larmour, D., P. A. Miller, and C. Platter, eds. (1998) *Rethinking Sexuality: Foucault and Classical Antiquity.* (Princeton).

Latour, B. (1993) *We Have Never Been Modern.* Trans. Catherine Porter. (Cambridge, Mass.).

Lazier, B. (2008) *God Interrupted: Heresy and the European Imagination Between the World Wars.* (Princeton).

Leibniz, G. E. (1989) *Philosophical Essays.* Trans. R. Ariew and D. Garber. (Indianapolis).

Leo, F. (1901) *Die griechisch-römische Biographie nach ihrer litterarischen Form.* (Leipzig).

Leonard, M. (2006) "The Uses of Reception: Derrida and the Historical Imperative," in Martindale and Thomas, 116–26.

Leslie, R. J. (1950) *The Epicureanism of Titus Pomponius Atticus.* (Philadelphia).

Levinson, R. B. (1928) "Spenser and Bruno," *PMLA* 43: 675–81.

Lezra, J. (1997) *Unspeakable Subjects: The Genealogy of the Event in Early Modern Europe.* (Stanford).

Lincoln, B. (1994) *Authority: Construction and Corrosion.* (Chicago).

Lindsay, H. (1998) "The Biography of Atticus: Cornelius Nepos on the Philosophical and Ethical Background of Pomponius Atticus," *Latomus* 57: 324–36.

Locke, J. (1997) *An Essay Concerning Human Understanding.* Ed. R. Woolhouse. (London).

Long, A. A. (1977) "Chance and Natural Law in Epicureanism," *Phronesis* 22: 63–88. Revised and reprinted in Long (2006) 157–77.

———. (1997) "Lucretius on Nature and the Epicurean Self," in K. A. Algra, M. H. Koenen, and P. H. Schrijvers (eds.), *Lucretius and His Intellectual Background.* (Amsterdam), 125–39. Reprinted in Long (2006) 202–20.

———. (2006) *From Epicurus to Epictetus: Studies in Hellenistic and Roman Philosophy.* (Oxford).

Lovejoy, A. O., and G. Boas. (1935) *Primitivism and Related Ideas in Antiquity.* (Baltimore).

Lowrie, M. (2009) *Writing, Performance, and Authority in Augustan Rome.* (Oxford).

Lyotard, J.-F. (1983) *Le différend.* (Paris).

———. (1991) *Leçons sur l'"Analytique du sublime": Kant, "Critique de la faculté de juger," paragraphes 23–29.* (Paris).

McClure, L. (2003) "Subversive Laughter: The Sayings of Courtesans in Book 13 of Athenaeus' *Deipnosophistae*," *American Journal of Philology* 124: 259–94.

McHugh, R. (2006) *Annotations to Finnegans Wake.* (Baltimore).

MacPhail, E. (2000) "Montaigne's New Epicureanism," *Montaigne Studies* 12: 94–103.

de Mairan, J.-J. Dortous. (1741) *Lettre de M. de Mairan à Madame la Marquise du Chastellet sur la question des forces vives, en réponse aux objections qu'elle lui fait sur ce sujet dans ses Institutions de physique.* (Paris).

Mansfeld, J. (1999a) "Sources," in Algra et al., 3–30.

———. (1999b) "Sources," in A. A. Long (ed.) *The Cambridge Companion to Early Greek Philosophy.* (Cambridge), 22–44.

———. (2002) "Deconstructing Doxography," *Philologus* 146: 277–86.

———, and D. T. Runia. (1996–) *Aëtiana: The Method and Intellectual Context of a Doxographer.* 3 vols. (Leiden).

Martin, L. C. (1945) "Shakespeare, Lucretius, and the Commonplaces," *Review of English Studies* 21: 174–82.

Martindale, C. (1993) *Redeeming the Text: Latin Poetry and the Hermeneutics of Reception.* (Cambridge).

———. (2006) "Introduction: Thinking Through Reception," in Martindale and Thomas, 1–13.

———. (2007) "Reception," in C. Kallendorf (ed.), *A Companion to the Classical Tradition.* (Oxford), 297–311.

———, and R. F. Thomas, eds. (2006) *Classics and the Uses of Reception.* (Oxford).

Mayo, T. F. (1934) *Epicurus in England, 1650–1725.* (Dallas).

Meeker, N. (2006) *Voluptuous Philosophy: Literary Materialism in the French Enlightenment.* (New York).

Meier, H. (1995) *Carl Schmitt and Leo Strauss: The Hidden Dialogue.* (Chicago).

Mejer, J. ((2006) "Ancient Philosophy and the Doxographical Tradition," in M. L. Gill and P. Pellegrin (eds.), *The Blackwell Companion to Ancient Philosophy.* (Malden, Mass.), 20–33.

Memoria della novi segni et spaventevoli prodigii comparsi in piu loci de Italia et in varie parti del mondo lanno mille cinquecento undese (ca. 1511, Bologna).

Miller, J. Hillis (1995) "Parabolic Exemplarity: The Example of Nietzsche's *Thus Spoke Zarathustra*," in A. Gelley (ed.), *Unruly Examples: On the Rhetoric of Exemplarity*. (Stanford), 162–74.

Milton, J. (2000) *Paradise Lost*. Ed. J. Leonard. (London).

Mitsis, P. (1988) *Epicurus' Ethical Theory: The Pleasures of Invulnerability*. (Ithaca).

Moles, J. (1989) "Nepos and Biography," *Classical Review* 39: 229–33.

Momigliano, A. (1993) *The Development of Greek Biography*. (Cambridge, Mass.).

de Montaigne, M. (1958) *The Complete Essays of Montaigne*. Trans. D. Frame. (Palo Alto).

———. (1978) *Les Essais*. Ed. P. Villey and V. L. Saulnier. (Paris).

Montesquieu, C.-L. (1946) *Lettres persanes*. (Paris).

Morales, H. (2001) "Sense and Sententiousness in the Greek Novels," in A. Sharrock and H. Morales (eds.), *Intratextuality: Greek and Roman Textual Relations*. (Oxford), 67–88.

Moravia, S. (1978) "From *Homme Machine* to *Homme Sensible*: Changing Eighteenth-Century Models of Man's Image," *Journal of the History of Ideas* 39: 46–50.

Most, G. W. (1984) "Sublime degli antichi, sublime dei moderni," *Studi di estetica* 12: 113–29.

———. (2002) "After the Sublime: Stations in the Career of an Emotion," *Yale Review* 90: 101–20.

———. (2007) "Il sublime oggi?" in E. Matelli (ed.), *Il Sublime: Fortuna di un testo e di un'idea*. (Milan), 41–62.

Muzzi, S. (1845) *Annali della Città di Bologna dalla sua Origine al 1796*. 8 vols. (Bologna).

Myers, D. N. (1992) "The Fall and Rise of Jewish Historicism: The Evolution of the Akademie für die Wissenschaft des Judentums (1919–34)," *Hebrew Union College Annual* 63: 107–44.

———. (2003) *Resisting History: Historicism and its Discontents in Modern Jewish Thought*. (Princeton).

Newman, B. (1992) *Selected Writings and Interviews*. Ed. J. P. O'Neill. (Berkeley).

Niccoli, O. (1990) *Prophecy and People in Renaissance Italy*. Trans. L. G. Cochrane. (Princeton).

Nichols, J. (1976) *Epicurean Political Philosophy*. (Ithaca).

Noggle, J. (2001) *The Skeptical Sublime: Aesthetic Ideology in Pope and the Tory Satirists*. (Oxford).

Norden, E. (1971) *Die antike Kunstprosa*. 2 vols. 6th ed. (Stuttgart).

Nussbaum, M. (1994) *The Therapy of Desire: Theory and Practice in Hellenistic Ethics*. (Princeton).

Nutton, V. (1983) "The Seeds of Disease: An Explanation of Contagion and Infection from the Greeks to the Renaissance," *Medical History* 27: 1–34.

Offen, K. (2000) *European Feminisms 1700–1950: A Political History.* (Stanford).

Omitowoju, R. (2002) *Rape and the Politics of Consent in Classical Athens.* (Cambridge).

Osler, M., ed. (1991) *Atoms, Pneuma, and Tranquility: Epicurean and Stoic Themes in European Thought.* (Cambridge).

Paganini, G. (2001) "Hobbes, Gassendi, and the Tradition of Political Epicureanism," *Hobbes Studies* 14: 3–24.

Passannante, G. (2009) "Homer Atomized: Francis Bacon and the Matter of Tradition," *English Literary History* 76: 1015–47.

———. (2011) *The Lucretian Renaissance: Philology and the Afterlife of Tradition.* (Chicago).

Petrarch, F. (1991) *De Remediis Utriusque Fortunae.* Trans. C. H. Rawski. 5 vols. (Bloomington).

Pinkard, T. (2002) *German Philosophy 1760–1860: The Legacy of Idealism.* (Cambridge).

Poignault, R., ed. (1999) *Présence de Lucrèce.* (Tours).

Popkin, R. H. (2003) *The History of Scepticism from Savonarola to Bayle.* Rev. ed. (Oxford).

Porter, J. I. (2003a) "Epicurean Attachments: Life, Pleasure, Beauty, Friendship, and Piety," *Cronache Ercolanesi* 33: 129–51.

———. (2003b) "Lucretius and the Poetics of Void," in A. Monet (ed.), *Le jardin romain: Epicurisme et poèsie à Rome; mélanges offerts à Mayotte Bollack.* (Lille), 197–226.

———. (2007) "Lucretius and the Sublime," in Gillespie and Hardie (2007a), 167–84.

———. (2008) "Reception Studies: Future Prospects," in L. Hardwick and C. Stray (eds.), *A Companion to Classical Receptions.* (Oxford), 469–81.

———. (2010) *The Origins of Aesthetic Thought in Ancient Greece: Matter, Sensation, and Experience.* (Cambridge).

Porter, R., and M. M. Roberts, eds. (1997) *Pleasure in the Eighteenth Century.* (New York).

Power, N. 2006. "Bachelard contra Bergson: Ancient Atomism and the Debate over Continuity," *Angelaki: Journal of the Theoretical Humanities* 11: 117–23.

Purinton, J. (1993) "Epicurus on the Telos," *Phronesis* 38: 280–310.

———. (1999) "Epicurus on 'Free Volition' and the Atomic Swerve," *Phronesis* 44: 253–99.

Quitslund, J. A. (2001) *Spenser's Supreme Fiction: Platonic Natural Philosophy and The Faerie Queene.* (Toronto).

Raimondi, E. (1950) *Codro e l'umanesimo a Bologna.* (Bologna).

———. (1974) "Il primo commento umanistico a Lucrezio," in Carlo Dionisotti (ed.), *Tra latino e volgare.* 2 vols. (Padua), 2: 641–74.

Ramachandran, A. (2006) "The Wide Womb of the World: Origins and Epistemology in Spenser's *Faerie Queene*," Unpublished MSS.

Reinhardt, T. (2002) "The Speech of Nature in Lucretius' *De Rerum Natura* 3.931–71," *Classical Quarterly* 52: 291–304.

Reuschlein, H. G. (1954) "Recent Cases," *Harvard Law Review* 68: 384–87.

Richlin, A. (1991) "Zeus and Metis: Foucault, Feminism, Classics," *Helios* 18: 160–80.

———. (1998) "Foucault's History of Sexuality: A Useful Theory for Women?" in Larmour, Miller, and Platter, 138–70.

Rochester, J. W., Earl of (1962) *The Complete Poems of John Wilmot, Earl of Rochester.* (New Haven).

Roller, M. (2004) "Exemplarity in Roman Culture: The Cases of Horatius Cocles and Cloelia," *Classical Philology* 99: 1–56.

Ronell, A. (2002) *Stupidity.* (Urbana, Ill.).

Rorty, R. (1979) *Philosophy and the Mirror of Nature.* (Princeton).

Rosenfield, L. C. (1968) *From Beast-Machine to Man-Machine: Animal Soul in French Letters from Descartes to La Mettrie.* (New York).

Rosetti, J. T. (1735) *Systema Novum Mechanico Hippocraticum de Morbis Fluidorum & Solidorum, ac Singulis Ipsorum Curationibus.* (Venice).

Roskam, G. (2007) *"Live Unnoticed" Λάθε βιώσας: On the Vicissitudes of an Epicurean Doctrine.* (Leiden).

Rossi, V., and U. Bosco, eds. (1933) *Le familiari.* 4 vols. (Florence).

Rothko, M. (2004) *The Artist's Reality: Philosophies of Art.* Ed. C. Rothko. (New Haven).

———. (2006) *Writings on Art.* Ed. M. López-Remiro. (New Haven).

Rousseau, G. S. (1976) "Nerves, Spirits, and Fibres: Towards Defining the Origins of Sensibility," *Studies in the Eighteenth Century* 3. Ed. R. F. Brissenden and J. C. Eade. (Toronto).

Rousseau, J. J. (1964) *La nouvelle Héloïse,* in *Œuvres complètes,* vol. 2. Ed. B. Gagnebin and M. Raymond. (Paris).

———. (1969) *Émile, ou, De l'éducation.* Ed. C. Wirz and P. Burgelin. (Paris).

———. (1971) *Discours sur l'origine et les fondements de l'inégalité parmi les hommes.* Ed. J. Roger (Paris).

———. (1979) *Émile or On Education.* Trans. A. Bloom. (New York).

———. (1988) *Discourse on the Origins and Foundations of Inequality Among Men.* Trans. J. C. Bondanella in A. Ritter and J. C. Bondanella (eds.), *Rousseau's Political Writings.* (New York).

Russell, D. A., and M. Winterbottom, eds. (1972) *Ancient Literary Criticism: The Principal Texts in New Translations.* (Oxford).

Ryan, A. (1996) "Hobbes's Political Philosophy" in T. Sorell (ed.), *The Cambridge Companion to Hobbes.* (Cambridge), 208–45.

de Sade, D. A. F. (1998) *Histoire de Juliette* (1797–1801), in *Œuvres,* vol. 3. Ed. M. Delon and J. Deprun. (Paris).

Scala, B. (2008) *Essays and Dialogues.* Trans. R. N. Watkins (Cambridge, Mass.).

Scarry, E. (1985) *The Body in Pain: The Making and Unmaking of the World.* (Oxford).

Schelling, F. W. J. (1869) *Aus Schellings Leben. In Briefen.* Ed. G. L. Plitt. (Leipzig).

———. (1982) *Werke.* Vol. 3. Ed. H. Buchner, W. G. Jacobs, and A. Pieper. (Stuttgart).

Scherer, J. (1969) *Association Guillaume Budé: Actes du VIIIe Congrès, Paris, 5–10 Avril 1968.* (Paris).

Schiller, F. (1993) *Essays.* Ed. W. Hinderer and D. O. Dahlstrom. (New York).

Schlegel, F. (1964) *Kritische Ausgabe.* Ed. J.-J. Anstett. (Paderborn).

Schorsch, I. (1994) *From Text to Context: The Turn to History in Modern Judaism.* (Waltham, Mass.).

Schuler, R. M. (1992) "Francis Bacon and Scientific Poetry," *Transactions of the American Philosophical Society* 82: 36–37.

Sedley, D. N. (1973) "Epicurus, *On Nature* Book XXVIII," *Cronache Ercolanesi* 3: 5–83.

———. (1997) "Plato's Auctoritas and the Rebirth of the Commentary Tradition," in J. Barnes and M. Griffin (eds.), *Philosophia Togata II: Plato and Aristotle at Rome.* (Oxford), 110–29.

———. (1998) *Lucretius and the Transformation of Greek Wisdom.* (Cambridge).

———. (2003) "Philodemus and the Decentralisation of Philosophy," *Cronache Ercolanesi* 33: 31–41.

Segal, C. (1990) *Lucretius on Death and Anxiety: Poetry and Philosophy in De Rerum Natura.* (Princeton).

Sellars, J. (1999) "The Point of View of the Cosmos: Deleuze, Romanticism, Stoicism," *Pli: The Warwick Journal of Philosophy* 8: 1–24.

———. (2006) "An Ethics of the Event: Deleuze's Stoicism," *Angelaki: Journal of the Theoretical Humanities* 11: 157–71.

———. (2007a) "*Aiôn* and *Chronos*: Deleuze and the Stoic Theory of Time," *Collapse* 3: 177–205.

———. (2007b) "Deleuze and Cosmopolitanism," *Radical Philosophy* 142: 30–37.

———. (2007c) "Gilles Deleuze and the History of Philosophy," *British Journal for the History of Philosophy* 15: 551–60.

Serres, M. (1977) *La naissance de la physique dans le texte de Lucrèce.* (Paris).

———. (2000) *The Birth of Physics.* Trans. J. Hawkes. (Manchester).

Shakespeare, W. (2002) *William Shakespeare: The Complete Works.* (London).

Shapin, S., and S. Schaffer (1989) *Leviathan and the Air-Pump: Hobbes, Boyle, and the Experimental Life.* (Princeton).

Shearin, W. H. (2007) "Atomic Politics: Speech Acts in Lucretius' *De Rerum Natura*," PhD diss., University of California, Berkeley.

———. (2009) Review of *The Cambridge Companion to Lucretius. Classical Journal Online*, 04.04.09. http://www.camws.org/CJ/Shearin on Hardie, Gillespie. pdf

Shelley, M. W. (2008) *Frankenstein, or, The Modern Prometheus. The Original Two-Volume Novel of 1816–1817 from the Bodleian Library Manuscripts.* Ed. C. E. Robinson. (Oxford).

Shelley, P. B. (1968) *Poetical Works.* Ed. T. Hutchinson. (London).

Sheppard, E. R. (2006) *Leo Strauss and the Politics of Exile.* (Waltham, Mass.).

Shirley, J. W. (1983) *Thomas Harriot: A Biography.* (Oxford).

Siebert, D. T. (1985) "Swift's *Fiat Odor*: The Excremental Re-Vision," *Eighteenth-Century Studies* 19: 21–38.

Smith, D. W. (2006) "The Concept of the Simulacrum: Deleuze and the Overturning of Platonism," *Continental Philosophy Review* 38: 89–123.

———. (2009) "From the Surface to the Depths: On the Transition from *Logic of Sense* to Anti-Oedipus," in C. V. Boundas (ed.), *Gilles Deleuze: The Intensive Reduction.* (London), 82–97.

Smith, M. F. (2006) "Quotations of Epicurus Common to Diogenes of Oinoanda and Diogenes Laertius," *Hyperboreus* 6: 188–97.

Smith, S. P. (2006) *Reading Leo Strauss: Philosophy, Politics, Judaism.* (Chicago).

Snyder, J. M. (1980) *Puns and Poetry in Lucretius.* (Amsterdam).

Socher, A. (2006) *The Radical Enlightenment of Solomon Maimon.* (Stanford).

Spenser, E. (1596) *The Faerie Queene.* (London).

Steinke, H. (2004) *Irritating Experiments: Haller's Concept and the European Controversy over Irritability and Sensibility.* (Amsterdam).

Stirling, B. (1934) "The Philosophy of Spenser's 'Garden of Adonis,'" *PMLA* 49: 501–38.

Stokes, M. (1995) "Cicero on Epicurean Pleasures," in J. G. F. Powell (ed.), *Cicero the Philosopher: Twelve Papers.* (Oxford), 145–70.

Strauss, L. (1936) *The Political Philosophy of Hobbes: Its Basis and Its Genesis.* Trans. E. M. Sinclair. (Oxford).

———. (1950) *Natural Right and History.* (Chicago).

———. (1965) *Spinoza's Critique of Religion.* Trans. E. M. Sinclair. (New York).

———. (1978) "Letter to Helmet Kuhn," *Independent Journal of Philosophy* 2: 24.

———. (1987) *Philosophy and Law.* Trans. F. Baumann. (Philadelphia).

———. (1995) *Liberalism Ancient and Modern.* (Chicago).

———. (1996) *Gesammelte Schriften.* (Stuttgart).

Striker, G. (1993) "Epicurean Hedonism," in J. Brunschwig and M. Nussbaum (eds.), *Passions and Perceptions.* (Cambridge), 3–17.

Strozier, R. M. (2002) *Foucault, Subjectivity, and Identity: Historical Constructions of Subject and Self.* (Detroit).

Swain, S. (1989a) "Plutarch's *De Fortuna Romanorum*," *Classical Quarterly* 39: 504–16.

———. (1989b) "Plutarch: Chance, Providence, and History," *American Journal of Philology* 110: 272–302.

Swift, J. (2010) "Strephon and Chloe (1731, 1734)," in C. Rawson and I. Higgins (eds.), *Jonathan Swift: The Essential Writings.* (New York), 61–17.

Tally Jr., R. T. (2010) "Nomadography: The 'Early' Deleuze and the History of Philosophy," *Journal of Philosophy: A Cross-Disciplinary Inquiry* 5: 15–24.

Tanguay, D. (2007) *Leo Strauss: An Intellectual Biography.* Trans. C. Nadon. (New Haven).

Terada, R. (2001) *Feeling in Theory: Emotion after the "Death of the Subject."* (Cambridge, Mass.).

Thompson, C. R. (1971) "Erasmus. The Dyaloge Called Funus (1534) & A very Pleasaunt & Fruitful Diologe called The Epicure (1545). Ed. Robert R. Allen," *Renaissance Quarterly* 24: 372–79.

Thomson, A. (1991) "La Mettrie, lecteur et traducteur de Boerhaave," *Dix-huitième siècle* 23: 23–29.

———. (2008) *Bodies of Thought: Science, Religion, and the Soul in the Early Enlightenment.* (Oxford).

Titchener, F. (2003) "Cornelius Nepos and the Biographical Tradition," *Greece and Rome* 50: 85–99.

Todd, J. (1986) *Sensibility: An Introduction.* (London).

Tompkins, J. P. (1980) *Reader-Response Criticism: From Formalism to Post-Structuralism.* (Baltimore).

Trinkaus, C. E. (1940) *Adversity's Noblemen.* (New York).

Tsouna, V. (2009) "Epicurean Therapeutic Strategies," in Warren, 249–65.

Tuplin, C. (2000) "Nepos and the Origins of Political Biography," in C. Deroux (ed.), *Studies in Latin Literature and Roman History* 10. (Brussels), 124–61.

van der Eijk, P. (2009) "Développements récents dans l'étude de la doxographie de la philosophie et des sciences dans l'Antiquité," in F. Le Blay (ed.), *Transmettre les saviors dans les mondes héllenistique et romain.* (Rennes), 107–16.

———, ed. (1999) *Ancient Histories of Medicine: Essays in Medical Doxography and Historiography in Classical Antiquity.* (Leiden).

Van Sant, A. J. (1993) *Eighteenth-Century Sensibility and the Novel: The Senses in Social Context.* (Cambridge).

Vartanian, A. (1960) *La Mettrie's L'homme machine: A Study in the Origins of an Idea.* (Princeton).

Vila, A. C. (1998) *Enlightenment and Pathology: Sensibility in the Literature and Medicine of Eighteenth-Century France.* (Baltimore).

Von Mücke, D. E. (1991) *Virtue and the Veil of Illusion: Generic Innovation and the Pedagogical Project in Eighteenth-Century Literature.* (Stanford).

Warren, J. (2002) *Epicurus and Democritean Ethics: An Archaeology of Ataraxia.* (Cambridge).

———. (2004) *Facing Death: Epicurus and His Critics.* (Oxford).

———. (2007) "Diogenes Laërtius, Biographer of Philosophy," in J. König and T. Whitmarsh (eds.), *Ordering Knowledge in the Roman Empire.* (Cambridge), 133–49.

———, ed. (2009) *The Cambridge Companion to Epicureanism.* (Cambridge).

Webb, D. (2006) "Michel Serres on Lucretius: Atomism, Science, and Ethics," *Angelaki: Journal of the Theoretical Humanities* 11: 125–36.

Wicks, R. (2007) *Kant on Judgment*. (London).

Wieland, W. (2001) *Urteil und Gefühl: Kants Theorie der Urteilskraft*. (Göttingen).

Wilson, C. (2008) *Epicureanism at the Origins of Modernity*. (Oxford).

———. (2009) "Epicureanism in Early Modern Philosophy," in Warren, 266–86.

Wilson, M. (2001) "Seneca's *Epistles* Reclassified," in S. J. Harrison (ed.), *Texts, Ideas and the Classics*. (Oxford), 164–87.

Wingrove, E. R. (2000) *Rousseau's Republican Romance*. (Princeton).

Wittgenstein,L.(1997)*Philosophische Untersuchungen/Philosophical Investigations*. 2nd ed. (Oxford).

———. (2001) *Philosophical Investigations*. 3rd ed. (Oxford).

Wolfreys, J. (2000) *Readings: Acts of Close Reading in Literary Theory*. (Edinburgh).

Wolfsdorf, D. (2009) "Empedocles and His Ancient Readers on Desire and Pleasure," *Oxford Studies in Ancient Philosophy* 36: 1–70.

Wood, A. (2005) "Kant's History of Ethics," *Studies in the History of Ethics: A Peer-Reviewed Electronic Journal and Research Portal*. http://www.historyofethics.org/062005/062005Wood.shtml.

Woolf, R. (2009) "Pleasure and Desire," in Warren, 158–78.

Wordsworth, W. (1926) *The Prelude, or Growth of a Poet's Mind*. Ed. E. de Selincourt. (Oxford).

Wurgaft, B. A. (2009) "Thinking in Public: Arendt, Levinas and Strauss on Intellectuals and Social Responsibility," PhD diss., University of California, Berkeley.

Yerushalmi, Y. H. (1989) *Zakhor: Jewish History and Jewish Memory*. (Seattle).

Zank, M., ed. (2002) *Leo Strauss: The Early Writings 1921–1932*. (Albany).

Zerilli, L. (2002) "'Une Maîtresse Imperieuse': Woman in Rousseau's Semiotic Republic," in Lange, 277–314.

Zhmud, L. (2001) "Revising Doxography: Hermann Diels and His Critics," *Philologus* 145: 219–43.

Zinsser, J. P. (2006) *Emilie Du Châtelet: Daring Genius of the Enlightenment*. (London).

Žižek, S. (1989) *The Sublime Object of Ideology*. (London).

Index